RARE MASTERPIECES
OF PHILOSOPHY AND SCIENCE

EDITED BY DR. W. STARK

★

THE NATURE OF SYMPATHY

THE
NATURE OF SYMPATHY

BY MAX SCHELER

TRANSLATED FROM THE GERMAN

BY

PETER HEATH, B.A.
Department of History
The University, Hull

WITH A GENERAL INTRODUCTION
TO MAX SCHELER'S WORK

BY

W. STARK, M.A.
Professor of Sociology
Fordham University

ROUTLEDGE & KEGAN PAUL LTD
Broadway House, 68–74 Carter Lane
London

First published in 1954
by Routledge & Kegan Paul Ltd
Broadway House, 68–74 Carter Lane
London E.C.4

Reprinted 1970

Reproduced and Printed in Great Britain by
Redwood Press Limited, Trowbridge and London.

ISBN 0 7100 6796 8

CONTENTS

v

CONTENTS

PART II. LOVE AND HATRED

PART III. OTHER MINDS

EDITOR'S PREFACE

In the last years, there has been a remarkable effort to make the writings of the leading sociologists and social philosophers of the Continent available to the English-speaking world. We now possess full translations of the main works by Toennies and Durkheim, and representative selections from the books of Simmel and Max Weber. Strangely enough, Scheler has so far been passed by. Yet he was as great as all the others, and, indeed, in some respects greater than any of them. The present publication needs therefore no apology. It was more than overdue, and it is hoped that it will be the first of many of its kind.

What has in the past decided English and American translators not to take up Max Scheler was possibly the fact that he is known as 'a German metaphysician'. Certainly, his books are not altogether easy reading, but their study is richly rewarding. The point need not be laboured here. Let anyone take up this volume and see for himself! Only one fact should perhaps be mentioned, namely that there is a deep kinship between Scheler's thought and some fundamental tendencies in American sociology, at any rate as far as substance is concerned. Personally, he has always reminded me of C. H. Cooley. When Cooley writes, in his essay on Spencer, that 'sympathetic qualities . . . are, after all, the only direct source of our knowledge of other people', he expresses a conviction which is also to be found in this and all the writings of Scheler's early and middle period.

W. Stark

Manchester
  May 1953

vii

EDITOR'S INTRODUCTION

THE life of many if not of most leading philosophers consists in the gradual elaboration of some great idea which has come to them in a sidereal hour of their youth. Such, for example, was Kant's flash of insight that space and time, commonly regarded as objective realities, are in point of fact subjective, i.e. merely the formal scheme which our mind imposes upon the world in order to be able to apprehend and understand its phenomena; such, too, was Bergson's sudden realization that the Greeks were wrong when they considered rest as the perfection of being and movement as an impoverished form of it; that, on the contrary, movement, becoming, is of the essence of life, while rest, immutability, can only be achieved in death. Scheler was a thinker of a different type. He, too, had his Damascus experience, but it was to him a point of departure rather than a point of arrival. Plagued by an extreme intellectual restlessness, he continued to change and re-change his point of view: he was one of those who, in Pascal's phrase, 'search groaning'. In order to understand his philosophical work, it is essential to distinguish three stages in his career, each of which is characterized by an outstanding intellectual achievement: the first by *Der Formalismus in der Ethik und die materiale Wertethik*; the second by *Vom Ewigen im Menschen*; and the third and last by the *Philosophische Anthropologie*, a book that was as yet unfinished when death struck him down, a man of barely fifty-four, in May 1928.

I

At the time when Scheler was born, the intellectual scene was dominated by two great hostile schools of thought. The one, an idealistic philosophy, traced its origin back to Immanuel Kant and had just been powerfully restated by Hermann Cohen: the other, an embodiment of the materialistic world-view, had come down from Jeremy Bentham and had gained considerable influence through the much-read and much-appreciated writings of John Stuart Mill. The choice before a young philosopher seemed simple enough: he could either turn to the right, or to the left. There was, apparently, no middle way.

In the narrower field of ethics, the Kantians started from the conviction that the cravings of the individual were, in the last analysis, at variance with the interests of the race. Man had to be tamed if he was to be transformed into a citizen: the moral law had to be imposed on his wayward will, and the moral law was the sum and substance of the claims of the community on its individual components. To the question: what is good?, Kant's disciples answered: good is what you ought to do! The concept of *duty* was thus at the root of their whole ethical system. But if man is a creature who can, in principle, act rightly, but will not, in practice, easily do so, if he is a creature whose spirit is willing but whose flesh is weak, a series of consequences is bound to follow: man cannot then be a unitary being; he must have two warring natures, one sensible, the other supersensible; there must be a phenomenal and a noumenal man. The moral law will reveal itself in conflict rather than in the day-to-day workings of the world: it will confront man as something alien, something independent of his human experience, something absolute and compelling, in a word, as a categorical imperative. He will not be able to say in concrete terms what is good and what not: he will only have a negative criterion for determining the goodness of an action —the rational conviction that it curbs his sinful bent. In such a philosophy, nothing can be good but the good will. In other words, the ethical teaching of the Kantian school was an abstract and formal doctrine of duty, not a concrete and material catalogue of values. It was this latter alternative of moral thinking which had been worked out and propagated by the opposite school, the children and grandchildren of Jeremy Bentham.

The Benthamites started from the sub- or semi-conscious assumption that the desires of the individual were in harmony with the needs of the race, either because an inborn principle of sympathy holds them together from the very beginning, or else because the mechanism of social intercourse ensures an ultimate reconciliation. The most that can ever be wanted is an appropriate system of laws to support and perfect the working of that mechanism. Thus there is, for them, little need to discipline man: on the contrary, discipline, as a source of pain, will be an evil in itself, and the highest postulate of practical reason will be to let everybody act as he wishes to do. To the question: what is good?, the Utilitarians could joyfully answer: what we all desire—what we feel will cause us *pleasure*. Their ethical system was frankly hedonistic. Man was in their view a simple and easily understandable being: a pleasure-seeking and pain-fleeing animal like any other, uncomplicated in every respect, and essentially one in nature. As objective goodness and subjective enjoyment coincide, it is not conflict that will reveal the norm of action—conflict can only arise where there is confusion of some kind—but the spontaneous everyday behaviour of men, and psychology will become the basis of ethics. Indeed, ethics will become a highly practical, one could almost say, economically useful, discipline. It will not concern itself with the metaphysical notion of a noumenally good will, but will elaborate instead a concrete list of values which sensible men do pursue, and which all men should pursue, and which will provide the basis for the practical maximization of both public and private felicity.

It must have looked, in Scheler's student days, as if a choice between these two theories—so perfect in themselves, so antithetic to each other—was unavoidable. In point of fact, however, both schools had come to the end of their tether: their very perfection had exhausted their original inspiration, and they had equally lost their attractiveness to young, keen minds. Life, so dialectical and so inventive, had provided a *via media*, a *via tertia*, after all, and that new departure in philosophy was connected with the name of Franz Brentano, whose outstanding importance for the recent history of epistemology and ethics is even now not fully realized. In the very year in which Scheler was born—in 1874— Brentano had published the first volume of his *Psychologie vom empirischen Standpunkt*, and this book was destined to become the starting-point of a new and powerful philosophical movement which Scheler joined after having given, for a while, a tentative and half-hearted allegiance to the idealistic teaching of Rudolf Eucken.

Brentano's ethical theory is lucidly set forth in his little book, *The Origin of the Knowledge of Right and Wrong*, a lecture delivered in 1889 to a circle of lawyers and translated into English in 1902. In it, Brentano makes short work of both the older theories. Kant's ethic, he claims, is practically useless because it does not tell us in definite terms what we ought to do. 'The Categorical Imperative . . . even when admitted, . . . leads to no ethical conclusions' (p. 45). Its demand, that we should act in such a manner that the maxim of our action could be a law for every man, is a purely formal principle, not a concrete guide for the perplexed;

and, even worse, it is the kind of abstraction that can, by a little logical jugglery, be perverted to almost any purpose, even the most immoral. But Bentham's pretended ethic is no whit more satisfactory. 'Ought we to say', Brentano asks, 'that whatever is loved and is capable of being loved is worthy of love and is good?' No, he answers, 'this is manifestly untrue, and it is almost inconceivable that some have fallen into this error. One loves what another hates, and, in accordance with a well-known psychological law . . . it often happens that what at first was desired merely as a means to something else, comes at last from habit to be desired for its own sake. In such a way the miser is irrationally led to heap up riches and even to sacrifice himself for their sake. The actual presence of love, therefore, by no means testifies unconditionally to the worthiness of the object to be loved, just as affirmation is no unconditional proof of what is true' (16 seq.).

What, then, is Brentano's own opinion? Its most pregnant formulation is contained in the proposition that 'the ethical sanction is a command similar to the logical rule' (XI). What Brentano means is that our mind can distinguish between good and bad in the same way that it distinguishes between true and false, or if not in exactly the same way, then at any rate in an analogous manner. If I hold the proposition that 'two and two make four' against the competing proposition that 'two and two make five', I know at once, and with certainty, that the former assertion is right and the latter wrong: my intellect 'commands' me to accept the one and to reject the other. Something similar is happening, Brentano tells us, if we compare two possible modes of action. A spontaneous judgement will tell me—indeed command me—that I ought to pursue the one and turn away from the other. The better alternative will have a definite inner superiority over its rival, a superiority which is brought home to my mind with a kind of evidence and conviction reminiscent of that experienced in the solution of a logical problem. It is true that in the one case reason, the intellect, decides, and in the other sentiment, the feelings. That is why ethical sanction and logical rule must not be altogether fused and confused: but though distinct, they are parallel, and even more than parallel, akin to each other. As Scheler was to express it later on: 'The heart possesses, within its own realm, a strict analogon of logic, which it does not, however, borrow from the logic of the intellect. As the ancient doctrine of the *nomos agraphos* can already teach, there are laws written into it which correspond to the plan according to which the world, as a world of values, is built up. It can love and hate blindly, or with evidence, just as we can judge blindly or with evidence' (*Ordo Amoris*, Schriften aus dem Nachlass I, 1933, 244).

It is easy to see why and how Brentano's ethic (though by no means an absolute novelty in the history of moral philosophy) provided, round about the year 1900, an attractive way out of the impasse into which the discussion had drifted, under the head-on clash between the idealist and materialist traditions. It seemed to combine what was true and sound in each of them. It found the origin of the knowledge of right and wrong in experiences of an emotional kind, and to that extent moved along Benthamite lines; yet it came near to the Kantian position when it insisted that these experiences are analogous to rational judgements. By distinguishing between a 'blind' preference on the one hand (a preference based on, say, a purely animal drive) and an 'enlightened' preference (a preference that deserves to be characterized as 'right') on the other, it did away with the most objectionable feature of the hedonistic theory, its inability to choose between the higher and the lower values: and it avoided the greatest weakness of the opposite doctrine, its formalism, by pointing out that our 'correct' judgements give us a concrete knowledge of right and wrong, an immediate and reliable guide in perplexity, not a vague and abstract formula that makes nobody the wiser. Indeed, even with regard to the a-priority or a-posteriority of ethical rules, their independence from, or dependence on, human experience, it managed successfully to steer a middle course: the proposition that 'pain is bad', the new school explained, is a-posteriori in so far as nobody can recognize it as correct who has not once in his life felt what pain is; yet the condemnation of pain springs from the very concept of suffering, and so it is not really induced from observation—hence it is an a-priori statement of a kind.

Scheler's philosophical work must be understood as a follow-up of Brentano's successful pioneering. Yet it would be wrong to describe the younger man simply as a disciple of the older. Scheler was a rather independent and self-willed disciple of Husserl and Meinong, and Husserl and Meinong were on their part again rather independent and self-willed disciples of the master. It is impossible here to discuss in detail the disagreements which split the original unity of the Brentano school. Suffice it to say that the bone of contention was the correspondence theory, the *adequatio rei et intellectus*. In his earlier years Brentano, with his Thomist background, had adhered to it: later on he had fallen away from it. Among his followers Oskar Kraus led a group who decidedly condemned it: the phenomenologists, as they came to be called, equally decidedly took it up and developed its implications. To the older Brentano and to Kraus the sentence 'X is good' meant: X is worthy to be loved; nobody who rightly feels and judges can deny that X is worthy to be loved. In other words, to them the statement was simply a statement concerning the operation of the human mind, and no more. But to Husserl and Meinong it did mean more because in their view there is a correspondence between the contents of our mind and the phenomena of reality. It meant to them that X is endowed with a *quality* which we call goodness. Now, a quality inheres in things; it belongs to the external world; hence to the phenomenologists a value judgement was essentially the statement of a fact. Meinong says in this sense that the emotions, by dint of their 'presentative function', have a part to play in the process of cognition. Such ideas raised Kraus's ire: he accused the phenomenologists of fiction-mongering when they said that 'good' was a quality in the same sense as 'red' or 'hot'. Yet their platonizing tendency gained ground in the Brentano school, and one of its most consistent representatives was the subject of this essay, Max Scheler.

We can best see what position Scheler was taking up if we bring to our minds the sociology and anthropology that was implied in Brentano's ethical speculations. For Kant, man had been born bad; Bentham had credited him with a sufficient grain of native goodness to make a spontaneously harmonious social life possible. Brentano shifted the interest from man's inborn nature to man's adult behaviour—for, surely, it is only the mature personality that can, with assurance, decide which line of action can 'rightly' be called good, and which not. Now, what enables the mature mind to make 'evidently correct' pronouncements in moral matters? What speaks in him when he speaks out? Obviously it is the fund of social valuations which has been deposited in him by education, and which has so penetrated his emotional life as to have completely merged with it. It was some conception such as this which (probably unbeknown to himself) had guided Brentano in his moral philosophizing. Now, the social *depositum* in the individual mind consists of certain habits of action and of thought—of customs and ideologies—which seem to have no existence in the outside world: the only existence they can claim is existence in human minds. This, clearly, was the older Brentano's conviction, and that of Oskar Kraus. But Scheler *did* ascribe to them an independent mode of being, thus recalling certain aspects of Emile Durkheim's contemporary work. He distinguishes between 'social valuations concerning good and evil' on the one hand, and 'the matter (*Wertmaterie*) "good" and "evil"' on the other—as if behind the social valuations arising in men's individual minds there were a further objective reality to which they 'correspond'. This is Scheler's much criticized 'ontologism'.[1] It constitutes, for better and for worse, the salient characteristic of his great book:

[1] Cf. Oskar Kraus, *Die Werttheorien*, 1937.

The Formalistic Principle in Ethics and the Non-Formal Ethic of Value.[1]

What Scheler sets out to do in this impressive tome is to build up a doctrine of moral values, their hierarchy, and of the norms which are based on that hierarchy—a doctrine which is to be concrete and evident, and yet independent of all positive psychological and historical experience (2). Values are to him clear, sensible (*fühlbare*) phenomena (11), which are already as phenomena real objective entities (*echte Gegenstände*) totally different from all states of feeling (14); they are, as qualities, ideal objects just as colours and tonal qualities are ideal objects (16), and they are given to us—recognizable by us—in and through feeling (30). His ethic is, like all knowledge, to be founded on a set of facts (*Tatsachenkreis*, 42). As Scheler expresses it with particular clarity in one connection: 'There is a mode of perception whose objects are totally beyond the grasp of the intellect, and for which the intellect is as blind as the ear and the sense of hearing are for colour—a mode of perception none-the-less, which presents to us real objects (*echte objective Gegenstände*) and an eternal order among them—namely the values and their hierarchy' (262). Clearly, it was Scheler's conviction that values are not only valuations but also value-facts, and that these value-facts can be seen by our mental eye in the same way in which our physical eye sees coloured surfaces. It is not without significance that he often speaks of a realm of values into which we can enter—a realm, that is, which is open to our experience and in which we can roam if we like. We can only know what is good subjectively by seeing what is good objectively, and the norms for action can only grow out of a certain kind of knowledge—the knowledge of value-facts and of their mutual relation and ranking.

Out of the wide range of subjects covered in Scheler's more than six hundred pages, only three further facets can be shortly considered here: his doctrine of the scale of values; his distinction between value-modalities; and the problem of relativity. One value is 'higher' or 'lower' in comparison to another, and this relation of theirs is perceived by us in a specific act of value-perception which is called 'preferring' (84 seq.). The values show certain characteristics on which their relative 'height' seems to depend. Scheler mentions four of them: (1) the lasting goods are

---

[1] First published in the *Jahrbuch für Philosophie und phänomenologische Forschung*, 1913 and 1916. *Die materiale Wertethik* is translated here as 'the non-formal ethic of value' in order to bring out the contrast, intended by Scheler, to the 'formal principle' of Kant. It is, of course, totally inadmissible and absolutely misleading to speak of Scheler's 'Ethics of Material Values' as does Brock in his *Introduction to Contemporary German Philosophy* (1935, 20).

to be preferred to those that are perishable and changing; (2) those goods are relatively higher which can be enjoyed by a greater number of men without the necessity of dividing them up; (3) if a certain value *b* must already exist before another value *a* can come into existence, then *b* will be higher up in the scale than *a*—the value that forms the foundation must be higher than the value which is founded on it; and (4) certain goods give us a deeper satisfaction than others, and the 'depth' of that satisfaction (which we directly experience) also influences the 'height' of the value which yields it. At first sight, these four points seem to be altogether disconnected from each other, yet Scheler does his best to show that they can be reduced to one ultimately decisive element which he calls degree of relativity (*Relativitätsstufe*).

As for the modes or modalities of value, Scheler also distinguishes four, each one accompanied by a corresponding opposite set of disvalues. There are (1) pleasure-values—the agreeable and disagreeable, seen, as is clear from what Scheler says elsewhere,[1] mainly from the point of view of the individual; (2) a group of values which could best be described in English as welfare-values. Scheler speaks of life values or vital values, because he thinks of all the goods which subserve and promote life, health, vitality and social well-being—the point of view here being essentially that of the community; (3) spiritual or culture-values, comprising beauty, justice and truth; and, lastly, (4) sacred values, or the values of holiness. In another and outstandingly beautiful passage[2] Scheler develops the same concept of order among the modes of value in, as it were, the opposite direction. In the ideal personality, he points out there, the religious being ought to occupy the highest level; underneath it will have to come the spiritually creative person; on the next lower level we ought then to find the citizen who should be alive in every one of us; and only in the last and humblest place the economic subject, the animal man who is concerned about his physical enjoyment. The lesson of these distinctions is that the realm of values is not a uniform whole, but divided into closed circles which rise hierarchically above each other and must, in the case of conflict, give way to each other. We ought to sacrifice our physical enjoyments to our duties as citizens of the state; we ought to sacrifice our social well-being to the claims of culture—beauty, justice and truth; and even these august values should be sacrificed, if the need arises, on the altar of sanctity, on the altar of God.

For a total understanding of Scheler's philosophical achievement it is, in conclusion, necessary to cast a glance at his solution of the problem of ethical relativity. As a moral philosopher he was

---

[1] *Vom Ewigen im Menschen*, I, 274–7.   [2] Ibid., 276.

anxious to present a system that would be absolute, and—in the sense given to the word by Franz Brentano—aprioristic; but as a sociologist he knew only too well that different societies have different value-systems and that no man can reasonably claim to be able to decide between them. The way out of this quandary which he suggests—though it is not without its difficulties!—is certainly ingenious. He compares the eternal and immutable values to a mountain-range which towers high above the valleys in which we humans live. To every age and to every people they reveal, according to their respective points of view, a different aspect of themselves: each one is true, and yet each one is unacceptable to all the others. We must not speak of a relativism of values then, but rather of a perspectivism (314)—an altogether different proposition. Only He who is exalted above the highest peak and who surveys the scene from the farthest heaven—only Almighty God, Himself the Value of Values, can know the truth in its entirety.

II

Scheler's transition from ethical to religious speculation was, in a way, a natural development. The very logic of his system led, as we have just seen, to a theistic conclusion. Yet, in his second, or Cologne, period, faith was to him more than a matter of intellectual curiosity: it was also a deep concern of the heart. It is this which makes *Vom Ewigen im Menschen* (1920) Scheler's most convincing book. Its title can best be rendered into English—if it be permitted to borrow one of Tolstoi's happiest phrases[1]—as 'Man's Divine Self'.

In the exposition of his religious thought (contained mainly in the second volume of *Vom Ewigen*) Scheler starts again with the presentation of a hierarchical order, this time of the capabilities of the human mind. He distinguishes intellect, reason, and the aptitude for religious experience. The intellect is of supreme importance in man's struggle for survival in that it helps him to make the tools and develop the techniques by which he can subdue and utilize his habitat. But as a source of knowledge it is profoundly problematic. Because the control of nature is its aim, it tends to conceive all phenomena, both of the external and internal worlds, as functions of a universal mechanism—for only in so far as the world resembles a mechanism can we dominate and exploit it for our purposes. Hence the narrow limitations of the intellect in the search for truth. Reason gives us both a wider and a truer knowledge. It can recognize that reality is more than a mechanism, more than a particularly intricate game of billiards (loc. cit., 23),

---

[1] *Resurrection*, Bk. I, ch. XXXVI.

that it is much more a field in which certain forms, aims and values are realized. Yet even reason has its *ne plus ultra*, and when it is reached a still higher power of the human mind must take over—its aptitude for religious experience which is an opening up to the outer, ever inbeating waves of revelation and grace, an opening up which is yet not entirely passive because it presupposes and implies a going out and coming to meet those waves which are flowing towards us.

Scheler's main thesis concerning the possible knowledge of God is the assertion that it can only be achieved if reason and religious experience co-operate—if they effect a pincer movement, so to speak. Reason can take us a good way along the road, but not to its end. Metaphysical speculation, he tells us, begins with wonder at the fact that something *is* rather than nothing, that—to formulate it even more precisely—there is not nothing. This root realization—which is not only an intellectual operation, such as the comparison of $+ a$ and $- a$, but also an experience—this deep insight leads at once to further consequences. It gives us the distinction between relative, contingent and imperfect existence on the one hand, and absolute, independent and perfect existence on the other; in other words, it gives us the concept of an *ens a se* which is visible in, through and behind every *ens ab alio*. But reason can take us even further. If it goes beyond the framework in which we accidentally find ourselves, if it delves into the realm of essences, it will perceive that other worlds than the one which has become reality were initially equally possible, and so it will be led to the concept of a *prima causa* of this particular contingent world which will coalesce with that of an *ens a se*. At this point the theory of value can help us on. The *ens a se* which is the *prima causa* of all contingent existence will, as the most important entity in the universe, also be the *summum bonum*. And even this recognition is not the last insight reason can gain. As it is an evident axiom that persons stand higher in the scale of values than things, it will be able to say that the great X it is pursuing—*if* it is—*ought* to be a person; otherwise it could not be the *summum bonum*. Yet here reason has reached its limits. It cannot tell us, Scheler asserts, *that* God is a person, and that for a very simple reason.

Already experience in the circle of men shows us that we cannot know a person unless he chooses to reveal himself to us. A man may be silent, and that distinguishes him from any object of the lower creation. Yet though a man may deny us all knowledge of what he thinks and feels and wills, he cannot keep from us the fact that he exists. As soon as we see his body, we immediately realize, on the analogy of the experience of ourselves, if of no other, that to this bodily configuration belongs an appropriate personality.

But God is a being without a body, and so this source of knowledge is not available here. If *He* chooses to be silent, no spontaneous act of ours will ever attain Him. Hence we can only know Him if we allow any revelation He may vouchsafe of Himself to enter into our mind. The receipt of this particular knowledge is the religious act. It begins where spontaneous perception ends, and is totally different from it. No metaphysics can take its place. Those who have claimed that it can were bad metaphysicians, because they cannot have had a sound idea of the confines of the human understanding.

The knowledge which we owe to the religious act, and which we can owe only to it, is the knowledge that God is, in point of fact, *a person*. It is this tremendous truth which the religious act grasps, in one blinding flash of insight, with all the evidence which a direct experience can give. Scheler uses in this connection a happy simile, though he does not elaborate it (103). A man may have seen the world day-in-day-out and found in it nothing but finite things, just as one passes a house a thousand times and perceives nothing but the bricks and doors and window panes. But, then, one day, a face is recognized behind one of the windows, and all is changed: the house now 'belongs to' that man: so the *homo religiosus*, once he is awakened to the divine presence, begins to see everything *in lumine Dei*. The parallel to the purely rational finding of the *ens a se*, and the contrast to it, is clear: the saint, like the thinker, perceives the dependence of the relative on the absolute, but the absolute is to him not an abstraction; it is a Person —He Who Is. Now, as the metaphysician advances beyond this point, so does the *homo religiosus*: as the one grasps the *prima causa*, so the other, the creator and sustainer of the universe. This knowledge will be realized in him as a definite feeling of dependence on God, of unworthiness, of creatureliness. Yet this feeling will also have its positive side, a blissful realization of security, of safety, of being enveloped in a stream of love. If the *summum bonum* is to the metaphysician the thing most worthy to be loved, passively as it were, it is to the *homo religiosus* a centre from which love actively radiates in all directions, an inexhaustible source of grace and compassion. And it is this religious realization which gives a new meaning to the findings of reason: it is here that the two wings of the search for the knowledge of God meet. We see now, from the vantage point of religious experience, that, although God *could* in principle hide Himself from us, as the metaphysicians insist, He yet *cannot* in fact do so because this would be in contradiction to His inmost essence, to His all-transcending love.

It might be thought that the direct knowledge of God which flashes upon man in his religious experiences would be perfect in itself and would not need any correlation with, and correction by, rational speculation. Yet this Scheler stoutly denies. There is a danger that the God of the *homo religiosus* will be all too personal, as it were; knowing love and anger as He does, He may assume in men's minds too anthropomorphic an appearance. On the other hand, the God of the metaphysician will tend to be a mere abstraction: he will be at best a concept, but not a person. So the two ideas must correct each other to give us full and adequate knowledge: 'The true God is not so empty and rigid as the God of metaphysics. The true God is not so narrow and not so alive as the God of mere faith' (64).

In his detailed analysis of the religious act, there are two points which Scheler is most anxious to establish: the one is that the religious experience is an experience *sui generis*, irreducible to any other, say, social or æsthetic; the other is the still more decisive thesis that all believing is founded on a seeing, all faith on vision. The religious act, Scheler insists, must not be conceived as merely a peculiar *form* of cognition which would share its field of experience with other such forms: it is, on the contrary, *materially* different from them in that it has its own particular phenomena which are inaccessible to them—as inaccessible as sounds are to the visual sense and colours to the sense of hearing. This exclusiveness in subject matter is also behind the three tests or hallmarks enumerated by Scheler, which enable us to decide whether any concrete act of human consciousness may be classed as religious or not. The specifically religious act is characterized (1) by the fact that it transcends the world, and not only this given world of ours, but any and every world, in the sense of an assemblage of finite things. (2) The quest for religious knowledge cannot be satisfied by any finite object or entity, not even if this finite object or entity is idealized out of all recognition. Scheler calls St. Augustine's cry: *Inquietum cor nostrum, donec requiescat in te*, a 'basic formula of all religious acts' (252). (3) Unlike any other mode of experience, the religious act demands an answer on the part of the 'object' towards which it is directed: it must 'receive' the truth which it is seeking—it cannot find it on its own.

It is supremely characteristic of Scheler's whole system of religious ideas at this time that he opposes to the sceptic's adage 'seeing is believing' his own confident assertion that 'believing is seeing'. It is based on the phenomenological philosophy which Scheler had taken over from his master Husserl, and in particular on the correspondence theory integral to it. 'To all knowledge', he says in an especially lucid passage (139), 'there must correspond a being, to all being a possible knowledge; analogously, to all loving and preferring, a value-fact (*Wertbestand*), to every value-fact a loving and preferring'. But if this is so, the very existence of the religious act will be a pledge of the existence of its intended object. As Scheler expresses it: 'Only a really existent being of the character of divinity can be the cause of men's religious aptitude, i.e. the aptitude to the realization of those acts which cannot be satisfied by any finite experience, and yet crave satisfaction. The object of the religious acts is at the same time their cause. Or: all knowledge of God is necessarily a knowledge from God' (269).

In all these opinions Scheler clearly shows forth his intellectual parentage: he has taken men like St. Augustine, Pascal and Cardinal Newman for his guides. But that means that, like them, he must defend himself on a double front: on the one side against the rationalizing theology of St. Thomas, on the other against the sentimentalizing theology of Schleiermacher. He has many arguments against the Neothomists. One is that their reasoning is circular. They confidently conclude from the creature to the Creator, but they overlook that the creatureliness of the creature, on which the argument is based, can only become apparent when its dependence on God has already been discovered—i.e. when God Himself has already been discovered. Furthermore, it is not permissible to jump, by means of syllogisms, across the great divides of reality. Would a being, however intelligent, that knew only the inanimate world, without having an inkling of what life may be, ever be able to infer from its knowledge the possibility of living things, let alone their characteristics? Surely not. Hence, *a fortiori*, it must be totally impossible for man with his finite intelligence and his finite experience, to grasp at Him who is infinite by simple ratiocination. But Scheler has another, and probably still more wounding, arrow in his quiver: he claims that the cosmological proof, if it is taken stringently, leads to an altogether irreligious result. This world of ours, from which all the reasoning starts, is a world where good and evil are hopelessly intermixed: if we were to conclude from it to the powers behind it, we would be led much sooner to Manichæan dualism than to Christian monotheism. We would certainly not find the God of St. John, the God of Jesus.

Although Scheler does not consciously develop his attack on Schleiermacher and modern Protestantism along the same lines as that on the Neothomist position, there is yet a certain parallel between the two trains of thought. Luther, he argues, has brought a new kind of circular reasoning into the world. He starts from the subjective certainty of faith in order to advance from there to its objective truth; yet is it not clear that the objective truth of faith must precede any subjective certainty, nay, that subjective certainty is utterly unthinkable without it? There is also a far too heavy reliance on causal reasoning. Schleiermacher makes much of the 'feeling of absolute dependence' evoked in man at the contemplation of the universe, and infers from it a cause for that feeling which he proceeds to call God. Yet need this be a personal god at all? Are we not rather pushed here into a kind of pantheism, such as in fact appeared in Schleiermacher's associates and successors, for instance in Hegel? Scheler has even less patience with Schleiermacher and his school (in the widest sense of the word) than with the Neothomists; understandably so, for their concentration on man's emotions, on his subjective and internal states of consciousness, makes their believing even less of a perceiving than Thomist rationalism, which, with all its alleged shortcomings, is yet an outward-looking towards reality and an apprehension of it which is at once rational and loving.

Where Scheler most openly disagrees with the traditional theology of either variety is in the low estimate he has formed concerning the value of the rational proofs for the existence of God. They are in his opinion not only unavailing, as they are for Kant, but altogether nonsensical. Who in his senses would demand a rational proof for the existence of colours instead of attempting to see them, or of sounds instead of attempting to hear them? Using a rather pleasing play on words which is possible in German, but unfortunately impossible in English, Scheler contrasts *Aufweis*, *Nachweis*, and *Beweis*. *Aufweis* is a demonstration in the original sense of the word, a pointing towards God, an invitation and a challenge to the yet unbelieving to open his eyes and to see for himself. It is invaluable as a pædagogical device, but it is not a proof. Whereas this *Aufweis* precedes, drives forward, and leads up to, the religious act, *Nachweis* follows upon it. It is a rational re-thinking and testing of the experience, a weighing and securing of its core. It, too, is invaluable, but, again, it is not a proof. *Beweis*, or proof as commonly understood, can reasonably be demanded only for *judgements* concerning an experience, but not for the experience itself. Judgements may indeed be right or wrong, but an experience (lying, as it does, in the pre-logical sphere of cognition) can at best be true or false. It may labour under deception, but it cannot be subject to error, and that is a different matter altogether.

A rational proof of the existence of God is in Scheler's opinion all the less necessary since every human being spontaneously believes in and adores some deity—only, in by far the greatest number of cases, alas! the wrong one. Those who have not found the Absolute will absolutize some relative good—money, promotion, woman, or what not—but everyone *has* his altar where he worships. There is a law, Scheler says, according to which 'every finite spirit believes either in the true God or in a false one' (281). Fallen man's dismal habit of cringing before idols is the moral malady which Pascal has called the *désordre du cœur*, and which is seated indeed in the deepest recesses of the human heart. Who would imagine that it could be driven out by clever argument? No, here we are in a sphere where reason is very largely (though perhaps not altogether) powerless. What is needed is a casting down, a smashing up, of golden calves. Once they lie in the dust, once their hollowness has become apparent, the obstacle will be removed which has stood between man and God, and he will be able to see Him whom, unwittingly, he has sought all the time— Him who alone can still the deepest desire of man's longing soul.

At this point our short survey of Scheler's thought in his Cologne period could fittingly be brought to a close, were it not for his incidental analysis of the concept of time, which is too valuable to be passed over in silence. If man cannot see God, it is because he has, on his part, erected a barrier which blocks his field of vision. This barrier can always be removed. Yet this barrier may consist of guilt: indeed, it always bears an element of guilt in itself —the pure in heart are never divorced from God. Can *guilt* then be wiped away as if it had never existed? Can an evil deed be blotted out so that it disappears without leaving a trace? In other words: can something that was done in the past be undone in the present as if the passing of time were not an irreversible process? Scheler suggests, in some of his most splendid passages, that repentance (*Reue*) can work this miracle. If our personal existence were a flow akin to the stream of objective time within which physical events take place, repentance would indeed be powerless. There could, in Kierkegaard's terminology, at most be a forgiving of sins, but not a forgetting: our liberation would remain limited because in nature what is past is past, and what is done is done. However, this is not so in human time. In every moment which we experience, the structure and the idea of the *whole* of our life are present, and, because present, in our power also. We cannot indeed change *ex post* the external *effects* of our actions, but we can alter their internal *meaning*. If we repent, then we expel out of ourselves, out of our personality, and out of human time, the deed with its motive, that is to say, the fact with its root, and it is, in a very definite sense of the word, true that it has never been. We are re-instated, as it were, into our pristine innocence. In this way, every moment of history can be redeemed and will remain redeemable while yet a spark of life continues to glow.

III

Scheler's philosophy of religion, as profound in thought as it was genuine in feeling, impressed friend and foe alike. Even an adversary such as Jacques Maritain speaks of him with respect—indeed, with affection.[1] Yet Scheler himself could not rest for long in his own achievement. Why did he fall away from it? The deeper reasons for his defection are not obvious. They could only be revealed by a sympathetic study of his life, by an investigation of those crises of faith at which Maritain is hinting, and for such a study, for such an investigation, it may already be too late today. But two more superficial reasons suggest themselves to the reader of his books. Scheler was quite willing to admit that the philosopher should give pride of place to the *homo religiosus*, the saint; but he was decidedly not willing to yield an inch to the theologian. Metaphysics as *ancilla fidei* was all right, but metaphysics as *ancilla theologiæ* by no means so. The rationalizing theologians around him were a thorn in his flesh and set up an irritation in his system which was apt to poison it altogether. If this was a comparatively petty cause, the other was of a more substantial nature. There is noticeable in Scheler's writings a growing desire to achieve a wider and wider synthesis—to break out of the narrow confines of the European tradition and to take into account at any rate the great achievements of Asiatic thought, if not indeed to advance to a universal vision. In the course of this endeavour, Christianity became of less and less importance to him, and this unavoidably estranged him from his own past. His removal to Frankfort in 1928 was but an external indication of his internal travellings.

The *Philosophical Anthropology* which was to outline Scheler's new position was as yet unfinished at the time of his death, but his essay *The Place of Man in the Universe* [2] clearly shows the direction in which he was drifting. It is significant that he first wanted to speak of 'man's *special* place', but that he later dropped the adjective because he increasingly found and felt that there is nothing so special about man as he had fancied for so many years. Indeed, he says quite brutally: 'There is not the slightest reason why one should, because of man's psychic life, make a more than gradual distinction between him and the animal, or why one should ascribe to his vital soul a special kind of origin and future destiny, as is done by theistic creationism and the traditional doctrine of immortality. The Mendelian laws apply to the building-up of psychic character in the same measure as they do to any physical features' (77). There is little talk in this essay of St. Augustine, Pascal and Cardinal Newman, whose influence had been so prominent in 'Man's Divine Self'; the figures now in the foreground are Buddha and Freud, whose doctrines, Scheler in-

[1] *De Bergson à Thomas d'Aquin*, New York, 1944, pp. 104–5.
[2] *Die Stellung des Menschen im Kosmos*, 1927.

sists, stand, in spite of all their differences, in a 'curious, sometimes even clearly recognized connection' (60).

And what insight is it that Buddha and Freud have in common across the centuries? It is the deep knowledge that all life is one, an indissoluble unity. Scheler proceeds to develop this theme in his own manner. Wherever there is life, he asserts, there, too, is psychic life: all living things are characterized by individuality and innerliness (*Selbst- und Innesein*). Even the plant possesses a vital urge instinct with feeling; even the plant has individuality in so far as it cannot be cut up without being destroyed; even the plant has a certain physiognomy, i.e. expresses and shows forth its internal states, such as vigour and listlessness. What the plant has not got, is any kind of reporting back of the stimuli which it receives to a centre from which appropriate movements of response would then issue. The existence and operation of such a centre is reserved to the higher forms of life, of which Scheler distinguishes three, described respectively by the terms instinct, habit and intelligence. As we ascend from the former to the latter, we perceive a threefold progress: progress in structure, in adaptability and in consciousness. So far as structure is concerned, the response of the living being to external stimulations becomes less and less predetermined and mechanical. Even instinct shows already the beginnings of a separation between sensation and reaction, but functionally there is here still the closest connection between the two. This connection is considerably loosened on the next higher level, that of habitual behaviour. Conditioned reflexes are not automatic as unconditioned reflexes are, yet they are still semi-automatic, and that distinguishes them from intelligent action, which is essentially free. Thus the separation between the sensory and the motor systems becomes ever more pronounced, and the position of the 'centre' ever more central.

Hand in hand with this growing liberation goes a growing pliability. Instinct provides its ready-made solutions only for the typical life-problems—survival-problems—of the species; habit gives us an answer even to relatively variable situations such as those of social intercourse, provided only they recur sufficiently often to allow the habit-making processes of trial and error to do their work; intelligence, however, can guide us in absolutely unique constellations, constellations never encountered before: it is thus the basis and the mainstay of all truly individual existence. Finally, there is an increase in consciousness and clarity as we rise from instinct to habit and from habit to intelligence. The plant has none of it: it is not possible in a being whose vital urge is directed, all of it, outward, which lives 'ecstatically' as it were; it arises only where resistances 're-flect' life inward, back onto itself, thus increasing and intensifying that innerliness which, for Scheler, is the hall-mark of all living things.

There is nothing at all remarkable about this description of the ascending series of life-phenomena, which is basic to the argument put forward in 'Man's Place in the Universe': it is quite obviously taken, with all its detail, from contemporary science. Yet a few points need emphasizing. The dark vital urge which he sees active in vegetative life is, according to Scheler, fundamental even in man. In a somewhat poetic passage he calls it 'the steam which drives everything up to the most exalted heights of spiritual activity, and which provides the energy even for the purest acts of thought and the most tender deeds of goodness' (14). It is, as he says again, behind every sensation, every perception, every mental image (18). Nor must it be thought that intelligence is the exclusive privilege of man; it is present already in the infusorium (25). It is true that Scheler is aware of the problematic character of so-called animal intelligence, even in so highly developed creatures as chimpanzees; yet, basing himself on the researches of some zoologists, e.g. Wolfgang Köhler, he confidently asserts that they may, in the full sense of the word, be described as intelligent. And goodness, too, is not a thing of which we alone can boast. 'The making of gifts, the readiness to help, reconciliation and similar phenomena can be found already among animals' (37)— which, incidentally, are also credited with genuine learning and tradition (30).

In view of all these assertions it is somewhat surprising to see that, in the end, Scheler does, after all, find an *essential* difference between man and all other creatures. He makes a distinction between psyche and spirit, and says that only the former is within the confines of nature, whereas the latter is not. This doctrine of the spirit is perhaps the only pillar of his earlier work that is now left standing. The spirit is not a phenomenon of life (as is, for instance, intelligence, that product of evolution); it stands outside and over against it; man is not only a feeling, acting and thinking creature, he is also a person. By dint of his spirit, the person is able to objectify his environment—an achievement of which merely vital beings are not capable, even if they are intelligent, because they must, through their very organization, remain bound up with, and in it. And this objectification is not restricted to things, it can also apply to man's physiological and psychological structure. Here lies the true contrast between animal and man. The animal is locked up in the concrete reality of its immediate present. Man can think of empty space and empty time. The animal has vague intuitions of quantity, but these are always embodied in concrete things. Man can conceive of abstract number. Indeed, man can even watch the interplay between his own body and his vital soul as if he were a third observer. How, it must be asked, is it that man can in this way break out of the prison-house of reality and look down upon it as from a higher vantage point? The answer is that man, by and through the spirit, is capable of suspending, as it were, his vital urge and organism which, if unsuspended, would keep him immersed in the stream of life, as it does the plant and the animal, and that, by and through the spirit, he can act ascetically, say 'no!' to life, and thus rise above it. Man is he that, by conquest of his lower self, can transcend the *hic* and *nunc*, and acquire true *a priori* knowledge.

Thus the person is spirit, and, as spirit, exalted above life. This, certainly, had been the conviction of the young Scheler—understandably so, for it is typical of, and integral to, the Christian tradition which he had upheld and developed in 'Man's Divine Self'; but was it really still the conviction of the older man, the Scheler of 1927? Probably not. Some parts of 'Man's Place in the Universe' certainly suggest that he was holding fast to this position, but others indicate that he was falling away from it. Immediately after defining 'the "person" in man' as the centre which is above the contrast of organism and environment', Scheler writes, in one of his most decisive passages: 'Is this not as if there were a progressive development in which a primal reality, in building the world, bends more and more back towards itself, to become, in ever higher forms and in ever new dimensions, aware of itself—and, finally, in man, to have and to grasp itself in all its entirety?' (44).[1] But if the spirit is simply the vital urge when it has come to self-knowledge and self-consciousness, then it is *not* outside life; it is life itself—a very different interpretation. The truth is that, by 1927, Scheler was rapidly sinking into the pantheistic or panentheistic mode of thought which he had fought, tooth and nail, all his life. It is characteristic that he now speaks with a new voice and a new sympathy of his erstwhile adversaries, Spinoza and Hegel (90).

But however Scheler may have conceived of the spirit in his closing days, whether as standing over against life, or as life become conscious, one thing is certain, namely that he did not ascribe to it the smallest particle of power. Pure spirit, he held, is pure impotency. It can only become effective, indeed, it can

[1] Cf. also p. 77. Scheler here says that even spiritual acts must, because of the essential unity of all psychophysical life, have a physiological *and* psychic component. It is not certain whether the word 'spiritual' is here used in its technical connotation, or means simply 'mental'. The context, however, strongly suggests that by 'spiritual acts' Scheler *does* mean acts of the spirit. But how can the acts of the spirit be independent of, and above life, if they are merely aspects of psychophysical processes?

only manifest itself, if it borrows energy from the lower vital urges of man, bending them, as it were, to its purposes. The utilization by the spirit of energies alien to it Scheler calls, with Freud, sublimation. Using two concepts which, as we shall see, were first applied in his sociological thinking, Scheler defines sublimation as the 'guidance and direction' of the power-stream of the organic impulses by the spirit and the spiritual will. 'Guidance' is the purposive stimulation of some drives and the corresponding lulling to sleep of others, which can be achieved by the conscious supply and the conscious cutting off of ideas and images; 'direction' the resulting inhibition (*non fiat*) and release (*non non fiat*) of spontaneous energies. What man's spirit can *not* do, according to this theory, is fight *directly* against the dark powers of vitality. Weak as it is, it can only lure them in certain directions, or play off one animal tendency against another. Thus the asceticism of which Scheler speaks as the root of our liberation from the trammels of reality, can only be passive and contemplative, not active and conquering. Here, better than anywhere else, we see how far he had drifted from the Christian tradition and become engulfed in Asiatic modes of thought.

With this doctrine of the spirit, Scheler believed he had found a way out of the age-old conflict of the idealist and materialist traditions. Materialism—the 'negative' theory—erred when it regarded the spirit as such as a product of sublimation, for who or what is to start that process of sublimation unless it is the spirit itself which is thus, illogically, presupposed? But whereas the spirit is a pre-existing entity, an attribute of absolute reality, of the very ground of things, it is in itself powerless, and that is where idealism—the 'classical' theory—falls down; when, for instance, in its Greek form, it ascribes to ideas an irreducible power and potency and influence in the world.

Although this new philosophy may have given some satisfaction to Scheler's intellect, it cannot have been more than cold comfort for his heart. An unmistakably pessimistic mood lies over the pages of 'Man's Place in the Universe'. 'Short-lived and rare are the flowering periods of culture in human history,' he writes with a tragic pen. 'Short-lived and rare is beauty in its tenderness and vulnerability' (66). But this pessimism is more than a mood: it has congealed into a theory, even a law. This law was formulated with great pungency by Nicolai Hartmann whom Scheler quotes: 'The higher categories of being and value are in themselves the weaker ones' (65). Is not the inorganic world independent of the organic, while the organic is dependent on it? Is not the plant independent of the animal, while the animal depends upon the plant? Are not both plants and animals independent of man whereas man depends heavily on them? And is not the inert mass of society relatively independent of the genius, whereas the genius can live only if he is tolerated by the mass? Wherever we look, we perceive the same picture: the higher forms of existence can only realize themselves through the powers of the lower ones.

It is abundantly clear that this world-view is utterly irreconcilable with any kind of theism. The idea of a creator-spirit who, by his powerful command, calls forth the world from the void, seemed to Scheler now the height of absurdity. He, who had followed the footsteps of St. Augustine, of Pascal, and of Cardinal Newman, has become a downright atheist. And, like most atheists, he is aggressive. Religion, he now declares, is no more than a sop for weaklings, unknown to, and not needed by, the strong.

For why is it that religions have arisen? They have arisen because the spirit of man, once it has objectified everything, once it has taken up its stand outside the confines of the concrete universe, feels utterly lonely and lost and thus longs for salvation and security. This salvation and security—alas! a purely delusionary one—is achieved with the aid of man's excessive imagination, which is one of his natural endowments and easily produces all sorts of phantasmagorias to which man can look for support —which cover up, as it were, the yawning depths of nothingness. Thus religion may have helped man in his difficulties, but it has not given him, as metaphysics does, the truth.

What Scheler, in the latter days of his life, envisaged to be the metaphysical truth, can perhaps be summed up in the following manner. Absolute reality—the *ens per se*—contains two elements, one low, one high; a vital urge and a fullness of ideas and values; *natura naturans* and *deitas*. In the beginning, the spirit (*deitas*) is all powerless. But relations change. In the end, the spirit will have gained the ascendancy. Evolution is a progressive spiritualization of matter and life—a progressive empowering of the logos. In this process, man occupies a central place. In him, the spirit has found itself, and he is capable of consciously embracing the cause of the spirit, thus furthering the ultimate 'realization' of the eternal deity. Scheler, as can be seen, was now preaching *a becoming god*.

With this metaphysic, Scheler recalls certain phases in the philosophical development of his great contemporary Henri Bergson. Both regarded the universe as a 'machine for the making of gods.'[1] Both must have asked themselves at one crucial moment whether the *élan vital* comes *from* God, or *is* god. But in the ultimate answer to this decisive question, the two thinkers disagreed. Bergson increasingly embraced the former, the theistic alternative; he died

[1] Bergson, *The Two Sources of Morality and Religion*, 1932 (Engl. ed., 1935), end.

on the threshold of the Catholic Church. Scheler travelled in the opposite direction. He sank deeper and deeper into materialism, scepticism and atheism, and it is perhaps not altogether fanciful to suggest that his untimely, all-too-early death was not entirely unconnected with the growing despair that had taken hold of his mind.

IV

From the very first moment of his career, Scheler was as vitally interested in sociology as he was in the various philosophical disciplines to whose development he later contributed. Already the book on *The Formalistic Principle in Ethics* contains, beside all its ethical speculation, a good deal of positive and descriptive sociology. The present survey, brief as it is bound to be, can only speak of two important sociological ideas contained in Scheler's earlier works, though there are several others that would be well worth considering—his concept of collective responsibility, and his concept of historical relativity, out of which his technical 'sociology of knowledge' was ultimately to develop.

The concept of collective responsibility stands on the border-line between sociology and ethics. It is as much a fact as a postulate. We not only *should feel* co-responsible for all that happens in our society, we *are* so, whether we like it or not, and whether we are aware of it or not. The connection between cause and effect does not depend on man's ability to discern it—in morals as little as in physics. 'There is no moral motion, however small, which would not—like the stone that falls into the water—produce infinite circles, and even these circles become finally invisible only for the naked and unaided eye. Already the physicist can trace them much further—and how far the all-knowing God! The love of A to B awakens not only—if there is no inhibiting cause—a corresponding love in B to A, but it naturally causes an increase, in the heart of the responding B, of the warmth- and life-giving power of loving in general, hence also of his love to C and D; and thus the wave travels on in the moral universe from C to D to E and F—into infinity. And the same applies to hate, injustice, immodesty, and every kind of sin. Every one of us has been an active participant in an uncountable number of good and bad things of which he does not have, and indeed cannot have, any knowledge, and for which he is none-the-less co-responsible before God' (*Vom Ewigen* I, 158). This consideration not only underpins 'the great principle of the solidarity of all the children of Adam in responsibility, guilt and merit' (ibid., 44), but it also opens up a deep and true insight into the underground criss-crossing of social forces, on which the degree of social control and harmony achieved in any society depends, and which it is the duty of the sociologist to lay bare.

The realization that the ideas of the past cannot be properly understood unless they are seen against the background of their contemporary conditions, and that many of them cannot be understood at all unless they are so seen, belongs to the oldest possessions of the social sciences; yet only in Scheler's hands did it turn from an empty common-place into a significant sociological principle. He will live on as the founder of the sociology of knowledge, if for no other of his achievements. In discussing Scheler's attitude to the proofs for the existence of God, we spoke of his antagonism to the Neothomists, but we did not mention any antagonism to St. Thomas himself. There was hardly any such antagonism. The reason for this lay in Scheler's sympathetic penetration of the situation which confronted the great philosopher-saint. He realized that in the thirteenth century the cosmological proof was by no means so unconvincing as it is today. Today the creatureliness of the creature, which is the foundation of the whole argument, is not admitted because it is not perceived, and without this initial insight all that follows is bound to be no more than an empty show of cleverness. But at the height of the Middle Ages, the creatureliness of the creature was no problem; it was a matter of course, because the whole atmosphere was drenched, as it were, in theistic sentiment. St. Thomas did not argue in a circle when he derived the existence of the Creator from the existence of the creature: that the creature was, in fact and in truth, a created being—presupposing, implying, demanding a Creator—was not doubted; it was a conviction which formed part and parcel of the unconscious metaphysic of the age. Why then were the rational proofs for the existence of God developed at all? Because, Scheler says, the thirteenth century was the first to be interested in suchlike exercises of the intellect. It was the beginning of the bourgeois age, and the bourgeois, even at that early date, was already a rationalist in the egg-shell, the scientist at the larval stage. It was to satisfy his bent of mind that St. Thomas showed how religion could be justified before the judgement seat of reason if such a justification be desired—a justification which, however, seemed at the time no more than the formal confirmation of what was beyond material doubt anyway.

This explanation of Thomist rationalism from the point of view of its social setting, shows already the specific method of the sociology of knowledge which was later so admirably perfected and so deftly utilized by Scheler and his school. But Scheler always read the equation between social fact and social thought—between

Marx's substructure and superstructure—from *either* side. If certain social situations demand certain ideas as their natural modes of expression, certain ideas on their part command certain social forms in which they can appropriately embody themselves. Scheler's discussion, in *Vom Ewigen im Menschen* (II, 409 seq.), of pantheism is a case in point. Pantheism, he explains, is necessarily aristocratic. Where God is not regarded as a personal God who reveals Himself to all who love Him, but as an impersonal and mysterious X that is visible only in and through reality, there the idea must and will arise that the scholars, the scientists, the intellectuals have the closest knowledge of supernatural things, or at any rate a closer knowledge than the common run of men. And, in point of fact, pantheism has historically tended, wherever it has appeared, to make a distinction between the religion of philosophers and the religion of the masses, a distinction quite clearly contained, for instance, in Spinoza's system of ideas. Thus ideas shape social relationships, just as social relationships shape ideas, and in the elaboration of the former connection and causation (if the word be permitted) Scheler showed much originality of mind and achieved great success in his pioneering.

The mature fruits of these seeds of thought are to be found in Scheler's work, *Die Wissensformen und die Gesellschaft*, published in 1926. It is perhaps some indication of the importance of this book to say that it led to a complete reassessment of the two great sociological theories which had dominated the nineteenth century, and which were left as its main heritage to the twentieth: Marx's 'historical materialism' and Comte's 'law of the three stages'. Of course, these theories had been repeatedly impugned before 1926: indeed, yet another exposure of their onesidedness and error would have been a useless flogging of dead horses. But Scheler's treatment of both Comte and Marx was highly original. He saw in them pioneers whose thoughts were well worth re-thinking—who had indeed become bogged down in error when they set out to find the truth, but who had all the same been on the way, and who had posed problems for which sociology must find some answer, if it was to be a true science of social life.

Scheler had no quarrel with Marx's general contention that it is not the consciousness of men that determines their existence, but on the contrary their social existence which determines their consciousness. What he objected to was the equation, so characteristic of Marxian thought, of 'social existence' with 'mode of production'. What, he asked, did Marx really mean when he spoke of *Produktionsverhältnisse*, or relations of production, as the ultimately determining element of the mental life? There are, he urges, at least four different meanings which can be given to that somewhat problematic term. It can either mean the human relationships characteristic of certain forms of economic enterprise; or it can mean the legal forms, say, the forms of property, at the basis of a definite social order; or it can, and often does, mean, phenomena dependent on the contemporary state of technological development; or again, class relationships in the narrower sense of the word, relationships between social groupings ranked as higher and lower. The Marxians will, of course, argue that these four elements cannot usefully be separated, since they are simply four facets of one and the same complex of facts; but then *all* contemporary phenomena are facets of one and the same complex of facts. A determinist doctrine ought to say what determines and what is determined, and if it fails in this task, it has failed altogether.

Returning to the Marxian starting-point, Scheler tried to approach the problem set by Marx in an entirely new, unbiased and balanced spirit. He accepts the division of that configurational unity which we call a society into a substructure and a superstructure, but he defines the terms differently and more comprehensively than Marx. Every human act, it is true, has its mental and its material component; yet we are justified in distinguishing actions which are predominantly cultural and ultimately directed towards 'ideal' ends and purposes, and actions which are predominantly determined by natural facts and urges, and aim at some tangible transformation of external reality. The former work themselves out in the world of ideas, the latter in the material world. These, and the institutions in which they are embodied, constitute what Scheler calls the substructure, the former the superstructure. To the substructure, then, belong first of all the great drives which are active in the human world, those for food, sex satisfaction and power, for instance: but also all other objective bases of society, such as there are—racial inheritance, geographical environment, power-political set-up and economic conditions. The substructure is in this way, for Scheler, the sphere of relative necessity, whereas the superstructure, where human expectations, volitions, ideas, ideals, and phantasmagorias play their part, is the field of relative freedom. Either of these halves of social reality has its own immanent and independent tendencies: both contribute in their measure to the reality which emerges from their co-operation and their conflict. But in what measure? Is the one the seal, the other the wax—the one determining, the other determined?

'It is the fundamental mistake of all materialistic interpretations of history', Scheler writes in reply to this question (loc. cit., 31), 'that they attribute to the material factors (*Realfaktoren*) . . . be it race, geo-political structure, political power-relationships, or conditions of economic production, the power univocally to determine the world of ideality such as we see it incarnated in the works of the spirit . . .' But, he goes on to say, 'it is the at least equally great error of all ideological, idealistic and individualistic conceptions of history, that they on their part imagine they can understand the history of material events and institutions, and of the state of the masses, be it directly or indirectly, as a simple prolongation of the history of the spirit'. Both protagonists in this discussion err. What happens is in point of fact more complicated than either of them would suppose. According to Scheler, the material factors determine which of the ideas thrown up by the stream of cultural development will come to influence and fruition; they are a selective agency; they 'open and close the sluices of the spiritual stream' (32). The blind tendencies of material development, on the other hand, can come under the 'guidance' and 'direction' (*Leitung und Lenkung*) of the human will, of human ideas and ideals. If the spirit can make use of some pre-existing, independently existing, tendency, i.e. of some fund of material energy, it can exert a very real influence on what is happening. Following Comte, Scheler speaks of a 'fatalité modifiable' of external history (*Realgeschichte*), to which there corresponds, on the part of the spirit, a 'liberté modifiable,' a freedom which, however unrestricted it may be internally, is limited by the objective constellation of the material forces, when it comes to excursions into the outside world.

The problem, of course, remains, in spite of this ingenious, and, it should seem, realistic theory. *How* modifiable is blind necessity? how *great* is the influence of the spirit? Scheler gave different answers to this question at different times, according to the stage he had reached in his descent towards the position expressed in *Die Stellung des Menschen im Kosmos*. In 1926, when the book under discussion was published, this process had already gone very far, yet Scheler was still ascribing considerable reality-shaping power to the spirit. Both eastern and western society, he points out, held initially the same seeds of technological development, yet whereas the west allowed them to unfold, they withered away and came to nothing in the east. The reason, Scheler asserts, lay in the different direction taken by the eastern and the western ethos, and by metaphysical and religious thought. Both were marked by a strong will to domination, but in the east it struck inward as it were, in the west outward. In the east, the main aim was to achieve control over the automatic motions of the soul and the processes of the body—the Indian ideal; in the west, to achieve control over the external forces of nature—an ideal traceable in the last analysis to the Jewish conception of the Deity as a Creator and Constructor, whose work man has to carry onward by subjecting the lower, especially the inanimate, creation to his will. If the Greeks did not develop a more advanced technology, in spite of the fact that they had a science containing many practical possibilities, this was due to the fact that their religion and metaphysics were nearer to the eastern than to the western outlook, and did not regard the world in the first place as a field of human endeavour and of human labour and workmanship.

With these ideas Scheler became the founder of a new and purified sociology of knowledge. While the valuable core of the Marxian theory is retained and rescued, its 'ideological' shell is broken and discarded. Scheler has no difficulty in showing that Marxism is in truth an ideology, i.e. the transmutation of particularist prejudices that have become unconscious into a pretended science. Far from being genuinely scientific, it contains a strong utopian element; indeed, far from being genuinely materialist, it shares the over-emphasis, characteristic of idealism, of the power of the spirit. Does it not assume that the day will come when the material factors underneath social life will cease to condition human thinking—the famous 'jump into freedom'? Does it not present again, in a new guise, the old idealistic dream of an (ultimate) supremacy of reason over reality? That age, Scheler asserts, will never come: it is wishful thinking to suppose that it ever will. And it is still more wishful thinking to suppose that men's eagerness to lord it over other men will disappear when one element in the complex substructure of society—the element of legal control over the means of economic production—is changed. The drives that lead to class domination are more manifold and deeper. In a simple sentence, which has since been amply confirmed by practical experience, Scheler exposes the whole utopianism of the Marxist utopia: 'Men's desire to dominate over men is, as any sound observation shows, in no way only a means to gain domination over things, but rather—as Kant rightly teaches in his *Anthropologie*—something which is basically characteristic of man and would never entirely disappear, even under an ideal technique of production' (loc. cit., 157).

But if the Marxist interpretation of history is an ideology, its Comtean counterpart is no less so: if the one reflects proletarian aspirations, the other eulogizes bourgeois achievements. What Comte did was to accept the naïve prejudices of his age, of nineteenth-century capitalism, according to which the type of knowledge in which it excelled, scientific and technological knowledge, was the most valuable type of knowledge conceivable, and then proceeded to interpret the other forms of knowing—religious and metaphysical—as historical preparations for it, valuable only in so far as they have served as stepping stones for the 'superior'

mental technique and accomplishment, and destined to be superseded by it. Against this theory of (fancied) progress, according to
which a metaphysical age followed upon a religious one, and a
'positive' upon the metaphysical, Scheler set two main arguments.
The one is the assertion that religious and metaphysical knowledge
have a permanent ground in life, just as scientific and technological
knowledge have; that they have co-existed in every age and always
will; that they are carried by entirely different human types (*homo
religiosus*, sage, scientist and technician), apply entirely different
methods (contact with God, speculation, inductive and deductive
reasoning), etc., etc.—in short, that the replacement of the one
by the other, so lightheartedly assumed by Comte to have taken
place in the course of history, is in fact an impossibility. Scheler's
second argument goes even deeper. It challenges Comte's assumption that mental development is an uninterrupted stream, that
every achievement can be handed on without difficulty to suc-
ceeding generations, and that for every achievement comes the
time when it is *passé*. Only scientific and technological knowledge
can, in point of fact, be handed on and treated in this way: only
in this one sphere is there 'cumulative' progress. So far as culture
in the narrower sense of the word is concerned, every nation and
every epoch has its own individual contribution to make: every
culture is a unique achievement, which is by no means robbed
of its value simply because time moves forward and other cultures
spring up later on. Scheler here echoes von Ranke's deep saying,
that before God all generations appear with equal rights, and that
that is the manner in which we, too, ought to see the history of
the human kind.

However, Scheler sees a spark of truth in Comte's doctrine, just
as he does in that of Marx. He, too, discerns in history three stages
or phases which tend to succeed each other, and which would have
succeeded each other with even more obviousness and regularity
if external influences had not cut across this immanent tendency
and disturbed it. At first, the *racial* factor is the one among the
substructural forces which, more than any other, determines the
shape of society and selects the spiritual tendencies which can
come to full development. Scheler thinks of India here, whose
all-important caste-system was due to the superimposition of the
conquering fair-skinned Aryan race upon the conquered dark-
coloured aboriginals, and whose indirect effect we can trace even
in the higher reaches of the brahmanic culture and religion. Then
the *political* factor moves into the foreground. Monarchical govern-
ments spring up which mould the contrasting racial components
of their territories into more or less uniform masses of subjects.
For centuries, power drives and political developments determine

what society is to be like, and what ideas will be able to pass, through the sluices of the material selecting agencies, out into the open light of day. Even economic tendencies are only secondary at this stage, just as they are in the first period. Under Colbertism, economic life is still no more than an instrument of power politics. Finally, however, the capitalist epoch arrives, when *economic* conditions are ultimately decisive for the social set-up and—always negatively, by separating what is to be realized from what is, in principle, equally possible—decisive also for the mental life of society, the content of culture. The modern age is indeed the age of economic classes and of a scientific world-view. Scheler in this way sees the common error of Comte and Marx in the transfer of observations and valuations which properly apply only to the last and latest phase of evolution, to earlier constellations.

Is there, in this successive shift of primacy among the material factors which act as the sluicegates of the spirit, anything that can rightly be called progress? Scheler actually uses the term (loc. cit., 45), but not in its positivist and rationalist meaning. He does not suggest that the modern age has achieved more sanctity in religion, more truth in knowledge, more goodness in action, more beauty in art. The eternal realm of values and verities has ever lain open before men's searching eyes, and it would be difficult to understand why later generations should have seen more deeply into it than earlier ones. Their greater adroitness in managing the forces of nature (which nobody will deny) cannot have given them —as Comte without good reason assumed—an advantage in the religious, metaphysical, moral or artistic quest. But if modern culture is not necessarily deeper than previous ones, it is broader. 'The inhibition and selection which the spiritual potentialities receive at the hands of the material factors, is in predominantly economically determined ages . . . the smallest, the release of the fullness of these potentialities the greatest. . . . Where, however, it is the racial position and composition (*die Blutzugehörigkeit*) of a group, as also its sex and age position or composition, that decides, directly or indirectly, the possible realization of its spiritual potentialities, there the inhibition of these potentialities is the greatest, their possibility of release the smallest. The specifically power-political periods stand in the middle. Hence spiritual culture is by no means positively most "valuable" when it has reached its highest stage in time, but it is richest, most differentiated, most colourful, most manifold' (46). At the same time, the influence of the human spirit, of men's volitions and ideas, on the course of objective development, on the *fatalité modifiable* of things, is (potentially at least) greater than ever before.

V

In many ways, Scheler's book on sympathy is the most characteristic of his numerous publications. All his main preoccupations are in a manner expressed in it. It has quite obviously grown from the same inspiration which produced the whole majestic structure of his theory of value. In fact the forms of love which he distinguishes, and the order in which he sees them grouped, are essentially a reflection and reduplication of the hierarchy of values which is at the core of his ethical system. There can be, he says, no love (in the proper sense of the word) of what is merely useful or agreeable. At the lowest level of loving we find a physical love or *amour-passion* which corresponds to the category of values called vital; on the next higher plane, as a finer form, a mental love which is aroused by, and directed to, the cultural values; and, at the apex, a spiritual love which goes out to those objects or persons which embody the values of holiness. Hence, as God is the Value of Values, so the love of God (in either of its two meanings) is the love of loves. But the book on sympathy, though published as early as 1913, also foreshadows Scheler's later thought. It is true that the total immersion and submersion of the ego in the stream of universal life, which is the characteristic aim of the brahmanic and buddhistic ethos, is depicted as a lower sentiment than the strictly personal, 'non-cosmic' love which is the specific ideal of the Christian tradition. Yet 'lower' means 'more basic' here, as well as 'less valuable', and there is an impressive passage (p. 105) in which Scheler demands that it be re-kindled and recultivated in Western man. Such ideas anticipate to some extent 'Man's Place in the Universe' and the 'Philosophical Anthropology'. Finally, the book is also a decisive contribution to sociological literature. Discussing, as it does, the difficult question how, and how far, each one of us can come to know and to comprehend the psychic processes of other human beings, it deals with a problem which is manifestly basic to all social science and speculation, and one without the solution of which no system of social theory can be either a complete or a well-grounded body of thought and knowledge.

It is by starting from this last-named problem, which Scheler describes as the problem of the 'essential, existential, and epistemological foundations of the interconnection between human selves and human souls' (p. 213) that we can most easily approach the book and penetrate to its message. There are two theories which Scheler endeavours to disprove throughout the work, both implying that our knowledge of other human beings is not, as the man in the street is inclined to assume, direct, but unavoidably indirect. The one asserts that it is acquired by means of reasoning from *analogy*—reasoning which may be only rudimentary and semi-conscious, but which is yet reducible to syllogistic form. We perceive on another man's face expressions of a kind which we know from our own personal experience of our own personal self, and so we conclude that what is going on inside him, is analogous to what is going on inside us. Scheler decidedly rejects this explanation: even babies can grasp the meaning of our facial expressions, not to speak of animals, and it would be nothing short of absurd to credit them with the faculty of syllogism-making. Moreover, a logical conclusion *per analogiam* could never lead us to the knowledge of a mind different from ours: it can, of necessity, lead us only to the assumption of an alien ego identical with it. The second theory is similar to the first, but avoids its crude rationalism. According to it, we do not *conclude* from a certain configuration of a man's features that he is angry, but we *feel* ourselves into him, thus comprehending the meaning of his expression by *empathy*. Scheler objects to this explanation, which suggests that we transfer something of our own mind and life onto and into the body of others, that it could never tell us whether the human being we are observing and trying to understand, is really alive or not: it would be a pure coincidence if the movement of empathy starting in ourselves were to meet, in the object which it seeks to embrace, a real soul akin to our own. And, once again, empathy could never hope to provide me with the knowledge of a human being different from myself. Like the other theory, it could at best induce me to believe that my ego is reduplicated in other bodies.

What the two theories criticized have in common is the assumption (which is very natural to the untutored mind, but which ought to be highly suspect to the critical philosopher) that the knowledge of self precedes the knowledge of others and is more fundamental than it. This, according to Scheler, is the root-error which has to be eradicated. Originally, the experience of self and the experience of others is in no way differentiated: the child feels the feelings and thinks the thoughts of those who form his social environment, and there is one broad roaring stream of living in which he is totally immersed. It takes a long time before vortices form within this stream, which draw together what later on will clearly be recognized as 'mine' and 'others'. Even when we come to integrate our own self—to cut it out of the texture, as it were, in which it had formed one indistinguishable strand alongside many others—we continue to see it against the background of a surviving, although progressively receding, common consciousness which contains, in principle, the experience of others as well as the experience of the self. It is this fundamental fact which, according to Scheler, explains our knowledge—our *direct* knowledge

—of the psychic life of our fellow-humans. Far from our living in them, as the theories based on analogy and empathy would suggest, *they* live in *us* because ego and non-ego have both emerged out of a common stream of life-experience and are thus (to use another, but kindred thinker's simile[1]) twin-born and not antithetic, for ever tied together and not divided by a yawning gap that would somehow have to be bridged.

However, the time comes when our individualism asserts itself. The time comes when we strive to establish ourselves as independent entities. We learn to objectify the experiences which are not our own and thus attribute distance to them. Then there supervenes the phase which Scheler describes as egocentrism. Having lived in others more than in ourselves, we now swing over to the opposite extreme. We develop a tendency towards solipsism in knowledge, towards egoism in action, towards auto-erotism in love. All these attitudes have their common centre in a *désordre du cœur*, in a confusion in our value-system. We fancy that our own world of values is the value-world itself. We become for ourselves the hub of the universe, the only absolute reality to which everything else is relative. Our fellow beings sink down to pale, shadowy creatures not comparable to ourselves in importance, nay, even in existence. This is the world-view which has found its clearest expression in Max Stirner's book, *The Ego and his Own*. The Ego —in German: *der Einzige*, the Single One—sees himself here as absolutely real: all others are merely objects for his use, his domination, and his pleasure. They are 'his own'. We are all Stirners at one stage of our development: we all suffer for a while from the 'timetic egocentrism' reflected in his famous book. How comes it that we rise above this narrow and warped view of the world and of society, that our wrong perspectives are righted, and that our heart is changed?

The great change is worked by sympathy and love. When the primal endowments of our soul which are known by these words come into play, the prison walls which our egocentrism has built around us are broken, and our eyes are opened to the fact that others *qua* human beings, *qua* persons, are as valuable as we are ourselves—and not only as valuable, but also as real. The shadowy figures around us come again to life and fill anew with flesh and blood. Thus it is sympathy and love that dispel the 'metaphysical delusion' of 'relative solipsism', just as they destroy the ethical evil of selfishness. They open the heart, and with the heart the mind. This is their great function in the scheme of things, and this, it seems, is the essential teaching of Scheler's book.

For Scheler sympathy and love are emotions in the literal sense

[1] C. H. Cooley.

of the term—in the sense of motions, of movements, which lead us out of and beyond ourselves. This is particularly true of love, which is a spontaneous act, whereas sympathy is merely secondary or reactive, a response to the experiences of others, which needs, moreover, as its vehicle, an underlying love and can go no further than that basic love will allow. Love, according to Scheler, makes us seeing, not blind. Its regard will penetrate through the outer shells which hide the real self, through physical appearance, through the social mask, through the awkwardness of language, which so often conceals rather than reveals our inner life—right to the most intimate sphere of the person, where absolute unknowability necessarily begins. Indeed, the essence of another's individuality, which can never be adequately described, which can never be exhausted in an enumeration of separate qualities however long, manifests itself for us in its fullness *only* in and through the act of love.

Stated in this bald manner, Scheler's thesis sounds simple and convincing enough. Yet how revolutionary does it appear if we compare it to the theories on the subject which Scheler found in possession of the field! Schopenhauer, von Hartmann, Spencer, Freud—they all approached the phenomena of sympathy and love along entirely different avenues. The bulk of the book is taken up with polemics against them. There is no need here to follow the discussion in all its detail. Suffice it to say that whereas in the hands of the others the two concepts tend to disintegrate, they stand out in their whole purity and definiteness in Scheler's argument. His is in truth a book on the *essence* of sympathy and love, an application of the phenomenological method at its best.

Great as are Scheler's achievements in many fields of intellectual endeavour, none is perhaps greater than his splendid characterization of the phenomenon of love. It is, in his opinion, much more than a fascination by, and infatuation with, a value or a set of values which we find realized in some object or person. Such a perceived value is no more than a starting point. If we love any human being, we certainly love him for what he is; but at the same time we love him also for what he *might* be, according to the possibilities of perfection inherent in his being. Our eyes are fixed on his ideal image which we grasp in, through and behind his empirical traits; yet we are indifferent as to how far it is reflected and realized in his actual state. At the same time, our love is the most potent force that can lift him from the one to the other. It carries before him his own purified, and, as it were, redeemed and transfigured likeness, as a challenge to follow and to reach it; it is like a voice calling: become what you are! become in reality what ideally you are in design! Thus it is to Scheler in its inmost

xli

nature a dynamic power. He calls it a movement in the direction from lower to higher value. Even sexual love (in the true sense of the word, as distinguished from the pure play of instinctive urges) has this character, because its intention is not simply the production of yet another human being no better than those that already exist. This, surely, could be achieved without a trace of true loving. It is, rather, an attempt to lift out of the universal fund of vitality a higher type of man, a vitally finer incarnation of the species.

Needless to say, what applies to this comparatively low form of love, applies still more—*mutatis mutandis*—to its higher forms. A love of beauty, for instance, is not simply a rapt contemplation of the beauty that is; it is also, and still more, an envisaging of further and higher beauty, which we feel to be possible when we gaze at our object, or at the person, that has inspired our sentiment; it is, indeed, the first motion towards its realization. Thus each act of loving is, on its proper plane, a reaching upward for ever higher values which are *in posse*, though not yet *in esse*, discernible as potentialities waiting for actualization. In this notion we see once more the deep Platonic tinge of Scheler's philosophy.

But what is the ultimate consummation to which he who loves with the highest love, with a holy love, would lead the one this love embraces? In view of Scheler's underlying theory of value and religion, there can be no doubt whatever about the answer: it is the fulfilment of the destiny ordained for the loved one by the Creator God—the realization of the idea which was in the Divine Mind when he was called into being. Thus love is a raising and a being raised towards the Summit of Perfection—the way of salvation for this nether world.

INTRODUCTORY NOTE TO THE
FIFTH EDITION

THE first edition of this book appeared in 1913 under the title *Zur Phänomenologie der Sympathiegefühle und von Liebe und Hass*, published by Niemeyer, Halle; the second, third and fourth editions under the same title as the present edition,[1] published by Friedrich Cohen, Bonn. After a period during which Max Scheler's works could not be reissued, this fifth edition appears under the imprint of G. Schulte-Bumke, Frankfurt-am-Main, to whom the Bonn publishers transferred their philosophy section.

For this edition, the text which formed the basis of the second, third and fourth editions has been revised from the manuscript, and a considerable number of printer's errors and textual inaccuracies have been corrected, in accordance with the author's intentions. For matters of detail, reference should be made to the projected Complete Edition of Scheler's works. The footnotes contain references to work published by the author after the issue of the second edition, including material incorporated in the first volume of his posthumous remains.[2] These are distinguished by square brackets from his own earlier references. The dates immediately following the titles of his works are those of first publication, except for those in the posthumous volume, which refer to the date of composition.

The preface to the first edition has been added to those of the second and third. The subject-index of the second edition has been supplemented and extended to include works published by the author after 1923.

---

[1] *Wesen und Formen der Sympathie.* [. . . Ed.]   [2] *Nachlassband,* I (1933).

PREFACE TO THE THIRD EDITION

This treatise on Sympathy was to have been the first of a series of books which Scheler planned under the title *Die Sinngesetze des emotionalen Lebens*; it was to be followed by studies of the sense of shame, the sense of honour, and the emotions of fear and reverence, but the project did not get beyond this first volume in the author's lifetime. Since no completed investigation of the problems of these emotions was found among the author's papers, this work now appears without the series-title. It should be mentioned that considerable portions of a study 'Über Scham und Schamgefühl' were included in *Nachlassband*, I.

MARIA SCHELER

Spring 1948

PREFACE TO THE THIRD EDITION

THE third edition of this book appears without alteration, in the same form as the second. The book has been well received, both at home and abroad, among those interested in philosophy, psychology and sociology—not that this means very much in the case of a philosophical work. What has greatly pleased the author, however, is that it should also have given rise to quite a number of serious discussions of the long-neglected problems with which it deals. Particularly in connection with those higher acts of sympathy which are of importance in Ethics I find, in the relevant sections of Nicolai Hartmann's imposing and profound *Ethics*,[1] a deeper and broader treatment of several of the analyses and propositions advanced in the present work. From an angle closer to that of the sociologist and philosopher of culture, Theodor Litt, in the third edition of his important *Individuum und Gesellschaft*, has made use of theories and analyses outlined here, and has developed them on fruitful lines. In their notable study, *Die Deutung des mimischen Ausdrucks, ein Beitrag zur Lehre vom Bewusstsein des anderen Ichs*,[2] H. Plessner and F. J. J. Buytendijk have provided an interesting development of my position in its bearing upon the epistemological problem of our apprehension of, and belief in, the reality of other selves. The psychiatrist, A. Ludwig Binswanger's *Einführung in die Probleme der allgemeinen Psychologie*, contains much that is of value in elaborating the conclusions of this book. And *The phenomenological approach in its application in*

---

[1] N. Hartmann: *Ethics* (tr. Stanton Coit), Allen and Unwin, 1923.

[2] *Philosophischer Anzeiger* (ed. H. Plessner), I. Halbband: F. Cohen, Bonn, 1925.

Max Scheler by Albert K. Weinberg has shown great skill in introducing the work to readers of philosophy and psychology in North America, analysing it especially from the methodological point of view, and comparing it with the methods employed in American psychology. A French translation of my book will be appearing in a few weeks, under the imprint of Payot, Paris.

MAX SCHELER

Cologne, 1926

PREFACE TO THE SECOND EDITION

PUBLISHED in 1913 under the title *Zur Phänomenologie und Theorie der Sympathiegefühle und vom Liebe und Hass*, this book has long been out of print and adverse circumstances have prevented the issue of a new edition, in spite of frequent demand. It now reappears in an essentially new form, more than twice as long, and under a title which corresponds better to its present content. It appears also as the first volume in a series of monographs, whose common unity of aim is set out in the general title *Die Sinngesetze des emotionalen Lebens*.

I must give the reader some account of the wider context of those investigations of which this book forms a part, and also of the material contained in the sections which have been added to it.

It has long been forgotten that, besides the causal determination and psycho-physical dependence of the emotional life on somatic events, there are also independent *laws of intension* among the 'higher' emotional acts and functions, as distinct from ordinary feeling-sensations. Hermann Lotze was the first to rediscover the intentional and evaluative character of our 'higher' emotional life. But since he only proclaimed this *logique du cœur* in very general terms, without entering into details, it received little attention. To him we owe the idea and the formula, that 'in its feeling for the value of things and their relation, our reason possesses as genuine a revelation as, in principle, in the principles of logical investigation, it has an indispensable instrument of experience'.[1]

The present author, in his *Der Formalismus in der Ethik und die materiale Wertethik*, has again adopted Pascal's old but splendid idea of an *ordre du cœur, logique du cœur, raison du cœur*, and made it a pillar of his ethical system. The series to be entitled *Die Sinngesetze*

[1] Hermann Lotze: *Microcosmos* (tr. Elizabeth Hamilton and E. Constance Jones), Clark, Edinburgh, 1885. Vol. I, p. 245.

xlv

des emotionalen Lebens is designed to apply this idea *in detail* to all the main branches of our emotional life, particularly in their ethical, social and religious aspects, and to provide more stringent evidence for the truth and profundity of this thought of Pascal. The intention is to follow this book by others on 'The Nature of Shame', 'The Nature of Apprehension and Fear' and 'The Nature of the sense of Honour'. In these my aim will be to treat all the more important *derivatives* of the major emotion in question, as has here been done in the case of sympathy; to give detailed attention to these emotions, not only from the standpoint of psychology and value-theory, but also with regard to their *order of development* in the individual and the species; and to assess their importance in the formation and maintenance, the ordering and specifying, of social groupings among men. We cannot yet set out our reasons for believing that by publishing our studies in the order indicated, we shall be able to give systematic coverage to all the varieties of feeling of real importance in the ethical and social field.

The first edition of the book has been augmented here by the following newly-written sections and chapters: a new chapter on emotional identification (Part I, ch. 2, 4) the special nature of which I had by no means realized at the time of the first edition; the entire chapter (Part I, ch. 4) on 'Metaphysical theories of Sympathy' (with the exception of the comments on Schopenhauer's theory, which were included in the first edition); and 'The sense of unity with the cosmos in some representative temperaments of the past' (Part I, ch. 5), 'Sympathy and its Laws of dependence' (Part I, ch. 6), and 'The Interaction of the sympathetic functions' (Part I, ch. 7), all of which are entirely new. The discussion 'On our grounds for assuming the existence of other selves', which appeared as an Appendix to the first edition, now stands as an independent part of the book (Part III), and has been enlarged by the addition of chapters 1 and 2, viz., 'Nature and scope of the problems', and 'The general evidence for the "Thou"'. Major and minor changes, additions and footnotes have also been incorporated at many points in the book.

It is only in the course of investigating these problems at length that the author has come to realize how *many-sided* are the philosophical questions connected with the phenomena of sympathy. The first exact analyses of the sympathetic emotions in modern times are due to the great British psychologists, Shaftesbury, Hutcheson, David Hume, Adam Smith, Herbert Spencer, Alexander Bain and others. Apart from the deep-seated errors which we shall show these analyses to contain—errors which, as I later realized, were already discerned in part by Guyau in his work on

British moral philosophy[1]—they are one-sided in two different respects. In the first place, they study the phenomena only in their empirical, genetic aspect, attempting neither phenomenological analysis nor accurate description; in the second, they only discuss the facts with a view to providing a deeper foundation for *ethics*. Important as the phenomena of sympathy are for ethics (cf. Nietzsche's criticism of Schopenhauer's theory of pity), we nevertheless reject from the outset an 'Ethics of Sympathy' *as such*, holding as we do, that the problem of sympathy in general has aspects and affinities which simply cannot be reached at all by a one-sided analysis and consideration from a purely ethical point of view. Apart from its importance for *æsthetics*, which in Germany at least, from Lotze to Lipps and Volkelt,[2] has largely been based upon the idea of 'empathy', there is a whole range of basic disciplines in philosophy and science for which an elucidation of the relevant phenomena is of the deepest interest.

First among these is the *descriptive and genetic psychology* of the individual and the race, both of which are concerned with the phenomena of sympathy and the forms of love. An attempt was made in the first edition to clarify this aspect of the question. The incursions of genetic 'association-psychology' were there repulsed by detailed criticism, especially of the British School (Hume Bain, Darwin and Spencer). This was implemented in the second edition by a review of those types of genuine 'identification' which we take to be the most primitive of all forms of sympathetic phenomena (see Part I, ch. 2, sec. 4). Our chief endeavour, however, has been to give an account of the *phases of development in the forms of sympathy* (in the chapter on its laws of dependence, Part I, ch. 6). The latter draws more fully than before on child and animal psychology, and on pathological deficiencies in the sympathetic functions. I intend shortly to publish an already-completed longer study of 'Phases in the development of the soul and its functions' which should provide a more general and comprehensive background of theory and interpretation for the account of sympathetic development presented here.

Sociology and social psychology are also bound to take a considerable interest in the phenomena of sympathy. For human groupings, from the unorganized 'crowd' held together by emotional infection, up to the most highly organized association, all cohere through forces which include, among others, certain specific *patterns* of sympathetic attitude; the characterization of these patterns forms an important part of 'psycho-sociology', i.e. the

---

[1] Jean-Marie Guyau: *A Sketch of Morality independent of Obligation or Sanction* (tr. from the French 2nd edition by G. Kapteyn), Watts, London, 1898.
[2] Cf. Volkelt's recent book, *Das ästhetische Bewusstsein*, 1926.

theory of the socially relevant actions of the individual. In the new edition *this* aspect of the problem is more fully worked out than in the first edition, though not exhaustively so. Thus, particularly in Part III, more attention has been paid to the various modes of awareness of other selves peculiar to different human groups and associations, such as the crowd, the communal unit, and society at large. While rejecting the theory that belief in the existence of others is either originated or justified through an argument by analogy, we grant it a certain limited validity in the rational economic phase of society. The first edition failed to connect the elementary phenomena of sympathy, which are *constant* in human nature, with the spiritual history of those ideas, evaluations and 'temperamental patterns' of sympathy which may dominate an entire cultural epoch. The connection is now brought out, in Part I, ch. 5, 'The sense of unity with the Cosmos in some representative temperaments of the past', by showing how the ideal potentialities of human nature have achieved their partial realization and characteristic stamp in Indian, Classical, Christian and modern Western culture.

Compared with the above-mentioned aspects of the problem, much less attention has so far been given to the *epistemological* function of sympathy, which has again been brought into prominence by Bergson's intuitive philosophy. Yet neither a theory of *biological* knowledge nor of knowledge in the *historical and social* sciences can afford to disregard the problem of sympathy. Ràdl's[1] researches bear striking witness to the way in which the mechanistic biology generally current in the West since Descartes' time has fought against the claims of sympathy to be a legitimate source of data for the knowledge of vital behaviour and of the organisms which display it; in place of the once self-evident conception of sympathy as a legitimate source of knowledge, on a par with perception and reason (in the realm of life at least), it has repudiated any ultimate objective distinction of *essence* between the organic and inorganic, holding it to be only an *illusion* due to projection of our subjective human feelings into certain natural phenomena perceived by the senses. The theory of projective empathy, here rejected in all its forms, thus combines with the mechanistic theory of life to constitute a pair of mutually supporting and inseparable ideas. I have again attempted to go into these questions in more detail than in the first edition (Part I, ch. 4, sec. 5, and Part III, chs. 1, 2 and 3), and hence I also discuss the problem recently revived by Driesch, Bergson and Becher, as to whether and how far the facts of sympathy point to the existence of a *supra-individual*

[1] Emanuel Ràdl: *History of Biological Theories* (tr. and adapted by E. J. Hatfield, Oxford, 1930).

unity of life. The two new chapters of Part III, and ch. 4, sec. 2 of Part I, deal more fully with the *cognitive* function of sympathy (as reproducing the experience or feelings of others), in 'intuitive interpretation' in psychology, history and the social sciences, and as a source of the pre-logical consciousness of the *reality* of other conscious subjects. Many workers in this field have now recognized that the problem investigated (with new and important additions) in Part III, i.e. the question of our grounds for assuming the reality of other selves, and the possibility and limits of our understanding of them, is virtually *the* problem for any theory of knowledge in the social sciences. Theodor Lipps, Hans Driesch, Benno Erdmann, Erich Becher, Arthur Kronfeld, Ernst Troeltsch, Joannes Volkelt, Edmund Husserl and Eduard Spranger, all bear witness to this. Troeltsch has lately formulated it in striking fashion, as follows: 'The main problem here is the question of our knowledge of other minds; for this is the peculiar presupposition of history, and in general a central issue for all philosophy, since the possibilities and difficulties of any common thought and philosophizing all depend upon it'.[1] In this second edition I have been at pains to take account of the numerous expressions of agreement or dissent evoked by the appendix to the first edition, and so at relevant points I have reviewed the critical comments made on my thesis by Erdmann, Driesch, Troeltsch, Edith Stein, Becher, Kronfeld, Spranger, N. O. Lossky and others.

Love and Sympathy can also be of significant, indeed crucial, interest to *metaphysics*, the central discipline of philosophy; but only *if* it can be assumed that their manifestations are *intrinsic* to our psycho-somatic and cognitive-cum-spiritual life, and incapable of further analysis in empirical or genetic terms. This is how we regard them ourselves, and indeed they have been systematically and rightly treated as such by virtually all the eminent metaphysicians known to history. The great Indian teachers, Plato (in the *Symposium* and *Phaedrus*), Augustine, Thomas Aquinas, Giordano Bruno, Spinoza, Hegel, F. von Baader, Schopenhauer, von Hartmann and Bergson, and Driesch and Becher in recent times, are but a few of those one might mention; each of them, in his own way, has tried to bring out that sympathy and love are functions of a special kind which bring us closer to the *very foundation of all things*; or again, they have sought to draw conclusions from the existence and nature of these functions concerning the *unity and constitution of the ultimate world-principle.* Though fundamentally at variance in their assessment of love and sympathy—

[1] Ernst Troeltsch: *Die Logik des historischen Entwicklungsbegriffes.* Kantstudien, XXVII, 3–4, p. 286.

some being theistic, some pantheistic, others again pandemonic or panentheistic, the tendency of each is expressed in the lines of Schiller's Ode to Joy:

> Was den grossen Ring bewohnet
> Huldige der Sympathie:
> Zu den Sternen leitet sie,
> Wo der Unbekannte thronet.[1]

In the new edition a complete chapter (Part I, ch. 4), has been devoted to these metaphysical interpretations of the phenomena of sympathy and love, and it is hoped that this will have done something towards clarifying these eternal problems. I believe I have at least shown there that the phenomena of genuine *spiritual* love (not the physical kind, to which we regard it as irreducible), are compatible only with a theistic or panentheistic metaphysics of the universe, dependent on a personal spiritual principle, and give *no* support to a metaphysical pantheism or monism. In Part I, ch. 6, I have tried to make some further progress towards a 'metaphysics of sexual love', a topic neglected since Schopenhauer's essay, and in so doing have given an idealized sketch of the true *ordo amoris*—the *correct* 'interaction of sympathetic functions' in the human soul—an account I should also regard as relevant to educational theory and the critical evaluation of culture.

In conclusion, it has been a particular pleasure to me that the first edition of this book should have received considerable attention, not only from professional philosophers and psychologists, but also among exponents of the new phenomenological approach in psychiatry and the study of sexual questions. The psychiatrist Kurt Schneider, in his *Pathopsychologische Beiträge zur phänomenologischen Psychologie von Liebe und Mitfühlen*[2] and *Bemerkungen zu einer phänomenologischen Psychologie der invertierten Sexualität und erotischen Liebe*[3] has made a happy extension of my original findings. In his acute and valuable *Psychologie des Geschlechtlebens*[4] Rudolf Allers has adopted my position as a starting-point, and both his positive treatment and his criticism of Freud's theory of the ontogenesis of

---

[1] Dwellers in the mighty zone
To Sympathy be homage given:
She that guides us up to heaven
To the realm of the Unknown.

[2] In *Zeitschrift für die gesamte Neurologie und Psychiatrie*, vol. 65, 1 and 2.

[3] Ibid., vol. 71. Cf. also A. Kronfeld's survey in *Zentralblatt fur die gesamte Neurologie, etc.*, vol. XXVIII, 9. *Über neuere pathopsychisch-phänomenologische Arbeiten.*

[4] Vol. 3 of *Handbuch der vergleichenden Psychologie*, ed. S. Kafka.

love in its various forms, have done much to elucidate the problems of sexual psychology dealt with in the first edition of this book.

MAX SCHELER

Cologne
August 1922

PREFACE TO THE FIRST EDITION

THE present work is the outcome of a wider range of enquiries designed to provide a phenomenological basis for a philosophical ethics. In publishing it alone, in abstraction from its context, and *prior* to the work which should supply that background, I am impelled by the consideration that the subject may yet be of interest, not only to moral philosophers, but also to epistemologists and psychologists, despite their less immediate concern with the value-aspect of the facts of sympathy, love and hate. I am also convinced that those conflicts of opinion as to the moral value of sympathy and love (between Schopenhauer and Nietzsche, for instance, or between the rival exponents of social progress and racial superiority), which have so greatly aroused the interest of the educated public, are due far less to differences of standards in evaluating these emotions, than to an inadequate conception and analysis of the relevant phenomena themselves.

At the same time this short work may perhaps provide an example of how to conduct investigations into the phenomena of the emotional life.

As for the bearing of the problem of sympathy and love upon questions of ethical principle, the reader may be referred to my *Formalismus in der Ethik, und die materiale Wertethik*[1] published at the same time as this book. An attempted description of how the varying opinions of love and sympathy can be traced throughout the vicissitudes of the moral systems which have prevailed at different times in Western Europe, may be found in my essay on *Ressentiment und moralisches Werturteil.*[2]

MAX SCHELER

Munich
October 1912

---

[1] *Jahrbuch für Philosophie und phänomenologische Forschung*, Vol. I, Niemeyer, Halle, 1913.
[2] W. Engelmann, Leipzig, 1912.

TRANSLATOR'S NOTE

IN translating Scheler's considerable apparatus of technical terms I have generally resorted to paraphrase or approximation, rather than neologism, as being more likely to be intelligible to the reader. This has often meant using alternative renderings for the same expression, either to point the meaning in a particular context, or for the sake of euphony, or to lighten the effect of repetition in the original. I have also departed from the author's punctuation, especially his practice of enclosing all references to 'phenomena' in (non-ironical) quotation-marks, wherever it has seemed advisable, or at least reasonably safe, to do so. In order not to encumber the text with bracketed explanations the more frequently-used terms and their main variants are listed in the table below.

Sympathie: Sympathy (generic term).
Mitgefühl: Fellow-feeling, companionate feeling, sympathy.
Miteinanderfühlen: Community of feeling, shared, mutual feeling.
Nachgefühl: Reproduced, vicarious feeling.
Einfühlung: Empathy.
Einsfühlung, -gefühl: Identification, sense of unity.
Cosmovitale Einsfühlung: Identification etc., with the (living) Cosmos; animistic identification.
Gefühlsansteckung: Emotional infection.
Gemütsgestalt: Temperament, pattern of feeling.
Mitvollzug: Co-operation, participation, conjoint performance.
Nachvollzug: Reproduction, re-enactment, conformity (of acts).
Menschenliebe: Benevolence, humanitarianism, love of mankind.
Mitleid, -en: Pity, commiseration.
Mitfreude, -n: Rejoicing (-with).
Geistig: Spiritual, intellectual.
Seelisch: Mental, psychic.

Vital: Vital, organic.

Sinnlich: Sensory, sensuous, physical.

Innere Wahrnehmung: Internal (inner) perception, awareness, insight.

Selbstwahrnehmung: Self-perception, introspection.

Innere Beobachtung: Internal observation.

Innere Anschauung: Internal intuition.

Wesen, Wesenheit: Nature, essence, entity.

Wesentlich, wesensgesetzlich: Essential, intrinsic, inherent.

Dasein: Existence, presence, occurrence.

Sosein: Character, quality, attributes.

PART ONE

FELLOW-FEELING

PREFACE

I AM not going to begin with an analysis of love and hatred but shall start by enquiring into the processes which one may describe as 'rejoicing-with' and 'commiserating'; these being processes in which we seem to have an immediate 'understanding' of other people's experiences, while also 'participating' in them. I take this course because, in the history of Ethics, it is these attitudes rather than love and hate which have commonly been treated as *more fundamental*—notably in the 'Ethics of Sympathy' of the British moralists, and by Rousseau, Schopenhauer and others; whence it has been thought possible to regard love as a particular case or consequence of the attitude of fellow-feeling. It is of considerable importance for the present condition of *ethical* studies that these matters should be clarified. For the above-mentioned attitudes have lately been the subject of very diverse ethical estimates. Witness the theories of pity upheld by Schopenhauer and Nietzsche, and their verdicts upon it.

Chapter I

THE 'ETHICS OF SYMPATHY'

BEFORE entering upon analysis, let me first briefly set out the reasons why an *ethic* which finds the highest moral value in fellow-feeling, and attempts to derive all morally valuable conduct from this, can never do justice to the facts of moral life.

(1) The ethics of sympathy does not attribute moral value primarily to the *being* and attitudes of persons *as such*, in respect of their character, action, volition, etc., but seeks to derive it from the attitude of the *spectator* (i.e. one who reacts emotionally to the experience and attitude of someone else); in this, however, it invariably *pre*-supposes what it is attempting to deduce. It is certainly *not* moral to sympathize with someone's pleasure in evil, his chagrin in contemplating goodness, or with his hatred, malice or spite. Can we really suppose that a fellow-feeling such as that of rejoicing with A's pleasure at B's misfortune is morally valuable? Clearly, the sharing of another's pleasure can only be moral when the latter *is itself moral*, and warranted by the value-situation which evokes it. This immediately indicates *one* of the essential differences between fellow-feeling and love. Loving another, we may often be constrained to regret that he should take pleasure in something, for instance, when he cruelly enjoys tormenting someone else; but mere fellow-feeling is, as such, quite regardless of the value of its objects. In acts of love and hate there is certainly an element of valuation present, positively or negatively (how, will be seen later); but mere fellow-feeling, in all its possible forms, is in principle *blind to value*.[1]

---

[1] Fellow-feeling can itself have a value, *independent* of the value content which gives rise to joy or suffering in others; but then its value cannot be derived from the latter.

5

(2) It would be quite wrong to suppose that an ethical judgement can only arise through the medium of fellow-feeling. There is, for one thing, the whole class of ethical judgements we pass upon *ourselves*. Is there any fellow-feeling to be found, for instance, in the 'pangs of conscience', in remorse, or in judgements of self-approval? Adam Smith thought this to be so, holding that no man on his own would ever immediately ascribe ethical value to his experience, volition, action or existence. Only by adopting the standpoint and attitude of an onlooker praising or blaming his conduct, and thus ultimately contemplating himself through the eyes of an 'impartial spectator', and by participating directly, through fellow-feeling, in the hatred, anger, indignation' and impulses of revenge which the *latter* directs towards him, does there arise in him also a tendency to self-judgement either positive or negative. Thus the 'pangs of conscience' for instance, are no more than an immediate participation in such detached acts of disapproval on the part of a spectator. As to this, we may observe that it is certainly true that in judging our own case we all too often succumb to the infection, as it were, which is transmitted by the attitude of other people towards us; *their* estimate of us seems to displace the immediately given value of our own self-appraisal and hides it from us. This used to happen, for instance, in the mediæval witch-trials, when many witches felt that they were indeed guilty of witchcraft and justly condemned to death. But is this more than just a *delusion* of conscience, due to the fact that its own counsels are overlaid by social suggestion? According to Adam Smith, a man unjustly condemned and universally considered to be guilty should also acknowledge his guilt himself. Indeed (apart from errors of fact), he really would *be* 'guilty'. This is certainly not so. Our conscience knows nothing of such an almighty social authority. On the other hand, if a man having no conscience at all, and therefore no sense of the vileness of his conduct, were to behave quite naïvely, exactly 'as though he hadn't done anything', then, given the necessary conviction for such effrontery, he might ultimately so infect others with his sense of innocence, that they too would hold him guiltless. From Adam Smith's point of view he ought then actually to *be* guiltless. But he certainly could *not* become so in such a fashion.

The ethics of sympathy is also found wanting in that it clashes from the outset with the self-evident law of preference,[1] whereby all positively valuable 'spontaneous' acts are to be preferred to merely 're-active' ones. But all fellow-feeling is essentially a reaction—as love, for instance, is not.

[1] For the nature of 'self-evident laws of preference', cf. my book, *Der Formalismus in der Ethik und die materiale Wertethik.*

Nor is it only self-judgement which can be carried out without the intervention of acts of sympathy; judgement of others cannot possibly be effected through fellow-feeling either, as the following analyses will show.

Chapter II

CLASSIFICATION OF THE PHENOMENA
OF FELLOW-FEELING

WE must first distinguish from true fellow-feeling all such attitudes as merely contribute to our *apprehending, understanding*, and, in general, *reproducing* (emotionally) the experiences of others, including their states of feeling. Such acts have often, and quite mistakenly, been assimilated to fellow-feeling. This has come about chiefly through the theory of projective 'empathy' which attempted to explain both at the same time.

But it should be clear (before we even begin to consider this class of acts), that any kind of rejoicing or pity *presupposes*, in principle, some sort of *knowledge* of the fact, nature and quality of experience in other people, just as the possibility of such knowledge presupposes, as its condition, the existence of other conscious beings. It is not *through* pity in the first place that I learn of someone's being in pain, for the latter must already *be given* in some form, if I am to notice and then *share* it. One may look at the face of a yelling child as a merely physical object, or one may look at it (in the normal way) as an expression of pain, hunger, etc., though without therefore pitying the child; the two things are utterly different. Thus experiences of pity and fellow-feeling are always additional to an experience in the other which is already grasped and understood. The givenness of these experiences (and naturally, their value) is not based, in the first instance, on sympathy or fellow-feeling—still less is the existence of other selves so established (as W. K. Clifford held).[1] Nor does this apply

---

[1] A. Riehl has followed him in this. *Vide Principles of Critical Philosophy* (tr. by Arthur Fairbanks, 1894). Part II, p. 160. Cf. W. K. Clifford, *Seeing and Thinking*,

merely to the knowledge given in the proposition: 'X is in pain' (for I can also be informed of this), nor to the factual judgement 'that X is suffering'—the other person's experience may also be completely realized in the peculiar form of 'reproduced' experience *without* any sort of fellow-feeling being entailed thereby. It is perfectly meaningful to say: 'I can quite visualize your feelings, but I have no pity for you.' Such 'visualized' feeling remains within the cognitive sphere, and is not a morally relevant act. The historian of motives, the novelist, the exponent of the dramatic arts, must all possess in high degree the gift of visualizing the feelings of others, but there is not the slightest need for them to share the feelings of their subjects and personages.

The reproduction of feeling or experience must therefore be sharply distinguished from fellow-feeling. It is indeed a case of feeling the other's feeling, not just knowing of it, nor judging that the other has it; but it is not the same as going through the experience itself. In reproduced feeling we sense the *quality* of the other's feeling, without it being transmitted to us, or evoking a similar real emotion in us.[1] The other's feeling is given exactly like a landscape which we 'see' subjectively in memory, or a melody which we 'hear' in similar fashion—a state of affairs quite different from the fact that we remember the landscape or the melody (possibly with an accompanying recollection of the fact 'that it was seen, or heard'). In the present case there is a real seeing or hearing, yet without the object seen or heard being perceived and accepted as really present; the past is simply 're-presented'. Equally little does the reproduction of feeling or experience imply any sort of 'participation' in the other's experience. Throughout our visualizing of the experience we can remain quite indifferent to whatever has evoked it.

We shall not, at present, give any very detailed account of those acts which serve to establish the existence of other people and their experiences.[2] It only needs to be emphasized that this acceptance and understanding does not come about as the conclusion to an 'argument from analogy', nor by any projective '*empathy*' or 'mimetic impulse' (Lipps).[3] That we cannot be aware of an experience without being aware of a self is something which

London, Macmillan, 1879; O. Külpe's criticism of Clifford's and Riehl's assertions, partly pertinent and partly beside the mark, in his book, *Die Realisierung*, Leipzig, 1920; and also the last chapter of this book.

[1] We feel the quality of the other's sorrow without suffering with him, the quality of his joy without ourselves rejoicing with him. On this, cf. Edith Stein: 'Neues zum Problem der Einfühlung'; Dissertation, Freiburg, 1917.

[2] Cf. Part III.

[3] Cf. Theodor Lipps: 'Das Wissen von fremden Ichen', in *Psychologische Untersuchungen*, Bd. I, Heft 4, 1905.

is directly based upon the intuitable intrinsic connection between individual and experience; there is no need of empathy on the part of the percipient. That is why we can also have it given to us that the other has an individual self distinct from our own, and that we can never fully comprehend this individual self, steeped as it is in its own psychic experience, but only our own view of it as an individual, conditioned as this is by our own individual nature. It is a corollary of this that the other person has—like ourselves—a sphere of absolute personal privacy, which can never be given to us. But that 'experiences' occur there is given for us *in* expressive phenomena—again, not by inference, but directly, as a sort of primary 'perception'. It is *in* the blush that we perceive shame, *in* the laughter joy. To say that 'our only initial datum is the body' is completely erroneous. This is true only for the doctor or the scientist, i.e. for man in so far as he abstracts *artificially* from the expressive phenomena, which have an altogether primary givenness. It is rather that the same basic sense-data which go to make up the body for outward perception, can also construe, for the act of insight, the expressive phenomena which then appear, so to speak, as the 'outcome' of experiences within. For the relation here referred to is a *symbolic*, not a causal one.[1] We can thus have insight into others, in so far as we treat their bodies as a *field of expression* for their experiences. In the sight of clasped hands, for example, the 'please' is given exactly as the physical object is— for the latter is assuredly *given* as an object (including the fact that it has a back and an inside), in the visual phenomenon. However, the qualities (i.e. the character) of expressive pheno- mena and those of experiences exhibit connections of a unique kind, which do not depend at all on previous acquaintance with real experiences of our own, plus the other's expressive pheno- mena, such that a tendency to *imitate* the movements of the gesture seen would first have to reproduce our own earlier experiences. On the contrary, imitation, even as a mere 'tendency', already presupposes some kind of acquaintance with the other's experi- ence, and therefore cannot explain what it is here supposed to do. For instance, if we (involuntarily) imitate a gesture of fear or joy, the imitation is never called forth simply by the visual image of the gesture; the impulse to imitate only arises when we have already apprehended the gesture *as* an expression of fear or joy. If this apprehension itself were only made possible (as Theodor Lipps believes), by a tendency to imitate and by the *reproduction*, thus evoked, of a previously experienced joy or fear (*plus* an

---

[1] We might also say that it is not the mere relation of a 'sign' to the presence of 'something', whereby the latter is subsequently inferred; it refers to a genuine, irreducible property of the sign itself.

empathic projection of what is reproduced into the other person), we should obviously be moving in a circle. And this applies also to the 'involuntary' imitation of gestures. It already presupposes an imitation of the inner intention of action, which could be realized by quite different bodily movements.[1] We do not imitate the same or similar bodily movements in observed connections of the inorganic, e.g. in inanimate nature, where they cannot be phenomena expressive of psychic experience. Further evidence against Lipps' theory of imitation lies in the fact that we can understand the experience of animals, though even in 'tendency' we cannot imitate their manner of expression; for instance when a dog expresses its joy by barking and wagging its tail, or a bird by twittering. The relationships between expression and experience have a *fundamental* basis of connection, which is independent of our specifically human gestures of expression. We have here, as it were, a *universal grammar*, valid for all languages of expression, and the ultimate basis of understanding for all forms of mime and pantomime among living creatures. Only so are we able to perceive the *inadequacy* of a person's gesture to his experience, and even the contradiction between what the gesture expresses and what it is meant to express. But apart from all this, the imitation of another person's expressive gestures certainly cannot explain the act of *understanding* his inner life. The only way of explaining imitation, and the reproduction of a personal experience similar to that underlying a perceived expressive gesture, is that through this a genuine experience takes place in me, objectively *similar* to that which occurs in the other person whose expression I imitate. For such objective similarity of experience, however, there need be no present consciousness of the similarity, still less an intentionally directed act of 'understanding' or a reproduction of feeling or experience. For my having an experience *similar* to someone else's has nothing whatever to do with understanding him. Besides, such a reproduction in one's experience would require the 'understanding' of another's experience to be preceded in the participant, by a similar *real* experience (however brief); i.e. in the case of feelings, a reproduction of feeling, which would always be itself an actual feeling. But one who 'understands' the mortal terror of a drowning man has no need at all to *undergo* such terror, in a real, if weakened form. This theory therefore contradicts the observable fact that in the process of understanding the thing understood is in no way experienced as real.

It also seems clear that what this theory could explain for us is the very opposite of genuine 'understanding'. This opposite

---

[1] On the distinction between imitation of action and imitation of movement, cf. K. Koffka: *The Growth of the Mind* (tr. by R. M. Ogden), Kegan Paul, 1924.

is that *infection* by others' emotions, which occurs in its most elementary form in the behaviour of herds and crowds. Here there is actually a common making of expressive gestures in the first instance, which has the secondary effect of producing similar emotions, efforts and purposes among the people or animals concerned; thus, for instance, a herd takes fright on seeing signs of alarm in its leader, and so too in human affairs. But it is characteristic of the situation that there is a complete lack of mutual 'understanding'. Indeed, the purer the case, inasmuch as a rudimentary act of understanding plays little or no part in it, the more clearly do its peculiar features emerge, namely that the participant takes the experience arising in him owing to his participation to be his *own* original experience, so that he is quite unconscious of the contagion to which he succumbs. This resembles those post-hypnotically suggested acts of will which are carried out without awareness of suggestion (unlike the obeying of commands, where one remains consciously aware that the other's will is not one's own); such acts, indeed, are characteristically regarded by the agent as being his *own*, and so too the experiences arising through participation in a common gesture of expression are ascribed, not to others, but to *oneself*. For this reason, even in daily life, we distinguish between merely aping someone ('taking him off', for instance) and really understanding him, and point the contrast between them.

Thus neither 'projective empathy' nor 'imitation' is necessary in order to explain the primary components of fellow-feeling, viz. understanding, and the vicarious reproduction of feeling or experience. Indeed so far as the first-mentioned acts come into it, it is not understanding they produce, but the possibility of *delusive* understanding.

Let us now turn to *fellow-feeling*, which is primarily based upon those constituents of 'vicarious' understanding already dealt with. Here there are *four* quite different relationships to be distinguished. I call them:

(1) Immediate community of feeling, e.g. of one and the same sorrow, 'with someone'.
(2) Fellow-feeling 'about something'; rejoicing in his joy and commiseration with his sorrow.
(3) Mere emotional infection.
(4) True emotional identification.

(1) COMMUNITY OF FEELING

Two parents stand beside the dead body of a beloved child. They feel in common the 'same' sorrow, the 'same' anguish. It is not that A feels this sorrow and B feels it also, and moreover that they both know they are feeling it. No, it is a *feeling-in-common*. A's sorrow is in no way an 'external' matter for B here, as it is, e.g. for their friend C, who joins them, and commiserates 'with them' or 'upon their sorrow'. On the contrary, they feel it together, in the sense that they feel and experience in common, not only the self-same value-situation, but also the same keenness of emotion in regard to it. The sorrow, as value-content, and the grief, as characterizing the functional relation thereto, are here *one and identical*. It will be evident that we can only feel mental suffering in this fashion, not physical pain or sensory feelings. There is no such thing as a 'common pain'. Sensory types of feeling ('feeling-sensations' as Stumpf calls them), are by nature not susceptible of this highest form of fellow-feeling. They are inevitably 'external' to us in some respect, inspiring only commiseration 'with' and 'upon' the suffering of pain by the other person. By the same token, there is certainly such a thing as rejoicing *at* another's sensory pleasure, but never mutual enjoyment of it (as a common feeling-sensation). It may, however, be the case that A first feels sorrow by himself and is then joined by B in a common feeling. But this, as will be seen, presupposes the higher emotion of love.

(2) FELLOW-FEELING

The second case is quite different. Here also, the one person's sorrow is not simply the motivating cause of the other's. *All* fellow-feeling involves *intentional reference* of the feeling of joy or sorrow to the other person's experience. It points this way simply *qua* feeling—there is no need of any prior judgement or intimation 'that the other person is in trouble'; nor does it arise only upon sight of the other's grief, for it can also 'envisage' such grief, and does so, indeed, in its very capacity *as* a feeling.[1] But here A's suffering is first presented *as* A's in an act of understanding or 'vicarious' feeling experienced as such, and it is to this material that B's primary commiseration is directed. That is, *my* commiseration and *his* suffering are phenomenologically *two different facts*, not *one* fact, as in the first case. While in the first case the functions of vicarious experience and feeling are so interwoven with the very fellow-feeling itself as to be indistinguishable from it, in the second case the two functions are plainly distinguished even *while*

---

[1] In *Zur psychologischen Analyse der ästhetischen Anschauung* Witasek defends the view that what we have called 'understanding' and 'vicarious feeling' is only an 'intuitive presentation of the experience in question'. This contention is decisively refuted by Edith Stein, op. cit., § 4: 'Der Streit zwischen Vorstellungs- und Qualitätsansicht', p. 19.

experiencing them. Fellow-feeling proper, actual 'participation', presents itself in the very phenomenon as a *re-action* to the state and value of the other's feelings—as these are 'visualized' in vicarious feeling. Thus in this case the two functions of *vicariously visualized* feeling, and *participation* in feeling are separately given and must be sharply distinguished. Very many descriptions of fellow-feeling suffer from failure to make this distinction.[1]

Nothing shows the fundamental diversity of the two functions more plainly, than the fact that the first of them can not only be given without the second, but is also present as a basis for the very *opposite* of an (associated) act of fellow-feeling. This happens, for instance, where there is specific pleasure in cruelty, and to a lesser extent in brutality. The *cruel* man owes his awareness of the pain or sorrow he causes entirely to a capacity for visualizing feeling! His joy lies in 'torturing' and in the agony of his victim. As he feels, vicariously, the increasing pain or suffering of his victim, so his own primary pleasure and enjoyment at the other's pain also increases. Cruelty consists not at all in the cruel man's being simply 'insensitive' to other peoples' suffering. Such 'insensitivity' is therefore a quite different defect in man to lack of fellow-feeling. It is chiefly found in pathological cases[2] (e.g. in melancholia), where it arises as a result of the patient's exclusive preoccupation in his own feelings, which altogether prevents him from giving emotional acceptance to the experience of other people. In contrast to cruelty, '*brutality*' is merely a disregard of other peoples' experience, despite the apprehension of it in feeling. Thus, to regard a human being as a mere log of wood and to treat the object accordingly, is not to be 'brutal' towards him. On the other hand, it is characteristic of brutality, that, given merely a sense of life, undifferentiated, as yet, into separate experiences, given even the fact of an enhanced appearance of life or a tendency towards it, any violent interruption of this tendency (as in vandalism towards plants and trees, to which one cannot be 'cruel'), is enough to mark it as brutal.

(3) EMOTIONAL INFECTION

Quite different again from these, is the case where there is no true appearance of fellow-feeling at all, although it is very

[1] In particular the theory of projective empathy, developed by Theodor Lipps.

[2] From the psychopathological side, Kurt Schneider's valuable work, *Patho-psychologische Beiträge zur psychologischen Phänomenologie von Liebe und Hass* is in part a verification, in other respects an elaboration and extension, of the phenomenology of sympathetic experience set out in the text (Cologne, Dissertation, 1921). Also in *Zeitschrift für die ges. Neurol. u. Psychiatrie*, Bd. 65, 1921.

frequently confused with this. Such confusion has given rise to the mistaken theories of positivism concerning the evolution of fellow-feeling (Herbert Spencer) and, moreover, to a quite false appreciation of values, particularly in connection with pity. I have in mind the case of mere *emotional infection*. We all know how the cheerful atmosphere in a 'pub' or at a party may 'infect' the newcomers, who may even have been depressed beforehand, so that they are 'swept up' into the prevailing gaiety. Of course such people are equally remote from a rejoicing of either the first or the second type. It is the same when laughter proves 'catching', as can happen especially with children, and to a still greater extent among girls, who have less sensitivity, but react more readily. The same thing occurs when a group is infected by the mournful tone of one of its members, as so often happens among old women, where one recounts her woes, while the others grow more and more tearful. Naturally, this has nothing whatever to do with pity. Here there is neither a *directing* of feeling towards the other's joy or suffering, nor any participation in her experience. On the contrary, it is characteristic of emotional infection that it occurs only as a transference of the *state* of feeling, and does *not* presuppose any sort of *knowledge* of the joy which others feel. Thus one may only notice afterwards that a mournful feeling, encountered in oneself, is traceable to infection from a group one has visited some hours before. There is nothing in the mournful feeling itself to point to this origin; only by inference from causal considerations does it become clear where it came from. For such contagion it is by no means necessary that any *emotional* experiences should have occurred in the other person. Even the *objective* aspects of such feelings, which attach to natural objects, or are discerned in an 'atmosphere'—such as the serenity of a spring landscape, the melancholy of a rainy day, the wretchedness of a room—can work infectiously in this way on the state of our emotions.[1]

The process of infection is an involuntary one. Especially characteristic is its tendency to return to its point of departure, so that the feelings concerned *gather* momentum like an avalanche. The emotion caused by infection reproduces itself *again* by means of expression and imitation, so that the infectious emotion increases, again reproduces itself, and so on. In all mass-excitement, even in the formation of 'public opinion', it is above all this *reciprocal effect* of a self-generating infection which leads to the uprush of a

---

[1] This shows that the process of infection does *not* lie in the imitation of others' expressed experiences, even though these may actually bring it about, where it is a case of infection through experiences undergone by animals or other human beings.

common surge of emotion, and to the characteristic feature of a crowd in action, that it is so easily carried beyond the intentions of every one of its members, and does things for which no one acknowledges either the will or the responsibility. It is, in fact, the infective process itself, which generates purposes beyond the designs of any single individual.[1] Although these processes of infection are not merely involuntary but operate 'unconsciously' (however conspicuous they may be), in the sense that we 'get into'

[1] I refrain here from describing the immense part which infection plays in the historical evolution of whole systems of morality, in the genesis of psychopathic group-movements (from *folie à deux* to the emergence of enduring pathological customs and usages on a national scale), in the onset of panics, and particularly within all revolutionary mass-movements. Cf. Gustave Le Bon, *The Crowd: a Study of the Popular Mind*, Unwin, 1896, and *L'Ame Révolutionnaire*; see also Tarde: *Les lois de l'imitation*; and Sigmund Freud: *Group Psychology and the Analysis of the Ego*, who there observes:

'Psycho-analytic research, which has already occasionally attacked the more difficult problems of the psychoses, has also been able to show identification as present in some other cases which are not immediately comprehensible. I shall treat two of these cases in detail as material for our further consideration.

'The genesis of male homosexuality in a large class of cases is as follows. A young man has been unusually long and intensely fixated upon his mother in the sense of the Œdipus complex. But at last, after the end of his puberty, the time comes for exchanging his mother for some other sexual object. Things take a sudden turn: the young man does not abandon his mother: he transforms himself into her, and now looks about for objects which can replace his ego for him, and on which he can bestow such love and care as he has experienced from his mother. This is a frequent process, which can be confirmed as often as one likes, and which is naturally quite independent of any hypothesis which may be made as to the organic driving force and motives of the sudden transformation. A striking thing about this identification is its ample scale; it remoulds the ego in one of its important features—in its sexual character—upon the model of what has hitherto been the object. In this process the object itself is renounced—whether entirely or in the sense of being preserved only in the unconscious is a question outside the present discussion. Identification with an object that is renounced or lost as a substitute for it, introjection of this object into the ego, is indeed no novelty to us. A process of the kind may sometimes be directly observed in small children. A short time ago an observation of this sort was published in the *Internationale Zeitschrift für Psychoanalyse*. A child who was unhappy over the loss of a kitten declared straight out that now he himself was the kitten, and accordingly crawled about on all fours, would not eat at table, etc. (Marcuszewicz: 'Beitrag zum autistischen Denken bei Kindern', *Internationale Zeitschrift für Psychoanalyse*, 1920, Bd. VI).

'Another such instance of introjection of the object has been provided by the analysis of melancholia, an affection which counts among the most noteworthy of its exciting causes the real or emotional loss of a loved object. A leading characteristic of these cases is a cruel self-depreciation of the ego combined with relentless self-criticism and bitter self-reproaches. Analyses have shown that this disparagement and these reproaches apply at bottom to the object and represent the ego's revenge upon it. The shadow of the object has fallen upon the ego, as I have said elsewhere. The introjection of the object is here unmistakably clear', p. 66 (tr. by James Strachey, International Psycho-analytical Library, No. 6, 1922).

these states without realizing that this is how it comes about, the process itself can again become an instrument of conscious volition. This occurs, for instance, in the search for 'distraction', when we go into gay company, or attend a party, not because we are in festive mood, but simply in order to find distraction; here we anticipate that we shall be infected and 'caught up' in the prevailing gaiety. When someone says that he wants 'to see cheerful faces around him', it is perfectly clear that he does not mean to rejoice with them, but is simply hoping for infection as a means to his *own* pleasure. Conversely, an awareness of possible infection can also create a peculiar *dread* of it, as is found wherever a person shuns melancholy places or avoids the *appearance* of suffering (not the suffering itself), by trying to banish this image from the field of his experience.

That this form of emotional infection also has nothing whatever to do with genuine fellow-feeling should be too obvious for any need of emphasis. And yet the aberrations of some most weighty authors make this emphasis necessary. Thus virtually the whole extent of Herbert Spencer's treatment of the emergence of fellow-feeling (and Darwin's also, to some extent), is no more than a persistent *confusion* of fellow-feeling with emotional infection. This confusion is dominant, especially, in the ever-recurring error of these writers, whereby they seek to derive fellow-feeling from the herd-consciousness and herd-behaviour of the higher animals. An entire trend of thought having thus gone astray, it is no wonder that, in presupposing this false conception of fellow-feeling, Friedrich Nietzsche, for his part, should have arrived at a completely *misguided evaluation* of fellow-feeling, and especially of pity. I select one passage—among many—from his outbursts against pity: 'Through pity, suffering itself becomes infectious; in certain circumstances it may lead to a total loss of life and vital energy which is absurdly out of proportion to the magnitude of the cause (—the case of the death of the Nazarene). This depressing and infectious instinct thwarts those instincts which aim at the preservation and enhancement of the value of life; by *multiplying* misery quite as much as by preserving all that is miserable, it is the principal agent in promoting decadence' (*Anti-Christ*, pp. 131 and 134).[1] It is obvious that here, as in all similar passages, pity is confused with emotional infection. Suffering itself does *not* become infectious through pity. Indeed, it is just where suffering is infectious that pity is completely excluded; for to that extent I no longer view it as the *other's* suffering, but as my *own*, which I try to get rid of, by putting the notion of suffering out of mind. Indeed it is just where infection *does* occur via suffering, that pity for the

[1] [Translated by A. M. Ludovici, London, T. N. Foulis, 1911.]

other person's sufferings, as being *his*, can stay the infection itself; just as the emotional re-living of an earlier painful experience, which still weighs heavy upon the present, can take this weight off one's mind.[1] Pity would be a 'multiplier of misery' only if it were identical with emotional infection. For only the latter—as we have seen—can produce in others a real suffering, a state of feeling akin to the infectious one. But such real suffering does not occur, however, in *true* fellow-feeling.

(4) EMOTIONAL IDENTIFICATION

The true *sense of emotional unity*, the act of identifying one's own self with that of another, is only a heightened form, a limiting case as it were, of infection. It represents a limit in that here it is not only the separate process of feeling in another that is unconsciously taken as one's own, but his self (in all its basic attitudes), that is identified with one's own self. Here too, the identification is as involuntary as it is unconscious. Lipps has wrongly sought to construe this as a case of æsthetic empathy. Thus, according to him, the absorbed spectator of an acrobat in a circus turn identifies himself with the performer, whose movements he reproduces within himself, in the character of an acrobat. Lipps believes that only the spectator's real self remains distinct here, his conscious self having sunk itself completely in that of the acrobat. Edith Stein has interposed a just criticism on this point.[2] 'I am not', she says, ' "one with" the acrobat; I am only "with" him. The correlated motor-impulses and tendencies are carried out here by a fictional "I", which remains recognizably distinct as a phenomenon from my individual self; it is simply that my attention is passively fixed throughout on the fictional "I", and by way of this, on the acrobat.'

There are other cases, however, insufficiently recognized either by Theodor Lipps or Edith Stein, in which such identification is undoubtedly complete; which do not merely exemplify a moment of true 'ecstasy', but may be of long duration, and can even become habitual throughout whole phases of life. They are of two opposite kinds: the *idiopathic* and the *heteropathic*. Thus identification can come about in *one* way through the total eclipse and absorption of another self by one's own, it being thus, as it were, completely dispossessed and deprived of all rights in its conscious existence and character. It can also come about the other way,

---

[1] It is not the mere reconstitution of repressed memories, nor yet the abreaction from them, but this *reliving* of them, that underlies whatever therapeutic efficacy psycho-analysis may possess.
[2] Op. cit.

where 'I' (the formal subject) am so overwhelmed and hypnotic-ally bound and fettered by the other 'I' (the concrete individual), that my formal status as a subject is usurped by the other's per-sonality, with all *its* characteristic aspects; in such a case, I live, not in 'myself', but entirely in 'him', the other person—(in and through him, as it were).

Such paradigm-cases of identification, either by way of an all-inclusive propensity to infect, or as a state of complete and total infection of the very roots of individuality, I find exemplified in very different kinds of experience—of which only a few main types can be indicated here:

(*a*) One such case is to be found in the very peculiar and as yet little understood processes of identification in *primitive* thought, observation and feeling among savages, such as Lévy-Brühl has recently described in detail.[1] They include, for instance, the iden-tification of each member of a totem with an individual member of the totem species. According to von den Steinen, the Boroso allege that they are really identical with red parrots (araras), each member of the totem with a particular red parrot. It is not just that the destiny (birth, sickness, death) of a member of the totem is mysteriously linked with that of his totem animal in a merely causal sense; this connection is really no more than a consequence of their actual *identity*. Such identification occurs even with (objec-tively) inanimate objects, for instance with particular stones (Foy calls them man-stones). The literal identification of a man with his ancestors is another case in point: he is not merely like his ancestor, or guided and ruled by him, but actually *is*, in his present life, at the same time one of his ancestors. This stage of historical identification between man and ancestor is prior to anything implied by the term 'ancestor-cult'. This cult, and its emotional bond with the ancestor in the form of piety, ritual obligation, etc., already represents a first stage of *liberation* from the primitive identification of the descendant with his ancestor, and presupposes a recognition that the two are *distinct* individuals. It seems to me that it is this type of primitive identification which survives, as it were, into historic times, in the phenomenon of mass self-identification with the 'Leader' (engendering through him a sense of identity among the members themselves); and that it is also the source of the world-wide belief in reincarnation, which is simply a rationalization of these original habits of identification.[2]

[1] Cf. Lévy-Brühl: *How Natives Think*, particularly p. 70 (tr. by Lilian A. Clare), Allen & Unwin, 1926. Cf. also D. Westermann: 'Tod und Leben bei den Kpelle in Liberia', in *Psychologische Forschung*, I. Band, 1–2 Heft, Berlin, 1921.

[2] Cf. the admirable examples given by Leo Frobenius in his *Paideuma: Um-risse einer Kultur-und Seelenlehre*, 3rd ed. Frankfurt-am-Main, 1928, pp. 42–7, of the forms in which this identification is expressed among the Ethiopians,

(b) True identification of the heteropathic type occurs in the religious *mysteries of antiquity*,[1] in the course of which the adept, by inducing a state of ecstasy, becomes aware of his true identity in the being, life and destiny of the god or goddess—becomes, in short, divine. Such identification does not merely relate to particular moments in the existence, character and life of the god (who is represented by an animal, e.g. the bull in the Orphic-Dionysian mysteries, or by a man); it extends to a specific cycle of his destined career, of which the phases are reproduced in the ecstasy. It is only through the gradual decay of these mystery-rites that many peoples have developed the arts of the theatre and the drama.[2] Here at last, the ecstatic *identification* is reduced to the level of mere symbolic *empathy*.

(c) Genuine identification is also present where the relationship between a hypnotist and his subject is not just a temporary one, in which particular acts and undertakings are suggested, but becomes a stable and permanent state, such that the hypnotic subject is continuously 'wrapped up' in all the individual personal attitudes of the hypnotist, thinks only his thoughts, wills only with his will, esteems his values, loves with his love and hates with his hate—but at the same time is convinced that this other self with all its attitudes and forms of action is really his own. But whereas in primitive identification we have a genuine identity of *existence*, in intensified suggestion through continuous hypnosis, involving not merely specific acts and performances, but an adoption of the whole concrete outlook of the hypnotist, we have only an identity of *character*, coupled with an awareness of separation in actual existence. The hypnotic trance[3] creates a mental attitude which is primitive only in an artificial sense, and thereby provides a new forcing-ground for suggestion (which does not have to be voluntary). According to Paul Schilder, it is the evolutionarily 'ancient' portions of the brain (the centres of sympathetic and parasympathetic innervation in the region of the third ventricle of the brain) which are functionally modified by hypnosis. Almost all the psychological features characteristic of the child and the primitive are to a large extent artificially regenerated by hypnosis. Such are: the faulty differentiation of perception and imagery; the ecstatic habit of surrendering in passively riveted attention to whatever is

[1] Cf. Odo Casel, O.S.B.: *Die Liturgie als Mysterienfeier*, Freiburg, 1922, a book which brings together a large number of examples of such identification from the mysteries of antiquity. Cf. further Erwin Rohde's classic work, *Psyche* (tr. by W. P. Hillis), Kegan Paul, 1925.

[2] Cf. similar material in Frobenius, op. cit.

[3] Cf. the details of recent research on this subject assembled by Paul Schilder in his notable work, *Das Wesen der Hypnose* (Halle, 1912), which also deals with the anatomical and physiological aspects.

presented; the increasingly affective and instinctive properties of the content experienced (Schilder actually believes that all the effects of hypnosis can also be evoked by emotion); the liability to faulty discrimination between 'I' and 'Thou', and the concurrent tendency to identify with the other self. Where sensory perception is subject to the will of the hypnotist (for it is not only possible, as Lipps held, to induce 'belief' in the presence of a chair or other object, there can really be perception as well), this takes place through control of those instinctive adjustments which ultimately condition all perception (even under normal circumstances). Psychologically, however, we must regard it as a more general characteristic of the hypnotic state, that in it the intellectual centre of all cognitive activity is put out of action, whereas the organic reflex system is stirred into increased activity, and this in respect of its most ancient functions and modes of operation; the 'seat' of the hypnotic subject's own intellectual activity is so *usurped* by that of the hypnotist that his organic and motor centres also come under the latter's intellectual authority, employment and control. The judgement, will and choice of the subject, his love and his hate, are then no longer his own but those of the hypnotist, whose intellect is mounted, so to speak, on the back of the subject's reflex-system. There can be no doubt, however, that the degree to which the subject effaces his own *character* in that of the hypnotist is largely dependent on his personal make-up, and that the phenomena of identification and emotional coalescence here referred to are intimately connected with all the rest.

The desire for positive *self-abasement* shown by the weak towards the strong, with its instinctive (unconscious) aim of participation in the latter's power, is a primitive impulse prior, in our opinion, to the aim of self-preservation and self-protection against a (feared) power: it is merely utilized, pressed into service as it were, by the will to self-preservation and defence. One indication of this is that the 'submissive instinct' may become quite pointless, and can even lead to ends antagonistic to those of self-preservation. Schopenhauer recounts the following observation made by an English officer in the Indian jungle: A white squirrel, having met the gaze of a snake, hanging on a tree and showing every sign of a mighty appetite for its prey, is so terrified by this that it gradually moves towards instead of away from the snake, and finally throws itself into the open jaws. It is of no consequence whether this be a case of conscious suggestion alone (quite involuntary, of course, on the snake's part), or whether it may not also involve a hypnotic narcosis of the squirrel's otherwise active higher centres;—plainly the squirrel's instinct for self-preservation has succumbed to an ecstatic participation in the object of the snake's own appetitive

21

nisus, namely 'swallowing'. The squirrel identifies in feeling with the snake, and thereupon spontaneously establishes corporeal 'identity' with it, by disappearing down its throat.

Masochism, whether of the gross or refined type, resembles its opposite, *sadism*, in being simply a (twofold) manifestation of the erotic craving for power. (The two conditions often alternate periodically in the same individual, according to the balance of power between the partners.) Even for the masochist, the object of enjoyment is not pure passivity as such, but his self-identifying participation in the dominance of the partner, i.e. a *sympathetic attainment of power*. Both masochism and sadism are found far more frequently in children than in adults—e.g. in their alternation between cruelty to animals, or even things, and passionate identification with them, between stubborn self-will and limitless surrender; in the case of adults they probably represent simply a fixation at a primitive stage of development (infantilism). Both states easily become sources of idiopathic and heteropathic identification. Schilder concludes with regard to them: 'This apparently illogical combination of contrary characteristics in one personality points to a general psychological law of wide application which may be briefly formulated thus: the lover identifies himself with the beloved, i.e. he adopts the latter's experiences, feels them as his own, and gives expression to this identification in his actions and other traits.'[1] However little we can acknowledge such a 'law' for love in general, we must recognize a tendency of this kind in erotic attachments (which are probably all that Schilder has in mind here).

But Schilder also attempts (like Freud) to establish a genetic connection between hypnosis and the erotic sexual relationship, in order to make both these phenomena of identification more intelligible. He argues for this as follows: (1) The procedures which favour the onset of hypnosis—gentle stroking, continuous admonition of the subject, the 'fascinating' stare, harsh words even —all have erotic value. The 'melting look' on entering the trance and on awakening from it has the same appearance as the expression of erotic satisfaction. There is a feeling of well-being like that associated with sex, and this is referred to the hypnotist; hence the common phantasy that he has sexually misused the subject during the trance (cf. the examples given by Forel in his book on hypnosis). (2) The region of the third ventricle of the brain, which is functionally modified during hypnosis, is also a focal point of the sexual system. Damage to this area leads to disturbances of the sexual functions, such as impotence, irregular menstruation, or modification of the secondary sexual characteristics. (3) There

[1] Op. cit., p. 25 seq.

is the evidence of animal hypnosis, as found, for example, in the arachnid *Galeodes Caspicus turkestanus*; the male makes an incision with his claws at a particular point on the abdomen of the female and so paralyses her, that she offers no resistance to the sexual act.[1] This suggests that in man also, hypnosis was originally an auxiliary biological function of sexuality, that is, a preliminary disposal of the female so as to facilitate sexual intercourse.

(4) Since inverted sexuality is latent in every individual, hypnosis of man by man or woman by woman is no argument against this.

If this promising hypothesis of Schilder's can withstand further criticism, and if his strongest argument, from the evolutionary evidence, can be corroborated by a larger number of examples, we should be in sight of that common ground of explanation for the phenomena of erotic and hypnotic identification which they have not hitherto possessed.

(*d*) The cases quoted by Freud in his book, *Group Psychology and the Analysis of the Ego* (in Section 7, which deals with Identification), should probably also be taken as instances of genuine (patho-logical) identification. There is the illustration (p. 64) in which a school-girl receives a letter from someone she secretly loves; her jealousy is aroused, and she reacts with an attack of hysterics, by which some of her friends are psychically infected, so that they also 'catch' the fit. Freud comments: 'It would be wrong to suppose that they take on the symptom out of sympathy. On the contrary, the sympathy only arises out of the identification, and this is proved by the fact that infection or imitation of this kind takes place in circumstances where even less pre-existing sympathy is to be assumed than usually exists between friends in a girls' school.' Freud's first observation is certainly just. I should only question whether 'sympathy' arises at all here. For sympathy presupposes just that awareness of distance between selves which is eliminated here by the identification.[2]

(*e*) The mental life of *children*, which in so many respects differs, not in degree but in kind, from that of the adult,[3] also exhibits a type of identification analogous to these pathological cases. Thus, in the 'make-believe' of children, and still more when they

[1] Op. cit., p. 23.
[2] Cf. the cases of self-identification quoted earlier from Freud's *Group Psychology and the Analysis of the Ego*.
[3] Cf. E. R. Jaensch: *Eidetic Imagery: Typological methods of Investigation: their Importance for the Psychology of Childhood* (tr. by Oscar Oeser), Kegan Paul, 1924. In certain children there occurs as a primary experience what Jaensch calls 'eidetic imagery', an intermediate form of awareness between 'perceiving' and 'imagining', out of which there develops, along diverging lines, the disparity in act and content between perception and imagination in the adult.

are taken to see a play or a puppet-show, the situation is very different from the parallel cases in which the adult 'play-acts' or indulges—as they say—in æsthetic 'empathy'. What is empathy in the adult is self-identification for the child. What is only 'play' to the adult is 'in earnest' to the child, and at least for the time being 'reality'. Consider the charming example given by Leo Frobenius, of the child playing 'Hansel, Gretel and the witch' with three burnt matches.[1] Even Freud's case of the child and the dead kitten belongs more to child-psychology than psychopathology. In the child's mind, individual self-awareness is still too unstable and incoherent to resist the childish capacity, which far exceeds the adult's, for ecstatic surrender to some eidetically projected personage. When the little girl plays at 'mother' with her doll, the make-believe character of the play, the 'Let's pretend that I'm Mother', is apparent only to the adult onlooker. In the act of playing the child feels herself (in the image of her own mother in relation to herself), completely identified with 'mother' (which still stands for an individual here, and is not an expression of general reference); the doll she identifies with herself. Hence it also comes about that the child's reaction in a theatre may so easily be quite unlike the adult's.

(*f*) Some particular cases of *divided consciousness* recorded by T. K. Oesterreich may also be regarded as instances of genuine identification, alternating, however, with awareness of self-identity; Oesterreich himself attributes them to identification, and the same applies, perhaps, to certain phenomena of 'possession', of which he has also recently given us a valuable account.[2] The particularly enlightening thing about these examples of self-identification is that they do not come about progressively, through the imitative performance of individual utterances, gestures or actions, but in a sudden leap, as it were; they thus betray the fact that (as in Flournoy's case of the woman who sometimes fancied she was Marie Antoinette), it is the prior state of self-identification with the other person which, throughout a succession of external circumstances quite out of keeping for the historical Marie Antoinette, is responsible for the wholly automatic reproduction of appropriate behaviour in matters of detail.

(*g*) I distinguish a further case of genuine identification, belonging neither to the idiopathic type in which the one individual self despotizes, as it were, over the other, nor to the heteropathic

---

[1] *Paideuma*, p. 59. [*Translator's note:* The child becomes so terrified by her own 'eidetic image' of the witch, that she cries to her father, 'Come and take the witch away. I daren't touch her.']
[2] T. K. Oesterreich: *Possession, Demoniacal and Other* (tr. by D. Ibberson), Kegan Paul, 1930.

in which the one self is entirely 'lost' in the other; it is that type of identification characterized by what I call the phenomenon of 'mutual coalescence'. The most elementary form of this is certainly to be found in *truly loving sexual intercourse* (i.e. the opposite of the sensual, utilitarian, or purposive act), when the partners, in an impassioned suspension of their spiritual personality (itself the seat of individual self-awareness),[1] seem to relapse into a *single* life-stream in which nothing of their individual selves remains any longer distinct, though it has equally little resemblance to a consciousness of 'us' founded on the respective self-awareness of each.[2] This phenomenon was doubtless the chief source of the primitive vitalistic metaphysics underlying the Bacchic orgies and mysteries, which led their initiates to believe themselves plunged back again into the one primæval source of *natura naturans*, with an ecstatic dissolution of all individuality.

(h) But the phenomenon of identification through coalescence is certainly not confined to the erotic sphere. It also reappears in the psychic life of the unorganized *group*, as Le Bon first described it. Here too there is not only an identification of all members with the leader, the despotic idiopath (who therefore cannot and must not merge himself in the collective consciousness); there is also a *further* outcome (engendered by cumulative and reciprocal infection), in the mutual coalescence of the members into a *single* stream of instinct and feeling, whose pulse thereafter governs the behaviour of all its members, so that ideas and schemes are driven wildly before it, like leaves before a storm. The nature and activity of the collective consciousness certainly displays a six-fold analogy with the consciousness found subliminally in dreams, in hypnosis, in animals, primitive peoples and children—the mob is a 'beast' and an 'overgrown child'—and lastly in many pathological states, especially the hysterical ones. But though Freud considers the emergence of this group mind to be closely related to erotic coalescence, the demonstrable links in his group-psychology are still too few for me. Freud defines the primary group as 'a number of individuals who have substituted one and the same object (the leader and hero or an "idea" derived from him) for their ego-ideal, and have consequently identified themselves with one another (in their ego)'.[3] The binding force here is said to be 'libido', in so far as it has already been permanently diverted from sexual objectives

---

[1] Cf. *Der Formalismus in der Ethik*, p. 284 seq.

[2] Cf. Wagner's descriptive tone-poem in *Tristan*, also Gerhard Hauptmann's *Heretic of Soana*, Martin Secker, 1923.

[3] Freud: *Group Psychology*, op. cit., p. 80. [*Translator's note:* The first parenthesis is an interpolation of Scheler's; the second restores a phrase omitted by him.]

and repressed into the unconscious. This hypothesis, if true, would explain in terms of a *single* notion a wide range of hitherto unconnected phenomena (e.g. hypnosis, which Freud describes as 'a group formation with two members');[1] but it seems to me not yet ripe for judgement, so long as the basic problems of the Freudian theory of love and sexuality remain unclarified.[2]

(*i*) A large number of earlier writers (among others Von Hartmann and Bergson), have adopted the identification-theory of love, i.e. the formula that 'love' of another consists in assimilating the other's self into one's own by means of identification; the typical case of identification of character which either leads these authors direct to the theory or provides the best supporting evidence for it, is the bond between *mother and child*. Here, indeed, we have the special, unique case in which the loved one really was once a spatial, corporeal 'part' of the one who loves. Here too there seems to be a smooth and continuous development among the various experiential factors, active and passive, which are involved; those which go to prepare the way for conception (procreative and sexual impulses), those which accompany pregnancy (gradual transformation of the procreative and self-preserving impulses into stirrings of the parental instinct, already awakened before birth itself), and those which are attendant, finally, on the nursing of the child once delivered (gradual transformation of the parental instinct into the conscious sentiment of mother-*love*). In this we pass over the still obscure question whether, just as digestion (according to Pavlov), requires 'appetite' (and a corresponding secretion of gastric juices), so effective conception may similarly require a psychic factor, say an awakening of the involuntary reproductive urge. But in any case one cannot appeal to such facts, as von Hartmann does, in order to establish that love is just an extended form of egoism, or (more reasonably), an extension of the instinct of self-preservation beyond the immediate self, by the adoption of another self into one's own. The facts themselves tell quite another tale. Even before birth the parental and nursing instincts are manifestly quite *distinct* from the impulse of self-preservation. The natural horror of abortion, for which the motives are naturally those of self-preservation, shows this plainly enough. Even before birth the mother regards herself and her child as *two* entities, the impulses appropriate to each being distinct even as phenomena. There is no sort of continuous development from self-preservation (and its

---

[1] Freud : *Group Psychology*, op. cit., p. 78.
[2] On this question cf. also Schilder's already quoted book, *Das Wesen der Hypnose* and our treatment of Freud's ontogenetic theory, Pt. II, ch. 6, sec 5 infra.

impulses) into maternal love. The psychic continuity lies, rather, between the reproductive and parental instincts. The 'self-sacrifice' of the mother for the preservation of her young, so often recorded even among animals, displays an independence, an antagonism of the two impulses which certainly does not arise in the first place as an outcome of gestation, being already present beforehand, and distinguishable in the phenomena themselves. So far from speaking of the mother-child relationship, with von Hartmann, as the mother's assimilation of the child into her own self (and will to survive), it would be more appropriate to describe it as a progressive approximation to an identification of the mother with her child in the shape of an ecstatic *self-devotion* to its individuality. The dreamy state of a woman absorbed in contemplation of her present and future role as a mother is just such a state of kinæsthetic ecstasy, as it were, in which the presence of the child-to-be is disclosed to her. But even the continuity between the parental instincts and what we are first entitled to call mother-*love* is not so complete as is often asserted. I would say, indeed, that instinct and love very often run counter to one another here. Instinct, the outcome of the female reproductive urge, is all the more obviously at work so long as the child is young and still lacks an independent personality of its own. The unremitting solicitude of those mothers who are most 'motherly' in this respect is often a positive hindrance to any kind of independent development of personality in the child, and frequently retards its mental and spiritual growth the more, in seeking to promote its physical welfare. Such continual solicitude, fussing and foolish fondness is proverbially attributed to hens.[1] Does it not seem as if the purely maternal instinct—unmixed with love—were seeking to draw the child back, as it were, into the protecting womb? It is maternal *love* which first checks this tendency, directing itself upon the child as an independent being, slowly making his way from the darkness of mere physical life into the increasing light of consciousness. Like love generally, it conceives the child in its *terminus ad quem*, not, as instinct does, in its *terminus a quo*.

It is only in respect of the *instinctive* components of the whole relationship that one should properly speak of the mother's identifying herself with the impulses, the changing desires and needs of the child. Yet where these components are concerned, it is assuredly not by an empirical understanding and attunement to the symptomatic expression of its changing needs and conditions that the mother is first led to the actions appropriate to the care of her child; it seems to me, rather, that these physical signs are but the transitory outcome of a deeper *metempirical* nexus between

---

[1] [To monkeys, in the German.—Tr.]

the vital rhythms of the mother and the internal phases in the life of the child. Thus the rhythm of lactation and milk-tension in the mother betrays an adaptation to the rhythm of the child's recurring hunger, which likewise holds between the satisfaction afforded to the mother by suckling and to the child by taking the breast. The stirrings of the urge to suckle *correspond* with those of the child's hunger, and it is this which chiefly enables the mother to discern the rhythmic phases of the child's need to be fed. She bears within her (in a manner but little understood), something like a biological code of signals for the progress of her child's condition, which allows her to 'know' about the child in a more intimate fashion than is possible for anyone else. When the mother wakens at the slightest sound from her child (but not in response to much stronger stimuli from other sources), the stimulus does not merely evoke the image of an utterance from the child which then has to be understood; it operates directly upon the ever-watchful parental instinct, transmuting it into an activity which only thereafter brings to light what would otherwise have been necessary before understanding could take place. Thus a mother can make intuitive prognoses for the turn of a child's illness, which often astonish the doctor. This is why mother-love has been held so indispensable in every age and clime, and not merely because of the greater solicitude it displays. The intuitive *psycho-somatic unity* of mother and child is not so entirely severed by their physical separation that its place can be *wholly* taken by the interpretation of organic symptoms through a system of physical signs.

(*k*) Jules Fabre's book *Souvenirs Entomologiques*—that inexhaustible storehouse of precise descriptions of instinctive behaviour—gives an account of certain hymenoptera which are able to sting (without killing), so as to paralyse spiders, beetles and caterpillars, in order to lay their eggs upon them; and Bergson has interpreted these facts as closely connected with sympathy. This stinging is carried out so skilfully, and is (in general), so evidently adapted to the anatomy of the nervous system and to the aim of paralysing without killing, that a surgeon with a scientific knowledge of the caterpillar's nervous system could do no better than the wasp does without any previous experience. There is such an unmistakably deliberate and objective co-ordination of the steps—the choice of nerve-centre for the sting: the living paralysis of the caterpillar: the deposition of eggs by the wasp—that it is quite hopeless to try to explain this as a chain-reflex or as due to the accumulation of inherited experience. This is Bergson's view, and also that of Hans Driesch, who applies it generally, for all true instincts.[1]

[1] [Cf. also Max Scheler: *Die Stellung des Menschen im Kosmos* (1927), Munich, 1947.]

Unquestionably, we must suppose the wasp to have some kind of primary 'knowledge' (in the widest sense of 'having') concerning the vital processes of the caterpillar. Bergson attempts to describe this 'having' in the following phrases:

'But there is no need for such a view if we suppose a sympathy (in the etymological sense of the word) between the Ammophila and its victim, which teaches it from within, so to say, concerning the vulnerability of the caterpillar. This feeling of vulnerability might owe nothing to outward perception, but result from the mere presence together of the Ammophila and the caterpillar, considered no longer as two organisms, but as two activities. It would express the relationship between them in a concrete form'.[1]

It is clear that 'sympathy' here means something quite different from fellow-feeling—for this is a case of hostile action and the exploitation of another creature exclusively in the interest of one's *own* species and without any benefit to the other side; nor, indeed, is it an example of vicarious feeling or understanding. The only thing which can be involved here is a sort of *identification* of the wasp with the caterpillar's organism and vital processes—an identification with that unitary vital process springing from a *single* organic centre which conditions and governs both the caterpillar's nervous system and its bodily sensations. It seems to me probable that this type of instinctive behaviour, in which the phases of a transaction between organisms display an evident intelligible connection, must be regarded as simply an abnormal accentuation of what we have described as genuine identification in the human sphere.[2] In other words, we must 'understand' the creature by analogy—taking as our starting-point, not the experience of adult civilized man, but the psychology of the primitive, the child and the group, together with cases of pathological defect in the activity of the higher co-ordinating centres in man; facts which present-day science, in contrast to the views of thirty years ago, has taught us to recognize as differing in *kind* rather than degree from the facts of mental life in the normal civilized adult.[3]

To add a further consideration: Throughout all modes of sensory apprehension the act of perception occurs as a simple and unitary act. Again, the content so given does not primarily consist

[1] Henri Bergson: *Creative Evolution* (tr. Arthur Mitchell), p. 188. Macmillan, 1911.
[2] An evidently intelligible connection among facts always calls forth an act which shall render it intelligible. Even the orientation of an act of consciousness is itself conditioned by the unity of the 'given' as such.
[3] Cf. the acute and suggestive observations of E. R. Jaensch in *Über die subjektiven Anschauungsbilder*, ch. II, 'Beziehung der eidetischen und wahrnehmungspsychologischen Untersuchungen zu Fragen der Naturphilosophie' (Bericht des 7. Kongresses für experimentelle Psychologie, Marburg, 1921).

in an aggregate, divisible into sense-data, but in a *whole* in which the reality, value and form of the object are already given *beforehand* as 'one and the same', i.e. as a structural configuration, into which the various sense-contents of sight, hearing, smell, touch and taste are subsequently fitted.[1] Parallel to this, we find the same simple and unitary vital principle displaying itself in a range of *instinctive impulses*, built hierarchically one upon another, and becoming ever more specific with every change in the structure and circumstances of the organism. These impulses are simply the more or less conscious correlates of what are, objectively speaking, the *constituent acts of its vital activity as a whole.* Now we know that evaluation takes *precedence* over perception in the constitution of the given—as it also does at the higher level of human mentality, and even on the intellectual plane. Is it not possible, therefore, that identification with the specialized vital principle peculiar to another organism (the caterpillar in this case), might yield a *pattern of the dynamic build-up* of that principle and an insight into the specific biological *value* of its various instinctive tendencies, which was *prior* to and independent of perception? This seems to me not at all 'mysterious' once one grasps what Driesch[2] has shown so admirably, that wherever we have to postulate a more-than-reflex reaction in an organism, this is never intelligible as a direct outcome of the sum-total of individual chemical and physical stimuli impinging on the bodily structure; it is intelligible only in terms of the individual object as an *integral whole*; this being itself understood only as part of a unitary situation within a total environment presenting, for each kind of organism, a *typical structure* determined in advance of any perceptual or sensory acquaintance with it. We do not deny that such identification with an alien pattern of life is occasioned, evoked and initiated in connection with stimuli, any more than we deny it of ordinary perception; for this too is something more than, and quite different from, that sum of sensations corresponding, in theory though never in fact, to the aggregate of stimuli. Even in Bergson's theory, it can hardly be denied that his 'sympathy' is conditioned by stimuli. Otherwise, his position would amount to an assertion of telepathic rapport between wasp and caterpillar, but that is certainly a phenomenon of quite another order. Though in such cases of 'instinctive identification' it is quite in order to speak of relative telepathy, in the sense that the identification extends *beyond* perception, and

---

[1] On the theory of perception see *Der Formalismus in der Ethik.* [Cf. also 'Erkenntnis und Arbeit' in *Die Formen des Wissens und die Gesellschaft* (1926).]

[2] Driesch: *Science and Philosophy of the Organism*, p. 342. A. & C. Black, 1929. Cf. also my comments on the concept of sensation in *Der Formalismus in der Ethik*. [Cf. also *Erkenntnis und Arbeit*, p. 354 seq.]

does *not* depend on prior perception of the nerve-centres to be attacked, as a scientific approach would have to do. Just as sight is a relative 'clairvoyance' in comparison with touch, so the capacity for identification is a kind of telæsthesia, in contrast to sense-perception generally.[1]

The epistemological conclusions of this book will show us how, to be aware of *any* organism as alive, to distinguish even the simplest animate movement from an inanimate one, a minimum of undifferentiated identification is necessary; we shall see how the simplest vicarious emotion, the most elementary fellow-feeling, and over and above these the capacity for understanding between minds, are built up on the basis of this primitive givenness of 'the other'; and by that time the capacity for a specialized identification with the particular dynamic pattern of another creature's lifestream will seem altogether less peculiar. It will then be possible to show that, in man generally, the instinct for specialized identification has atrophied more than in most animals, and has applied itself, moreover, to very *general* patterns in the life of others, whereas in primitive peoples, children, dreamers, neurotics of a certain type, hypnotic subjects and in the exercise of the maternal instinct, there remain much greater residual capacities for identification than in the average adult product of modern civilization. This is not to be wondered at. Our conceptions of life as everywhere 'evolving' towards the human, and of man himself as progressing throughout his history towards present-day civilization, have been profoundly modified in one essential respect: we now realize that in this evolution, life and mankind have not only acquired essential capacities, but have also *lost* them. Thus man has all but lost the animals' capacity for specialized identification, and many of their instincts, thanks to the hypertrophy of his 'intellect'; just as the civilized man has all but lost the primitive's capacity for identification and the adult that of the child. Hence too, has the adult lost that sensory eidetic imagery, which is still present in children as a midway-stage between perception and ideation, and out of which the distinction between them seems first to be developed.[2] It seems as though certain kinds of knowledge can be acquired *only* in youth or not at all. 'Too old to learn'[3] applies in a more than merely quantitative sense. Again, as we have shown elsewhere,[4]

---

[1] In *Der Formalismus in der Ethik* I have shown on similar lines how appetite and disgust indicate the biological significance of things as 'edible', *prior* to actual experience of their beneficial or harmful effect, and are in this sense 'televaluations'.

[2] See E. R. Jaensch's recent works on the eidetic type of image, particularly op. cit., p. 33.

[3] [I.e. 'Was Hänschen nicht lernt, lernt Hans nimmermehr'.]

[4] *Vide* 'Probleme der Religion' in my book *Vom Ewigen im Menschen*, p. 707.

this is evidently how civilized man has lost his 'sense of the supernatural' in religion, so that he has to 'keep the faith' and 'trust' in what his forbears could still discover and see for themselves (it being 'natural' to them). Indeed, the modes of knowledge appropriate to particular types of object seem to be necessarily related to specific phases of development and to no others. Every advance in intellectual capacity involves an increasingly extensive decline in these other powers. The ideal to aim at should be a *synthesis* between progress and the maintenance of tradition— including the revival of what threatens to become extinct— together with an integration of the sequence of tasks assigned to each phase of development, from animal to man, primitive to civilized, child to adult. It may be added that women, as such, still possess powers of intuition which, being based on the maternal instinct with its specialized aptitudes for identification, are found only rudimentarily in man—nor has he anything to replace them. This capacity first develops, no doubt, in a woman's own experience of maternity, but it is not confined to her own child, or to children generally, for it extends, when fully developed, to all the world.

The same can also be said of the racial element in the composition of cultural communities. For in the total enterprise of human knowledge no one people can altogether take the place of another. Only long-term and simultaneous *co-operation on a world-wide scale* between the individual yet complementary portions of humanity can bring into play the total capacity for knowledge inherent in mankind at large, without distinction of time or place. We must therefore dismiss the simplified view of evolution as an upward march of the world process directed towards the undisputed sovereignty of the civilized male, and even of the civilized male European. The phases of evolution are never merely stepping-stones, for each has a unique character and *value of its own*. Evolution is never merely a progress, for it always involves decay as well;[1] while Man himself is the 'first citizen' of creation rather than its 'lord and master'.

Only by *identification*, at the organic level,[2] and only by learning, on the intellectual plane, to *understand* the form and pattern of other ways of life, can we hope for a gradual *smoothing-out* of the private idiosyncrasies and limitations besetting each of us like a horse in blinkers. Blinkers may serve a biological purpose, but

[1] Cf. in *Der Formalismus in der Ethik*, p. 300, my criticism of Herbert Spencer's fallacious method of appraising animals and plants according to their appropriateness to human concerns.

[2] Identification—as Uexküll has already shown, always occurs both in the 'inner world' and 'outer environment' of the organism (whence the inner world can be inferred from the structure of the outer). Understanding, however, applies only to the cognition and field of intentional reference peculiar to man.

in knowing the knower must look beyond them, becoming conscious of them by taking account of their presence, and extending his outlook accordingly.[1]

If we reconsider the types of identification so far described it will be obvious that their nature is radically different from any understanding due to the vicarious reproduction or rehearsal of personal feelings or actions, and equally remote from anything which can possibly be called 'fellow-feeling'. Both of these—vicarious emotion and fellow-feeling—completely exclude the sense of unity or true identification. But from this survey of the types of identification proper, a second and more important feature seems clearly to emerge. The only 'region' in the whole framework of man's unitary intellectual and psycho-somatic nature where identifications can take place is invariably to be found *midway* between the bodily consciousness, which embraces in its own specific fashion all organic sensations and localized feelings, and that intellectual-cum-spiritual personality which is the centre of activity for all the 'higher' acts of intention. For it seems to me certain that neither the spiritual nucleus of our personality[2] and its correlates, nor our body and the phenomena (such as organic sensations and sensory feelings), whereby we apprehend the modification or restriction of its field, are such as to allow of the identification or sense of unity involved in each of the typical cases cited. A man's *bodily* consciousness, like the individual essence of his *personality*, is *his and his alone*.

Assuming the first point (that everyone is confined to his own organic sensations, pleasure-pain feelings, etc.), to be unquestioned as it is unquestionable, it is only the second part of the foregoing statement which is at all open to doubt. We may be confronted with the experiences characteristic of *spiritual mysticism*, I mean the oft-proclaimed experience of the soul's fusion with God, the 'mystical union' so-called, as a hitherto unconsidered instance of merging and identification, with the implication that in this we have overlooked the highest of all forms of identification. But to this we must give the answer of several of the greatest authorities on spiritual mysticism,[3] that the phenomenon here referred to does not exist, so far as the activity in us is really confined to our own centre of personality, and so far as 'God' Himself is regarded therein as a purely spiritual Being. Wherever the

[1] [Cf. on this the author's *Die Stellung des Menschen im Kosmos* (1927), Munich, 1947; see also the essay 'Der Mensch im Weltalter des Ausgleichs' in *Philosophische Weltanschauung*, Bonn, 1929, and 'Probleme einer Soziologie des Wissens' (1925) in *Wissensformen und die Gesellschaft*.]
[2] The nature of this (and the autonomous laws of its activity) are outlined in my book *Der Formalismus in der Ethik*, p. 401 seq.
[3] *Vide* Zahn: *Einführung in die christliche Mystik*, § 29. Paderborn, 1918.

phenomenon does seem to manifest itself, it is neither God as a pure spirit that is present to the inward eye of the self, nor is it the purely spiritual centre of personality that is directed upon God. On the contrary, as is clearly the case in all the ancient mysteries, it is always an idea of God conceived as the collective life of the world, or as Himself endowed with the attributes of life; nor is it ever through our individual centre of spiritual activity by itself that true identification and fusion are attainable, but only in conjunction with our centre of vital activity. The strictly naturalistic and pantheistic type of mysticism maintains that its deification of *existence* (by fusion of the soul with God) is truly adequate, compared with the (inadequate) endeavour to invest conduct and *character* with deiformity by participation in the divine activity ('In Thee we live and move and have our being' or Saint Paul's 'I live, yet not I, but Christ in me'); but, as can be shown in detail, it is always characterized by a twofold error, in that it involves a naturalizing of the divine personality, as well as the human, and thus a total or partial privation of the spiritual element. True mysticism of the spirit always retains at least a consciousness of the ontological gulf intervening between man and God as a limit of approach, and so never aspires to more than a partial identity of attributes.[1]

Supposing we could get rid of all physical differences between human beings (including their essential here-and-nowness), and could further eliminate all qualitative differences in regard to their private objects of consciousness (including the formal aspect of these objects—in short the whole of *what* they think, will, feel, etc.), the individual diversity of their central personalities would still remain, despite the fact that the *idea* of personality would be the same in each of them.

In spite of their variety, the characteristics common to all the typical examples of identification we have mentioned, show them to lie in that *intermediate* region of human nature, which I have sharply distinguished from the spiritual personality and the physical body by calling it *vital consciousness* (as the cognitive counterpart, whether super- or sub-conscious, of the actual process of organic life), and the focus of which I have elsewhere referred to as the 'vital centre'. It is that climatic region of the soul to which belong the energies of life and death, the passions, emotions, drives and instincts; (these are of three types: the instinctive appetites of hunger and thirst, the erotic life-instincts and their derivatives, and the instinctive desire for power, dominance, increase and reputa-

---

[1] When we come to discuss the treatment of identification in monistic metaphysics (Indian philosophy, Schopenhauer, Hegel, von Hartmann, etc.), this assertion will find confirmation at a deeper level. Cf. Part I, ch. 4.

tion). It is impulses such as these which may lead, in their conscious manifestations, to the sense of unity and to identification proper.

It will become increasingly clear to us, what a revealing light is cast by this observation upon all those theories of love and sympathy which derive from metaphysical monism (Schopenhauer, Driesch, Bergson, and, in a certain sense, Erich Becher). Here our first concern is with phenomenological facts, to which even metaphysical 'theories' must necessarily pay heed. And it certainly seems to us a notable confirmation of the foregoing account, that all types of identification proper should exhibit several common features in the way they come about:

(1) Their occurrence is always automatic, never a matter of choice or of mechanical association. In our terminology we describe this by saying that they are due to a specific 'vital causality', different in kind both from rational purposiveness and from (formal) mechanical efficacy. Among other essential features of this basic causal relation we may notice its automatic, vectorial and goal-seeking (not purposive) character; it is a concrete causality *a tergo* of the past as a whole (as distinct from immediately antecedent causes of the uniformly recurrent, qualitatively identical type).

(2) They occur only when two spheres of man's consciousness which are by nature always present concurrently in him, are almost or wholly empty of particular content: the cognitive, spiritual and rational sphere (which is personal in form), *and* the sphere of physical and corporeal sensation and sensory feeling. Only inasmuch and insofar as the acts and functions operative in these spheres are put out of action, does man become disposed to identification and capable of achieving it.

To attain to identification, man must elevate himself 'heroically' above the body and all its concerns, while becoming *at the same time* 'forgetful', or at least unmindful, of his spiritual individuality; he must abandon his spiritual dignity and allow his instinctive life to look after itself. We might also put it by saying that he has to become something less than a human being having reason and dignity, yet something more than an animal of the kind which lives and has its being only in its physical circumstances (and which would indeed come closer to being a plant instead of an animal, the closer its approximation to this marginal type).

The point is that gregariousness in animals represents an advance towards the human level, whereas man becomes more of an animal by associating himself with the crowd, and more of a man by cultivating his spiritual independence.[1]

[1] Empirical evidence for this may be found, above all, in the modes of identification characteristic of those groups which are in process of disintegration (though still to some extent 'organized' in practice).

Thus everything that tends to promote an absolutely collective existence (a limiting concept) will tend to make the individual *more of a hero, and at the same time more of a clod,* in that it stultifies him as a spiritual personality with an ideal and vision of his own. On the other hand, all consideration of things in the light of his own material interest (i.e. self-love, individual self-respect, and the tendencies to self-preservation and betterment which derive from this), will also have to be purged from his outlook, if he is to immerse himself in the primordial feelings and attitudes of the group. He is simultaneously raised above his physical circumstances *and* despoiled of his spiritual inheritance. (Is there not an analogy here with passionate love—*l'amour-passion* as Stendhal calls it—as distinct from self-gratifying lust on the one hand, and spiritual acceptance of the loved one as an individual on the other?)

If there is any one thing within recent experience which serves to confirm these observations, it is the experience of the (First) World War. However it comes about, and whoever is to blame for it, a war-situation transforms all 'organic communities', i.e. groups and individuals having a sense of unity in their collective mode of life, into real entities of a unitary and powerful kind.[1] It glorifies the individual, while largely paralysing his spiritual independence. It elevates a man above his mundane preoccupation with himself, while deposing and disabling him as a spiritual personality. Revolutionary groups and mass-movements exhibit a similar condition of communal frenzy, in which body and soul go under together in a *single* passionate surge of collective activity.

This delimitation of the only *region of human nature* in which identification can occur will play an important part in our assessment of a whole range of metaphysical interpretations which have been applied to the facts of sympathy. I refer to the 'monistic' accounts (of Hegel, Schelling, Schopenhauer, von Hartmann, Bergson, Driesch and Erich Becher).[2] They do not call for acceptance or rejection here. But from the above evidence we may conclude that such theories can only have *meaning* in the *organic* sphere, i.e. as evidence for the metaphysical reality of a supra-individual 'life' in all things living, of a primal entelechy in everything subject to biological laws; whereas they can never entitle us to infer that one and the same spiritual cosmic principle is likewise active in all finite spirits (the theory of *intellectus infinitus*).

[1] Cf. the section 'Die Realität der Nation' in my book *Der Genius des Krieges* (1915) and the essay 'Das Gesamterlebnis des Krieges' in my *Krieg und Aufbau* (1917).
[2] Cf. ch. IV *infra*.

Chapter III

GENETIC THEORIES OF FELLOW-FEELING

THERE are several genetic theories of fellow-feeling which, whatever their explanatory value, prove unequal to the phenomenological factors we have dwelt upon.

To commiserate is, as we have seen, to be sorry at another person's sorrow, *as being his*. The fact that it is his is part of the phenomenological situation. There is no question of any sort of identification in feeling with the other person, nor of my sorrow with his. Even in the first-mentioned example above,[1] the process of feeling in the father and the mother is given separately in each case; only *what* they feel—the *one* sorrow—and its value-content, is immediately present to them as identical. In pure emotional infection, on the other hand, the incoming infective emotion is *not* ascribed to others, but regarded as 'one's own'; only in its causal origins does it relate back to some other person's experience.

I have already construed suggestion and the behaviour of crowds on the lines of the herd-animal's relationship to its leader. I would add that a similar transference of experience also plays an important part in the process of *forming traditions*. 'Tradition' represents a transmission of experience, whether of thought or behaviour, which is the opposite of mere communication or teaching, and likewise of conscious imitation. For in any kind of communication there is a giving, not only of information, but also of the accompanying fact that my *informant* thinks this, says that, etc. In tradition the latter is absent. Here I believe that 'A is B', *because* the other person does so, but *without knowing that* he does so; I simply share his opinion without distinguishing the act of understanding the sense of his belief from my own act of opining. Thus I may feel resentment, anger or love for a thing, or a cause,

[1] Cf. p. 12.

37

because those about me do so, or because my forbears did. But I take the emotions in question to be *my* emotions, engendered by the nature of the case (e.g. the cause itself), and have no suspicion of their origin. This is what gives tradition its binding power, that we take traditional reactions to be our own, and to be entirely derived from the subject-matter to which they refer. It is a corollary of this that the content of tradition does not appear as something past, like a memory, but as a thing present (just as a remembered colour appears as a present sensible appearance of colour). Here we are living *in* the past—without being aware of the act of remembering which brought us thither, and hence *without realizing that it is the past* in which we are living.[1] Thus a family may have a traditional attitude of predilection, aversion or mistrust for certain occurrent or dispositional values, regardless of who or what may happen to possess them; or some ancestral custom concerning wife and children, for example, may be handed down without the descendants realizing that it has no basis in themselves or in the realities of the situation. Take, for instance, the traditional feud between Guelf and Ghibelline, or the 'hereditary enmity' of German and Gaul.

Emotional infection between individuals can thus occur over a gap in *time*, there being here no trace of the usual sense of 'reliving' the experience—(this actually dissolves the power of tradition)—and no consciousness of the fact of transmission. Such an infection, where a tradition of love is involved, is quite unlike the attitude of *pietas*, which is a particular way of *understanding* the past, plus an attitude of fellow-feeling towards it. *Pietas* already presupposes an intervening lapse of time and a sense of detachment from the matter to which it refers, which have no part in a genuine traditionalism. So long as children continue to *take after* their parents, to feel, think, speak and act as *they* would, without realizing the origin of all this, there can be nothing of *pietas* about them.

Tradition is a sort of halfway house between the inheritance of a mental disposition and conscious communication. It shares with inheritance its automatic and unconscious mode of transference and with conscious communication its primarily mental influence. Whereas our mental inheritance, in the shape of inherent emotional dispositions and conative tendencies, cannot be eliminated, it *is* possible, at some later stage of development, to get rid of our traditional loves and hates. Freud's psychoanalytic method, for instance, is an artificial means of eradicating certain genuinely

[1] For identification with a childish disposition of one's own past self, cf. the essay 'Über Reue und Wiedergeburt' (1919) in my *Vom Ewigen im Menschen*, Leipzig, 1921.

traditional emotions, by making their traditional aspect an object of conscious recollection (whence there follows an 'abreaction' from the emotions involved in the original situation and subsequently repressed). The collective traditions of an entire group are unfortunately incapable, as yet, of being dissolved by such means. Critical historiography (as in Renaissance humanism, or the higher criticism of the Bible), can dissolve traditions by letting loose upon the past, as it were, the power of those ideas and emotions which overshadow and constrict our lives today; but it can only do so among small groups of educated people, never for the population as a whole. It seems to be the rule in such 'criticism' that it only becomes possible when the living tradition, if not actually extinct, is already on its death-bed; it is thus rather a *consequence* of the process of dissolution than the real cause of death. Its task is merely to dig the grave for the corpse.[1]

It follows from the above that any theory is mistaken which fails to recognize the phenomenologically observable diversity of the two processes of commiseration and of suffering in others, and the fact that the former is directed upon the latter; while any such conception must also fail in its estimate of the *ethical* value of fellow-feeling, on one side or the other. There are a great many such theories, but only the more typical specimens will be dealt with here. They are partly *psychological*, partly metaphysical.

Quite a number of philosophers have alleged that the phenomenological course of fellow-feeling largely consists in a kind of *comparison*, which, if put into words, would run as follows: 'How would it be if this had happened to *me*?' Whatever the place such a comparison may occupy in life, it certainly has nothing to do with genuine fellow-feeling. If only because the answer would very often be, 'Had it happened to *me*, with *my* character and temperament, it would not have been so bad; but being the sort of person he is, it is a serious matter for him'. True fellow-feeling betrays itself in the very fact that it includes the existence and character of the other person as an individual, as part of the object of commiseration or rejoicing. Can one rejoice more profoundly with a person than at his being the perfect, talented, unspoiled individual *that he is*? or commiserate more deeply than for his having to suffer as he does, being the sort of man he is? In the phenomenon

---

[1] The distinguishing of what is inherited from what is traditional is always very difficult in the individual case, and most difficult of all in the problems of instinct and experience in animal-psychology. Cf. Lloyd Morgan: *Instinct and Habit*. Herbert Spencer, for instance, considers the categories of primitive thought to be inherited, while William James and Lévy-Brühl regard them as merely traditional. (Cf. Lévy-Brühl's Preface to *How Natives Think*.) I incline to the latter view, on account of the great historical and cultural differences in the forms taken by primitive thinking.

of compassion, which is a heightened commiseration bestowed from above, and from a standpoint of superior power and dignity, commiseration displays its characteristic consideration for the *condition* of its object, in a special degree. Thus wherever fellow-feeling has a direct reference to the other person, as such, or to the *individual uniqueness* of his sorrow or joy—which can hardly happen indeed, unless it is based on love—it follows that 'comparison' must already be ruled out as insufficient for an understanding of the situation. Even if the assumption were otherwise correct, it would still cover only those cases in which the emotions involved lie closest to the region of sensory feeling, and farthest from that of the spiritual emotions, which are also the most highly individualized.

But the fact of the matter is that such 'comparison' simply *cannot* be found in commiseration proper at all. It is a fabrication of those theorists who echo the psychology and ethics of the French Enlightenment in taking the natural egoism of man for granted, and therefore seek to construe the altruistic sentiments, and fellow-feeling likewise, as a *consequence* or *counterpart* of some kind to the self-regarding sentiments and attitudes. If, at the moment of reacting in commiseration or rejoicing, we could do so only under the momentary impression, or illusion even, of undergoing the process *ourselves*, our attitude would indeed appear, phenomenologically speaking, to be directed merely upon our own sorrow or joy, and would therefore be an *egoistic* one. A phenomenological reference to the other person as such would no longer be apparent as the immediate purport of the feeling itself. The more so when this theory, having rightly perceived that the comparison is certainly not a matter of judgement and inference, goes on to allege that instead of my merely supposing 'what it would be like' for this to happen to me, I really have a fleeting and involuntary illusion of its actually doing so; in short, an emotional hallucination, like the typical case of the soldier in battle who feels his adversary's uplifted sabre cut painfully into his arm, though it never actually strikes him at all. On this view, fellow-feeling would really be a self-regarding emotional reaction, which has acquired the specious appearance of being a special type of feeling owing to a *misapprehension*. For in entertaining this illusion or hallucination I should have a phenomenological awareness of myself as the sufferer; my practical response would be to try to remove its cause, and even though this might lie in the other person's pain or distressing circumstances, such a reaction would be in no way different from one that was aimed at removing discomforts of my own. But from this it is evident that in so far as this attitude is based on illusion and error, *no sort of moral value* can be ascribed to it. Ethics would then have to counsel us: 'Take good care that you don't mistake the miseries of others for your own, or devote your energies to their removal'; and if it proved impossible to carry out this injunction, one could only tell the person concerned to 'Go and see a doctor'.

There is a further case which resembles this *spurious* type of fellow-feeling, and presents a similar contrast to the real thing: it arises where, although there is an understanding of the other's sorrow, whose effect is to release a reaction of distress, this feeling is not directed upon the other person's condition, but upon the consequential reaction in oneself. An example of this is when someone adopts the maxim 'I must have cheerful faces around me' and thereupon dispenses happiness to those about him; or conversely, when he relieves the woes of others because he 'can't bear to see that kind of thing'; or accedes to the importunities of a beggar or petitioner in order to 'get rid of him' or 'put him out of sight'. And such cases shade into those of mere excess of sensibility, which Nietzsche so misguidedly identified (along with emotional infection), as akin to fellow-feeling; as when a person 'cannot stand the sight of blood', or 'cannot bear to see a fowl's neck wrung'. The really instructive feature here is the way the agent brings his own pleasure or pain into the foreground of attention, so as to *mask* their presence in the other person, and concentrates upon these obtrusive feelings of his own. From just such a spurious case as this we may see that genuine instances of commiseration or rejoicing are never self-regarding states of feeling. But this can be grasped only if we do not lose sight of the sharp distinction between feeling-*functions* and emotional *states*. As I have said on a previous occasion:[1] the suffering of pain is a different thing from the pain itself: suffering as a function has quite different thresholds from those of pain, just as the *capacity* for suffering, joy or satisfaction is distinct from *susceptibility* to pain or to sensory pleasure (the latter being largely constant in history, whereas the former varies widely according to the level of civilization).[2] Now true fellow-feeling is wholly functional throughout: there is no reference to the state of one's own feelings. In commiserating with B, the latter's state of feeling is given as located entirely in B himself: it does not filter across into A, the commiserator, nor does it produce a corresponding or similar condition in A. It is merely 'commiserated with', not undergone by A as a real experience. It may seem extraordinary that we should be able

---

[1] *Der Formalismus in der Ethik*, p. 262 seq. Cf. also the essay 'Vom Sinne des Leides' (1917) in *Moralia*.

[2] There is a phase in anæsthesia by narcosis in which the pain is still quite objectively present, though there is no longer any suffering at all.

to feel the emotional states of others, and really 'suffer' over them; that the result of rejoicing *with* them should be, *not* that we are joyful on their account, for this would then be simply our own joy, but that we are able to *savour* their joy without thereby needing to get into a joyful mood ourselves; but this is just what happens in the phenomenon of *genuine* fellow-feeling. Whereas the causation or infective propagation of analogous feeling-states in ourselves by reason of their presence in others, is no true fellow-feeling at all, but merely seems to be so because of a misapprehension.

In my essay on 'Self-deception'[1] I have dealt with yet another type of case, where again there is no authentic fellow-feeling present, but this time because there is a sort of identification with the other person. It is to some extent the opposite of the previous case. I have in mind the situation in which our own life acquires a tendency to dissipate itself in a vicarious re-enactment of the doings of one or more other people; where we are so *caught up*, as it were, in the other's changing moods and interests that we no longer seem to lead a life of our own; or where our own life largely consists in a series of reactions to such material content as becomes available, *at second hand*, through the other person's experience. Here we react to what actually touches him, as though touched by it ourselves; not because of any illusion or hallucination concerning the priority of the individual feelings, but simply because we are leading *his* life and not our own, while remaining quite unaware of the vicarious relationship by which this process is effected.[2] The distinctive element in this sort of case lies above all in the attitude to one's own self and the evaluation of one's own interests, acts of will, conduct, and indeed one's very existence. This attitude and assessment are now no more than derivative, being determined by the changing *regard* in which the other person holds or might hold us, and which he may demonstrate. We think well of ourselves in finding favour with him, and badly when we do not. Our very acts and decisions are determined by the implicit demands inherent *in his conception of us*. Now this picture he has of us is not, as it normally is, a *result* of our own spontaneous life and activity, which we then receive back at second hand, rejoicing, for example, to find him endorsing it. On the contrary, what happens is that this life and activity becomes entirely dependent on his fluctuating opinion of us.[3] This produces a purely reactive style of life having, on that account alone, a low moral value.

[1] *Vide Zeitschrift für Psychopathologie*, Heft I (1913): also in *Vom Umsturz der Werte*, II, Band, under the title 'Die Idole der Selbsterkenntnis'.

[2] Cf. the cases of pathological identification mentioned above.

[3] Cf. the subtle analyses of V. von Gebsattel in his essay 'Der Einzelne und sein Zuschauer', *Zeitschrift für Psychopathologie*, II, I. It is a different matter when we merely take over the other person's ideal picture or model of himself as

Such a reactive attitude towards society is characteristic of the abnormally *vain* man, who—in contrast to the proud type, is utterly in thrall to the notice and opinion of other people; it is only *as* one who is seen, marked and attended to that he has any sense of his moral reality, and his own personality, wishes and feelings are completely hidden from him by the 'personage' he enacts. It is also characteristic, though in a very different fashion, of a type I should describe as the mental *parasite*. This human species lives, mentally, entirely on those around him, or on a *single* member of his acquaintance, in the sense that he partakes of the latter's experiences as his own, not merely echoing the other's thoughts and opinions, but thinking and uttering them on his own account, and sharing his moods likewise. It is a consciousness of internal emptiness and nullity, which gives rise to this type of personality; a vacuity which drives him out of 'himself', and hence to fill his empty belly with the experience of others. And this passive type finally passes into the far more dangerous active form of the disposition: that of the spiritual *vampire*, the hollowness of whose existence, coupled with a passionate quest for experience, drives him to a limitless *active* penetration into the inmost reaches of the other's self; unlike the passive type, he does not fasten on a single individual, but always on one after another, so as to live a life of his own in their experiences, and fill the void within. Strindberg has given a masterly description of the type in his play *The Dance of Death*. It is also common for certain psychoses to exhibit a variant form of the general attitude here outlined; I refer to that excessive deference in attitude, thought and action, towards the 'spectator' and the impression supposedly made upon him, which is so especially noticeable in *hysteria*. Here the presence of an onlooker immediately upsets the patient's natural self-possession, his consciousness of himself being replaced by the *image* of himself as seen by the onlooker, and as judged by the latter's standards of preference. He speaks, acts and conducts himself by reference to this image and on the spur of the moods it evokes—refusing to eat, for instance, or even committing suicide in some cases. It would be a mistake to describe this, as many psychiatric textbooks do, simply as 'excessive vanity', 'play-acting' or 'coquetry' on the part of the patient. For those who affect such attitudes are conscious, not only of the picture they present, but also that it is *they* who present it; they oscillate between this picture and an awareness of themselves as they really are. For the hysterical patient, however, the picture has come to life; the image

appropriate to ourselves also, and judge ourselves accordingly. Cf. on this point the second volume of *Vom Ewigem im Menschen*, 'Vorbilder und Führer', to be published shortly [published in *Nachlassband*, I, 1933].

of what he might be has come, for him, to *displace* what he actually
is. Preoccupied as he is with the other person, the real course of
his receptive, expressive and active life is actuated by variations
in the fully-formed image supposedly seen there, depending on
whatever authoritative version of it may have caught his fancy
at the time; though he does not consciously set out to produce
such variations in the image, for the sake of a pleasurable reaction
thereto. Such a patient therefore, will not be content, like the still
normal 'prima donna' type, to put on a stricken air so as to make
others feel sorry for him, or a gay one to cheer them up; instead,
he will implement the wished-for calamity by *actually* staging one,
will actually kill himself, actually get into a state of wild hilarity,
etc., but all still entirely for the benefit of the spectator and
depending on his presence. The vain man, the play-actor and the
coquette do not act thus, for they have not lost their capacity for
self-awareness and merely vacillate between their own true condition and the image of themselves as others see them.

All such sub-species of this general type consist of forms which
have nothing to do with fellow-feeling proper, seeing that the
conditions for this, the consciousness and feeling of being oneself,
of leading one's own life and thus of being 'separate' from others,
are only apprehended here in a degenerate form. For this reason,
too, their *ethical value is negative,* however much they may be mistaken for refinements of fellow-feeling or even for love. There is
certainly nothing to prevent such attitudes from leading to actions
of great benefit to the other person. All these people are capable
of acts of what is commonly called 'sacrifice'. But in fact that is
merely what they look like. For a man who neither leads his own
life nor finds it worth living cannot sacrifice himself for another.
He simply does not possess the one thing needful for sacrifice,
namely a life of his own. Such neglect of self may have the quality
of being useful and well-intentioned towards others, or it may be
damaging and malevolent—as in the case of pure villainy, which
may render the villain quite forgetful of his own advantage and
even reckless of damage to himself; but even where the process
begins in goodwill, it is an almost invariable rule in such cases,
that it *ends in hatred,* and the more so, the more the agent persists
in throwing himself *away* in this spurious fashion, for it is the very
opposite of really meritorious self-*devotion.* Without a certain self-
awareness and self-respect, acquired at first hand, and not derived
from the effect produced on others, it is not possible to live morally.
But the more our self-respect is impaired in the process referred
to, the harder do we struggle to retain it, and the sterner grows
the conflict between this endeavour and the countervailing tendency to lapse into absorption in another person. Figuratively

speaking, although the 'slave' has voluntarily delivered himself into the bondage of living another's life rather than his own, he comes at last to chafe against his fetters, and to rise up against his 'master'. And so the expense of spirit which at first resembled love turns necessarily to hatred, as a final means of self-assertion.[1]

A peculiar mixture of genuine fellowship with subservience of this type is to be found in the relationship of 'patriarchal' authority between parents and children, or master and man. Its characteristic feature is the *mixture* of authority and considerate or indulgent fellow-feeling in the superior towards his subordinate, and, in the latter, a submissive deference to the life and will of the master, together with a genuinely solicitous fellow-feeling for him. The Russian appellation of 'Little Father' expresses this very strikingly.

But let us return to the genetic theories of fellow-feeling, and to the point made earlier, that in true unalloyed commiseration and rejoicing there is no state of sorrow or joy in oneself. This phenomenological fact is a stumbling-block for all those theories which undertake to explain the fact of fellow-feeling, without reverting, as before, to 'inference' or 'automatic illusion'. For they do so by asserting that perception of the symptoms and occasioning circumstances of joy or sorrow in another person either has the effect of *immediately* evoking the *reproduction* of a similar joy or sorrow previously experienced in oneself, or else that it does so *indirectly* by way of a tendency to imitate the symptoms so perceived. Let us disregard the second alternative and confine ourselves to the reproduction of past states of feeling. Lipps,[2] like Störring,[3] makes all fellow-feeling consequent on a prior reproduction of feeling, and assumes that, given such a reproduction, which would necessarily present the feelings in question as having been previously felt to be my own, there is a further process of 'empathy' by which they are then carried over into the other person. In so doing he recognizes a problem which Störring disregards. For in fact we do at least have the impression that in fellow-feeling the other's emotions are in some sense 'given'. Störring does not explain this impression at all. While in view of

---

[1] This process often finds expression in an 'ambivalent' oscillation between love and hatred, in which hatred always sets in when self-abandonment has gone too far, to be again transformed into love, once the personal self has been reinstated. The fear of love, so-called, is in fact the fear of 'throwing oneself away'.

[2] Cf. Theodor Lipps: *Einleitung in die Psychologie* and *Grundfragen der Ethik*.

[3] Cf. G. Störring: *Beiträge zur Ethik*, II Band. The pure theory of fellow-feeling in terms of reproduction and association has been worked out with even greater thoroughness and precision by Antonin Prandtl in his book on Empathy, and by Benno Erdmann in his *Grundzüge der Reproduktionspsychologie*, Berlin, 1920.

all I have previously said about his theory of empathy, Lipps explains it wrongly. For it follows from what has already been shown that a genetic theory is irrelevant here, since the other person's state of mind is directly grasped *in* the expressive phenomenon itself—without any sort of projective 'empathy'. But this raises the question whether such a reproduction of one's own joy or sorrow does or can play any part whatever in genuine fellow-feeling.

Let us first consider those cases where such reproduction undoubtedly does occur. Everybody must have had the experience of going in serious trouble to someone and telling this interested relative or friend of his distress. And he may well have noticed how the adviser in question, instead of entering into his visitor's circumstances, takes the latter's tale as an opportunity for indulging in a spate of reminiscence about *himself*, as to how a very similar thing once happened to him, and what he then did about it. 'Yes', they say, 'that's life all over: I once had pretty well the same thing happen to me.' Somewhat put out, we draw our friend's attention to the fact that here the circumstances are 'rather different'; we do our utmost to divert the rapt historian's gaze from his own career to our present troubles. But all too often he calmly goes on with his tale. Again, we have all met people who temper the quantity and direction of their interest according to what has given *them* most joy or sorrow in their own lives. But is such an obtrusion of one's own experience, even though it be reproduced quite automatically *without* any act of recall, any more authentic as a case of fellow-feeling than the previous one, seeing that it again involves a diversion of interest from the other person back to oneself? I do not think so. This genetic theory does nothing to account for positive unalloyed fellow-feeling, which is a genuine *out-reaching* and entry into the other person and his individual situation, a true and authentic *transcendence* of one's self; it merely explains some of the casual empirical circumstances associated with the working of fellow-feeling, and these are more liable to disturb and detract from it, than to produce or promote it. In so far as our own reproduced experiences may intervene between our fellow-feeling and the other person's state of mind, the purely positive character of the feeling is veiled in an obscuring medium originating in the particular state of our psychophysical organization at the time. This genetic association-theory overlooks the very existence of *pure* fellow-feeling as such, just as it ignores the possibility of pure remembering (independent of the memory-image, as Bergson has effectively shown[1]), and of a pure intuition

[1] Henri Bergson: *Matter and Memory* (authorized translation by N. M. Paul and W. Scott Palmer), London, Macmillan, 1911.

indivisible into sensory constituents. To add a further point, the experience reproduced, for instance the grief or anguish felt in pitying a person afflicted by these states, would have to be a *genuine* feeling (though less intense than the original state). For it is not supposed to be a question of remembering a feeling one has possessed or shared, but of actually reproducing it, so that there really is a new feeling present, albeit a weaker one. Thus, to pity a drowning man, I should have to be stricken for a moment with fear like his own; to have pity for someone in pain, I should need to feel a twinge of it myself. But the purer and truer the fellow-feeling, the less does this happen; the more it does occur, the closer we approach to a condition of emotional infection, which actually does consist in such a reproduction of feelings, either directly or by virtue of the tendency to echo the expression of feeling in others; and the effect of this is to *lower* the moral value of the attitude accordingly.

This theory is at fault in yet another respect. For it entails that our fellow-feeling must necessarily be confined to processes and incidents in other people's experience such *as we have already met with ourselves*. But this conclusion is as little in accord with the facts as the corresponding view, that we can only understand what we have actually been through ourselves. We can have a lively and immediate participation in joy or sorrow, can share with others their appreciation of value, and can even enter into another person's commiseration for a third party, without ever having sampled that particular quality of experience before. A person who has never felt mortal terror can still understand and envisage it, just as he can also share in it. It is a futile evasion to argue that for this we must at least have had real experience of the 'elements' of the state or value in question, such as those comprised in fear, or in some sort of 'death-like feeling', in the present case. For what sort of 'elements' are these? How far must we descend in search of those mental particles which the atomistic psychology believes to be constituent of experience? And on what principle or rule are these 'elements' to be compounded, if we do not already have some idea of what the end-product is to be, namely mortal terror? Are we to go on shuffling these elements in imagination, until they happen to fit the case? Such a game would be most unlikely to come out. Certainly, the variety of emotional tones within the compass of a species such as man, is no less *finite* however large it may be, than the limited number of basic colours he is able to perceive. Nevertheless, it is quite wrong to suppose that these basic colours must necessarily be encountered in actual perception and sensation, before they can be 'visualized' at all; the fact is that this intrinsic limitation of range holds *equally* good throughout for *all* modes of colour-awareness alike, whether in perception, in judgement, or in the use of imagery (in memory, fantasy, etc.); it is only because of the biologically purposive character of the order in which these acts are brought into use, that we usually begin by perceiving qualities in sensation, on receipt of an external stimulus, before they are presented in imagery.[1] It is exactly the same in the present case. Given the range of emotional qualities of which man is intrinsically capable, and from which alone his own actual feelings are built up, he has an *equally innate* capacity for comprehending the feelings of others, even though he may never on any occasion have encountered such feelings (or their ingredients) in himself, as real unitary experiences.

Moreover, this applies increasingly, the more such feelings ascend from the sensory level, through the vital, to the spiritual plane. It is only for *sensory* feelings ('feeling-sensations') that reproduction is required, in order to be sure of understanding and participating in them.[2] Thus it is scarcely possible for a normal person to acquire a real understanding of a perverse sensual pleasure and impossible for him to share in it, any more than he can in the enjoyment of pain. It is equally difficult to partake in the enthusiasm of the Japanese for consuming raw fish; and difficult even, for a man of culture to summon up a genuine sympathetic enjoyment in the pleasures of the populace, such as their taste for rowdy music, for instance. The varieties of sensory pleasure and pain in animals are also largely alien to us, and fellow-feeling is no longer operative in such cases. Nevertheless, so far as the various modes of *vital feeling* are concerned, understanding and fellow-feeling are able to range throughout the *entire* animate universe, even though they rapidly fall off in respect of specific qualities as we descend the organic scale. The mortal terror of a bird, its sprightly or dispirited moods, are intelligible to us and awaken our fellow-feeling, despite our total inability to penetrate those of its sensory feelings which depend on its particular sensory organization. Again, the very people whose sensuous enjoyments are unintelligible and uncongenial to the person of culture, are perfectly comprehensible to him in respect of their

---

[1] It has not yet been established for certain whether those born blind have any conception of colour.

[2] A detailed analysis of the four levels of feeling: spiritual, mental, vital and sensory, and an outline of the specific laws appropriate to each, is to be found in my book *Der Formalismus in der Ethik*, p. 344. My theory has recently been confirmed on the pathological side by Kurt Schneider in his essay 'Pathopsychologische Beiträge zur psychologischen Phänomenologie von Liebe und Mitfühlen' (*Zeitschrift für die gesamte Neurologie und Psychiatrie*, Bd. 35, 1921) and further in *Bemerkungen zu einer phänomenologischen Psychologie der invertierten Sexualität und erotischen Liebe* (ibid., Bd. 71, 1921).

vital emotions, and awaken his wholehearted interest therein. While the understanding and sharing of *mental,* and still more of *spiritual* feelings, is completely independent of all such gulfs between the contingent personal backgrounds of individuals. Jesus' despair in Gethsemane can be understood and shared regardless of our historical, racial and even human limitations. And for every candid heart which steeps itself in that desolation it operates, not as a reminder or revival of personal sufferings, great or small, but as the revelation of a new and greater suffering hitherto *undreamed* of.

Only so are we enabled, by understanding, emotional reproduction and fellow-feeling for other people's circumstances, values and standards (fellow-feeling plus evaluation), to effect a real *enlargement* of our own lives and to *transcend* the limitations of our own actual experience; thereby reconciling the appearance of both such fields of actual experience under that *governing* master-concept of life in all its fullness, vouchsafed to the open-hearted through a sympathetic understanding of value and circumstance in the present and the past. According to the theories we are rejecting, we are supposed, firstly, to be necessarily confined in the prison of our own casual experiences, in all their individual, racial and historical heterogeneity, so that the objects of our understanding and sympathy would represent merely a *selection* from such experience as *we* have actually had. Thus an age could only understand and sympathize with those aspects of a bygone epoch which were familiar from its own experience. 'Wha's like us?'[1] would become an axiom for the historian, and the habit of analogical comparison with the present day, which is really a grave abuse of history, would be enthroned as the basic principle of historical method. The idea of an inner *moral unity of mankind*[2] over and above the actual contacts of its members, would likewise become a pure fiction. A second conclusion would necessarily follow from such a view: that though fellow-feeling so often seems to affect our volition and action, and even the entire course of our inner life, setting it right, for instance, by inducing us to abandon a plan or renounce decisions already made lest they should prove detrimental to others, this would merely be an illusory effect, since such sympathy could only extend to matters for which our own life hitherto had furnished the material. Fellow-feeling and its objects, being merely epiphenomenal to what has actually been experienced, would have no hope of ever exerting any *real effective* influence on its present course of development. And now let us confront this view with a

---

[1] [An approximate rendering of: 'Wie haben wir's so herrlich weit gebracht'. The reference is to Wagner in Goethe's Faust, Pt. I, 1, 573.—Tr.]

[2] Cf. my analysis of this in *Der Formalismus in der Ethik*, p. 555.

case like that of Buddha's conversion. A man who, having grown up amid luxury and splendour and all the amenities of life, was led by the sight of a few instances of poverty and sickness to discern and respond to all the pain and misery of the world, so that his whole life thereafter took an entirely different course. Or again, we may take an example from Tolstoi's story *Master and Servant* which tells how the master's mean little heart is *opened*, after life-long closure, in the act of his first experience of pure sympathy at the sight of his servant perishing of cold; and this not only for the limited feeling of the moment, but for everything to which he had hitherto been blind, neglectful or obtuse in his own life.[1]

But we have no need of such exalted examples. We can perceive in our own daily lives a rhythmic alternation between the closed and the open viewpoint, between self-regarding aloofness and sympathetic interest in the lives of other people. We may notice how our flow of sympathy is by no means dependent on variations in the external stimuli, but fluctuates widely in spite of them. Thus it often fails us when confronted with the fact and the evidence of intense suffering, and then often without any such powerful inducement, some trifle may open all our soul to human joys and sorrows for days and weeks on end, as if a light were suddenly shone, or a window opened, in a darkened room. It is brought home to us here with especial clarity, how fellow-feeling differs, in the *autonomy* of its functioning, from states of mind occasioned by factors external to ourselves.

[1] Jacob Wassermann's novel *Christian Wahnschaffe*, gives a masterly portrayal of a man addicted to selfish enjoyment and a slave to the conventions of his station and class, who slowly learns, by repeated acquaintance with human distress and misery, to open his heart to the other side of life and society (tr. by Ludwig Lewisohn as *The World's Illusion*, Rahway, N.J., 1921, re-issued by Allen and Unwin, 1929).

Chapter IV

METAPHYSICAL THEORIES

(1) SCHOPENHAUER'S THEORY

THE best-known theory dealing exclusively with our first type of pity is that of Schopenhauer. According to him, it is fellow-feeling which reveals the *unity of being* underlying the multiplicity of selves. It is this which destroys the illusion to which we are otherwise enslaved, whereby each of us considers himself as having an independent reality. Thus according to Schopenhauer, it is above all in pity that we gain an immediate intuitive insight into the underlying unity of the world (by which he understands the obscure driving urge he calls 'Will'), and are enabled to 'see through' the illusory character of time and space, which he mistakenly considers to be principles of individuation.

Schopenhauer deserves credit for an understanding of pity which is in many respects juster than that commonly accepted in psychology and ethics. The very fact of his reaffirming, against Kant, the general relevance of feeling in ethics, must be set down as one of them. He is sound, in principle, in recognizing that commiseration is an 'immediate' participation in the woes of others, and does not depend on inference or on any artificial mode of 'projecting' oneself into the other person's situation. And despite his altogether one-sided emphasis on this particular sentiment, he goes beyond the ideas of his time in acknowledging that pity has an intentional character, and in not regarding it as a blind condition of the soul, explicable in merely causal terms. He is also right in his realization that the phenomena of commiseration presuppose a unity of life which is not grounded in the experience of a multiplicity of different organisms in spatial separation; though his manner of conceiving this in terms of a metaphysical ontology,

51

and still more his habit of identifying it as a blind Will, certainly involve him in groundless assumptions.

But the advance which his view represents over the theories then current must be weighed against errors and confusions so great as to make his achievement seem a slight one. For the positive moral value which Schopenhauer ascribes to pity does not primarily reside in the constituent function of *fellow*-feeling, but in the *suffering* inherent in it (in which he fails, moreover, to distinguish the factual and functional components). Since suffering in general represents, for him, the essential 'way of salvation', it is only as a form of suffering and as a mode of apprehending its ubiquitous presence that pity acquires the positive value he attributes to it. He thus takes up a position opposed, not only to a properly philosophical appreciation of the moral value of pity, but also to the judgement of sound common sense. For it is generally conceded that pity is felt in the first instance as a compassionate outreaching beyond the individual self; secondly, that it does not increase suffering, but proverbially halves it; and that more often than not it contributes to a twofold satisfaction—that which is found generally in the mere enlargement of one's self by participation in another's experience, and that found by the pitied one in merely witnessing the tokens of love and sympathy, not to mention what he derives from the fulfilment of his desires through the help of his sympathizer. The basis for Schopenhauer's fundamental appreciation of pity is in direct opposition to all this. It rests on the function of *suffering*-with, as such, wherein sickness, poverty or misery are merely the occasions of its emergence. It does *not* lie in the display of love, nor in the comfort which compassion may bring, and he more than once expressly emphasizes that it is not the diminution, but the *increase* of suffering as a 'way of salvation', which gives it value as a source of moral redemption. All the same, his account is not without a certain touch of eudæmonism in its evaluation of pity: the compassionate man finds in the sufferings of others a corresponding solace for his own discomforts, since it is through pity that he realizes the extent and the *universality of suffering*. Thus by feeling himself and his own sorrows to be involved in that universal whole of suffering to which the world of nature is unalterably destined, he achieves a quietude of 'resignation' concerning his own selfish desires. But despite its appearance of nobility and pathos, this consummation is rooted in an emotional experience of a type that is far from valuable, and one, moreover, with which true pity can in no way be reconciled. When suffering comes to a morally sensitive person, the fact that others are similarly afflicted, and his emotional entry into the distress thus sympathetically intimated, lay a double burden on his own heart. Schopenhauer obviously confuses here the morally indifferent process of mere insight or understanding by emotional reproduction with that of fellow-feeling proper. For even if the world *were* ultimately reducible to a single self-mortifying Will, such a vicarious intimation of our unalterable fate might bring solace and resignation, but could never account for our reaction to this suffering, namely fellow-feeling. For such a reaction would simply throw us back into the misery we had hitherto discerned only by inspection, as it were, and would automatically provoke a further instinctive struggle to escape it, so that mankind would be forever enmeshing itself more deeply in what Schopenhauer, following the Indian writers, calls 'Sansara'. By thus vaguely uniting fellow-feeling with emotional reproduction, Schopenhauer is obliged to equate genuine pity with this essentially inert reaction. Moreover, his presentation of the theory takes on a character which betrays a hidden element of sadistic *glee* in the affliction of others. Both aspects come out at times in his letters, where he can hardly conceal his elation at hearing from friends who write to him as a well-wisher in their toils and troubles; he does not answer them with help or consolation, but merely observes that they may now obtain first-hand confirmation of the soundness of his teaching!

If Schopenhauer had gone on to draw the logical conclusions of his reasons for approving of pity, the result would have been to make it obligatory to *cause* suffering, so as to ensure a continuous renewal of opportunities for the exercise of this essentially valuable sentiment of pity. At all events, a man whose susceptibilities run on the lines of Schopenhauer's description of pity, will feel a peculiar satisfaction at the sight of suffering in others, since it is only this, as he fancies, which enables him to react in a kindly or compassionate way. His spiritual vision will soon be blind to the *positive* values, such as joy and happiness, which lie about him; his disposition to contemplate suffering will so govern his attention as to provide unlimited opportunities for his propensity to indulge in vicarious suffering. It is a narrowly defined type of personality which thus finds its exact expression in Schopenhauer's ethics. Tolstoi, for instance, is in many respects a representative of this type. In his posthumous play *And the light shines in the darkness*, in which he draws an extraordinary and savage picture of his own psychological conflicts, and in so doing pillories himself, he attributes to his hero a morbid passion of this very type; it comes out clearly in the music-room scene, where the hero (who is himself) intervenes without reason upon the gaiety of his family and the other children, to remind them of the miseries of the poor, which ought to forbid such frivolity.

We find in Schopenhauer one of those misplacements of value which I have dealt with elsewhere,[1] in that he plainly construes that *taste* for pain and suffering which is also gratified in sympathy, as the appearance of a genuine moral pity. It is well known to those familiar with hospitals that the reasons for choosing nursing, or even surgery, as a profession (like other callings involving a close contact with visible afflictions), often include a desire for the sight of distress and pain and of such outward evidences of these as wounds, blood and so on. Naturally, such a motive in the choice of a career is not in the least inconsistent with the strictest observance of duty in the giving of aid and the performance of all other moral acts related to this, 'from a sense of vocation'. An intrinsically morbid inclination may very well provide the latent energy which is the ultimate power behind an essentially good and even praiseworthy vocational activity.[2] Such practical and concrete instances offer an appropriate confirmation of Schopenhauer's theory.

A further indication that Schopenhauer is not primarily concerned with the positive evaluation of the element of fellowship in pity, but with the suffering it contains, is that he treats pity as having a higher *ethical* value than rejoicing, besides holding it to be more widely distributed in practice. Instead of the factual and merely utilitarian grounds on which the prevailing opinion bases its moral preference for pity over rejoicing, he thought himself able to ascribe to the former a *metaphysical* function which he denied to the latter. I do not enter here upon his mistaken attempt to derive love itself from pity, nor, more generally, upon his altogether inadequate endeavour to trace all moral values back to this source, including even the idea of justice itself.

The above bears out what Nietzsche[3] was in many ways right to recognize, though he unfortunately extended our observations to include the case of true pity as well, namely that Schopenhauer's idea of pity is ultimately based on a morbid energy of life in decline, which is taken to be morally positive only through self-delusion; his *interpretation* of pity in terms of *metaphysical monism* is a further illustration of this. For he holds that it is not only values and the feelings they evoke which come to light in vicarious

[1] Cf. my study 'Das Ressentiment im Aufbau der Moralen' (1913), in the volume of collected essays *Vom Umsturz der Werte*.

[2] In his *Principles of Psychology* (Vol. II, § 532) Herbert Spencer claims to find some such enjoyment of pity as an element in all commiseration. 'The contemplation of the suffering exercises a kind of fascination. There arises an abnormal desire to dwell on that which is intrinsically painful.'

[3] The justice of Nietzsche's statement is very well brought out by E. Kramer: 'Das Phänomenon des Mitgefühls in der modernen Philosophie, insbesondere bei Schopenhauer und Nietzsche' (Dissertation, Cologne).

or companionate emotion, but that pity is further able in some directly intuitive fashion to rend 'the veil of Maya'; the latter, in the guise of that spatio-temporal intuition which he takes to be the principle of individuation, being responsible for concealing from us the *unity of being*, namely the one blind, self-mortifying Will.

In adopting this line, Schopenhauer's theory becomes a special case of the erroneous theory of fellow-feeling as identification, and a metaphysical version of this to boot. Now actually, as we have shown already, the sort of identification which Schopenhauer describes,[1] can only come about by way of some sort of emotional infection and identification, which would positively exclude an understanding of the other person's state; so that his theory implies a further confusion of moral pity with susceptibility to emotional infection and identification. If this doctrine of the revelation, through pity, of my metaphysical unity with others were carried to its logical conclusion, such a unitary identity of existence, with its reduction of individual suffering to mere illusion, would make it quite inconceivable how pity *for* another person, and the acts of succour so engendered, could have any special moral value. For if 'I' am essentially one and the same as the other person ('Tat twam asi', as the Indian proverb says), it is logically ines-capable that he must also be one and the same as I. But this means that if I am *myself* in pain, and preoccupied, either in trying to escape from it or in enduring it as a means of salvation, this suffering has just the *same* value when there is no fellow-feeling in it as when it is actually due to fellow-feeling; for the meta-physical unity of being would be just as evident in either case. Pity presupposes a distinction between individuals, and if this is an illusion, pity itself must be another. The dissolution of the self in a common stockpot of misery eliminates *genuine* pity altogether.

(2) THE SCOPE OF METAPHYSICAL THEORIES IN GENERAL

The metaphysical theory of fellow-feeling and its varieties can-not be fully set out here. That must be reserved for a systematic treatment of metaphysics, particularly in regard to organic life. Only this, together with a metaphysics of Spirit, could take in the metaphysical sense and meaning of love in all its forms.

At all events, metaphysical theories of fellow-feeling have a considerable advantage, in their approach to the problem, over empirical theories of the psychological and genetic type with

[1] Cf. for instance the prize essay on 'The Basis of Morality', § 18 (tr. by A. B. Bullock), Allen & Unwin, 1915.

which we have been dealing. They accept, in principle, what our analysis has confirmed and what our criticism and rejection of the empirico-genetic theories has reinforced from the other side, namely that vicarious and companionate feeling are *basic phenomena*, which can only be *exhibited* as they actually are, without being derivable from more elementary facts on psycho-genetic lines. So far as such elementary phenomena are further explicable at all, this can only be on *metaphysical* lines, i.e. by a systematic scrutiny of the reality of the thing; and though such a reality must conform like any other to the constitutive laws we find prevailing in the order of empirical existence, it will no longer stand in any direct or indirect causal relation to our actual psycho-somatic organization. Fellow-feeling *is* a phenomenon of the metaphysical order. In this the metaphysical theories are indubitably right. And failure to recognize this fact is the prime fallacy of all empirico-genetic theories of fellow-feeling (including the phylogenetic[1]), wherever they seek to trace its origin as distinct from merely expounding its development.

The best-known type of metaphysical theory of fellow-feeling is that of *metaphysical monism*. Throughout history it has had a comprehensive array of defenders.[2] Leaving aside the metaphysics of ancient India and of Buddhism, and the Indian and Christian mystics, we may mention among modern philosophers, Schelling, Hegel, Schopenhauer, Eduard von Hartmann and Wilhelm Wundt; and more recently still, Bergson, Driesch, Becher, Münsterberg, Volkelt—to say nothing of lesser writers.[3]

(1) A first and most fundamental point of difference among the monistic theories of fellow-feeling is as follows. Does fellow-feeling as a purely emotional function possess significance for *knowledge*, a cognitive bearing on the unity of Absolute Reality (Schopenhauer's 'Will', Bergson's 'Elan Vital', etc.)?—is there indeed, *in* the act itself, a dim and confused intimation of a metaphysical reality, which would either have been hidden altogether or have remained opaque to us in some particular respect, if not approached by this route? Or does a monistic ontology, such as

[1] Cf. ch. VIII *infra*.

[2] Since the publication of the first edition of this book, some new and very noteworthy theories of this sort have been added to the earlier ones.

[3] On Hegel, *vide* Wilhelm Dilthey: *Die Jugendgeschichte Hegels*. Cf. further Schopenhauer: *The Basis of Morality*, op. cit.; E. von Hartmann: *Phänomenologie des sittlichen Bewusstseins*; Bergson's remarks on 'Instinct and Sympathy' in his *Creative Evolution*, and on maternal love in *Time and Free-will*; Hans Driesch: *Science and Philosophy of the Organism*, Part II, in which fellow-feeling is taken as a sign of the unity of the entelechy as distinct from a plurality of entelechies; Erich Becher: *Die fremddienliche Zweckmässigkeit der Pflanzengallen und die Hypothese eines überindividuellen Seelischen*; H. Münsterberg: *Psychology, General and Applied* and *The Eternal Values*; Joannes Volkelt: *Das ästhetische Bewusstsein*.

the attribution of a corporate life to the animate universe, or the identification of all minds as ultimately one, merely serve to *explain* how the phenomenon of fellow-feeling is actually possible? The first view is to be found in Buddhist metaphysics, and more unmistakeably still in Schopenhauer and Bergson; the second in von Hartmann, Driesch, Becher and others.

We have tried to show elsewhere[1] that there really are feelings which are essentially *intentional* (i.e. not first engendered by a concept or idea), and there we have already disavowed the theory that such feelings convey a dim and confused knowledge of existence in the shape of factual *ideas*. Similar considerations apply in the case of an emotionally *vicarious* understanding of feelings in another person, which are intentionally directed on an object of positive or negative value; and they also apply to the *fellow*-feeling based on this, and relating to the actual emotional state which supervenes, in the other person, upon his intimation of value or its opposite. In both cases, the feeling is assuredly a feeling *of* something, i.e. is intentional in character, referring in the first case to an objective content of value or disvalue, and in the second to the emotional state of another person. This being so, the Schopenhauer-Bergson view has at least one great point in its favour—(so long as the word 'knowledge' is not equated with knowledge of ideas, i.e. with representational, conceptual or propositional knowledge, and so long as the old Spinoza-Leibniz doctrine of the continuity of difference between idea and feeling, thought and emotion, is wholly renounced and discarded). For it does at least do justice to the intentional nature of vicarious and companionate feeling, as well as its presentative function (of ushering in values as qualities, and as qualities of feeling, without presenting the actual feeling itself). This function is 'cognitive' in the same pre-logical sense as applies to the perception of situations. The soundness of this interpretation is enhanced by virtue of another law[2] we have found to be basic wherever presentative acts are involved (in memory, perception, anticipation, imagination, or the apprehension of meaning); viz. that the *value*-qualities

---

[1] Cf. *Der Formalismus in der Ethik*, p. 260.

[2] Cf. K. Koffka: *The Growth of the Mind*, p. 134 (tr. by R. M. Ogden), Kegan Paul, 1924. '. . . the child recognizes its mother's face as early as the second month, and in the middle of the first year it reacts quite differently to a "friendly" face than it does to an "angry" face. . . . Furthermore the difference is of a kind which obliges us to conclude that "friendly" and "angry" faces are phenomenal facts to the infant . . . is it not possible that phenomena such as "friendliness" and "unfriendliness" are very primitive—even more so than a blue spot.' Koffka adds: 'However absurd this possibility may seem to a psychologist who regards all consciousness as being ultimately made up of elements, it ceases to be absurd as soon as one considers the matter biologically.'

57

of objects are already given *in advance* at a level where their imaged and conceptual features are not yet vouchsafed to us, and hence that the apprehension of values is the *basis* of our subsequent apprehension of objects. Thus it could well be that vicarious emotion, in the shape of fellow-feeling, might be a *means* of gaining objective value-insight into metaphysical reality, no less than a necessary *preliminary* for conceptual knowledge of its character. At all events, the nature of sympathetic phenomena does not rule this out as impossible.

Even before we bring our classification of its types to bear on this problem, it seems clear to me that sympathy does not afford us a positive insight (in the twofold sense above), but *frees* us, rather, from an *illusion*; an illusion which is always to be found embodied in the naïve view of the world and manner of ordering it. Fellow-feeling (and in a higher sense love, of the reverent spiritual kind yet to be described), in so far as it concentrates, not upon the occurrence of actual emotions and evaluations in other people, but upon their intrinsic *quality* (being an intentional and cognitive act it can do this just as thought or apprehension can), does in fact already have the important metaphysical office of dissipating the naïve illusion which I propose to call 'egocentricity'.

(2) By 'egocentricity' I mean the illusion of taking one's own environment to be the world itself, i.e. the seeming givenness of this environment as 'the' world. As an apprehension of the reality of objects, egocentricity is equivalent to solipsism; with regard to volition and practical behaviour, it is egoism; and as an attitude of love it is auto-erotism.[1] However, since valuation underlies perception and volition, solipsism, egoism and auto-erotism have an identical common root in *timetic egocentricity*. This latter, the tendency to identify subjective values as environmental ones, and these in turn as belonging to the objective order of values, I shall therefore call 'egocentricity' without further qualification. It is also the basis of the solipsistic attitude. Now some people may wonder at this and ask: 'Is there really such a thing as "naïve" solipsism? Are not all men, even in a state of nature, firmly convinced of the reality of their neighbours as beings having feelings of their own?' I answer: Certainly they are, firstly at the level of conscious judgement, and secondly, on the timetic level, generically, in so far as they are by nature capable of fellow-feeling, and specifically, depending on how far this extends. Though the range

[1] Bleuler's term 'autism' seems the most suitable for the pathological symptoms of that type of self-preoccupation where all interest in the environment disappears. He gives an instructive description of 'autistic' states in his book on Dementia præcox.

of fellow-feeling falls off much more *rapidly* than the rational conviction that other people exist and have experiences. But in both respects the natural man is at least a *relative* solipsist, if one compares his consciousness of his own *reality* with his degree of parallel conviction concerning other people. These others certainly exist as souls, but, it is, for all that, a shadowy sort of existence; the phrase is significant, for such an existence is in reality and character merely relative to his own ego, his own field of values, and his own supposedly absolute notion of reality. Thus the difference between the solipsist and the man who has conquered his naïve solipsism, thanks to the metaphysical insight attainable in fellow-feeling, is not that the former thinks that he alone is real and other people merely products of his fancy (as in subjective idealism). It is a double distinction, one of *degree* in the consciousness of reality, and the other, and sharper, in kind, between the *absolutely* real and that which is in essence and character only *relatively so*. And the naïve illusion in respect of the real which is dispelled by fellow-feeling is simply this twofold *difference* between the natural man's consciousness of his own reality and that of other people. The cancelled item is simply the egocentric ascription to others of an ontological status of mere dependence on oneself, as a *seemingly absolute reality*; there being no *awareness* of this status of dependence, so long as the ascription persists. In the egocentric and solipsistic attitude, we take this fellow-man, whose existence for us is in fact dependent on our own nature and range of interests, as possessing an ultimate and absolute reality. And this is just where the metaphysical misapprehension lies. It is overcome in the *change of heart* displayed in a thorough-going sympathetic insight—*a change in the innermost nature of psychical reality itself*; it is by no means a mere change in the contents of consciousness, for these simply reflect and exhibit it. When solipsism of this type is recognized and formulated as a theory, it leads to that view of the world which Max Stirner has graphically depicted in his book *The Solitary One and His Estate*.[1] The Ego here takes itself as absolutely real; it is not a generalized ego, but literally the solitary one. All other selves are mere objects for use, domination or enjoyment, as is clearly shown by the expression 'estate'.[2]

The metaphysical illusion in the solipsistic view of reality is,

---

[1] [Translated by S. T. Byington, London, A. C. Fifield, 1912, under the title *The Ego and its Own*. The present rendering of the German title 'Der Einzige und sein Eigentum', is adopted for the sake of making Scheler's references to it intelligible.—Tr.]

[2] Cf. the chapter on 'Person in sittlichen Zusammenhängen' in *Der Formalismus in der Ethik*, p. 534.

as we have said, a result of timetic egocentricity. The dissipation of this illusion follows, necessarily and uniquely, from the effect of fellow-feeling in enabling us to grasp how a man, or living creature, as such, is our *equal in worth*; though naturally this does not at all exclude the secondarily given differences of worth between men (or living creatures) in respect of their *character*. This equality of worth once established, the other person also becomes *equally real* to us, thereby losing his merely shadowy and dependent status. But fellow-feeling can only effect this if its intention is directed upon the *essence* of the other person's ego (including its value-essence and the elements which make it up); of which it is no less capable than intuition, in the discernment of essences, or thought, in the contemplation of ideas. An act of fellow-feeling directed upon some casual feature in the other is not by itself sufficient. Hence we see, as in the above-mentioned case of Buddha's conversion, how the change of heart referred to only takes place where an isolated case, a chance occurrence of sympathy with another person's condition and experience, is treated purely as an example (as 'just another' beggar, invalid, corpse, etc.); the *essence of suffering* in other people is thereupon grasped as an idea, in all its generality, and the pure sentiment of fellow-feeling is released as a permanent disposition, spreading far beyond the occasion which first inspired it, towards *every*body and *every* good thing. Without the aid of images or concepts we gain here an immediate insight into a truth which, expressed in propositional form, would run somewhat as follows: 'As a man and a living creature, the other person's value is the same as your own, he exists as really and truly as yourself. Other people have the same value as you do.'

Solipsism, however, is not the only result of timetic egocentricity. It also leads to *Egoism*, i.e. egocentricity of character and attitude in volition and action. For our striving and willing are based upon our emotional grasp of values, so that a person without appreciation of value in others is incapable of satisfying their wants in practice. Egoism is therefore the *outcome* of a closed heart and mind, not a cause of this disposition—a cause which could then be eliminated by a mere effort of will, through attention to duty or the cultivation of will-power. Such egoism, as a practical aspect of egocentricity, can be eliminated only by a complete uprooting of its illusory conception of reality, an endowing of its shadowy personages with that flesh and blood which they take on only for a heart already open to them by virtue of its own conquest of timetic egocentricity.

This is not to say that the timetic egocentricity of an all-excluding self-esteem is actually at the bottom of every egocentric attitude, egoistic and solipsistic alike. Without arguing the point here, I merely affirm my conviction that the timetically egocentric character and disposition is itself the outcome of an exclusively auto-erotic self-assertiveness, the total elimination of which would have the effect of inhibiting the instinct of self-preservation itself.

Our positive analysis of fellow-feeling and our refutation of the empirico-genetic theories having shown that pure fellow-feeling is an intrinsic characteristic of the human spirit, it is thereby established further that it is an *a priori* act having 'the worth of others in general' as its *a priori* content. It is not a product of such acquaintance as we may happen to have with other people and their emotional states, nor is its scope determined thereby, being merely assisted in its development and provided with opportunities for its application and display.[1]

(3) As against the position upheld, with good reason, by the intuitive theory of fellow-feeling, von Hartmann has shown especial confidence in his ability to construct a similarly metaphysical and monistic account of the phenomenon, though on a non-intuitive basis. 'Fellow-feeling,' he says, in his full and penetrating *Phänomenologie des sittlichen Bewusstseins*,[2] 'embodies an illusion to which our intellect is somewhat prone. We experience a feeling which exists nowhere but in our own minds. Yet we do not think of this feeling of ours, but of that which evokes our fellow-feeling. So we fancy ourselves able, as it were, to have feelings in another person's mind, or to participate immediately in someone else's feelings, when we are merely sensible of the reaction which it produces in our own.' Very characteristically he adds: 'This illusion is like that of a blind man, who locates his sense of touch at the end of his stick, instead of in his hand, or the still more general illusion of thinking that we see things outside us, whereas we are conscious only of the content of our own representations.'[3] We can see how this pre-phenomenological conception of the facts is a mere consequence of von Hartmann's general brand of epistemological realism, whereby it is only through a 'causal inference' that we are allegedly able to proceed from the data of our own consciousness to the reality of the self, no less than that of the external world; arriving subsequently at the reality of other selves and ultimately at that of a metaphysical ground of the universe transcending the subject-object relation. Since we are opposed on principle to this type of 'transcendental critical realism', we are

---

[1] Cf. Part III, Chapter II, on how the 'idling' or non-fulfilment of the *a priori* intentional function of 'pure' fellow-feeling may help to furnish an intuitive conviction of belonging in general to a community, even for a man who has never had occasion to make contact with anyone else. There being no empirical occurrence, this can only be a matter of pure fellow-feeling.

[2] Berlin, 1879, p. 219 seq.   [3] Ibid., p. 227.

naturally unable to accept this application of it to fellow-feeling. Although von Hartmann reproves Schopenhauer for thinking he had found in pity a spring of action directly motivated by the welfare of other people, through its effect upon our own,[1] he nevertheless observes: 'The realization that its motives are psychologically actuated does not lessen the strangeness of the problem of pity from a metaphysical point of view; but we shall now no longer be puzzled as to how the welfare of another person can have a direct influence on my will; the question is how it comes about that my idea of this welfare awakens in me a fellow-feeling whose pleasure-pain character is orientated as if it were my welfare and not his which was at stake. If we approach the problem in this way, Schopenhauer's metaphysical solution still carries its full weight.' We must flatly disagree with this view of von Hartmann's. The only people who are entitled, and obliged, to look for a *metaphysical* concept of fellow-feeling are those who agree with Schopenhauer, Bergson and myself in regarding it in its pure form as a primary act, whose presentative function is essentially one of carrying us *beyond* our own actual welfare-situation. Obscure and mysterious references to 'causal inference' are of no more explanatory value than they are in regard to our assumptions concerning the reality of the external world, the soul, or God. They are quite insufficient to give metaphysical meaning to those experiences of fellow-feeling which have just been described as illusory, since von Hartmann has already given them an interpretation in terms of empirical psychology. If fellow-feeling is intrinsically illusory, then let us get rid of the illusion, and not pile a further metaphysical explanation of imposture on top of the thing itself. This compromise between psychological and metaphysical explanation is as inadequate as most of the other examples in von Hartmann's compromise-philosophy.

(4) Though there is no denying that fellow-feeling has a metaphysically cognitive function, it is quite another question whether, in addition to exposing the egocentric fallacies already referred to, it can either give endorsement to a *monistic metaphysics* as its source of knowledge, or require such a metaphysics in order to give an ontological explanation of its actual possibility. The ancient pantheists and monists persistently proclaimed this to be so, from the famous 'Tat Twam asi' of the ancient Brahmins to the more enlightened wisdom leading, in Buddhism, to the break-up of the old Indian caste-system. And it has been asserted with equal vigour by those who, like Hegel and von Hartmann, have maintained against Schopenhauer, the *secondary* character of fellow-feeling as compared with the spontaneous act of love. The monistic

[1] Ibid., p. 227.

view is that, if love is not to be an imposture, the lover and the beloved must actually be *identical* in the metaphysical order of being; so that there is no real distinction of substance between the persons, but either a pure illusion in the appearance of their separateness (Schopenhauer's theory of time and space as principles of individuation); or else an illusion which, though not actually relating to empirical reality, is still metaphysical, in that the persons separated in empirically objective reality (and hence outside the sphere of consciousness), still amount to no more than concrete functional units of the absolutely unknown divine mind, and are thus identical in their metaphysical essence, and distinct in essence only as regards the objective phenomenal world (von Hartmann's concrete monism).[1]

These monistic and partially pantheistic metaphysicians believe, therefore, that fellow-feeling and love can tell us something, by way of intimations, about ultimate reality itself (its unity, for instance); very different are those who remain content to see no more in fellow-feeling and love than simply an intentional indication of the unity of life in all things living, and a grasping of this unity (Bergson's élan vital); or who see it as a fact to be explained and understood only by postulating, against an irreducible plurality of vital entelechies, a single unitary Life-entelechy—a collective life of the universe, in which the locally active life-forces of individual members of the system of animate nature, and even of tissues, organs and cells, represent merely the discrete functioning of its complex and ramified structure. Among many other factors telling against a plurality of entelechies and in favour of their substantial unity, Hans Driesch has pointed to the facts of fellow-feeling, love and conscience, from his own vitalistic point of view. This latter commits him to a metaphysical dualism, in distinguishing aggregation from collectivity as different modes of order (the popular antithesis of mechanism and vitalism). Erich Becher also seems inclined to adopt this standpoint,[2] again citing the fact of fellow-feeling, as a sort of subjective and psychological

[1] Cf. E. von Hartmann's *Psychologie*, among the well-known volumes expounding his theory.

[2] *Vide* E. Becher: *Die fremddienliche Zweckmässigkeit der Pflanzengallen und die Hypothese eines überindividuellen Seelischen*. Munich, 1921. With Bergson it is a different matter. Since he regards fellow-feeling as a particular species of 'intuition' (in his own sense), it has a bearing on our knowledge of reality as such; while mechanism, in his opinion, is of no metaphysical significance, being merely the biologically practical, relative view of the world appropriate to the 'understanding'. For an admirable exposition and criticism of Bergson's concept of Intuition, see Roman Ingarden, 'Über die Gefahr einer petitio principii in Erkenntnistheorie', *Jahrbuch für Philosophie und phänomenologische Forschung*, IV Band, Halle, 1921.

factor of awareness, in those examples of co-operative purposiveness of which he has given a discerning account, and on which he bases his metaphysical hypothesis of a supra-individual life-agency. Similar ideas were also worked out by Jean-Marie Guyau.[1]

Are the examples of fellow-feeling so far referred to sufficient to justify a critical discussion of these theories? In answering this question we shall pay particular attention to identification, fellow-feeling and love, and shall give separate treatment to the theories of metaphysical monism, and those which regard fellow-feeling as at least favouring the assumption of a unitary principle of life throughout animate nature. For the moment we shall by-pass the question whether it is pity (as Schopenhauer thinks, and to a much lesser extent von Hartmann also), which is supposed to reveal something about ultimate reality, or whether rejoicing comes into it as well. This question raises an altogether different issue, whether the amount of misery in the universe is on the whole greater than the amount of happiness, whether the world as a whole is more evil than not, either as it stands (Schopenhauer's view), or as it really is (von Hartmann's). This question of metaphysical optimism, pessimism, meliorism[2] or indifferentism is here set aside. We confine ourselves to fellow-feeling in general, which is the same in commiseration as in rejoicing.

Our decisive ground for an uncompromising *rejection* of the metaphysico-monistic theories is that, in fellow-feeling proper, the 'distance' of the persons and their respective and reciprocal awareness of separateness is kept in mind throughout, as is also the case with both its components, vicarious, and (in the narrower sense) companionate feeling. The reason being that fellow-feeling is not infection, nor identification. Even in mutual endurance of the 'same' evil and the 'same' quality of feeling-state—in other words, in the extreme case of fellow-feeling, where there is no distinction as yet between vicarious and companionate feeling—the functions of 'feeling something' remain distinct, and the phenomenon itself includes an awareness of difference among its separate sources in two, three or x individual selves.

---

[1] Cf. Jean-Marie Guyau: *A Sketch of Morality independent of Obligation and Sanction*, op. cit.

[2] Naturally, the first question to be asked is whether this problem has any meaning, i.e. whether the intrinsic differences of quality and kind among joys and sorrows permit of their being added together at all; and further, if such aggregates exist, whether we are able to recognize them. Schopenhauer's 'proof', from the negative character of pleasure, on the ground that, in fulfilling a want, it is always merely a release from pain (rejoicing being likewise a release from commiseration) has long been shown to be fallacious. Cf. on this, *Der Formalismus in der Ethik*, p. 361, and the essay 'Vom Sinn des Leides' (1917) in *Moralia*, Leipzig, 1923.

The observable facts of the situation convey no suggestion, therefore, that the persons are so far from being independent entities as to be merely modes or functions of a supra-personal spirit; nor do they give us any occasion to fall back upon the metaphysical existence of a supra-personal and supra-individual spiritual being, in order to explain how the phenomenon is actually possible. On the contrary, the latter itself *rules out* any metaphysics which would obliterate a real substantial difference between such concrete foci of action, referred to as 'persons', in the interests of a metaphysical Being-as-such.

Indeed, we must go much farther than this. Even if we abstract from the physical and spatio-temporal differences between persons, and from everything which distinguishes the possible *contents* of their consciousness (in every conceivable field of consciousness in the inner, outer, or common world), they always continue to differ in their *intrinsic character* as concrete act-centres. And they would still do so even if their bodies and the entire contents of their consciousness could be made to tally exactly. They are indeed the only examples of the independent existence of substances whose individuality is completely self-determined. They cannot be distinguished, like bodies in other respects identical in character, upon spatio-temporal, numerical and quantitative grounds, since as pure act-centres they transcend time and space (however much they may operate in the objective spatio-temporal world by *virtue* of that life-force whereby a living body is fashioned from dead matter); they therefore can and must be distinct in their *pure character* (or personal essence) alone. Physical objects, and bodies even, may be identical in character and yet really distinct owing to differences of spatio-temporal position. But the only ultimate distinction between persons is one of character, i.e. the fact that they are *absolute* individuals. Schopenhauer's theory of spatio-temporal order as the sole principle of individuation is therefore completely fallacious.[1]

Hence fellow-feeling does not proclaim the essential identity of persons, as Schopenhauer and von Hartmann allege, but actually presupposes a pure essential *difference* between them (this being also the ultimate basis of their difference in actual fact). The occurrence of a feeling in some sort of supra-individual spirit or universal consciousness, in which the two persons merely participate together, coalescing therein, as it were, would not be fellow-feeling at all. And if, as we saw, it is the very office of true fellow-feeling to dissipate the solipsistic illusion by apprehending the equivalent status of the other person *as* such, it cannot be at the same time a dim perception of the fact that neither of us really

[1] On other grounds as well, of course, which are not dealt with here.

exists, but only some third party, of whom we are merely the functions.

The sole significance of fellow-feeling as a datum for metaphysics can therefore lie only in its disposing us to realize, that independently existing persons in mutual relation to one another are by nature *predisposed for a communal mode of life* and are teleologically adapted to one another (regardless of whether and how far they actually live together). It is this natural predisposition which is intuitively grasped in fellow-feeling as a harmonious fulfilment of human worth, and there attains conscious expression. And now it surely follows, that an intrinsically teleological relationship of mutual adaptedness (as distinct from one which is explicable in empirically contingent and ultimately mechanical or associative terms), necessarily requires an intelligence transcending all finite persons, to ordain this object and destiny; an intelligence which, in bringing persons into existence, at the same time conceives their individual diversities of character according to a pattern; if so, pure fellow-feeling, by the very fact of being inexplicable in genetic or associative terms, lends support to the conclusion that all persons intrinsically capable of sharing in this feeling have *one and the same creator*. If fellow-feeling has a metaphysical meaning then, it is that, in contrast to identification and infection which are also found in the animal kingdom, it points, not to pantheism or monism, but to a *theistic* (or ultimately panentheistic) metaphysics of ultimate reality.

The fact of separation presented in fellow-feeling rules out an explanation in terms of monistic metaphysics and offers equally little cognitive support for this view. Still further evidence against it is to be found in the fact of an irreducible *twofold transcendence*, firstly, in the essential *individuality* of the person with whose emotional state we sympathize, and secondly in his absolute *privacy*, of which, even in our greatest intimacy with him, we know *a priori*, both that it necessarily *exists* and that it must remain *absolutely inaccessible* to any sort of community of experience. The realization that as finite beings we can never see right into one another's hearts, that we cannot even have full and adequate knowledge of our own hearts, let alone other peoples', is given as an essential feature in all experience of fellow-feeling (not excluding spontaneous love). And it is no less apparent that the actual feelings in the other person, to which we respond, are qualitatively different in a way which no amount of understanding can bring home to us; it is not a matter of any discrepancy in the quality of the feeling reproduced, owing to misunderstanding or lack of insight; even an ideally perfect understanding could not assimilate the nature of this difference in feeling-quality, for it is rooted in the very fact of difference between the individuals whose feelings they are.[1] Thus the absolute uniqueness of a man's personality remains, like its absolute privacy, *essentially impenetrable* to understanding (though not therefore merely a-rational or ineffable). All we encounter is a plain awareness of the fact of absolute uniqueness, X, and of there being a sphere of absolute personal privacy, Y, but there is no hope of X or Y ever being filled in by addition of the missing *content* of understanding. There is the old English story[2] of the dialogue between John and Thomas, in which it is always John's John talking, and Thomas' Thomas; for John speaks only to John's Thomas, and Thomas only to Thomas' John, while the real John, the real Thomas, and the whole tale of their conversation can be seen and heard only by their omniscient Maker;—and this, alas, is something more than a poor jest, for it is pretty nearly the literal truth.[3] But it will be obvious that these observations are strictly incompatible with a monistic interpretation of fellow-feeling.

Fellow-feeling based on emotional reproduction, whether in commiseration or rejoicing, is essentially something *undergone*, and not a spontaneous act. It is a *reaction*, not an action. But this has other implications for our problem besides those already mentioned. It means that fellow-feeling is of itself incapable of extending the bounds of understanding even to the threshold of absolute privacy (as spontaneous love at its most spiritual is able to do); for in fact it stops short at that relatively intimate notion of personality whose intelligible content varies according to its pattern, be it acquaintance, comradeship, friendship, marriage, society, community, nationality, civilization and so on—in short, according to whatever type of bond it may be which links people together. There it must halt, without of itself being capable of further advancing this boundary in the direction of the sphere of absolute personal intimacy. Fellow-feeling depends entirely on the nature and depth of the love involved.[4] It is quite unable to bring about a *change in the form* of the relationship, from a peripheral to a deeper kind, for example. In providing material for that understanding which can be evoked even in its first (vicarious) stage, the character and degree of fellow-feeling is always confined to the particular nature (and pattern) of the bond established. And the scope of this will have already set relative limits to what is

---

[1] Persons as such are single only *because* they are 'individual'. They can only constitute a plurality by reason of their diversity of character.

[2] [Cf. O. W. Holmes: *The Autocrat of the Breakfast-Table*, ch. 3.—Tr.]

[3] Matter much to the point on this will be found in Nicolai Hartmann's extremely valuable work *Metaphysik der Erkenntnis*, pp. 156 and 265. Berlin, 1921.

[4] Cf. below.

private and must therefore remain beyond understanding. Only spontaneous love can break down this barrier—and then only up to the limits of absolute privacy; but it is able thereby to effect an active transformation of a bond from one pattern to another.[1]

(3) THE TREATMENT OF LOVE IN METAPHYSICAL MONISM

Although we shall deal with love and hate at a later stage, we propose, for the sake of continuity, to ask at this point whether the phenomenon of *love* either requires or permits of interpretation in terms of metaphysical monism.

We may take von Hartmann as a typical representative: 'We have already[2] seen that love in its deepest sense involves treating the beloved as if his being were identical with our own: but if this instinctive premiss of love is an illusion, then the whole of love, being based upon it, is likewise illusory. If on the other hand, love is to be ranked as the highest, noblest and most god-like of all our moral instincts, there can be nothing illusory about it or about its fundamental premiss (whether this be conscious or unconscious), and we must recognize, in its emotional anticipation and partial realization of the principle of the essential Identity of individuals, an unconscious intimation pointing prophetically to the absolute basis of morality and bearing witness to its truth.' Farther on he says: 'Love exhibits in an emotional and partial fashion what is theoretically and universally established by insight into the essential Identity of individuals. Though love may restrict its application of this absolute moral principle of the Identity of Being to a few persons, it does hold out to them an emotional guarantee of practical fulfilment; whereas theoretical insight into this universal Identity of Being must first strive, with the help of reason or religious feeling, to acquire the power of influencing practice. A (merely theoretical)[3] insight into the Identity of Being may show egoism to be theoretically an illusion, but meanwhile leave it unaffected in practice; so that we are still left with the task of resisting and crushing the power it exercises, wherever it may find an outlet. Love on the other hand is normally quite unconscious of its metaphysical basis, yet it represents an instinctive and genuine conquest of egoism in regard to the loved one, its superiority being all the greater in proportion to its strength. The

[1] von Hartmann gives a good treatment of this. Op. cit.
[2] See *Phänomenologie des sittlichen Bewusstseins*, pp. 266–97, in the chapter headed 'Das Moralprinzip der Liebe', in which the lover's yearning to identify the beloved with himself is described as an 'extension of self-love' by incorporation of the other person into oneself.
[3] The bracketed expression is an insertion of my own.

absolute moral principle of the Identity of Being imposes a common ethical obligation (the repression of egoism by virtue of the One Being which is in all individuals alike): love already provides the required solution, though only in a particularized sense, for it is unaware of the universal nature of the obligation, and perhaps of its very existence' (p. 793). On the relationship between love and fellow-feeling von Hartmann says: 'In fellow-feeling the sense of the universal unity of Being merely flickers up, only to be quickly stifled again in the dismal vapours of egoism; but in love it bursts out into a calm and steady flame whose radiance gives warmth to life. Fellow-feeling is a passive affection received through the observation of passive states of emotion in others; love is an active spontaneous yearning to give practical effect to the feeling of identity' (p. 271).

Now von Hartmann's predecessor in this view is Hegel, whose opinions on love are most fully expressed in those early fragments on theology and history of which W. Dilthey has recently given a detailed account in his admirable study entitled 'Die Jugendgeschichte Hegels'.[1] Love, for Hegel, is 'the sense of the whole':[2] 'It is a feeling peculiar to the living, and it is as living beings that those who love are one.' 'From this one feeling life breaks forth, to lose itself in dissipation among a diversity of emotions, and in the whole of this diversity to find itself again. This whole is not contained in love as a multitude of separate items in an aggregate; life finds its own self therein, reduplicated in its own image, and again merged in unity.' Even the love of God, for Hegel, rests on the essential identity of the human and the divine spirit, which in man attains to self-awareness only in religion. 'To love God is to feel oneself in all things living, to infinity, and without restraint.' The gospel's injunction, 'love thy neighbour as thyself', does not tell us 'to love him as much as oneself (in degree), for to love oneself is an expression without meaning; it says, love him as if he *were* yourself; a feeling of being neither stronger nor weaker, but on a level'.[3] Thus Hegel's rejection of the theistic interpretation of love is no less clear-cut and decisive than von Hartmann's;[4] or than that of Spinoza, for whom men's love for one another and for God is merely part of that love with which God eternally loves himself, and who holds that though man is certainly able to love God, in *amor intellectualis Dei*, there can be no such love of God for man.[5]

---

[1] Wilhelm Dilthey: *Gesammelte Schriften*, IV Band.
[2] Ibid., p. 95.　　　　　　　　　　　　　　[3] Ibid., p. 81.
[4] Cf. E. von Hartmann: *Phänomenologie des sittlichen Bewusstseins*, particularly towards the end.
[5] [Cf. the author's essay 'Spinoza' in *Philosophische Weltanschauung*, Bonn, 1929.]

Our case against such theories, and all those like them is that so far from 'saving' the phenomenon of love, they simply *abolish* it. For love 'in its deepest sense' does not consist in taking the other person and treating him as if he were identical with oneself. It is not a mere quantitative 'extension of self-love', nor is it a relationship of parts within a whole, whose collective exertions are devoted merely to its own (egoistic) self-maintenance, self-aggrandisement or growth. This is nothing less than a palpable *misrepresentation of the phenomenon*. It is the utterly and essentially different facts of emotional identification, and of what we have called the idiopathic variety at that, which would answer more nearly to the description of love furnished by Hegel and von Hartmann. If I take hold of someone and treat him 'as if' he were essentially identical with myself, this means that I am mistaken, firstly about his status in reality, and secondly about his nature. The first point is obvious enough. Since, at that very moment, his reality as another person would have been extinguished in the *phenomenon* itself, there could really be no such thing as an other-regarding love here at all; it would simply have to be explained psycho-genetically as a fortuitous instance of *self*-love—as a case of selfishness, indeed, since there is no thought or recognition here of love as an act by nature independent of its target ('myself' or 'another'), unaffected by changes therein, and totally different from any sort of hatred, for instance (though this can also be hatred of self or of others). Now it is just such an attitude of emotional outrage upon one's neighbour that we do actually find in idiopathic identification. The second point is no less obvious. Love calls explicitly for an understanding entry into the individuality of *another* person *distinct in character* from the entering self, by him accepted as such, and coupled, indeed, with a warm and whole-hearted endorsement of 'his' reality as an individual, and 'his' being what he is. This is profoundly and beautifully expressed by the Indian poet Rabindranath Tagore, when he depicts the sudden revulsion from (erotic) subjection and the yearning for the willing self-devotion of love:

Free me from the bonds of your sweetness, my love!
No more of this wine of kisses.
    This mist of heavy incense stifles my heart.
    Open the doors, make room for the morning light.
    I am lost in you, wrapped in the folds of your caresses.
Free me from your spells, and give me back the manhood to
    offer you my freed heart.

The Gardener, XLVIII.

This giving and receiving of freedom, independence and individuality is of the essence of love. And in love, as it gradually re-emerges from the state of identification, there is built up, within the phenomenon itself, a clear-cut consciousness of two *distinct* persons. This consciousness is not merely a starting-point of love, for it only reaches full maturity as love pursues its course. It is the point at which psychical and spiritual love, as found in man at least, is, as the poet says, at its farthest remove from subjection, i.e. from the archetypal forms of suggestion and hypnosis. This *freedom* of love has nothing to do with arbitrary decision or freedom of choice or with free-will in any form, for it springs rather from the freedom of personality as against the sway of impulse in general; yet it is completely annihilated in metaphysical monism. What has obviously happened here is that in concentrating on the phenomena of identification at the vital level, an entire *range of love-emotions* has been passed over and misunderstood. Nor, finally, is there any regard whatever here for those limits of *absolute personal privacy*, our marginal awareness of which is first quickened and made clear in the fullness and depth of love, and there alone. For by the very fact that no man can have knowledge of this privacy in another, there can be no talk, in such a connection, of being or becoming or apprehending oneself as one and the same. So to von Hartmann's assertion: 'If the instinctive premiss of love —the essential identity of the persons—were an illusion, the whole of love would also be illusion', I oppose its converse: 'If the difference of the persons were an illusion, and if the consciousness of this which accompanies love in its increasing reverence and delicacy of approach to the absolute intimacy of the other's self—if this consciousness of personal diversity, greatest when love is deepest, were likewise an illusion, then love itself would indeed be illusion too.'

Thus love is far *less* capable even than fellow-feeling, of an interpretation in terms of metaphysical monism, just because it is so much the more personal, free, independent, spontaneous, and the more decidedly intentional in its direction; and this is because it is love alone which encounters the absolutely private self as a permanent limit of advance, and first 'discovers' it, as it were, in the process. It is in keeping with this that the classical monistic interpretations of love to be found in the Indian writers and in Schopenhauer are all inclined, either to merge love in fellow-feeling, or to derive it from this—if not actually to confound it with identification.

(4) THE SENSE OF IDENTITY AND METAPHYSICS

There may be facts of sympathy having a genuine bearing on the metaphysical postulate of a self-same, all-inclusive, supra-individual reality inherent in the existence and nature of all men; but at all events the phenomena of companionate, vicarious and fellow-feeling are not among these facts, and nor are those of love (in the strict sense). Still less would I claim, as Driesch does in many passages of his works, that the moral consciousness *in general*, conscience, the sense of duty, etc., are indications of a supra-personal whole and of a genuine evolution,[1] as distinct from mere accretion, in biological development and human history. In addition to the other-regarding and social attitudes, the moral consciousness certainly inculcates in every man as a worthy ideal a no less immediate attitude of veneration for God and for himself (e.g. as intrinsic values and objects of his duty). There is nothing *essentially* or even exclusively *social* about the moral phenomenon; it would remain standing even if society collapsed, and is by no means a product of our relation to others or to the community. Only if and in so far as there actually is a community do we become morally aware of certain necessary demands upon our standards and conduct in relation to it; though the existence of such a community may well be no mere contingent datum, but an essential truth of fact, posited along with rational consciousness itself, as we have often declared it to be. But the notion of an *objective hierarchy of values*, central to the whole of theoretical ethics, can be elaborated without regard for the facts of the situation between 'self and neighbour' or 'individual and community'; being valid for man as such, it holds equally for the isolated individual and for the community or any other collective group. There can be no truck with any proposal to set up ethics on a social basis, and none therefore with the attempt to found it on a metaphysics of the 'whole' as a sort of reality underlying the appearances of social life.

But it seems to us another and very different matter in regard to that extensive range of phenomena dealt with in our chapter on Identification; a group of facts having no relevance as such to ethics, but all the greater perhaps, in metaphysical significance. Now it is already inherent in the general phenomenal character of the facts referred to in identification proper, that they themselves indicate the branch of metaphysics, i.e. the metascience of the particular region of being, to which they are relevant. The fact is that they belong entirely to the *metaphysics of organic life*, having no bearing on the metaphysics of spirit, of man, or of

[1] *Vide* H. Driesch: *The Science and Philosophy of the Organism*, op. cit.

history, and no primary relevance even, for the metaphysics of inorganic nature.[1] Such phenomena can only appear once our powers of intellectual consciousness and corporeal sensitivity have been lulled into minimal activity. The first defines the human personality as in itself individual, while the second circumscribes it as 'this particular' embodied unity. It is only when man's *vital plane is isolated* to the fullest possible extent (never completely of course), in contrast to his purely sensory, mechanical and associative side on the one hand, and the purely cognitive level of his intellectual awareness on the other, that the above conditions are realized. It may be a matter of identification of the organic life-centres, as between subject and hypnotist;[2] it may be the phenomenon of mutual fusion, in the sexual act, into a single torrential life-stream; or it may be the mother's identification with her child (in the maternal and parental instinct, not in mother-love). It may be a question of the predatory creature's instinctive familiarity, from the inside, with the process of life and the internal arrangements of its victim, and with the best points of attack upon it. It may be the feeling of mass-unity in the herd or the horde; the ecstatic sense of immersion in the life of deity; the alternations of dual personality resulting from identification; or the varieties of identification found in psychopathology, in dreams, and in the outlook of savages, as already described. In every single case, it is always the *same* level of being and consciousness which becomes 'one' in the phenomenon of identification; and this is the sphere of *vital activity* in the man or the creature concerned.

Thus we may suppose that there are good reasons to be found elsewhere, compelling the assumption of a universal transcendent totality of life and hence a real unity of all life everywhere; but it would then be, not in love and fellow-feeling, but in the facts of identification (or consciousness of vital unity in general) that we should have to seek, both for an indication of the validity of this metaphysical insight in subjective consciousness, and for an immediate emotional confirmation of its reality in all life everywhere.

[1] Only if such a metaphysics were to conclude that the inanimate must be regarded as deriving from the animate, and were to trace physical laws back (in a metaphysical sense only) to biological ones, would it then be possible to identify, metaphysically, with the inanimate universe.

[2] There are well-established facts to indicate that the intellectual personality of the hypnotic subject is not displaced or altered in quality, either by hypnosis or post-hypnotic suggestion, being merely interrupted in its action for the time being. Nor can the morally relevant aspects of personality be in any way upset by such means, as is shown by the persistence under hypnosis of conscientious qualms and resistances, and even of a totally different moral attitude on the part of different persons, although the same situation is suggested to them (e.g. a house on fire, in which someone is in danger of burning to death).

It therefore seems to us an unquestionable advance upon the earlier monistic standpoints of Hegel, Schopenhauer, Schelling, von Hartmann and the Indian philosophers, that Bergson, Driesch, Becher and others should confine their consideration of the field of shared experience in general to its significance for a possible collective unity of *organic* life, and no longer to its bearing on the ultimate nature of reality. Though in doing so they certainly make far too little distinction between the phenomena themselves, and therefore lump identification, fellow-feeling, love and even the moral consciousness generally so much together as to court the risk of error, in adopting a monistic metaphysics for the whole of the intellectual and spiritual life as well. The more so in that they differ from my own general philosophical position in drawing only a most inadequate distinction between the cognitive and the vital spheres of consciousness, and between both of these and the sphere of mechanical association.

Within this twofold restriction, of the question to that of the metaphysical unity of organic life, and of the facts to those of genuine identification, I tend to think of the latter as a subjective indication that the unity of all things living is metaphysically consistent; while our direct confirmation of this (in mutual identification), I take to be an ontological precondition of the real possibility of the phenomenon itself. I confess, however, that I do not consider this opinion as strictly proven, nor would I grant it even the degree of probability which I do in fact attribute to it, if a large number of other reasons did not dispose me to postulate the reality of a collective, *unitary* and universal life-force, embracing all kinds and conditions of terrestrial life, and purposefully guiding and governing the empirical development of one species from another.

(5) THE UNITY OF LIFE

The metaphysical unity of life is taken for granted nowadays by leaders of thought so widely divergent in their methods as Bergson, Simmel, Driesch, Becher and Sir Oliver Lodge. If only to mark off our position from those who uphold this view we must emphasize the following points:

We entirely reject metaphysical biologism, i.e. the conception of ultimate reality, in the manner of Bergson, Simmel, Lodge and others, as itself an *élan vital* or life-principle, or as the life or soul of the universe. For neither in its knowing, intuiting and thinking capacity, nor in its emotional and volitional one, is Spirit, or νοῦς, an outcome or 'sublimation' of life. The modes in which cognition operates can nowhere be traced back to the bio-psychical pattern found in processes of the automatic and objectively goal-seeking type; each obeys laws of it own. Nor, again, are cognitive, ethical or æsthetic values subordinate varieties of biological value.[1] The regions of being and the realms of objects to which all truly cognitive acts have intentional reference (which includes the realm of all those things and processes belonging to life itself), have their being and subsist altogether regardless of the nature of life and living organisms or the fact of their existence. Only so can life itself become, in its turn, an *object* of factual knowledge and evaluation. If the nature and existence of everything, or the knowledge thereof, were 'relative' to life (in respect of either existence or knowledge), then life itself would be unknowable. But it is precisely the realm of spiritual actuality that is articulated as strictly personal, substantive, and intrinsically individual, right up to God, the Person of persons. We therefore count it the gravest of metaphysical errors in any theory, from that of Averroes onwards, that it should seek to construe persons, i.e. concrete centres of spiritual activity, as 'modes' or 'functions' of a universal spirit; whether this be an absolutely unconscious spirit (von Hartmann), a transcendental absolute consciousness (Husserl), or a transcendental reason (Fichte, Hegel's pantheism of Reason). A man's personality is not first singled out by reference to his body, for the latter, indeed, can only be distinguished in the last resort, as itself 'belonging' to the person, as that one among all possible bodies over which he has the most immediate control. Again, we do not define personality by reference to the quality of its acts or the content and objects thereof; nor by the temporal coherence of its experiences, in memory or in any other respect. On the contrary, this whole quality and continuity of the stream of consciousness already owes its peculiar content to the peculiar *character* of the intrinsically individual personalities to whom it belongs. Personality is thus elevated and, in its pure form, exalted above the body and above life, in itself or any other; this being at once its mere earthly condition of existence and the material upon which it works.

On the other hand, there is the agency which governs the development of form and the vital reactions, such as spontaneous movements, expressive utterances, and activities; a force of which we are only partially and inadequately aware at the vital level of consciousness (e.g. in the felt forces of life and death and the impulses specific to each); but a force we must posit as real in order to explain what is demonstrably non-mechanical in those processes of life which can be studied objectively; now we hold

[1] Cf. the treatment of this in my book, *Der Formalismus in der Ethik*, and my criticism of the theories of Spencer, Nietzsche and Guyau, p. 283 seq.

this to be a *single, self-same* reality,[1] but our present point is that in essence, existence and operation, it is quite *distinct* from the Spirit, with its personal structure. Between *spirit and life*, between person and life-centre, we discern no unity of substance but only a bond of *dynamic causality*. Our grounds for asserting this relationship between spirit and life, between Person and life-centre, lie in the essential difference between the *intelligent* patterns of connection found in the 'free' activities of the spirit and the automatic nature of psycho-somatic processes, which are merely *intelligible* to an observer as purposive (but not themselves intelligent). Only by taking this view does it become possible, and necessary, to postulate an essential difference in the one-many relationships of personal centres and vital agencies respectively. For if they were identical in substance (as is held by Thomist scholasticism), we should simply have a dilemma: either we may postulate that all vital entelechies are ultimately one, in which case the spirit in each person is also, in reality, one and the same; or else there are just as many independent vital-centres as there undoubtedly are independently existing spirits. If, on the other hand, the connection between spirit and life is merely dynamic, it might also be the case that, although individual spirits were personal substances, life (in a sense still to be ascertained) might be metaphysically one and the same in all persons—though exerting itself dynamically in many different ways. This dynamic diversity of field and function could be given greater precision by means of those entities and principles which are truly applicable to the organic realm, and which it is the task of an ideal system of morphology to develop.[2]

[1] This conception has been defended in recent times first by von Hartmann and later also by Driesch. Cf. Hans Driesch: *The Science and Philosophy of the Organism*, op. cit., and also *Mind and Body* (tr. by Theodore Bestermann), Methuen, 1927.

[2] This is not the place to enter further into the metabiological problem of the unity and multiplicity (and the kind of diversity) in the agency underlying vital phenomena. I intend to publish in another work the system of 'unity of life' and its theory, which I have long since worked out, on a phenomenological as well as on a scientific basis, and have already expounded in lecture-courses at the Universities of Munich and Cologne.

Chapter V

THE SENSE OF UNITY WITH THE COSMOS IN SOME REPRESENTATIVE TEMPERAMENTS OF THE PAST

THE *Indian ethos*, as exemplified in Brahminism and Buddhism, and the closely related outlook of Laotse's teachings, have often been described as an attitude of boundless sympathy, and especially of pity, for all creatures and indeed for the whole of creation. Such a view is correct in this at least, that it is not an ethos of love. It is neither a non-cosmic mysticism of spiritual love like the unworldly asceticism of early Christianity; nor an ethos combining godliness and worldliness, like the temperamental outlook of the Middle Ages, where love of God and love of the world are reconciled by 'loving all things in God'; nor, finally, is it a pantheistic ethos of love, either in the rousing and impassioned style of Giordano Bruno's 'heroic love', the cooler and more spiritual manner of Spinoza's *amor Dei intellectualis*, or the love-philosophy of Schelling and Goethe. As I have shown elsewhere, the only thing which Buddha finds positively valuable in love is the fact that the heart is thereby redeemed, though without attaining actual beatification; besides the benevolent and altruistic actions to which it leads, by accident, as it were, it embodies a method whereby man may release himself from confinement in his own individual self, and, at the highest level of absorption, may altogether lose his individual and personal identity.[1] It is only the 'hence' of love, not the 'hither', that is

[1] Cf. my essay 'Das Ressentiment im Aufbau der Moralen' and 'Liebe und Erkenntnis' in *Moralia*, Leipzig, 1923. Consult also Richard Pischel: *Buddha*, in the series 'Natur und Geisteswelt'; Friedrich Heiler: *Die buddhistische Versenkung*; and particularly Karl Eugen Neumann's translation of Buddha's discourses, *Die Reden Gotamo Buddhas*, Munich, 1921.

prized and practised in the techniques prescribed, which are thus wholly confined to the element of *alienation*, disavowal and renunciation of self, to the point of complete surrender, activities for which the other person merely serves as a 'stalking-horse'. Hence there is here neither love of God nor a genuine love of self, as distinct from egoism. The first is no longer present, and least of all in Buddhism, since it has no God; the latter is absent, because there is no individual spiritual self to be worthy of redemption by love, no less than the spiritual self of the other. The Buddhist technique of attenuation is calculated to reduce the reality of one's own self to the same shadowy status as that which others have for us: it is not like the Christian love of persons, which is to 'Love God above all things, and thy neighbour as thyself', and therefore seeks to enhance the reality of the other person 'in God', up to one's own level. Nevertheless the *value* aimed at in the Buddhist conception of love remains entirely individual, and indeed *solipsistic*, in so far as the whole point of this love lies in the dissolution, the annihilation, the 'unrealizing' of the reality and character of the *lover*, and not in any cultivation or endorsement of value in the loved one. This may suffice for the saintly, but to others it can at best be only an example.[1] In any case, this merely negative 'redemption of the heart', as Buddha regularly calls it, is not the ultimate end of the *Via perfectionis* of the holy monk; this is reached only in the '*extinction*' of the self, in the putting-off of reality, the annihilation and dissolution of self, as it is depicted in the everrecurring phrases of Buddha's discourses, in the central collection of the Pali-canon. Even the purest and most spiritual love still ranks here as an 'attachment', howsoever refined and sublimated, a final phase of concupiscent attachment to the world (or the gods), which must be severed, as it were, if the pure subject, freed from all that is personal and individual, is to succeed in attaining complete estrangement from God, the world and the self, and thereby at last to step clear of the causal nexus in which all things actual are yoked to pain.[2]

Moreover, though the fact is much less commonly recognized, it seems to me equally clear that the Indian ethos has no more of a claim to be (what Schopenhauer was grossly mistaken in

---

[1] A similar but less radical form of this negative ethos of love, though one which retains the theistic standpoint, has appeared only twice, so far as I know, on Christian soil in the West; in the mystical 'detachment' of Meister Eckhart and in the quietist movement associated with Molinos, Fénelon and Mme Guyon. A doctrine of love which received its most pointed expression in Fénelon's curious essay on 'Amour pur', only to be assailed by Bossuet, and thereafter officially condemned by the Church.

[2] Cf. particularly the third and fourth discourses in the fifth section, in Neumann's excellent translation.

thinking it), a genuine ethos of *fellow-feeling*, with a specific accent on pity. I find strong evidence for this in the fact that, unlike the western conception of fellow-feeling proper, which presupposes the possession of spiritual individuality, the Indian does not confine itself primarily to *man*, and to the higher animals only so far as they resemble him. Its scope extends to *all living creatures* including animals and plants on their own account, and in the last analysis, to the whole world of existence; the latter, indeed, being co-extensive with pain (namely the vast and *single* misery of the world). (Panvitalism is already presupposed here, since only the living can suffer.) For the Christian ethos of the West, true fellow-feeling is in part a prior condition for spontaneous, positively-directed love, and in part the result of this, namely a more penetrating sympathy; here, however, 'love' is only a first stage on the road of writhing oneself into the universal agony of contingent existence in general.

Thus in the Indian ethos we have, in fact, an early example of a truly *identificatory* outlook in the shape of a negative identification, in suffering, with the cosmos itself. At the heart of it lies the vast communal mass-misery of all things, whose wretchedness is due to the fact that their nature is wholly real, and not merely apparent. Two factors underlie this ethos of woeful identification with the afflictions of the universe: an attitude to Nature which is utterly different from the western one, and an unfavourable estimate of the real as such: *omne ens est malum*. (A mere consequence, therefore, of this primary metaphysical axiom, is the doctrine Schopenhauer borrowed from Buddha concerning the negative character of pleasure in general, viz. that it is merely the satisfaction of an urge, impulse or need, the quieting and repression of an unresting impetus.) The difference in the attitude to Nature has been well indicated by Rabindranath Tagore at the beginning of his book *Sadhana*. Unlike the urban cultures of antiquity and Christendom, the Indians are a jungle people. They have neither the Northern European conception of Nature, as something to be dominated and controlled, nor, like the Greeks, a detached admiration and love for her plastic patterns and forms. The Indian lives *in* Nature, identifying his life with hers, and with the felt plenitude of her universal creation. Hence he does not put mankind on a metaphysical plane of existence *above* that of the animal or plant: he does not think of man, like Plato and Aristotle, as the glittering apex of Nature's aristocracy, nor conceive him, like the Jews, as her lord and master, made (as in Genesis) in the image of God, by whose divine decree all other life, all existence even, is at his *service*. The Indian deals with the animate creation, and even with the signs of life still latent for him in the inanimate, on terms of 'brother', 'comrade' and 'friend', at all events, *on equal terms*. He does not look down on Nature in compassionate love (as when the Old Testament says: 'A just man is merciful to his beast'); he looks her straight in the face.[1] Here there is no metaphysical distinction of substance or even of function separating spirit from life, or the Person from the corporeally animate; nothing corresponding to the Aristotelian conception of νοῦς ποιητικός, let alone to the doctrine of an Aquinas, Descartes or Kant. For these western creeds, though profoundly at variance, do not abolish *this* identity. Tagore has also remarked upon this, and rightly so. The technique of *Tat twam asi* ('That is what you are'), like the *Neti* technique ('I am not that, it does not belong to me'), and the methods of *Yoga* for obtaining control over the automatic vital processes, thereby leading to awareness of all the bodily organs and their sensations, are simply three related procedures directed towards *the common aim of full community in suffering with the Universe*. The technique of *Yoga* dispenses the essentially living element in man from its individual status and makes it universal, in that it leads to an apprehension of the body as a mere *object* of consciousness alien to the self, a mere setting for the universal flow of life throughout all existence. The *Neti* technique puts an end to the parochialism of identifying oneself with some *particular* good or person or thing, in favour of identification with the universe in its undivided *wholeness*. But the technique of *Tat twam asi*, which presupposes the other two, is the most immediate preparation for the act of identification itself. Moreover, the justified assumption that will (desire) and reality are intrinsically concordant is here explicitly scouted; for it is by itself enough to make us disown existence, that the world is not an absolute fool's paradise or a cosmos of perfectly logical design, so that it still incorporates a *general* possibility of frustration, contingency and evil. If at the same time we fail, in the absence of any distinction between spirit and life, to distinguish further between conscious will and the spur of impulse, it follows that the identification we make with the world will necessarily be a *distressful* one.[2]

Thus it is not a question, as it is in western civilization, of treating evil and its causes as something public and objective, to be progressively mitigated and got rid of by commercial, technical, inventive or scientific means. It is simply a matter of

[1] Cf. Theodor Lessing's book, *Untergang der Erde am Geist: Europa und Asien*, Hanover, 1924, in which the concept of a universal democracy of being is well worked out. Cf. further L. Ziegler: *Der ewige Buddha*, and the section 'Die Mysterien der Gottlosen' in the second volume of *Gestaltwandel der Götter*, Berlin, 1920.

[2] Cf. my essay 'Vom Sinn des Leides'.

eliminating the *suffering* involved, once this has been recognized in its full breadth as intrinsic to all things real, by breaking down all resistance to evil, including psychical and physical resistances of an involuntary kind, by means of a progressive *inner* mastery over almost all such psycho-somatic processes and responses. Even the occurrence of the simplest pain-sensation entails, in addition to the normal stimulus and throughout its transmission to a terminal point in the nervous system, an associated quantum of automatic, involuntary, but spontaneous *attention*, which has a resistant quality about it (and probably also a motor nerve-process corresponding to this attention). The seat of all such involuntary and instinctive attention lies in the psychic life-centre; the conscious will may be able to extend its command over the latter to the point of governing and repressing this spontaneous resistance, which is normally quite involuntary and beyond all mental control. Once this is achieved, the sensation of pain itself disappears —as can be seen in the methods employed by fakirs. *Mutatis mutandis*, this art of complete quiescence can also be applied to the highly strenuous spiritual achievement of total impassivity towards painful feelings of a much more profound kind.

As with Buddha's conversion, a few examples are sufficient to establish that general misery is inherent in the scheme of things; it requires no quantitative reckoning of pleasure and pain. By this categorical rejection of reality and will the ruling passion for life and pleasure is overthrown; but the rejection itself comes about only because *sensory pleasure is treated*, consciously or otherwise, as an *absolute* in the scale of values. The same sort of thing can be observed in the final phases of Epicureanism, in the founder of the Trappist order, and in Schopenhauer (only there unfortunately it takes the far more odious form of an indignant pessimism).

Before turning to other typical forms of identification with the cosmos, let us ask what this feeling *consists* in, and how far we may allow it an internal justification.

Identification with the cosmos cannot really take place except within a view of things which envisages the world as a whole, a *collective organism*, permeated by a *unitary* life; it requires an organic mode of approach to things. Given such a viewpoint, the ideal and real (teleological or causal) connections between things, as studied in science and philosophy, are supplemented by a new sort of relationship, co-extensive with what is real in life generally. It is that which holds between life and its *mode of expression*, a specifically symbolic relation. It is intrinsically impossible to identify with the inanimate, when presented as such (and fellow-feeling is plainly ruled out as well: this latter point, indeed, being much more obvious than the other). Identification can extend to the cosmos only if those Ideas and Forms of Intuition which have pure and immediate application to the organic element in experience, are superimposed also on dead matter, its changes and motions, doings and undergoings, its coming-to-be and passing-away. Only then do *all* natural phenomena appear both as the undivided total life of a single world-organism and the universal fluid matrix in which it is expressed. Such an expressive matrix must necessarily have a *universal* grammar of expression, a sort of *cosmic mime* and panto-mime, whose laws have a hidden influence upon our conception of nature; and yet, as the spacious projects of Novalis, Lavater, Goethe and Fechner show, it must also be possible to discover them by rational means. Once the expressed meaning is made out, the conative-affective self makes an immediate, non-inferential leap into the living *heart of things*, taking in their form and pattern and realizing that their perceptible attributes (colours, sounds, scents, tastes and so forth) are only the outward aspect and frontier of the inner life thus imparted. There is an admirable remark by Rodin, an artist whose entire approach is expressive rather than formal:[1] 'A thing', he says, 'is simply the shape and outline of the "flame" which gives it birth.'

Philosophically speaking, the organic conception of the world in one or other of its thousand forms, has to this day held prac-tically undisputed sway over all but the western portion of humanity. And it also played a governing part in shaping the outlines of the whole western outlook and way of thinking, until the beginning of modern times. Here at last, it began to be re-placed, though only among a small intellectual aristocracy at first, by an essentially mechanical conception of the universe. It was only in the European and American 'community' towards the end of the eighteenth century that this point of view had become so gradually diffused among all classes as to constitute a common and 'relatively normal' way of looking at things.[2] And this creates an altogether new spiritual *cleavage* between man and man, no less than between man and Nature.

The organic point of view is to be found, among the ancients, in Plato's doctrine of the 'world-soul' as the mediating agency between the world of Ideas and the μὴ ὄν of matter, and in the Aristotelian conceptions of form, entelechy and motion. The idea running through all ancient philosophy, that only like can have

---

[1] Cf. Adolf von Hildebrand's appraisal of Rodin in: *The Problem of Form in Painting and Sculpture* (tr. by Max Meyer and R. M. Ogden), New York, G. E. Sterchert, 1907.

[2] In the nineteenth century, on the other hand, the organic view is revived and upheld only by a succession of small groups of intellectuals (the Romantics, Goethe, Fechner, Bergson), in revolt against the prevailing outlook.

knowledge of like, is equal evidence of how the feeling of unity with the cosmos which lies deep in the myth[1] and religion of antiquity, still dominated even its most highly rationalized and sophisticated philosophies, despite their immense superiority to Greek polytheism.[2] Admittedly the sort of identification which prevailed in antiquity is different from that of India or southern China (Laotse). It belongs more to the *exacting* type than the submissive one; it is *active* rather than passive; and there is more joy than sorrow in its sense of unity with the universe, 'the blessed animal' ($\mu\alpha\kappa\dot{\alpha}\rho\iota\omicron\nu$ $\theta\eta\rho\dot{\iota}\omicron\nu$)[3] as Plato calls it, in pointed contrast to Buddha. Such an identification does not meet things demo-cratically face-to-face, in the manner of Indian Buddhism, but makes for a superior and condescending attitude in man towards the animal, the vegetative and the inorganic. This is just what we find in Aristotle's conception of the soul as only *one* active form among many, the 'first entelechy of an organized body'; while the human soul actually contains the animal and vegetable souls, as under-strata of spiritual $\nu o \tilde{\upsilon}\varsigma$.

The ancients' sense of unity implies a felt unison of the human spirit with the single hierarchic scale of Being and that governing *Eros* which animates the entire universe from the material to the divine, and sustains it, grappling with valiant rivalry, in a ferment of life. It is an identification with the creative Eros, which carries us up from $\mu\dot{\eta}$ $\ddot{o}\nu$ to $\ddot{o}\nu\tau\omega\varsigma$ $\ddot{o}\nu$ and constitutes, as it were, the real soul of the world; an Eros that is the ultimate prime mover of the universe itself. *Omne ens est bonum*, as the later Scholastic for-mula puts it: an axiom which permeates all the basic notions of the Greek and Western world, and attests in this feeling of unity a sense of man's communion with all things in *rejoicing* unto God (conceived as an eternal, static, quasi-geometrical principle, not as the active power of historical development envisaged by modern evolutionism). In quality, aim and pattern, therefore, such an identification is quite unlike the Indian. Moreover, the ancients were the first to draw that distinction between spirit and life, *Logos* and *Psyche*, which has remained fundamental to all life and thought in the West ever since. Though this does not do away with identification, the general importance of the latter as a road to metaphysical knowledge and unity is thereby greatly dimin-ished. The distinction creates an entirely new plane of purely

---

[1] For Hesiod, the act of procreation is the prototype of causality in general.

[2] Cf. the excellent account of the 'decline of the biological viewpoint' given by Emanuel Ràdl in the first volume of his valuable *History of Biological Theories* (tr. and adapted by E. J. Hatfield), Oxford University Press, 1930.

[3] [The allusion is probably to the *Timæus*, but the phrase seems incorrectly quoted.—Tr.]

spiritual relationships of men to things, to one another, and to God; and it is only upon this plane that true fellow-feeling and spontaneous spiritual love first become possible. The cult of Orphism, and the mysteries, with their genuine sense of unity, are already a romantic harking-back in reaction *against* this spiritual disintegration of identification, and against the town-bred 'Apollinism' of Greek thought.

I have already dwelt, in another connection,[1] upon the historical significance of western Christianity; the way in which it combines the Jewish and Roman notions of mastery over Nature (which are alien and even hostile to identification), with the romantic, Græco-Hellenistic view of God and the world, and both of these with the Gospel of Jesus; and the profound change it has thereby wrought in our conception of the love-emotion. We shall have less to say here. Its doctrine of God as the invisible spiritual 'Lord and Maker' of the world which is taken over from the Jews, presents a contrast to the Greek view (in which will is absent, and the attributes of 'Lord' and 'Maker' are also lacking in consequence). Compared with the Greeks, therefore, the *whole of Nature becomes vastly less animate and less alive*, while man as a spiritual being is given such decided precedence over Nature that all feeling for unity with Nature is branded as paganism for centuries afterwards. Indeed it is not until the Franciscan movement that man's ties of brotherhood with plant and animal, wind and weather, attain once more a brief revival. Man struggles to *disengage* himself emotionally from Nature, in the name of the invisible God and his own immortal soul (which in Augustine and all the early fathers is contrasted with the vital soul in a far more dualistic fashion than it is in Aristotle or the later mediævals, such as Albertus Magnus and Aquinas). He does so in order to concentrate all the energies so liberated on that spontaneous, *non-cosmic* love of Jesus Christ, which culminates, for St. Paul and his successors, in the act of becoming one with Christ and with the stages of his earthly career, from baptism to the final sacrifice and redemption of his poor and humble life (whose course was later to be crystallized and made objective in the Christian liturgy). In this way Nature comes to be thought of as an essentially lifeless *instrument* of man's spiritual will; and so too is man, in his natural and fleshly capacity (*sarx*), though not as a soul made in God's image, a spirit (*pneuma*). This shows itself, first in asceticism of the body, and later in the ever-advancing material conquest of Nature by means of technology. The materializing (or deadening) of Nature and the spiritualizing of man and his elevation, through Christ, to the status of adoption as a child of God the Father and

[1] Cf. *Das Ressentiment im Aufbau der Moralen*, op. cit.

Creator, are the *common* fruit of one and the same process. *Only* man can be 'brother' to man here; the works of Nature are not his kindred, but rather his 'born slaves' and the rights he exercises as their lord and master are like the rights of God over Nature herself. The stars, as 'visible gods' are now eclipsed. Malebranche was not unjust in reviling Aristotle, from the Christian standpoint, as a pagan; while Schelling, who revived the universal animism of antiquity, was no less justified than von Baader, von Hartmann and Fechner in arguing that the Christian outlook and habit of mind, as formulated in Theism, implies a dead and comparatively mechanistic approach to all the lower orders of Nature. This mechanizing and petrifaction of Nature is the result of ascribing to a purely spiritual deity the new attribute of Creative Will, and of presuming the soul of man to possess a purely spiritual will. Whereas in Aristotle, for instance, the will is in no sense a purely spiritual attribute in God or man, but only arises in the *conjunction* of the purely cognitive intellect with the sensitive and vegetative principles of the human body.

The non-cosmic mysticism of spiritual love propounded in Christianity is therefore in polar opposition to the Indian and even the ancient Greek sense of unity with the animate cosmos, 'suffering' or 'blessed' as the case may be. Only in the nature and development of the Christian mysteries and sacraments do we find preserved a truly vital identification with the inner destiny of the very *body* of our Lord, and even with his actual flesh and blood. It is most evident in Baptism, the Eucharist, the Passion on the Cross and the Redemption and Ascent into Heaven. In this way, even the non-cosmic spiritual and moral love of the Christian for his God and Saviour acquired a footing in the living and organic, through its 'magical' identification with the body and blood of Our Lord under the forms of bread and wine. By the institution of Holy Communion, it is divinely ordained that the natural objects of bread and wine shall be eternally capable of changing their substance into the body and blood of our Lord; and these have come to be virtually the *only* natural substances which permit of that sort of 'union' which the ancient world could establish with the *entire cosmos*. It is also quite plain that to 'take up' Our Lord's cross, to suffer, to rise again and to be exalted 'in Him' are of all things farthest removed from fellow-feeling in the ordinary sense. They are genuine examples of identification, though based on personal love. No reasonable person will be led to the almost ludicrously profane notion, that Paul's ἐνδύεσθαι Χριστὸν, his 'putting on of Christ', his being 'rooted and built up in', 'suffering in', 'crucified with', 'dead and risen again in' Him represent nothing more than fellow-feeling or pity for Christ, or that they are identical with the mere belief that all this once happened in the world, and happened 'for me' and for my salvation. On the contrary, it is as clear as day that in their orphic obscurity and morbid ecstasy of passion, these utterances of St. Paul refer to something totally different from mere fellow-feeling or understanding; nor can they relate to articles of faith, to assertions taken on trust (for Jesus *could* not have said any such thing in His lifetime and did not do so). Nor is it at all a matter of emulating the humility of Christ's life: (Paul, indeed, has generally very little to say of Christ's *life*). He is expressing a *true identification in form and essence* (though not existence), of Christ's Person with his own; not in the sense of mere knowledge and awareness, but as a *becoming*, a remaking, an ingrafting of his own personal substance into the Person of Christ; in short, an ontological process. But this 'becoming' is brought about by an act of continuous substitution of his own person *for* Christ, and of indwelling *in* Him, which thereupon immediately entails that his own real actions are carried out in conjunction and conformity with Christ. In virtue, that is, of that quite specific and unique state which Paul calls 'believing in Christ', that simultaneous substitution of his own person 'for' Christ and indwelling 'in' Him, which he is perhaps alone in understanding in this fashion.

Religious faith must always imply 'belief in', never merely 'belief that'. The two things are utterly different. And if I am to say what such a 'belief in' a charismatic person really comes to, in contrast to any sort of belief in matters of fact (belief that), I can find no other characteristic but this very factor we describe as spiritual and practical *self-identification with a Person*, the complete putting of oneself in his place and at his disposal. Such an indwelling in the substance of a person entails an immediate identity of thought, will and feeling, and hence a remaking and ingrafting of one's own self in the image and pattern of the Master. It is a continuous dynamic chain of ever-fresh impressions made by the spiritual Master-pattern in the material of one's own inner experience; it resembles a transverse wave-motion, in which the wave-pattern is continuously transferred to new regions of the water. By comparison with this indwelling identification that we find in St. Paul, even the 'Imitation of Christ' of later times is already a derivative and indirect attitude, though here also there is no 'copying' in the literal sense (for this always proceeds from the outside inwards, and so starts with gesture or action); it is a reproduction and reincarnation of that person's spiritual acts and dispositions, going so far, in some cases, as to lead even to physical resemblances, though these are produced outwardly from within. (We may recall the infliction of Stigmata.) Once the nature of this 'belief in' has been grasped, it becomes simply analytic to say that it must be experienced as a gift, a grace, a favour granted, not as a personal achievement of one's own. So powerfully does the Master's figure grip and seize and overwhelm the disciple here, that the act of consent, which is really and truly present in all such belief, simply does not reach self-consciousness at all. Election by grace is thus merely a questionable theologico-metaphysical rationalization of this fundamental experience of the living sources of faith. When Paul says (Galatians, ch. II, v. 20), 'I live; yet not I but Christ liveth in me,' we are confronted with what is simply the spiritual version of that coalescence with the ideal, which begins thereafter to acquire dogmatic status in a magical form, as the sacrament of Holy Communion.

Christianity brought with it a non-cosmic personal love-mysticism of universal compassion; though it no longer looks down, for it is directed upwards, and welded into unity with the love of Jesus. It was left to one of the greatest artificers of the spirit in European history to make the memorable attempt of uniting and harnessing this, within a *single* life-stream, to the animistic sense of union with the life and being of Nature. This was the very remarkable achievement of the saint of Assisi.[1]

Even on the most cursory consideration of St. Francis and his record on earth in the light of our problem, we are immediately struck by the fact that he addresses both sun and moon, fire and water, animals and plants of all descriptions, as his 'brothers' and 'sisters'. He achieves an *expansion* of the specifically Christian emotion of love for God the Father, and for our neighbour and brother in God, to include *all the lower orders of Nature*; while at the same time he succeeds, or seems to succeed, in *uplifting* Nature into the light and glory of the supernatural. Was this not a grave heresy from the point of view of the traditional Christian doctrine which had prevailed throughout the church's history? For by the very fact of regarding man as a rational being this doctrine creates an enormous *gulf* between man and Nature; and still more so by considering him a vessel of supernatural grace and a generation exalted high above all reason and nature by the redemption of Christ, Son of the Father and Son of Man. And if not a heresy of the intellect, in a saint so little given to mere 'intellect', science or learning, was it not yet a grave *heresy of the heart*? There must have been very deep reasons why the fundamental break with the past implied in the saint's new outlook should not have been so

---

[1] There is much valuable material in D. v. Hildebrand: *Der Geist des hl. Franziskus und der dritte Orden* (Munich, 1921); and more recently, in L. Ziegler, *Gestaltwandel der Götter*, vol. 1, the chapter entitled 'Weg der Nachfolge'; the portrait of St. Francis is exceptionally well done.

regarded. For those about him certainly did not fail to realize how very strange, new and unconventional this attitude was. The statement of Thomas of Celano deserves the closest attention: 'He called all creatures his brothers, and in a *strange way, wholly denied to others*, he looked with the heart's keen insight into the inmost being of every creature, just as though he had already entered into the freedom of the glory of the children of God.'

It does seem to me that in this respect St. Francis really has no predecessor in the entire history of Christendom in the West. Saint Bernard's mysticism of love and betrothal is quite another thing; we look in vain for any sense of cosmic unity there. The natural objects and processes referred to in the Gospels, even in those passages which betray the Redeemer's pure understanding and profound and noble love of Nature, are only mentioned, so far as I know, as *parables* for ties and relationships which hold specifically between man and God or between man and man. Neither through my own researches, nor through detailed enquiry from Biblical authorities, have I been able to find a single passage which goes beyond this parabolic intention. There is no trace of cosmic identification with a natural object, or even of a spontaneous emotional love for Nature itself, without reference to its repercussions on man or meaning for him; still less is there any suggestion of a duty to love Nature as such (or as having a direct relation to God, regardless of any human connection). The primacy of the Son of Man over the Sabbath is explained in Matthew, ch. XII, v. 11, as follows: 'What man shall there be among you, that shall have one sheep, and if it fall into a pit on the sabbath day, will he not lay hold on it, and lift it out? How much then is a man better than a sheep?' As the last few words indicate, the parabolic element is as evident here as when it is said of the sparrows, that not one of them shall fall to the ground without our Father, or of the fowls of the air and the lilies that they take no thought for the morrow, 'yet your Heavenly Father feedeth them' (Matthew, ch. VI, v. 26–28). The crucial difference is that with St. Francis we can no longer speak of a *mere* parable or symbol in this sense. We may try—as one acute and informed commentator seems willing to do[1]—to treat St. Francis's lyrically expressed feelings of brotherhood and sisterhood for sun, moon, water, fire, bees, lambs, bugs, flowers, birds, fish and so on, in some such sense as this: that he took water to his heart, for instance, 'as a symbol of the holy sacrament of penance and as the means of baptism'; or that the two trussed lambs for which

[1] Cf. Dietrich von Hildebrand: *Der Geist des hl. Franziskus*; cf. also in the same book, 'Die Wirkungen des franziskanischen Geistes auf die Kunst'.

he bartered his cloak to the peasant who had brought them to market for slaughter, bore a symbolic reference to the words of John the Baptist, 'the Lamb of God, that taketh away the sins of the world'. But such an interpretation would very soon break down in view of the multitude of creatures which certainly had *no* such symbolic reference,[1] though he 'looked with the heart's keen insight into their inmost being'. For what is really new and unusual in St. Francis's emotional relationship to Nature, is that natural objects and processes take on an expressive significance of *their own*, without any parabolic reference to man or to human relationships generally. Thus sun, moon, wind and so on, which have no need whatever of benevolent or compassionate love, are greeted in heartfelt recognition as brother and sister. All created things are taken in their metaphysical contiguity (man being also included), to be *immediately* related to their Creator and Father as self-subsistent beings having, even in relation to man, a *quite intrinsic value of their own*. This is the new, the startling, the strange, the anti-Judaic element in the saint's attitude. Certainly, as our commentator seems most anxious to emphasize, St. Francis was 'far removed from any sort of pantheism' in this (even of the type still strongly tinctured with theism, that we find in Telesio, Campanella or Giordano Bruno). His loving soul discerns in every created thing a work of the invisible spiritual Creator, a stepping-stone from Nature towards God, a footstool for His feet, a manifestation of His glory—a visible and audible 'Glory to God the Father . . .'

In this sense, even for him, Nature is not an immediate object of identification with a life universal either dissevered from God as Spirit, or actually equated with Him (as in the Renaissance pantheists); for Nature itself is but a symbol and a parable, as the 'Hymn to the Sun' makes sufficiently clear.

With St. Francis we are as remote from the Indian type of identification (in suffering) as from that of the Greeks (in joy), and equally far from the naturalistic identification typified in the dynamic pantheism of the coming Renaissance. Yet he exemplifies a difference, of kind and quality, rather than degree, in the emotional and intuitive conception of the relationship between man, Nature and God, that has no parallel in anything to be found in Western Christianity from the earliest times onwards, and is sharply at variance with the whole of the Christian feeling for Nature hitherto, in the primitive church, the early Fathers, or the later Middle Ages. It is difficult to say just what this novelty

---

[1] Johannes Jörgensen also brings this out very strikingly in his well-known book, *Saint Francis of Assisi: a Biography* (tr. from the Danish by T. O. Conor Sloane), Longman, 1912.

consists in, though it can be seen and felt with the greatest ease. There seem to be three essential factors involved:

(1) A natural object, for St. Francis, is a symbol, a mark, a signpost, a significant pointer to the spirit and person of God; not because it is interpreted, recognized or inferred to be such by man, nor yet because it yields a parable (as in the Gospel), for man's relation to God or his fellowmen, but simply *in* and *because* of its being objectively there, just as it is.

(2) Nature is not thought of in the scholastic manner as a realm of informing influences and informed objects, sharply isolated one from another. St. Francis was a declared opponent of scholasticism and its aristocratic, hierarchical doctrine of the scale of Being. He thinks of Nature as a living whole, whose relation to its visible manifestations is rather like that of a man's countenance to the various expressions it may betray. There is a *single* divine life embodied in the forms of Nature, and 'expressed' in her aspects and incidents. Nature is a *single* field of expression for this same surging life which finds a continuous embodiment of itself in the plenitude of natural forms; and the 'insight of the heart' is far superior to mere fellow-feeling or benevolence in its power of *grasping this god-like life of Nature from within.*

(3) God is not merely felt and thought of as the Lord and Creator of the natural order, and the 'Father' (through Christ) of men alone; He is also the loving Father of all Nature's creatures as such, so that (by the redemption and grace of Christ) they all come to be children together in His sight, which therefore naturally implies that their relation to mankind should be that of *brother and sister.* It is this which represents, for St. Francis, the final destruction of that Jewish and Roman conception of the unilateral authority of man over Nature which is tempered, but not eliminated, in the Gospels. Indeed, though he frequently appeals to Holy Writ, as if to justify, support and give colour to his view of Nature and love of it, he seems to me to be really importing *into* the words of the evangelists a meaning which transcends parable, and to be largely mistaken in reading his own genuine sense of identity into the authors of the Gospels as well.

However, the real mystery of St. Francis is that, despite this momentous revival of true identification with a unitary conception of a divine life that is merely incarnate in the works of Nature, there is not the slightest impairment, on the non-cosmic level, in his personal spirituality; as can be seen in his Christian vision of God, coupled with a love of Christ that can truly be described, in St. Francis's case, as amounting almost to intoxication, and an *Imitatio Christi* which extended even to the physical stigmata.

On the contrary, for all its strictness, harshness and ascetic rigour, his spiritual life stems throughout in a perfectly natural and unbroken course from the *soil* of this new and (in its day) quite original and unheard-of identification with Nature, and bears from thence a harvest of incomparable deeds; indeed it is the spiritual personality which first lends inspiration, as it were, to the act of identification.

If St. Francis had been a theologian and philosopher—which, fortunately for him, and still more fortunately for us, he was not —if he had attempted an exact formulation of that vision of God and the world, which he simply intuited, lived and perfected, he would certainly never have become a pantheist, but might well have had to admit an element of 'panentheism' into his scheme. So far as rational formulæ can encompass the intrinsically religious and severely Christian character of his view of God and Nature, it might be stated more or less as follows: Christ's supernatural act of redemption, though none the less an historical event, is at the same time an eternal miracle in the order of metaphysical reality, perpetuated in the Church and her sacraments, and especially in the Eucharist, wherein God everlastingly takes flesh upon Him and is made man; a miracle which must serve as a pattern for the ideal of a moral and religious *Imitatio Christi*, extending to a complete identity of structure between the believer's personality and that of Christ. At the same time—and herein lies the novel element—this supernatural being and becoming also prefigures, in its innermost meaning, the continual life-giving incarnation of God the Father in *Nature*—an active continuance of creation, parallel to the sacrifice of Christ. Hence there is in truth but *one* divine life dwelling in all created things, and it is as forms of expression for this divine life, as 'natural sacraments', so to speak, and as a system of real symbols pointing to God the Father, that they can and should be regarded by men. But this can only be achieved by sympathetic insight into the heart of the creature —St. Francis's most characteristic gift, and one which was unknown to the history of Christianity before his time. It is also the source of his *social* mission, which aims at moderating social distinctions and class-antagonisms while bringing charity to the common people, in a way which resembles, though on a much smaller scale, the Buddha's campaign against the ancient Indian caste-system. It contributes further, to the greater freedom and plasticity of Trecento painting (Giotto), and has an indirect though by no means negligible effect on the new philosophy and science of Nature then in process of displacing the rigid scheme of Forms (in favour of a dynamic view of Nature and an incipient nominalism). Both of these were cultivated with growing zeal in the Franciscan schools, and to the eventual destruction of High Scholasticism—but *not*, alas, in the original spirit of the master.

Where does this new panentheistic phase of identification originate? If we leave the inborn talents and spiritual endowment of the Saint out of account, there can be no doubt that its source lies in the *Provencal cult of chivalrous love* (itself derived, according to Burdach, from the Arabs); a mode of feeling which Francis certainly cultivated in youth and early manhood prior to his conversion.[1] This again confirms the fact that Eros is the ultimate source of all identification and always remains so. The self-styled 'troubador of God', who kept to the end of his life the habit of humming his beloved French troubador songs to himself, was never to lose hold of this strand of his past life; it can be seen, even in the rigorous and heroic asceticism of his later career, in the almost indescribable tenderness of his relations with St. Clara. And yet, with incomparable *spiritual artistry*, as unself-conscious as it was undesigned, he succeeded, for all his early absorption in the historic emotional attitude of the Provencal cult, in so divesting it of all substance, all worldly or amorous import, that virtually nothing but its serene and ethereal *rhythm* was left behind.

So appropriate was this to the spiritual love of God, of Christ and of persons (which had, of course, a wholly indigenous origin of its own), that the effect was to reanimate this Christian inheritance to an equally unprecedented state of vitality. Just as the Provencal mood acquired, for him, a spiritual and Christian flavour and in doing so became entirely 'functional' and dissociated from womanhood, its original object, so now it provided a spiritual key and a new insight into the *whole* of Nature, whereby her secrets also were unlocked and stood revealed. The rhythm, as I say, remained; the specifically amorous qualities of mood and feeling, the noble gallantry and respect for womanhood, the chivalrous submission of the knight-errant before her delicate frailty and the power of her natural charms—these kept their place in the soul of St. Francis as an acquired gift for 'submission' and 'devotion' of his centre of organic consciousness to the heart of the living creature—an ever-beating rhythm of adoration before the god-like life *within* all created things.

Even if we do not make use of the term in Freud's quite impossibly crude interpretation of it,[2] there can be no question here of 'sublimating' an emotion of erotic origin into an enhancement of Christian brotherly love (a quite impossible process in any case).

[1] Cf. Paul Sabatier, whose opinions on this point remain unchallenged in spite of much facile criticism. *Life of St. Francis of Assisi* (tr. by L. S. Houghton), Hodder & Stoughton, 1894.
[2] Cf. *infra*.

Nor can it merely be, as Hildebrand supposes, a supernaturally inspired extension of the Christian's original non-cosmic love for God and his fellow-men, so as to include the brute creation also. How could such a thing be rendered psychologically conceivable? We are here confronted with a *unique confluence of Eros and Agape* (an *Agape* steeped in *Amor Dei* and *Amor in Deo*), occurring in a soul of native saintliness and genius; an *interfusion* of both, in short, which has become so complete as to present the greatest and most sublime example of a simultaneous 'inspiriting of life' and 'enlivening of the spirit', of which I have any knowledge.

Never again in the history of the West have the emotional forces of sympathy regained the pattern we find in St. Francis. Nor do we ever encounter such a simultaneous and complete integration of their activity in Religion, Love, Social endeavour, Art and Knowledge. Indeed it is perhaps the commonest characteristic of all subsequent ages, that what is knit together in St. Francis should disintegrate into an increasing *diversity* of patterns of sentiment and feeling, and disperse itself in a variety of 'movements' and *one-sided* fields of activity.[1]

We have no intention here of offering either a history or even a synoptic account of the elements of emotion; our aim is merely to present examples of forms and varieties of sympathy for which there is genuine phenomenological evidence. We shall therefore conclude now, by outlining the sequence in which the simplest and clearest of the above patterns have evolved. I shall simply mention them briefly at this point, while indicating at the same time their place in the system of human nature.

(1) Three tendencies emerge from the Renaissance, of which the first two are directly connected with the Franciscan movement, whereas the third has an independent origin in the late Renaissance and provides, as it were, the necessary contrast to the brilliance of the other two. They are, firstly, the Christian cult of Platonic love (Dante and Petrarch), which is likewise strongly imbued with the Arab and Provencal cult of romance; secondly the pantheistic philosophy of Nature, with its emotional delight in the sensible universe, and the new feeling for Nature which goes along with it;[2] and lastly, the new style and mode of conscious enjoyment of the sexually erotic, purposive, yet divorced from

[1] There is valuable material for a philosophical history of such modes of feeling in the West in Emil Lucka's *Evolution of Love* (tr. by Ellie Schleussner, Allen and Unwin, 1927) and recently in Paul Kluckhohn's excellent and welcome study, *Das Problem der Liebe im 18 Jahrhundert und in der deutschen Romantik*, Halle, 1922.

[2] Cf. Alfred Biese: *Development of the Feeling for Nature in the Middle Ages and in Modern Times* (Routledge, 1905); see also the valuable works of Karl Joel on the dynamic pantheism of the Renaissance.

ulterior purposes and largely untrammelled by considerations of rank and race. St. Clara, Beatrice, Laura and Fiametta represent an array of feminine types which does much to exemplify the emotional phases of the Renaissance in this respect. They personify both the good and evil, the lofty and the low sides of this great era, and in both cases it is something which would not have been possible either *before* it, in the early Middle Ages, nor at any time *afterwards*. It is only in the context of an increasingly unmediæval *dualism* between spirit and life, that either a Beatrice or a Fiametta become possible: it is this which provides a common basis for the mutually disruptive emergence of a fanatical enthusiasm on the one hand, and a voluptuous sensuality on the other.

(2) Protestantism has a bearing on our enquiry in four main aspects: (i) it excludes love in any form, whether benevolence, love of our neighbour, or the love of God as a mystical reality, from among the means essential to salvation. (ii) It rules out any sort of pagan identification with Nature, thereby powerfully reinforcing the primary Judæo-Christian tendency to subjugate Nature into an exclusive preserve for human *control and activity*. (iii) It arrests the development of a spiritual Eros by rejecting both the practice and the ideals of other-worldly asceticism (monasticism). (iv) It deflates and domesticates the emotional relationship between the sexes (in complete contrast to the Renaissance!).

(3) The triumphal progress of natural science and of the mechanistic conception of the universe makes any sort of organic point of view untenable; all identification is regarded as illusory and anthropomorphic (Descartes discounts it even in relation to animals and plants), so that eventually the only thing that remains is a newly-developed type of sympathy, namely *humanitarianism* or *the love of mankind in general*, based on an essentially 'social' conception of man's status as a being divorced from God *and* Nature.

There are only three other patterns and movements on a similar scale recorded in the modern period. And they are all *counter-movements* against two of the basic patterns referred to, namely those of humanitarian sympathy and Protestantism. One is the Romantic movement (to which the later positivism of Comte also belongs), which attempts to reinstate the organic view of the world, the feeling of unity, and *also*, with rather less success, the non-cosmic love of God and of one's neighbour, peculiar to Christianity. Next there is the great wave of resentment among the working classes which, having lost faith in the efficacy of sympathy, borrows from Darwin and treats the *struggle for existence* in Nature and between the classes as the sole motivating factor in all historical development. Thirdly, there are in our own time the various movements which seek to bring about a renewal in the pattern of the human heart, with or without associating themselves with the great counter-movement of romanticism (Fechner, Bergson, phenomenology, vitalism, the disciples of Stefan George, and the Youth Movements).

Chapter VI

SYMPATHY AND ITS LAWS OF DEPENDENCE

Is there a constitutive relationship of *dependence* between identification, vicarious emotion, fellow-feeling, love of humanity and non-cosmic personal and divine love? I believe that there is such a relation.

(a) *Identification underlies vicarious feeling*

It seems to me that identification underlies vicarious feeling in the (timeless) order of functional dependence, as well as in that of genetic evolution. Though admittedly this statement applies only to emotional *functions*, not to emotional states. Thus it is not the case that the state of emotion in A which is vicariously induced in B must at some time have comprised the total or partial content of an identification, or must even have been present immediately beforehand. Nevertheless, the total subjective field (A) of which the vicariously felt emotion forms part must at least be accessible to identification on the part of the vicariously participating subject (B). It is not in the least necessary that such an identification (by B) should extend to all, or even a particular part, of the actual states felt by the subject (A) in whom they occur. Hence such an identification may be either concrete or abstract, and this to any degree. I can identify myself with the animate universe, with mankind as a whole, with a nation or a family, without thereby having to include in this all the particular emotional states actually possessed by the subject with whom I identify. It is invariably characteristic of identification:

(1) That it takes place below the level of waking consciousness.

(2) That it is automatic (involuntary) in operation.

(3) That it is confined to the sphere of vital consciousness, in subject and object alike.

These are unmistakeable features, which do not apply to vicarious feeling. However, if such a (detached) reproduction of feeling is to be possible, I must at some time have gathered the *quality* of the emotional state thus vicariously felt (in conscious detachment from the subject to whom it refers), by having identified with a subject of this *type* (directly or indirectly, e.g. by identification with someone who has himself had previous experience of identifying with those of this type). As has been shown already, it is by no means necessary that the qualities of the states we respond to should have actually been realized in our own experience before we can enter into them. But so far as they do extend beyond the qualities of our personal experience (which are naturally the most easily and directly accessible in others), these unfamiliar qualities cannot have become known to us originally by being vicariously felt, but only, in the *first* instance, by way of *identification* proper.

It is thus a fundamental principle of the evolution of feeling everywhere, whether from child to adult, animal to man, or from savagery to civilization, that in the early stages we still find identification where later on we encounter vicarious feeling. We have already seen how the little girl playing at 'mother' still retains a genuine identification of the doll with the child, and of herself with the mother. One might describe the first as 'ecphoric' and the second as 'enphoric' identification, for in the one case the Alter (the doll) is identified with the Ego, while in the other the Ego is identified with the Alter (mother) (A = E, E = A). But if an older child plays the same game, it is more a matter of vicarious feeling instead. Again, the primitive's sense of *unity* with his ancestors is a case of identification, whereas the later 'piety' of the ancestor *cult* displays a merely vicarious feeling for the life of one's forebears. There is true identification still to be found in the herd, the horde and the crowd, whereas in communal life, such as that of the family, it is only vicarious feeling that is involved. (The multifarious systems governing the blood-feud are hardly dependent any longer on true identification with the injured relatives or kinsmen, being already based on vicarious feeling and the idea of substitution.) So likewise, in the mysteries of antiquity we still have genuine identification, whereas in the art of the theatre, which has everywhere developed historically from mystery and ritual, its place is taken by merely æsthetic empathy and vicarious emotion. (The attitude of the spectator towards the still semi-ritual tragedy of antiquity may well represent a transitional stage between these two.) Again, the instinctive identification of

97

mother-love is similarly replaced, in the later stages of childhood, by merely vicarious feeling, this being perhaps all that the father can ever have towards his child. These are but some of the examples which could be multiplied indefinitely. To take a parallel case: we may still retain a sense of unity, in wartime for instance, with the struggle and hardships of our own people, even when we can no longer maintain it for a more extended group, e.g. for such other nations as belong to the same cultural tradition. For them there is only a vicarious fellow-feeling. In general we may say that even where there is no more than vicarious feeling or fellowship with the wider group, there will still be identification with the more immediate one.

(b) Vicarious feeling underlies fellow-feeling

The validity of this law of dependence has already been demonstrated in detail in Chapter II, and a reminder of this is all that is required for the purposes of the present survey.

(c) Fellow-feeling underlies benevolence (humanitas)

As has been shown, it is through fellow-feeling, in both its mutual and its unreciprocated forms, that 'other minds in general' (already given previously as a field) are brought home to us, in individual cases, as having a *reality equal to our own*. Such acceptance of a common status (and the judgements based on this) are a prior condition for the emergence of spontaneous benevolence, i.e. love of someone simply because he is human and has the semblance of a man. Vicarious feeling is not sufficient to confer this equality of reality-status: it only conveys the quality of the other's condition, not its reality. Thus we can easily *reproduce* in ourselves the joys and sorrows of characters in fiction, or the persons in a play (Faust or Gretchen, say), as the actor presents them; but so long as we maintain a generally æsthetic attitude, and do not, like the novelette-reading teen-ager, take their part as if they were real, we cannot have genuine *fellow-feeling* for them. For the latter emotion *essentially* involves the ascription of reality to the subject whose feelings we share. It therefore disappears when the supposedly real subject is replaced by one which is presented as figurative or fictitious. It is precisely *in the act* of fellow-feeling that self-love, self-centred choice, solipsism and egoism are first wholly overcome.

The emotional realization of the unity of mankind as a species must therefore have been already achieved in fellow-feeling, if benevolence (or humanitarianism) in this particular sense is to be possible. The closeness of their connection is evident from the fact that neither general benevolence nor fellow-feeling depend upon a previous discrimination between the positive or negative *values* of men, or the values of the emotions we share with them. A genuine love of humanity does not discriminate between fellow-countrymen and foreigners, the virtuous and the criminal, the racially superior and inferior, the cultured and the uncouth or between good and bad generally. Like fellow-feeling, it embraces *all* men, simply because they are men, though marking them off distinctly from the lower animals and from God. This, however, does not alter the fact that fellow-feeling (which can also be bestowed on animals) differs from love of humanity, since the latter, like all forms of love, is associated with a positive evaluation, such that it conceives the human as possessing a special value—as compared with the animal, and also the divine. Its quite specific and peculiar note of feeling is sounded in Goethe's: 'For I was a man and that is to be a fighter.'[1]

In fellow-feeling this specific valuation of the human as such is not yet present. Certainly, once benevolence has gained its impetus from pure fellow-feeling, it can, by its own activity, enlarge the scope of the latter to an unlimited extent; for the experience gained in active well-doing, which proceeds from *love* only, and not from the essential passivity of fellow-feeling, has the effect of continually increasing the range of objects accessible to fellow-feeling. But this does not alter the fact that fellow-feeling in general, as a felt intentional act, is a necessary condition for the possible emergence of benevolence.

(d) *Benevolence underlies the non-cosmic love of persons, including God*

It is unnecessary to say anything further here about the intrinsic difference between benevolence and that non-cosmic love for the spiritual person of our neighbour in God (whoever he may be), which first made its historical appearance in Christianity. The subject is fully discussed in the essay *Das Ressentiment im Aufbau der Moralen*,[2] though on our present view of the matter it must be admitted that our treatment there goes too far at a number of points.[3] Among other things, we put forward the opinion that the 'modern idea of benevolence' (humanitarianism, philanthropy,

---

[1] [*West-östlicher Divan*, Buch des Paradieses: 'Einlass'. The speaker puts this forward as sufficient reason for entry into Paradise.—Tr.]

[2] In *Vom Umsturz der Werte*, Bd. 1.

[3] I now acknowledge the essential justice of Jonas Cohn's criticism of my views on this subject.

etc.) has been 'worked up' entirely from motives of resentment against patriotism and the Christian love of God and the person. This amounts to repudiating it as a genuine, 'autonomous' movement of love with a positive basis of its own in the fabric of the human spirit, and regarding it merely as a gesture of defiance and protest against the Christian conception of personal and divine love on the one hand, and patriotism on the other. We still retain our previous conviction, that the idea of general benevolence has very often been *employed* polemically in this fashion from motives of ill-will. And we still maintain that the *ranking* of general benevolence *above* the Christian love of God and persons, and above patriotism, the love of our country and those who share our way of life—in effect, the ranking of a Utopian concern for the extremities[1] above what lies nearest the heart, is entirely due to that ill-feeling working itself out; hatred for the divine, hatred for man's spiritual personality and its potential perfection, hatred for one's country and one's neighbour are thus transformed into an ideology. From this position we do not retreat an inch. But it is only this *exaggeration* of the value of benevolence which proceeds from resentment, not the sentiment itself either in essence or origin. Hence it is not benevolence, but only the 'idea' of it, which can be 'worked up' against the forms of love referred to. Benevolence itself is a type of love-emotion, inherent, as an ideal possibility, in man's *essential nature*, and itself by nature and intention positive, both as to its origin and its value. This is not to ignore the fact that, like all the ideal potentialities of the love-emotions in man, it is only at certain points in history that benevolence has shown up powerfully and prominently as an actual historical movement; it is to be found in the *humanitas* of earlier antiquity, which subsequently came to be taken as an ideal by the Cynic, Stoic and Epicurean schools; again in the humanitarian and philanthropic movements of the Age of Enlightenment in Europe; in the intellectual history of the Chinese, with the spread of Laotse's teaching from South China and its amalgamation with Buddhism; and once again in the modern sentimentally-based democracies of the nineteenth and twentieth centuries.

But once this is admitted, a further point must also be recognized, which it is the specific purpose of this section to maintain; namely that the non-cosmic love of God and persons—and the cognate idea that all finite spirits are one, through redemption, in God—*depend*, for their possible 'realization', upon general loving-kindness among men. The reason for this law of dependence is as follows: from an ontological viewpoint, the vital self as such and its real substratum, the vital soul in mankind generally, are

[1] (The reference is to Nietzsche's 'Fernstenliebe'.—Tr.)

no more than a *supporting structure* for the spiritual personality; at once a condition of the occurrence of its conscious acts, and an instrument for its use. But in the genetic order of presentation and development, the situation is reversed. This is to say that a person (his pure conscious acts and the significance thereof), cannot become available to the spiritual comprehension of others save by the prior establishment, through fellow-feeling, of parity of esteem for the reality of the vital self, or its substrate, on either side; and by an ever-deeper penetration of the spontaneous goodwill so engendered, up to the very threshold, as it were, of human personality itself. If the multitude of individual spiritual persons comprising mankind as a whole are to stand revealed, and even their existence brought to light, without culpable or wanton omission of anyone, as capable of being loved as persons, a general love of humanity is requisite, and indeed indispensable. And the love so required, being based on a fellow-feeling which takes no account of value, is itself unmindful of distinctions of value or love-preference between one man and another. This can be confirmed by supposing the contrary. Prior to the emergence of general benevolence, men could be classified as lovable or hateful objects, as 'friend' or 'foe', freeman or slave (in the Aristotelian sense of a natural status, not attributable to ancestry or to the social institutions of any given period); morality enjoined and sanctioned love of one's friends, hatred of one's enemies, respect for the free-born and contempt for slaves. And so long as this continued, the personal element could be discerned only in friends not in foes, in the freeman not in the slave (of whom Aristotle strikingly remarks, that his will is that of his master). The essential characteristic of the Christian conception of spiritual love is that it is love of the individual as a person—any individual *whatsoever*, of course. In this it is sharply distinguished from the generalized love of humanity which merely regards individuals as lovable qua 'specimens' of the human race; but it presupposes this love of the human 'specimen' nonetheless. Hence it is only by reference to the general love of mankind that the position and scope of a *possible* love of the person is defined in the first place.

In spiritual love of the person, however, a new principle comes to light. For apart from his acceptance of the mere existence of the other person as given, it no longer depends entirely on the spontaneous act of the person who loves or understands, since it also rests upon the free discretion of the person who is to be loved or understood. 'Persons' cannot be intuitively understood (by reproduction of their spiritual acts), unless they *spontaneously disclose themselves*. For they are also capable of silence and concealment. The automatic (involuntary) modes of expression, as such, provide evidence only for the state of a man's organic and psychological self; they do not give knowledge or understanding of his cognitive activity as a person. Hence language, which also includes the possibility of silence or reticence, is essential in order to grasp the content of personality. The psychic life of animals is in this sense completely open to human inspection, in principle, if not actually in fact; but a man's spiritual personality is not so. It can either *en*close or *dis*close itself. Moreover, it is an essential condition for the very possibility of self-disclosure, that there should be a pure mutual love between the parties, this being itself necessarily derived from spontaneous goodwill; for according to the principle laid down in *Der Formalismus in der Ethik*: 'Other things being equal, and in the absence of particular inhibiting circumstances, love will evoke a similar type of love in return.' Hence the possible development of that generalized individuality, which is already involved in apprehending the existence of another person, into a concrete individuation of him through his own voluntary self-disclosure, is necessarily bound up with a spontaneous general goodwill towards him on the part of the loving subject himself.

History does but confirm what this order of dependence would suggest. The Christian love of persons, for example, was only made possible, in a real sense, by building upon the *humanitas* of the ancients and the later prophets; the latter having itself, by a sufficiently devious historical process, already gone far to destroy the old Græco-Roman order of precedence in love, that of loving one's friends, hating one's enemies, honouring the freeborn and despising the enslaved.

Since the non-cosmic love of persons is necessarily connected, in nature and meaning, with theism, the love of humanity in general is no less essential as a prior condition for the love of God; so far, at least, as this latter is something more than the *amare Deum*, already known to Plato and Aristotle, namely an *amare in Deo*; and so far as it is felt and thought of as effectual only through a prevenient love of God towards mankind.[1]

---

[1] I have already said all that needs saying on this point in *Das Ressentiment im Aufbau der Moralen*, op. cit., and also in 'Probleme der Religion' in my *Vom Ewigen im Menschen* (1921).

Chapter VII

THE INTERACTION
OF THE SYMPATHETIC FUNCTIONS

Identification, vicarious feeling, fellow-feeling, benevolence and non-cosmic personal love

W<small>E</small> have been seeking to acquire a knowledge of the powers which make up that spirit of participation, intrinsic to all emotional acts and functions of an intentional or evaluative kind. We have attempted to assess them in all their variety of metaphysical significance; and we have depicted those doctrines of life and conduct wherein the *a priori* normative scheme of such powers has been realized historically, in a diversity of ages and climes, through large-scale movements, exhibiting a one-sided emphasis on one or another of its many and various aspects.[1] Our newly-won familiarity with the laws of dependence among these powers now enables us to erect upon this order of value-precedence an *ideal*, though not an obligatory, normative scheme of the 'correct' *ordo amoris*. Such a scheme is of particular importance for ethics and for education in all its forms—though only for the cultivation of the emotional life, of course. We proceed to offer a few observations on this subject.

(1) If man is to achieve the full realization of his ideal capacities, his various emotional powers must *all* be cultivated, and not just one or another of them. The reason for this has already been given, namely the strict order of dependence which obtains between emotional acts and functions. There can be no full

[1] For an account of the relationship between the conceptual genesis of a view of life, and the description of its course in history (also applied to ethical and æsthetic doctrines), cf. my essay 'Weltanschauungslehre, Soziologie und Weltanschauungssetzung' (1921) in *Moralia*, in the series 'Zur Soziologie und Weltanschauungslehre (Leipzig, 1923).

development of the higher, though necessarily rarer, emotional powers in man, where the lower but more common ones have not been fully cultivated. The sense of unity with the living universe, so excessively predominant among the Indians and the Greeks, may be lost in an individual or an entire cultural epoch; it may be thought to be no authentic source for metaphysical knowledge of those aspects of the subsistent universe which can only be grasped in this way; more commonly still, it may be held that its cognitive significance and value have been superseded by science, or Christianity, or humanism; but the effect is to cut away the ultimate roots upon which all the 'higher' forms of sympathetic and emotional life depend for their subsistence. It goes without saying that natural science must deliberately 'shut off' this animistic feeling, and avert its eyes from the objective data it presents. But the grounds for this are not that identification is illegitimate as a source of cognitive entry into the being and becoming of Nature, but that one of the *principles of selection* whereby the organic and inorganic sciences choose their original data, is the furtherance of a technical aim. They endeavour to obtain a symbolic picture of Nature, which is not only true (in conformity with the facts), and definitive, but also makes her *tractable* and susceptible to control.[1] Despite this necessary but *artificial* attitude on the part of science, the fullness of Nature in its phenomenological aspect still presents a vast number of fields in which the life of the cosmos may find expression; fields wherein all appearances have an *intelligible coherence* which is other and more than mechanical, and which, once disclosed by means of the universal mime, pantomime and grammar of expression, is found to mirror the stirrings of universal life within. This emotional conception of Nature continues to exist along with that of science; *each does so in its own right*, and the task of bringing them into unity is proper only to philosophic metaphysics. It is not those who respect the animistic feeling as an authentic means of participating in things, who deserve to be called childish or primitive: it is those who, 'childishly' misconceiving the limitations both of animistic identification and of science, would set them in opposition to one another. In point of fact, the scientific point of view does actually depend on the animistic one to this extent, that without the positive 'meaning' and 'value' which Nature *only* manifests when we identify with her, she would simply not be 'worth' mastering; so that the very attempt to conceive Nature as formally and mechanically adapted for our subjection would itself become *meaningless*. I have elsewhere confirmed by examples how

---

[1] [Cf. 'Lehre von den drei Tatsachen' (1911), in *Nachlassband*, I.]

the scientific pioneering of a new field begins historically in a mood of identification with it, so that the enthusiastic 'amateur' must always necessarily precede the 'expert'.[1]

As a matter of principle, we must therefore rid ourselves henceforward of our one-sided conception of Nature as a mere instrument of human domination; historically a legacy of Judaism, it has defied the assaults of early Christianity, the Franciscan movement, Goethe, Fechner, Bergson and the romantic philosophy of Nature, to gain ever-increasing acceptance as a virtual axiom of the Western point of view, and has finally led, amongst other things, to the setting up of a materialistic and mechanical conception of Nature as an absolute principle. Like Goethe, Novalis and Schopenhauer, we must learn once more 'to look upon Nature as into the heart of a friend'[2] and to limit the scientific picture of her as a formal mechanism, indispensable as it is for technology and industry, to the 'artificial' specialist attitude of the physicist, chemist, etc. The *cultivation* of human nature (which includes the emotional side), must set itself against this 'scientific experts'' view of Nature as an enemy to be overcome.[3] Hence the first task of our educational practice must be to revive the capacity for identification with the life of the universe, and awaken it anew from its condition of dormancy in the capitalistic social outlook of Western man (with its characteristic picture of the world as an aggregation of movable quantities). We must dissociate ourselves, firmly and unreservedly, from the gross error of regarding the sense of unity with the universe as merely an 'empathic' projection of specifically human emotions into animals, plants, or inanimate objects—as sheer anthropomorphism, therefore, and a fundamental misapprehension of the real. On the contrary, it is man the microcosm, an actual embodiment of the reality of existence in *all* its forms, who is himself *cosmomorphic*, and as such the possessor of sources of *insight* into all that is comprised in the nature of the cosmos.[4] Apart from the prototypes we possess in those fluctuations of feeling in the Western world to which frequent reference has already been made, our greatest need at present is to bring about a long-term reciprocal *adjustment* between the Western ethos and that of Asia, and especially India; so that eventually Asia should learn to cultivate the western ideals of *humanitas* and the non-cosmic love of persons in God, while we

[1] Cf. 'Vom Wesen der Philosophie', in *Vom Ewigen im Menschen* and 'Liebe und Erkenntnis' (1917) in *Moralia*, Leipzig, 1923.

[2] [Goethe: *Faust*, I, line 3220.—Tr.]

[3] [Cf. *Bildung und Wissen* (1925), Frankfurt, 1947.]

[4] [Cf. *Die Stellung des Menschen im Kosmos* (1927) 3rd ed., Munich, 1947.]

of the West should cultivate in ourselves the sense of emotional identity with the living universe.[1]

Failing this sense of unity between mankind and the natural universe, man finds himself cast off from Nature, his eternal mother, in a manner which is essentially repugnant to his nature. Such an ethos would seem to enjoin love and forbearance towards plants and animals only in so far as a display of harshness or cruelty towards them might ultimately vent itself upon other men as well. There would then be no ascription of *intrinsic* value to a love of plants, based on a sense of unity with their springing life, or to a love of animals based on identification with their lives and association with their feelings. It is not surprising, therefore, that such an exclusive 'love of humanity', divorced from all sense of kinship with the universe, should find expression in an arbitrarily destructive attitude towards the whole of organic Nature; as has been exhibited in the industrialism of the capitalist era, particularly in its hey-day, when the havoc and destruction visited upon natural resources has been such as to scandalize all who were acquainted with it. Nor is it surprising that the good things in life (including even the human ones) are no longer rated superior to the achievement of a maximum of production and profit (the creation of the largest possible quantity of commodities and amenities). There is equally little recognition of the positive value, lower indeed, not higher, but none the less *fundamentally* necessary, which life and its attributes possess in relation to cultural values of a spiritual kind.[2] For there is ultimately *one* life only, and *one* vital value which comprehends all things living. From the nature of the case it necessarily follows that a decline in the sense of cosmic unity must eventually be detrimental to love of humanity and to the sense of human brotherhood, so far at least as they relate to man's *organic* well-being and the welfare of particular organic groups and communities among men, especially the family. But the ideal of dominating Nature, and the 'science' which serves that ideal, themselves become meaningless when their application in industry and technology is no longer referred back to *man*, and man indeed simply and solely as a *living creature*, for its ultimate justification. Only the promotion of works of cultural value, the cultivation of human personality, and the practice of holiness and religion, can claim an intrinsic right to make use of man as a living creature, and to flourish at his expense. The promotion of utility and amenity can never make

[1] [Cf. the essay 'Der Mensch im Zeitalter des Ausgleichs' (1927) in *Philosophische Anschauung*, Bonn, 1929.]

[2] Cf. the chapter 'Höhere und niedrigere Werte' in *Der Formalismus in der Ethik*, p. 84 seq.

any such claim upon him. For they are in fact subordinate to the values of human life. Fearful, therefore, in its iron rigour, is the chain of thought which has prevailed throughout the period of historical decline in the West since the end of the age of humanism; an age whose conception of humanity was itself but a belated afterglow of the epoch of emotional community with the living cosmos and an organic outlook upon the world. Inevitably, it has been the women and children, and of these especially the most feminine and most child-like, who have had most to bear under the steam-roller progress of utilitarian civilization; for it is they who preserve the closest emotional ties between 'homo sapiens' and Nature. Children do not exist simply in order to become adults, for childhood has an irreplaceable value *of its own*. The child, moreover, is father to the man. Nor do women exist to subserve an entirely masculine conception of civilization, as servants and handmaidens for the chosen pursuits of the masculine mind, with its excessive regard for the accumulation of worldly goods. Their existence possesses an intrinsic value of its own, namely the power of identification, by virtue of their innate maternal instinct, which is far more part of their nature than their purely biological function; and it is this which endows all women, *ceteris paribus*, with a natural 'right' to children. It is only as a creative artist or in the service of religion (as a 'nun' in the widest sense of the word), that a woman can or should 'freely' renounce that natural right; not under the pressure of merely economic considerations or the so-called 'claims' of utilitarian civilization and 'progress'.

Life and all its values may and should indeed be sacrificed none the less, firstly for the sake of a nobler life, and secondly for ends and values of a purely spiritual and religious kind. But such a sacrifice should never be undertaken for utility's sake, nor even for that of 'science', so far as the latter continues to be governed by the principle of an ulterior technical motive. There are 'martyrs' to philosophy, the *gaya scienza*, and martyrs to faith, who deservedly rouse our admiration. Martyrs to 'science', however, are not sublime, but ridiculous.

Wherever the sense of cosmic unity has again come to life, certain practical developments naturally follow, such as the care and protection of animals and plants, anti-vivisection campaigns, the conservation of forests and the preservation of 'beauty-spots' (i.e. particular expressive unities in Nature). And these tendencies are intimately connected with those social and political movements which also seek to bring about a decisive realization in the human sphere of the following *ethical axiom*: that consideration for the *conditions which favour the propagation* of the human race, the organic development of peoples and the maintenance of their vital welfare, that is, the mental and physical health of races and peoples, the preservation of the family, the protection of women and children, and all that pertains thereto shall take *absolute precedence* over all concern for the maximal accumulation of wealth and material goods. The reversal of this scale of values is the product of *ill-feeling towards the weak and helpless* and betrays a corrupted morality.[1]

A decisive factor in cultivating a capacity for identification with the cosmos is that sense of immersion in the total stream of life, which is first aroused and established among *men in respect of their mutual status as individual centres of life*. For it seems to be more or less a rule (of which we have as yet no further understanding) that the actual realization of the capacity for cosmic identification cannot take place directly in relation to external Nature, but is mediated indirectly, in that sense of unity between man and man, whose main varieties we have already described. Man's point of entry into identification with the life of the cosmos lies where that life is nearest and in closest affinity to his own, namely *in another man*. He who has never known the Dionysian ecstasy of emotional union between man and man, it matters not how, will also find the living, dynamic side of Nature, *natura naturans* (as opposed to *natura naturata*, with which science and the symbolic approach to the study of Nature are solely concerned) for ever a closed book to him.

There have been a hundred descriptions of how the recurrent *cycles of youth and age* in human life bring with them a profound modification, a transformation even, in our conception of the world of Nature; but such accounts have hitherto been sadly wanting in precision and accuracy. We have made appreciable

[1] I am glad to have found this idea, which was expounded in detail in my treatise on resentment, set forth with great clarity by the distinguished English philosopher and sociologist Bertrand Russell, who states it in his *Principles of Social Reconstruction*, (1916) in ch. 4, under the title 'Property'. 'I wish to show how the worship of money is both an effect and a cause of diminishing vitality, and how our institutions might be changed so as to make the worship of money grow less and the general vitality grow more. . . . The things of nature are not valued in comparison with money. It is not thought a hardship for a woman to have to accept, as her only experience of love, the prudent and limited attentions of a man whose capacity for emotion has been lost during years of wise restraint or sordid relations with women whom he did not respect. The woman herself does not know that it is a hardship; for she, too, has been taught prudence for fear of a descent in the social scale, and from early youth she has had it instilled into her that strong feeling does not become a young woman. So the two unite to slip through life in ignorance of all that is worth knowing. Their ancestors were not restrained from passion by the fear of hell-fire, but they are restrained effectually by a worse fear, the fear of coming down in the world' (pp. 112–14).

progress towards a phenomenology of the child's mind and his picture of the world, but much less has been done on the phenomenology of adolescence, and almost nothing of a serious kind on the phenomenology of maturity or old age.

Already in puberty there begins a change of outlook towards nature, which might be described as a sudden *vivifying* of natural phenomena, such that they acquire a new and intensely expressive character. Nature itself seems to respond to the formless and chaotic longing which now begins to stir, in devious ways, within the child. Nature seems as though filled with a thousand dynamic powers, evoking now a fear unknown before, now an equally strange and new-seeming delight. The theory of projective empathy offers us no assistance here, any more than in understanding the prehistoric animism of primitive man. It is not just a new experience of Nature, but the experience of a *new Nature*. It is the aspect of *dynamic* process in Nature, its becoming, growth and development, rather than its static completeness in space and time, which now emerges fully for the first time. A whole period may bear such an impress, the early Renaissance for instance, which Werner Sombart, in a charming though far from adequate sketch of its love-life, has aptly described as the 'adolescent age' of sexual love in the post-mediæval West.[1] This aspect of things is very closely connected, in the period in question, with the germination of that new feeling for Nature which Jakob Burckhardt has so shrewdly depicted in his *Culture of the Renaissance*. It is also tied up indirectly with the emergence of the new natural philosophy in Nicholas of Cusa, Giordano Bruno, Campanella, Vico and Telesio. But adolescence betokens a preparation for that emotional identity of human beings in the unity of universal life, whose natural aim and end in the biological order of development is their *loving union in the sexual act*; this being the only case of *mutual* fusion into universal life which we have so far been able to identify as normal to human beings. And here we stand, in fact, at the gateway to *every* kind of emotional fusion with and into the cosmos itself.

There may be those who, whether from foolish prudery or for other reasons, are unwilling to recognize that, for the civilized man, the loving sexual act discloses, not knowledge indeed, but a source of possible knowledge, and metaphysical knowledge at that, which he can otherwise obtain only very imperfectly (e.g. in mass-emotion), or not at all. But to shut one's eyes in this fashion, to the fact that such experiences provide the natural key

[1] Here, as always, in dealing with periods, it is the 'younger generation' (a vitalist concept) which exhibits the new style of feeling. Cf. Werner Sombart: *Luxus und Kapitalismus*.

to the sense of cosmic unity in *all* its forms, is to treat the question with less seriousness than it deserves. Despite his gross error in assimilating the life-force to a 'blind will', Schopenhauer's 'Metaphysics of sexual love' is certainly right on this point, if on no other, that the 'focal point' (as he happily describes it) of the life-force in man as in everything else lies, not in the sexual instinct, which is merely the way *Eros* operates among creatures of opposite sex, but in *Eros* itself. It does *not* lie in appetite or hunger and thirst, as Marx supposed, nor is it to be found, as Nietzsche fancied, in the urge to mastery and power.

What we have now to say is this: *we must restore the idea of the sexual act to that true metaphysical significance*, which has been denied to it only during a single brief period in the history of the West, despite a unanimous chorus of acknowledgment everywhere else among civilized mankind. This significance and meaning attaches to it quite apart from the delectable joys by which it is accompanied in consciousness; it is equally remote from the consummation of the objective biological purpose of procreation, and still more so from any subjective design for the propagation, preservation, increase or betterment of mankind. We regard the *metaphysical degradation of the sexual act* as a principle essentially fatal to the correct governance of sexual relationships and to the enlargement and improvement of population in the Western world of modern times: it is the prime source of every error and aberration in matters of this kind. It arises from a dilemma first broached in the teleological ethics of early Judaism, from which, unfortunately, no single denomination of historical Christianity, ecclesiastical or otherwise, has succeeded in freeing itself, and which the development of the bourgeois institutions of marriage and prostitution has altogether precluded from further review. The old Jewish dilemma runs as follows: The essence of the act of mating lies in its *end*, and this must be either procreation *or* sensual pleasure. Now to start with, the 'essence' of a thing never lies in its 'end'. The essence of punishment, for instance, is retribution, and this has nothing to do with the ends which punishment may be *applied* in order to achieve, such as deterrence, reform, or the protection and security of society. This is already enough to expose the falsity of the foregoing theory. Moreover the act of mating, as such, cannot possibly be included under purposive action, so-called, for it represents an *expressive act* which does not differ essentially from the many other expressions of love and affection, such as kissing, caressing, etc. In animals it is still essentially a matter of instinct, resulting automatically in the presence of specific sets of stimuli, and bound, by the periodic cycle of the mating-season, to the rhythm of the changing year.

Nor has the act of mating become voluntary in man—an intrinsically impossible feat; it is merely an act whose inception can be permitted or restrained at will. This accounts for the well-known fact that any attempt to make the act intentional and deliberate, or even to concentrate attention on the movements involved, has the effect of inhibiting its onset, by robbing it of the psychic energy it requires. Although the natural rhythm has largely subsided in man it has not been silenced altogether, as is borne out by the work of Fliess, Swoboda and others on the vital rhythms. Women especially, in view of their menstrual period and the fact that their whole being is more deeply linked with the course of Nature, remain more firmly in bondage to her rhythms than do men, with their greater deliberation, awareness and alienation from Nature.

That the sexual act in man should also be of this kind is naturally not upset by the fact that the inherently instinctive and automatic expression of this may itself figure *as a whole* in the service of ends chosen by him in his cognitive and conative capacity. Such automatic expressive movements may likewise be employed by the actor, for instance, for the purpose of artistic effect. Pleasure and procreation *may* also be aimed at, but there is no ethical reason why they should be. Pleasure should not be the primary aim, and it is only as a by-product of love-making, not as a goal and object, that it attains a depth and power of passion sufficient to produce a genuine fusion and identity of feeling. If the pleasure pursued is entirely self-centred, the phenomenon of fusion and identification is invariably absent. The partner then becomes simply a means of auto-erotic satisfaction. There is equally little justification for treating procreation as the object; for one thing, because it is doubly immoral in this sphere to employ another human being as a means to an end. And for another, because the *objective and natural goal* of the sexual act (not its purpose) is by nature not the sort of undertaking which can be subject to choice. Moreover, this natural goal will be attained to better effect the more the love-guided choice of a partner is a fulfilment, *ceteris paribus*, of the mating tendency itself, so that such love simply finds itself directly *expressed* in the act; but this implies a corresponding disregard of procreation as the subjectively intended aim. In this the sexual act conforms to the general rule whereby all expressive movements, of an automatic no less than of an instinctive kind, are not advanced, but rather distracted and diverted, by the subjective intervention of the will, and even by attentiveness, from the attainment of their objective and natural goal. But the decisive argument is the one already alluded to: that to think of human procreation as a deliberate object of the will is an utter *contradiction*. Firstly, because neither conception nor gestation are matters over which man has any positive power of choice. It is only the possible *frustration* of these natural processes which is subject to consciousness and will. Secondly, because even from the physical point of view man is not an integral product of his parentage. For, apart from the merits and defects acquired by direct or indirect inheritance, which are ultimately attributable to the *whole* of his ancestry, man, like other organisms, owes his existence, in an ultimate and metaphysical sense, to a *creative act of universal life*; an act for whose occurrence the business of pro-creation and all its attendant processes are merely the physical occasioning causes. The idea of an organism as an aggregation of cells has again led to serious error here. Each man is, even in a physical sense, an entirely *new* and original individual, and it is only from a statistical point of view in respect of the material substance of his body that he exhibits the same organs and pro-cesses as other men do. The hen really *does* come before the egg—the whole before the part. Every product of universal life is a *fresh* creation, its procreation through the sexes being no more than one of Nature's techniques; it is a creation of Eros, the life-giving, body-building principle which animates all life everywhere; and it owes nothing whatever to human volition, or even to human agency. Children remain always a *gift* of the mighty natural forces incarnate in Eros, an offspring of his sublime, joyous and dæmonic sport. But after all that has been said, we may certainly take it that a mutual merging in emotion into the common medium and background of universal life is nothing less than a true and com-plete counterpart, in consciousness, of that ontological act whereby a new corporeal individual clambers up out of the metaphysical depths of life.

Parenthood *partakes*, therefore, in a mysterious and instinctive way, of this primordial creative tendency in all life, now shortly to manifest itself on the physical terrestrial plane by the produc-tion of a new creature in and through the act of mating. This participation comes to conscious awareness in the *feeling* of fusion and identity, the phenomenon of sinking together into union with the eternal Mother of all things living and into her imperial darkness. Emotionally absorbed in one another, the pair are equally in conspiracy of feeling with universal life itself, and it is this which makes for the creation of new being between them.

And now, what is this *love* between the sexes, which attracts them one to another and finds its ultimate expression in the sexual act? Certainly it is not what Schopenhauer thought it, an emotion whereby the 'spirit of the race' lashes men on to the dark and doubtful labour of propagating their kind.[1] For what would the mere preservation of the species amount to without its advancement or ennoblement? And what need of love, as distinct from mere impulse, if it is simply to ensure the upkeep of the breed? The selfish pleasure-seeking of the voluptuary, the most loveless couplings of the bourgeoisie, mindful, even in the marriage-bed, of an heir to family, fortune or estate, a new steward for the administration of old possessions, are no less effective in preserving the race; though even the voluptuary, human at least in his quest for pleasure, does not so wantonly overthrow the lowest standards of human decency. Such acts 'preserve' the species as human fodder for business, industry, war and the like. But they merely *reproduce*, whereas love *creates*. For love is simply an emotional assessment of a value, anticipated as offering the likeliest chance for the qualitative *betterment* of mankind. It is a sort of emotional project for man as he might be—a better creature than those who have preceded him; already a visionary moment of contact with the Eros of universal life itself, in its eternal travail and endeavour to bring forth that which is new and better and fairer than what has gone before.

The movement of love is always and everywhere towards the *creation* of values, not their reproduction; and so it is also when its business is with the making of men, the agents and vessels of history. Even where the issue is barren—for such various reasons as death, sickness, or the malfunctioning of those physical mechanisms which govern the conception and gestation of the child, it has at least been a beautiful and noble *effort* towards the bettering of man as a vital being.

Love as such, as a pure function, never errs and is never deceived, so long as man does not deceive himself as to its presence, its genuineness, or concerning its object. Nor does it err or deceive itself even in those cases referred to in Georg Simmel's profound but very one-sided *Fragmente über die Liebe*,[2] where it seeks existence only for its own sake, as 'pure feeling', and seems merely to make artful use of biological sex-differences and the automatic tensions which result therefrom, in order to engender itself and to irradiate the soul. For here it enters only into an earth-bound relationship, a union, for instance, in which the racial energies are in decline, and for this very reason it is constrained to sterility. For love as such seeks to produce a 'nobler race', and this being impossible here, its very providence will at least hinder and restrain such men from mere reproduction of their kind and from

---

[1] Cf. Schopenhauer: *Metaphysics of Sexual Love* [cf. also Max Scheler: *Über Scham und Schamgefühl* (1913) in *Nachlassband*, I].

[2] Cf. Georg Simmel: *Lebensanschauung: vier metaphysische Kapitel*, Munich, 1918.

handing on their hereditary taint still further to a distant posterity. But we must not follow Simmel in treating this 'negative instance' as a norm; it is only a border-line case of love, to be taken instead as the marginal *exception*, which does but prove our rule. Simmel supposes that love resembles justice and the arts, which first sprang entirely from vital needs and motives, and continued to serve these purposes (in an objective sense) for centuries, only for a 'reversal' to take place in which life and its energies came, in their turn, to subserve these spiritual values for their own sake. So love-making also, even to the kiss and the sexual act, is supposed to have originated in the course of evolution for the objective purpose of procreation, but thereafter to have emancipated itself into an independent value which now commands life to *its* service. But such a notion is too simple and too ingenious to be true as well. The converse theory has also been put forward by believers in a 'rationalization' of the will to propagate, for instance, by H. Grotjahn.[1] But such analogies—Simmel's deeper one, no less than the more superficial ideas of Grotjahn, have no real justification. Against Simmel it must be said that in the last phase of his 'philosophy of life' (approached by way of Bergson), he completely misconceived the primordial nature of *spirit*, and the objects, meanings and values appropriate to it. Nor, indeed, is it correct to maintain, as Simmel does, that pure art, pure knowledge (i.e. philosophical, rather than positive scientific knowledge), justice, ethical norms of a more general kind and even the disposition of the individual, were ever developed out of 'life', or were originally fostered and cultivated in the service of organic drives and needs. The original confines of the development of the spirit, its limited apprehension of meaning and value, may well have been progressively enlarged, in the course of human evolution, by the effect of organic drives and wants in giving direction to its aspirations; but the activity of the spirit has everywhere and at all times followed its *own original laws*, and its objects of meaning and value have always been sublimely *elevated* above all that relates to life as such. Sexual love, on the other hand, even in its purest and noblest aspects, is fundamentally and inescapably a part of man's *vital* constitution, within and without, even though friendship and metaphysical love of the person as individual may at times be combined with it. As a function of the vital soul, therefore, sexual love can never acquire a more-than-vital value, to which the whole of life could or should be subordinated. Even in its highest conceivable form, it can be no more than the finest flowering, the absolute *climax*, summit and peak of man's career

[1] [Cf. Max Scheler: 'Bevölkerungsprobleme als Weltanschauungsfragen' (1921) in *Schriften zur Sociologie und Weltanschauungslehre*, Vol. III.]

as a vital being. But even this is enough to provide a quite definite refutation of the very bourgeois opinion that sexual love should be 'enlisted' in the service of practical life, society, the state (war), the nation, commercial life even, and I know not what else—as is assumed with amazing naïveté by most nationalist exponents of a mass-population policy. It is also enough to dispose of the proposition that sexual love should be employed subjectively, in the interests of propagation (as an inducement to the highly unimportant occupation of merely turning out men of the same value as before), or that it should simply be thought of as objectively engaged in such a task of *propagation*. For even though true sexual love be no more than the finest flowering and the climax of the *vital* life, it cannot on that account be sacrificed to the fact that the mere bringing of a larger *number* of human beings into the world is possible through acts of intercourse and procreation in which it plays *no* part. The qualitative peak of organic life cannot be subordinated to the mere quantitative multiplication of human lives. Nor should love, at its best the supreme phenomenon of life, be sacrificed to power, honour, interest or gain (nor the comforts of love to 'health' or 'social welfare'), any more than it should be dedicated to merely increasing the population. Rather than allow that this love exists simply for the sake of reproduction, we should proclaim it already entailed in the vital meaning and value of reproduction itself, that as many human beings as possible should discover the crowning-point of their lives in the experience of sexual love.

Mere reproduction, as a steady turning-out of human replicas, cannot therefore be the natural end of true sexual love, for the elementary and completely unselective operation of the sexual and procreative instincts would be perfectly adequate for this purpose. Sexual love, however, is no *mixtum compositum* of sexual instinct, spiritual friendship, respect and other spiritual attitudes of emotional approbation; it is a simple, *unanalysable and genuinely vital form of love*, orientated upon the human type which represents for each member the individualized norm of the race, the appropriate racial ideal. It is the cardinal error of the naturalistic and sensualist philosophy of Schopenhauer and Freud, to which Simmel himself was quite right in objecting, that they see in sexual love only a secondary phenomenon, an airy and fanciful *superstructure* reared by repression upon the massive foundation of the sexual impulse. They recognize it, not as a *primary* emotional function of the vital soul, able to discriminate and select among values, but merely as a product of the inhibition of impulse, and a spiritual elaboration of these inhibitions. And on this very point we find a strange alliance between this 'cynical' philosophy and the old misguided priestly morality, which likewise endeavours to depreciate love, as far as possible, to a mere gratification of impulse and libidinous pleasure-seeking. This is partly due to professional jealousy, disparaging what it has had to forego, partly to anxiety lest the mere business of reproduction should be interfered with (the question of numbers being of especial concern to priests, with a view to the power and expansion of their Church), partly to the nobler and deeper motive of avoiding a *clash* between sacred and profane love, a considerable danger, indeed, and notably in the highest forms of sexual love. For the likelihood of such a clash is naturally the smaller, the lower the level of feeling at which the erotic relationship is maintained. No one would allow his relationship to God and his personal contact with Him to be clouded or suppressed on account of a woman he has degraded to being a means either of enjoyment or the getting of an heir; but in a great love (an *amour-passion*) the dangers of such a lapse are threatening indeed.

Moreover, this naturalistic conception of sexual love is far more deeply embroiled with that historic sentiment of *Romantic Love*, to which it seems totally alien, than the protagonists of either side appear to realize. For romantic love is no less lacking in the true *amour-passion*; it is no more than a tardy rationalization of the fluctuating tides of impulse and of a libido without natural restraints. Instead of these being immediately concentrated on a *single* object by means of genuine sexual *love*, they are capriciously pushed and pulled hither and thither by *cerebral* activity, in conjunction with cultural, artistic and intellectual endeavours associated with the company of the other sex. Fundamentally, the 'romantic' lover is no more than a sort of 'amorous friend'. Hence he invariably lacks the elemental force and directness of the true passion of love. His attachments never have that instinctive, all-excluding quality which true love evokes. He always has a number of 'affairs' which are carried on with a peculiar mixture of intellect and sensuality, passing into those 'moments of bliss', of which our romantics have so much to tell us, and whose value they so grossly overestimate. Besides, love comes to the romantic only in the form of *yearning*, so that its consummation in the sexual act—if this is not avoided from the outset—does not satisfy and increase his love, but usually dissolves and dissipates it. Thus 'remoteness', as a means of facilitating voluptuous *longing*, is very often an almost essential ingredient in romantic love. Now the Schopenhauer-Freud theory of repression and sublimation provides a very good empirical explanation for this romantic *pseudo-love*; but not for purely sexual love, which has no more to do with 'sublimated libido' than appetite has with 'sublimated hunger'.

Simmel also succumbs to this false romantic conception of sexual love, so akin to the cynical view of the naturalist and to the ideas of the average priest. That love should exist for its own sake, simply as an emotion, and that life should be dedicated to *its* service, is a notion we meet with in almost all romantics.[1] It presupposes a sensualizing of the spirit and a spiritualizing of the sensual which are both equally false. It is at once far too soulful *and* far too cynical. It makes love, and even the awareness of love (i.e. that *brooding* upon love which is confounded with the thing itself), into a sort of 'art for art's sake'. True sexual love on the other hand is a *creative life-force*, the nobility of life eternally blazing the trail upwards and outwards from its present level towards a higher form of existence—a teleology in the real, not the imputed sense of the term. It prefigures, for those who feel it, the best combination of hereditary traits open to them, not in the shape of an 'idea' or 'concept', but as an instinctive preference. Plato and Nietzsche have therefore shown much greater insight on this point than Schopenhauer, Freud, Simmel and the ideologists of romantic love. Plato calls Eros a 'generation'—but a 'generation in beauty'[2]—and sees in the sexual urge only a technical arrangement on the part of nature to make this 'generation in beauty' possible. Hence he does not regard Eros as an outcome or consequence, a repression or sublimation of the sexual urge. For Plato it is the *world-soul* itself, giving life and soul to the 'blessed animal' of the entire cosmos, that is the 'creative Eros' at the heart of things; through human love, its messenger, permeating the souls of lovers to bring the new being to birth. Nietzsche, moreover, declares in *Zarathustra* that the 'garden of marriage' should serve, not to multiply, but to better the strain, and calls for a new sense of responsibility in deciding 'Art thou a man who may and should wish for himself a son?'

Now Simmel ranks sexual love far too high upon those planes of being of which man is composed, and thereby overestimates its value as well, comparing it with ends-in-themselves which are *more-than*-vital, such as art, pure knowledge and justice. Hence he is obliged to repudiate the moral demand that sexual love should be sacrificed in order to realize these values. But at the same time he places these spiritual values far too low—to begin with, at least —in that he derives them, or the acts corresponding to them, from 'life', so that by his arbitrarily assumed 'inversion' he may subsequently turn them into autonomous and intelligible spheres of culture. The result is that sexual love and these spiritual values

---

[1] Cf. Paul Kluckhohn: *Das Problem der Liebe im 18. Jahrhundert und in der deutschen Romantik*, Halle Niemeyer, 1922.

[2] [*Symposium*, 206.—Tr.]

come to rest on the *same* plane, whence it follows accordingly that the 'Art for art's sake' view of love appears to be justified. Simmel is the complete romantic at this point and is also thinking as such, endowing the spirit with a spurious vitalism, and the truly vital with an equally fictitious spirituality. Hence he inevitably misjudges the point at which *sacrifice* becomes justifiable and necessary, and which vindicates renunciation and asceticism even in regard to sexual love (this being unquestionably the highest among values pertaining to life on the purely vital plane of feeling). Such sacrifices may be required for personal (religious) salvation on the one hand, or for full development of the powers of the individual spiritual personality on the other. Even the purest and deepest sexual love may and should be 'sacrificed' for the sake of these two supreme *personal* values; but only for these—certainly not for the sake of the mere product- or achievement-value pertaining to acts of spiritual culture, except indeed for the concrete values of religious faith, the protection and preservation of those 'treasured beliefs' to which the person subscribes. Obviously it can never be justified in the interests of 'cultural progress', so-called, nor by the needs or supposed welfare of 'society'; nor for the sake of 'science', which differs from philosophy or wisdom, in being precluded by its very nature from ever having personal value, and which has a bearing upon (personal) culture only in being one means, among others, of achieving it.[1] But to renounce true love for the sake of God is a still finer and more glorious sacrifice—if it can cheerfully be made—than that of honour itself. But such a sacrifice is genuine only if made in the spirit: 'Beloved, you are the dearest thing in life to me, but Thou, God, art dearer still.' By contrast the cynical or clerical depreciation of sexual love, whatever its motive, no less than the modern bourgeois custom of bartering it for the sake of wealth, advancement, health, national well-being, science, the continuance of a business, mere achievement of any sort, political power, even the maintenance of a royal dynasty, are utterly and completely damnable. For man's betterment of his own capacities can only be given positive effect through love, the appointed agency, as it were, of God and Nature, whose work is independent of and *prior* to all the intrinsically *negative* constraints of a eugenic policy imposed by custom or legal enactment. And such betterment is a far more *central* concern, and far higher in the scale of value than all these other fine and desirable things.[2] However, the sacrifice of love *can* also be made in order to develop the spiritual potentialities latent in

[1] [Cf. Max Scheler: *Bildung und Wissen* (1925), Frankfurt, 1947.]
[2] Cf. the excellent treatment by Bertrand Russell, op. cit., ch. VI, with which I am in complete agreement.

personality, as Goethe made it in the case of Frederike von Sesenheim; but only so if such love is itself an important factor in *setting off* the development in question.

Simmel may be wide of the mark here, but Grotjahn goes still further astray in alleging it to be everywhere evident that the organs, functions, actions and reactions originally appropriated entirely to organic existence (such as mouth, ear and eye; eating, hearing, seeing and locomotion), have been released from their duties under civilized conditions. Whence it follows that the sexual organs and the sexual act can and must resign their office of assisting procreation to become available, at choice, *either* in the interests of the will to procreate *or* for purposes of pleasure. These analogies are misleading. In the first place, there is no such psychic entity as that referred to by many recent demographers as 'the will to procreate'. There is, indeed, a procreative *instinct*, and the *avoidance* of procreation is a positive act of will. Besides this, it does also make sense to speak of a 'wish' for children, though this can neither be a 'will' nor is it ever an 'instinct'. But it is quite misleading, both psychologically and theoretically, to postulate both a positive *and* a negative will to procreate, between which there is supposed to be some sort of 'choice'. For to 'will' without awareness of capacity is a psychological impossibility; where there is *no awareness of capacity*, 'trying' becomes just 'wishing', and is thus frivolous, belonging only to the domain of volitional fantasy. But it is obvious that procreation is *not* under voluntary control. The 'willing' of the sexual act occurs only in the impotent, for it is an *expressive* act, not a purposive one. The willing involved is, at best, *negative*, namely in enforcing continence. Hence any attempt to 'rationalize' it here is essentially negative and never positive. Grotjahn, moreover, adopts the pernicious alternative propounded by the old Judaic sexual morality, and accepts the possibility of choosing between the ends of procreation and pleasure; but, strictly speaking, there can be no such rationalization in the 'positive' case. Grotjahn's analogies lead him even farther astray. Certainly, we eat not merely because we are hungry, but also because the food is agreeable. But here Grotjahn proceeds to overlook the fact of *appetite*. If we have no appetite at all, or are subject to nausea, even those foods that are objectively 'nicest' and 'best' have no appeal for us. We also need appetite if we are to go on eating even after we have had enough, and are no longer hungry. Conversely, even in extreme hunger, we cannot eat if we are at the same time *nauseated* by the food, for in the spasm of revulsion we choke upon the morsel and spew it out, before it can appease the pangs of hunger in the stomach and thereby satisfy us. Now on the other side, the place of appetite is taken by the automatic impulse (however rudimentary), of sexual *sympathy*. Without it, or where revulsion is present, it is likewise impossible to satisfy the sexual impulse, even though the sexual 'hunger' may be the strongest imaginable. 'Appetites' may be taken to denote those polar emotional functions which are discriminative of value, in contrast to the blind forces of instinct which only. vary in degree. Even so the appetites stand quite apart from the exercise or inhibition of will. The purely wilful consumption of food, simply on account of its pleasantness, is therefore a complete invention on Grotjahn's part; if appetite is present, then even food eaten from relish and not from hunger will nevertheless be digested and assimilated. The only analogy to deliberate abstention ('prohibition') would be to take the food, savour it on the tongue, and then spit it out again. But as against this, even the strictest anti-prohibitionists do not forbid us to take notice of the pleasantness of the sexual act—as well deny us the enjoyment of the food we eat. Hence these analogies completely break down. This is not to pass any sort of judgement on the 'prohibition' question itself. We merely repudiate this attempt to give it a philosophical justification.

Man, even on his physical side, is not just an integral product of his parentage, nor yet the mere (potential) sum-total of his whole ancestry, but represents in every case a *new and original manifestation* of universal life itself; and his *spiritual personality* is assuredly even less of an 'artefact'. This has to be conceded, whether, with Thomas Aquinas, we locate the individuation and singularity of persons in a *prima materia*; with Averroes and the pantheists (Spinoza, Fichte, Hegel, Hartmann), in the body; with Kant, in the empirical content of conscious thoughts and experiences; with Schelling, in a free act of divine creation; or with Schopenhauer, in a free act of self-creation on the part of an already determinate 'intelligible character'. The procreative act remains throughout a mere occasioning cause, whose result is the real union of a spiritual subject with the nascent individual body. Only pure materialism can suppose that a man's mentality also is nothing but the outcome of his parentage and of the act in which he was begotten. Pantheism and metaphysical monism, on the other hand, maintain that only the original character of each individual is purely hereditary, the singularity of the con-scious subject being held, in general, to be attributable to the physical constitution which it has to support. Our view, however, is that both materialistism and monistic pantheism are utterly untenable. This already follows from our earlier treatment of the problem of personal individuation. Spiritual love does not exhibit a trace of emotional identification or fusion. Moreover, though our detailed knowledge of the laws of inheritance for mental characteristics is still very scanty, what little we do know on the subject gives us grounds enough for dismissing such theories in any case. For it all goes to show that the heritable mental qualities and capacities are invariably found only at the level of the organic psyche, and not in the purely intellectual sphere.[1] Idiosyncrasies of character are certainly more heritable than powers of intellectual thought and vision. So far as 'talents' are heritable at all, I believe this to be wholly attributable to a disposition favourable to the assimilation and exercise of spiritual activity on the part of that single 'entelechy' in which conscious mind and living organism are merged in one. We have already emphasized, however, that we cannot postulate an absolutely real substantial multiplicity of such entelechies, but only a set of qualitatively determinate functional tendencies on the part of a universal life that is metaphysically one. Our reasons for this emphasis will be set out more precisely elsewhere.

There now remains the important question as to whether we should ascribe an indigenous character, or rather a true *essence* to the person as a purely spiritual entity, or endow it, like Thomas Aquinas, only with *singularitas* (i.e. the nature of an unspecified particularity = X). Since, in dealing with 'spiritual' (i.e. non-spatio-temporal) reality, it is differences of *kind* which furnish the only possible basis for positing distinctions of *existence*, and hence of plurality generally, we are already committed in advance to the first alternative. But quite apart from this ontologico-metaphysical argument there are *phenomenological* grounds for this presumption:

(1) The more deeply we penetrate into a human being, through knowledge and understanding, guided by personal love, the more unmistakable, individual, unique, irreplaceable and indispensable does he become in our mind. The various wrappings which shroud the core of his individual personality fall gradually away. Such are the more or less uniform social 'self', with its common bondage to similar instincts, passions and necessities of life; and the *idola* of language, which conceal the individual nuances of experience from us, in attaching the same signs and words to them all. This also applies to self-knowledge motivated by a genuine self-regard. In other words, a man is the more an individual, *the more he is his inmost personal self*, the more he holds his peace ('When the soul speaks, it is no longer the soul speaking'), and the more he is reduced to his own discarnate self-subsistency.

---

[1] Thus, while talents can be accumulated by inheritance, this is by no means the case with genius. Genetics has itself emphatically recognized the radical dissimilarity between genius and talent, even at its highest. Cf. the interesting observations of A. Mjoens on this point.

(2) Our knowledge of a man (in his nature as a soul), does not proceed by induction from his successive temporal states or by synthesis of the constituent elements of these states. On the contrary, at each stage he appears to us in intention as *a concrete whole* whose internal disposition is initially a mere matter of conjecture on our part. This 'hypothesis' concerning his real character is then tested as to content, varied and corrected, by observation of his successive states and their (real and abstract) constituents. The hypothesis must conform to all this, but we are guided throughout by an a priori '*blue-print*' of the true and essential nature of 'man', such as could also be applied to ourselves; (compare 'the Frenchman', 'the German', 'the shopkeeper', 'the soldier', etc., built up, as they are, from inauthentic material). But as such knowledge increases, so the content of this hypothesis becomes ever more *individual*, ever harder to put into words (*individuum est ineffabile*) —yet at the same time ever more certain. The outward manifestations of particular states, or elements thereof, come, in this way, to have an altogether new bearing upon our insight into a man's personality: *one* such state we attribute merely to 'circumstances', to a momentary 'self-forgetfulness', to an obstruction of his true personality; while in another of his states and the way it is expressed we fancy ourselves to have gained a fleeting glimpse into his true nature. In other words, it seems that the self-same intrinsic character of a man can only be *disclosed* in the succession of his temporal states. Man's spiritual nature is thus revealed in the course of his real temporal development as a psycho-physical organism. We do much the same ourselves, sketching in the particular states of our own self upon a prevailing outline conception of what we are like. Our consciousness of self is not a synthesis, gleaned from memory, of the details of our momentary states. Here too, the *pattern of personality* is apprehended before we grasp the basic contents of the pattern itself. And this pattern becomes ever more distinct and individual with every advance in the process of knowledge.

(3) The more we come to know of men in whom the spiritual element operates freely, unhampered by the needs and necessities of *life*, through having acquired that mastery of life and its demands which is the characteristic mark of genius, the more individual and definite does our picture of such men become.[1] But from this marginal case we must also conclude that the spiritual person, such as it exists in *every* man, is equally individual in itself, and that it is only because it is more deeply hidden through its more laboured mode of activity, and also because of

[1] [Cf. the section on Genius in the essay 'Vorbilder und Führer' (1911–12) in *Nachlassband*, I (1933).]

our lack of interest, or love, that it appears less individual to us, and merely an example of some general type. Hence, as knowledge progresses from the associative level of the soul to the vital, and from thence to the existence of the spiritual person, the impression of individual quality grows, increasing by leaps and bounds as each new level is reached, until full individuality is attained. It is not, therefore, in a man's body, nor in his social relationships, paternal, national or professional, nor in the somatic ties and circumstances which condition our spiritual activity as persons, nor in the successive character of the stream of consciousness, that we shall discover the *principia individuationis* for that quality of spiritual personality which persists the same throughout, being differentiated only by the multiplicity of its instances. We hold, on the contrary, that the ultimate and authentic *principium indivi-duationis* in man (and not in angels only, as St. Thomas supposed), lies in his spiritual soul, (i.e. the real substratum of the core of his personality), whereas his body, his station in society and the successive stream of his development are the factors which first enable us to classify men systematically into types, according to character, and to acquire a relatively general picture of their traits and temperaments. Projected upon the *metaphysical*, or abso-lute plane of human existence, such generalizations are only of a statistical character; the 'type' has a real meaning only at the various levels of relative existence on which man may be taken or considered. It does, on the other hand, have a quite real meaning in the metaphysical field of the inanimate, and in that of the animate universe taken as a whole. Indeed in the inanimate world, it is rather the category of the 'individual' which ceases to have real meaning on the metaphysical plane.[1]

The spiritual substances inherent in persons or their acts are thus the *only* substances having a truly individual essence, and whose existence as separate entities follows directly from their intrinsically individual character. It is from this essence that each spiritual substance acquires its individual 'vocation',[2] though the man in whom it is embodied may well fall short of this to any extent, both in will and deed. He may even fail to fulfil his 'destiny', the manner in which his spiritual substance is adapted to the complex conjunction of his physical, biological and historical environments; and he may fail especially in that supposedly 'free' willing and acting, which is already part of his destined calling.

Now since we must assign to every true essence a place in that

---

[1] Even in physics and chemistry the 'things' of everyday life lose their indi-vidual character.

[2] *Vide Der Formalismus in der Ethik*, p. 508 seq., on the idea of 'individual vocation' [and the chapter on 'Ordo Amoris' (1916–17) in *Nachlassband*, I].

realm of essences, whose personal subject is none other than the personal spirit sustaining the Universe,[1] we may say that the nature and essence of every spiritual soul represents an eternal idea on the part of God. Indeed, in its nature and in the disposition implied thereby, it simply is the content of this divine idea, and in no sense a mere 'reflection' of it. Not in its existence, but in its eternal essence, the soul 'rests' eternally in God.[2]

This eternal idea, alone out of an infinity of other candidates, is brought into *existence* by the 'choice' of God upon one condition only: that it shall remain loyal to the ever-present endeavour of life as a whole to show itself, in all its main aspects, a creative Eros, wherever *opportunity allows* in a world whose life has withered into a fixed and deadening routine, in short, in a 'mechanistic' universe. Thus it is not the human procreative act, but the actuation of one of these ever-present tendencies of *Life as a whole* in all its main aspects which is the primary occasioning cause whereby the cosmic principle exercises its creative 'fiat' in calling just this one spiritual soul among many into existence.[3] Nor does the secondary occasioning cause, which brings the powers of universal life into play and concentrates them upon a single bodily individual, itself proceed from the sexual act; it is due to the workings of true *sexual love*. If there is not a spark of this, in the shape of 'sexual sympathy' (as opposed to repulsion) on the part of at least one of the participants, intercourse is quite impossible. Unlike love, whose significance is metaphysically dæmonic, though not 'spiritual' or 'divine', the sexual *impulse* is intrinsically unselective, subject only to quantitative fluctuations, and merely physical in nature. This impulse, therefore, and its cognates, the parental and propagative instincts, together with their accessory organs, represent merely the technique with which bisexual animals on earth 'happen' to be endowed, and through which the distinctly sexual variety of love is active and does in fact 'happen' to operate—though there is nothing in the latter which necessarily presupposes a differentiation of the sexes. *Eros*, on the other hand, must be regarded as a concerted effort to create, in conjunction, that is, with that universal life with whose metaphysical unity we identify ourselves in the experience of mutual fusion. It should be looked on as the inwardly dynamic aspect of the objective process

[1] Cf. 'Probleme der Religion' in *Vom Ewigen im Menschen*.

[2] It is the monstrous error of historical Platonism and the theory of reincarnation that they construe this pre-existence in essence as one of actual existence; while the fallacious doctrine of a merely posthumous immortality goes wrong in misconceiving the pre-existence of the individual essence, ascribing to every man a 'standardized' soul, deriving its characteristics and values entirely from its fortunes and farings (including hereditary factors), during its career upon earth.

[3] We can only speak of plurality at this stage, not of number or quantity.

of procreation, omnipresent wherever life exists, so long as the procreative aim is to improve the standard and not just to multiply the prevailing type. The governing tendency of life is not growth or nutrition (so far as the latter is not just mechanical accretion it already presupposes growth), nor is it the mere endeavour after increase of power or extension of the environment; the rightful claimant to the title is Eros, the quintessential depth of life itself —the dæmonic element, as it were, that lies within.

It is no longer seriously in question nowadays that the Darwinian attempt to attribute the evolution of species to the survival of those who chance to be fittest, has proved utterly and completely inadequate.[1] Indeed the *metaphysical theory of Mechanism* has been found equally wanting at all points, in psychology as in physics, in sociology no less than throughout the entire biological field. The matter should be *res judicata* by now. And yet this mechanistic metaphysics still dominates all the *naturalistic conceptions of love*, not only in theory, but also in the conduct of social life in the West. For such conceptions begin by giving priority to sexual instinct over sexual love, and that also means placing 'survival' before 'improvement' and granting the individual, even on the vital plane, that primacy over the species which belongs to him only in his spiritual capacity. Virtually all the customs and institutions, and the whole climate of *sexual and erotic life* in the West, show a similar dominance of Mechanism. The reason is that this latter is now no longer merely a theory of a scientific or philosophical kind, in short a sophisticated world-outlook, such as it may well have been in the seventeenth and eighteenth centuries. It is an example of what I call the *relatively normal world-outlook* of a group or a period, i.e. those matters which are taken for granted in thought and feeling, and, having no need of proof, are no longer the subject of serious enquiry. But this mechanistic viewpoint is by no means confined to any particular intellectual group, such as are formed by churches, sects and political parties, or by groupings of a professional, social or class character. For it is the hallmark of *bourgeois man, homo capitalisticus*, who is to be found in all these groups, and preponderates to a greater or lesser extent in each of them. It is the groups of relatively normal outlook, however, who form the basis for all the more sophisticated viewpoints, and even when the latter have become an established tradition, the normal views continue to have at least a practical application, since they not only influence the more sophisticated versions of themselves, but also affect the practice of other groups

---

[1] Cf. Oscar Hertwig's book, *Die Zufallslehre in der Theorie der Entwicklung der Organismen*, and the useful surveys of Hans Driesch: *Science and Philosophy of the Organism*, and Emanuel Ràdl: *History of Biological Theories*, op. cit.

having a different point of view. No wonder, therefore, that in *every* group and denomination, every party and class, the conception of love and the relation of the sexes should be governed throughout by a materialistic metaphysics, despite some natural variations in degree, and despite the fact that the practical political conclusions which have been drawn from it differ according to the various group-interests involved.[1]

It is our earnest hope that we may devote another work to outlining the historical evolution of this 'relatively normal world-outlook' of the capitalist era in its heyday and decline; an outline which would also survey its view of love, and the actual relationship of the sexes, and set forth a programme for a genuine re-shaping of both. That will be the place to examine the *sociological* outcome of the relations between the sexes and in procreation, embodied in such institutions and customs as monogamy, prostitution, free love, etc. These, in the last resort, will turn out historically, in fact and conception, to have been partly the offspring and result of the false and disastrous metaphysics and ethics of these matters which has prevailed throughout the period; and partly a consequence of the dominance and leadership of a human biological type, which can only be understood in terms of racial genetics; whence it is only through similar eugenic measures that it can be superceded, or at least removed from leadership (and not, as socialists imagine, by economic methods, let alone *merely* political ones).

But this supercession can only be accomplished under a condition which is of no practical importance in itself, though necessary if anything is to be done: and that is the adoption of the metaphysical conception which we have here put forward, that man's birth is always a new beginning. For the general spirit which so largely underlies all our institutions and customs at the present time is due, in the last resort, to our subordination of the values of life to those of utility, and to the monstrous delusion that man can 'produce' men at his own will and pleasure (like so many cardboard boxes or machines); in short to our lack of reverence in face of the unfailingly new and unprecedented *miracle* of man's first beginnings in birth. But both forms of the delusion are themselves only ideological beliefs of a human type which is in process of biological *decline*, and knows it, and was itself begotten in the ways of error and perdition.[2]

[1] [Cf. the essay on 'Bevölkerungsprobleme als Weltanschauungsfragen', op. cit.]

[2] In contrast to the previous optimism concerning racial matters, the Conference on Social Biology held in New York in 1922 came round, by a large majority, to the conviction that European man is in the throes of a racial decline for which there is at present no remedy.

Let this be granted: and let it be conceded also that man's sense of unity with the living cosmos is in general so bound up with the sense of union in sexual love that the latter is, as it were, the 'gateway' to the former; for it is not so much the foundation thereof as the means, prescribed by Nature herself, of *arousing* in man a capacity for identification with the cosmos, which is not, in itself, at all dependent upon sexual love. It is easy, then, to see how such a false metaphysical conception of sexual love and human birth would also, in due course, inevitably impair the sense of cosmic unity itself. The ancient and true idea of a Creation has been wasted and whittled down into the notion of a colourless and derivative 'soul-substance' uniformly provided in all men alike, a substance whose entire character is allegedly made up of the traces left upon it by inheritance and environment, and by what it achieves independently through a 'freedom' construed as the liberty of indifferent choice. Corporeal birth and the new-born body are looked upon as the unaided work of the parents in begetting (this being also the doctrine current in almost every church in Christendom), not as a manifestation of life universal, on the occasion of begetting. Again, the qualitative improvement of racial standards is thought to be attainable by a merely quantitative increase in the number of chance variations. It is beliefs like these which have undermined the foundations of our sense of unity with the living cosmos. By the same token, the 'mystical union' between the essence of man's individual personality and the Divine idea of that personality, is replaced by the indeterminate notion of being simply 'made in his Image'. Now this 'mystical union' of ours between the essence of spiritual personality in a man and the 'same' essence recurring in God as His idea of this spiritual soul, in no way implies or encourages pantheism. For we are not postulating a mystical union in the sense of a real fusion, or a subsequent knowledge that finite personality *is* in reality only a mode or function of the Divine Spirit. We are merely indicating a way of grasping the identity of character between the spiritual soul and its idea in God. Nor does this involve the assertion of an identity in essence between man and God, but simply an essential identity of the spiritual soul with the essence of God, *so far, and only so far,* as the essence of this created world (amid the infinite multiplicity of God's ideas) is prefigured in His realm of ideas. The essence of every finite spirit is certainly a genuine *part* of this essence. But the realm of all possible essential kinds of being in God is, and remains, infinitely richer and wider in range than the instances and patterns of being which we are able to recognize in the objects of the created world (together with all the fancies of which our imagination is capable).

In all this the inmost essence of the Divine Person remains totally inaccessible to us. For it does not enter into any of those ideas that are brought into being by the divine intellection and contemplation. And it would be the height of presumption for man even to wish that, merely by virtue of his own spontaneous spiritual activity, he might have, or attain to, mystical union with this essence.

Nevertheless it is this union in essence, under the limitations here prescribed, which assuredly provides the metaphysical foundation for the *possibility of non-cosmic personal love*; and this, in our opinion, is the natural basis of the Christian love of our neighbour. For however 'general' this type of love may be, in the sense that it is extended to *all* men without qualification, it is not confined only to men as such. Still less does it apply only to the terrestial embodiment of the genus *homo*—'of a reasonable soul and human flesh subsisting', for it takes in all finite spiritual persons whatsoever, including those with an immaterial body, or with none at all, if such there be. What is much more important for us, in view of our present lack of acquaintance with spirits of a higher order, is that it is nevertheless directed to the *individual centre of being* in every spiritual person. So far as a man's empirical life is concerned, our own as well as another's, this is always represented by the *ideal of his eternal vocation*. 'Become in fact what you are by virtue of your individual nature': such is the call of non-cosmic personal love to every man, and in its going-out to him it is this image of his particular vocation, and not a standardized pattern of excellence, which is held up before him, as it were, as his own intrinsic ideal. For in the physical order of experience men may all be dispensable, more or less, according to their kind; but in the non-cosmic realm of the metaphysical order they may differ in value, yet are indispensable, one and all.

Hence the non-cosmic love of persons is unlike the general love of humanity or any particular human affection for a specially-constituted group, in that the very idea of its own possibility necessarily demands that *all finite personality should have a spiritual focus in the Divine*: a 'God within God', if by the first we understand the God of pure religion, and by the second, God as the metaphysical principle of the universe, to which universal life itself belongs only as an essential attribute. Without this theistic premiss, the non-cosmic love of persons itself is neither thinkable nor tenable. Naturalism, pantheism in all its forms, an irrational monism like that of Schopenhauer, no less than a monistic postulation of the irrationality of existence (Hartmann), all make such love impossible and are incompatible with its fundamental character. Our *consciousness of a common salvation* is necessarily based upon this metaphysical and ontological unity of conjunction between the individual essences of all spiritual persons in God, despite the separateness of their existence, in consequence of their diversity in essence and sense of vocation. Absolute metaphysical individualism (which is very nearly the position of Leibniz), excludes this consciousness, since it denies our unity in God; metaphysical monism and universalism do likewise, for they impugn the reality of the spiritual person as a metaphysical substance, and with this, its freedom (subject, of course, to its own intrinsic limitations) to realize or repudiate its eternal essence, to follow or fall short of its vocation: and this is to deny it responsibility also. For the individual responsibility of persons stands or falls *along with* their collective responsibility (which they have from the beginning, and cannot spontaneously assume).

Thus among all the forms of sympathy and varieties of love, the sense of vital unity with the cosmos stands, so to speak, at the *opposite pole* to the non-cosmic love of persons, founded upon the love of God. All the other forms lie, as it were, in stages between them. Those who seek to ascend this scale will surely fall if they insist upon taking the second step before they have made the first.

Chapter VIII

THE PHYLOGENETIC ORIGIN
AND EXTENSION OF FELLOW-FEELING

I T has now been shown that fellow-feeling is an ultimate and *original* function of the spirit, whose empirical genesis is in no way due in the first place, to other processes, such as reproduction, imitation, illusion or hallucination, in the life of the individual. This does not *merely* mean that fellow-feeling is 'innate' (in every single human being), but that it is also part of the *constitution* of all emotional beings generally. Moreover, fellow-feeling certainly *is* innate, and in no sense first acquired in individual life; what is inborn, that is, is the more or less marked tendency to avail oneself of this function and to exercise it in practice. I say advisedly, the more or less marked tendency; for there can be no doubt that the considerable *variations* in the exercise of fellow-feeling, among different races, peoples and individuals, are not attributable to the variety of their experiences. The part which heredity plays in this has not yet been sufficiently investigated, but these tendencies differ basically from the outset, as any close observation of children will show. Shaftesbury, Hutcheson and Adam Smith long ago insisted on this point as an objection to all explanation of fellow-feeling in terms of utilitarianism and the associationist psychology.

It seems that fellow-feeling undergoes an extensive *development* in each individual; there is good reason to speak of a 'childish egoism', only later giving place, increasingly, to fellow-feeling. However, the essential part of this development is not due to fellow-feeling proper at all, but to growth in our understanding of the nature and differences of mental processes in other people.[1]

---

[1] This interest in the experiences of other people is also subject to development, which advances slowly with increasing understanding; child-psychology has only recently begun to describe its phases.

We should also bear these factors in mind, for example, when judging primitive peoples and their attitude and behaviour to strangers and to other tribes. And the same holds good in considering the historical development of modes of feeling. The progress of civilization has often been ascribed to an enlargement of fellow-feeling—for instance, in the abolition of torture, the mitigation of capital punishment and flogging, and the stamping-out of barbaric sports such as bull-fighting or the wild-beast combats of the Roman arena. But quite wrongly, in our opinion. The prime credit for such moral reforms is due, not to enlarged sympathies, but to the enhanced susceptibility to suffering which civilization brings in its train. Those who are more susceptible to suffering, who suffer more than others under the same pain, are also more sensitive to pain in others than those who are less susceptible. The degree of susceptibility is constant, however, in both the idiopathic and heteropathic attitudes. An increase in its amount has nothing to do with an enhancement of sympathy. Nor does a greater susceptibility have any positive value in itself. It is only where susceptibilities are *equal* that a greater capacity for pity implies moral superiority. Besides, there are other motives for the above-mentioned reforms, some of which are also of moral value, though they are not relevant here.

Now while admitting that fellow-feeling is inborn in the individual man, attempts have been made to represent it phylogenetically as an 'acquired characteristic of the race'. Darwin and Spencer in particular have developed this idea at length. This is not the place in which to enter into the empirical details of these theories, nor into the wealth of interesting factual material presented by Darwin in his *Descent of Man* and *Expression of the Emotions in Man and Animals*, and by Spencer in his ethics and sociology. We wish only to say a few words about the *principles* of this explanation.

Darwin's account relies upon two principles: (1) The rise and development of the sympathetic emotions is a *consequence* of the rise and development of the *social instinct*. Thus in animals for whom a communal mode of life was found to promote the survival of the species, so that a gregarious habit became natural to them (by the formation of a tendency to avoid solitude), the sympathetic emotions must have proved exceedingly useful. For this reason they have not arisen or developed among non-social types (such as the predatory animals which do not hunt in packs). The sympathetic emotions are therefore epiphenomena of the social habit and the 'social instinct'—which continues to betray itself in the shape of an instinctive desire to regain the herd, as well as in the tendency to pining and wasting under solitary conditions (away

131

from the herd), even when the other requirements of life are fully supplied by artificial means.

(2) Darwin's second principle asserts that, once the sympathetic emotions have been formed, their *increase* is in accordance with progress in the intellectual development, the articulation and solidarity of interests, among members of the collectivity. This is brought about as the internecine struggle for existence among the members of a species comes to be more and more transformed into a struggle of the species as a *whole* against other species, or against Nature. The same basic ideas, with some divergences, are to be found in Spencer, who applies them to human history, and sees in excessive egoism and lack of sympathetic feeling an 'atavism' which the 'progress of the species' tends more and more to eliminate. His ideals, therefore, are the abolition of war, the advent of the 'industrial age' and the final attainment of 'social equilibrium'.[1]

Now are these principles tenable? I think not. For one thing, Darwin utterly confounds the element of *understanding* in the act of sympathy as a whole, with fellow-feeling proper. To put it more precisely, he mistakes the latter for the process in an animal whereby the experiences of another animal somehow come to influence and affect it; in man this may take the form of an act of understanding, but it need not do so, for man can also behave as a true herd-animal (in crowd-behaviour, for instance); in animals, however, the transference is generally by way of 'infection'. Now it is doubtless true that this process varies in any case, according to the abundance and fullness of intercourse in the social way of life. Hence the communicability of experience by 'infection' also *increases* with the range and intensity of social life, along with the power to understand and the ability to sympathize. But the former, as we have seen, is just as much of a prior condition for feelings and impulses which are the exact *opposite* of true fellow-feeling, such as brutality, cruelty, malice, envy, jealousy, spite, etc.[2] There is a certain sociality of life, a certain degree of communication, necessarily implied in these emotions, no less than in pity or rejoicing. This could not be otherwise, unless these internal dispositions were to be analysable as mere effects of an attitude intrinsically egoistic and idiopathic, coupled with the *absence* of any sort of participation in the experience of others.

---

[1] The empirical evidence offered for their assertions by both writers shows that they confound fellow-feeling and emotional infection. Cf. Darwin's *Descent of Man* and Spencer's *Ethics*, I, and *Psychology*, II.

[2] Cf. my essay, *Die Ursachen des Deutschenhasses* (Leipzig, 1917), which disputes Spencer's sociological thesis that the increasing contacts between nations through civilization and communication have led to greater love and fellow-feeling among them.

But cruelty, brutality, envy, jealousy and malice are far from being dispositions of a *merely* egoistical or idiopathic kind—unless we are to suppose that they envisage their objects as lifeless and insensible, like so many blocks of wood. This does not apply even to brutality (as has been said already). If you suppose a man to be a corpse or a tree-stump it is just not *possible* for you to be 'brutal' towards him; while in the cases of cruelty, envy, malice and spite, such a supposition would simply not make sense. They are all genuinely heteropathic attitudes, whose immediate intentional reference is to pain in others, not to the agent's own pleasure, whatever the pleasure that may actually result when the impulse is satisfied. If there is no truth in the oft-refuted assertion that man aims at his own pleasure even in helping others—though pleasure may certainly result from this, there is equally little truth in the notion that these hostile attitudes are entirely based on the individual's pursuit of his own pleasure—as if he had no eyes for the other's experience, or saw it, if at all, without having any regard for it. No indeed. The heteropathic attitude can be directed with equal immediacy upon pain or the diminution and destruction of value in another person, just as it can upon pleasure or the increase and realization of this value. While the social form of life is presupposed by *negative* heteropathic attitudes no less than by positive ones.

We light here upon an ambiguity in the concept of 'fellow-feeling' which profoundly affects our problem. One may rejoice at another's joy and also repine at it; grieve at his sorrow, and also gloat upon it. Both require that the state of mind should be conveyed or understood. Normally one only speaks of 'fellow-feeling' in connection with the first-mentioned alternatives in each case, where the state of mind and the functional reaction to it both have the same polarity. But Darwin's account would only hold good for a sense of 'fellow-feeling' which included the second alternatives as well. Now this is a matter of the highest importance for ethics. For it is surely obvious that fellow-feeling has *positive* moral value in the *first* sense only, and equally obvious that all attitudes where the polarities are reversed are *negative* in value. But Darwin connects the mere fact of sociality and its increase with the presence of fellow-feelings of the positive kind only; whereas he should have attributed it to the presence and development of *all* the heteropathic feelings and qualities, including the negative ones. This leads him to the fundamentally erroneous belief that 'social development' as such is in some sense a condition of moral *progress* and a source of *positive* moral energy, and finally to the proposition 'Good is to live in company: evil, to dwell alone' —a notion which deservedly roused Nietzsche to violent protest.

This can also be applied, of course, to man and his history. The growth of social relations among nations and infra-national groups, and the increased solidarity of their interests, have not accentuated the heteropathic responses, as such, for all their effect upon our capacities for understanding. But the enrichment of understanding due to the greater intimacy of human contact has provided these responses with far more varied material. They have become, in consequence, unusually *diversified*, though the diversity extends to the *negatively* valuable as well as to the *positive*. In the course of its history, civilization has given rise to quite new forms of cruelty, brutality, envy, malice, etc., which never previously existed. Closer contacts and increased solidarity of interests have brought new 'vices' as well as new 'virtues', in their train.

There is equally little foundation for the Darwinian assumption that the sympathetic emotions are merely epiphenomenal to the 'social instinct', the latter being itself a consequence of the social mode of life. We may confine ourselves to remarking that, so far as concerns the mere capacity for perceiving the liveliness of other living things and assimilating their experience, this feature is certainly not a consequence of the social mode of life, but is in some form, however elementary, a *natural endowment of all living creatures*. Nor is it a consequence, but a *presupposition*, of the possibility of any kind of sociality; for this, as such, must always be more than a mere spatial proximity and purely causal efficacy of things upon each other. There is no such thing as a 'society' of stones. Things are only 'social' when they are in some sense present 'for one another'. Hence the sociality and capacity of living things to pursue a reciprocal existence of any sort lie outside the relation of cause and effect. The development of such capacities is not the empirical consequence of an outwardly social form of life. On the contrary, the governing relation is one of parallel co-ordination.

Chapter IX

PITY AND REJOICING AND THEIR TYPICAL MODES

So far as the *modes* of pity are concerned, some characteristic distinctions are drawn by language itself; we speak, for example, of 'compassion', mere 'regret', or 'concern'; again, there are different ways of experiencing pity, betrayed by such expressions as 'I was concerned about it', 'I was overcome with pity', and, stronger still, 'A sorrow that wrung my heart'. Sometimes it is more a spontaneous outgoing from ourselves, at other times the suffering of other people seems, as it were, to flood in upon us. 'Compassion' is pity at its strongest. Its opposite is 'regret', which is so distant and cold that the phrase 'I much regret' has become little more than a polite formula for the refusal of assistance sought or desired. Above all, 'regret' by itself is incapable of bestirring the will. It rests content with wishing. Even 'concern' is stronger than 'regret'.

It is very characteristic, and has often been remarked, that pity and rejoicing are unusually different in the extent of their incidence. *Mitleid* (pity) is a *genuine* word, native to the language. *Mitfreude* (rejoicing-with) is a feeble product of *analogy*. Most languages possess a *number* of words for different kinds of pity, but not for different kinds of rejoicing. This is an indication, at least, that pity is wider in scope than rejoicing.[1] In ethics, too, pity is always mentioned far more frequently than rejoicing, and often more highly thought of. It is very difficult to make out the reasons for this.

(1) There are no grounds whatever for the metaphysical thesis of Pessimism, that the amount of sorrow in the world is much

---

[1] As Jean-Paul significantly observes, 'Pity is for men; rejoicing for angels'.

greater than the amount of joy, or that pain is a positive state, whereas joy is only a negative one.

(2) It is also said that pity for suffering is the greater for being often accompanied by the consoling thought: 'It is a good thing *I'm* not in that state', while rejoicing, on the other hand, is checked by the envy which is easily roused by good fortune. This account is based on correct observation, but it is quite inadequate, since it is certainly not consistent with *genuine* sympathy.

(3) One might also think that the field of application for pity is greater owing to the fact of pain: for there is no corresponding feeling of sensory pleasure so capable of intensification or so generally distributed over the whole organism; more particularly, there is none which automatically receives immediate expression. Every part of the body is susceptible to pain, though not to sensory pleasure, at least not to the same degree or with the same range of intensity. It is also easier, in general, to specify sources of pain than sources of sensory pleasure, while the latter vary more widely in different peoples and periods than the former. But these distinctions apply to sensory feelings, rather than to modes of vital feeling or the spiritual emotions. And yet here the distribution still varies as before.

(4) The linguistic facts referred to might, however, be traceable merely to the fact that the *social evaluation* of pity is other and *higher* than that of rejoicing, and not to its actual distribution; and this evaluation might again relate to the greater *practical* importance of pity. Pity is a source of beneficence, and is on that account preferred to rejoicing and congratulation by anyone who is a recipient of sympathy and at the same time a utilitarian in his judgements, since rejoicing has no such immediate practical effect. Now in fact this seems to me to be the real reason for the distinction. In respect of its quality as an emotional act, the purely ethical value of rejoicing is quite equal to that of pity. As a *total act*, however, it contains *more* value, as such, than pity, for joy is preferable to sorrow. The value of its occurrence is likewise the greater, as evincing a nobler disposition, by the very fact of its greater liability to frustration through possible envy. The common estimate which finds expression in language conceals, therefore, a utilitarian reversal of the true order of value.

As to the *morbid* forms of fellow-feeling it can be said that all types of perversion exhibited in relation to states of the self are also found in relation to these states in *others*. A person, that is, who is in the habit of inflicting pain upon himself will also be inclined to inflict it upon others; while he who finds enjoyment in his own pain, finds it also in the pain of other people, and all the more so when this enjoyment is itself painful to them. This situation is a very remarkable one. It is not to be confused with the enjoyment of pain suffered by others where the capacity for feeling is normal (i.e. in cruelty). The moral value of such enjoyment is entirely negative. Whereas to enjoy pain in others because one enjoys pain generally is not in itself an immoral act, but a pathological symptom. These two conditions are very often confounded, both in life and in theory. In such a case, therefore, the first thing to look for is whether malice and genuine cruelty are present, or a mere enjoyment of pain (*algophilia*), which may also disclose itself in sympathy. For there is another type of person who may show all the signs of pity, though filled only with a disguised enjoyment of pain. Thus it is well known that many women become sick-nurses because they enjoy seeing pain, etc., though their services are given from a sense of duty none the less, their perversity being merely made the basis of their vocation. Corresponding to this on the other side there is the type who hungers after pity, who enjoys the sight of other people grieving at his own sufferings, and who therefore provokes pity—not for utilitarian purposes, like a beggar feigning blindness, for example, but because he enjoys suffering.[1]

[1] The case is altered, however, when the provoking of pity is only a manœuvre, an 'experiment', either to test the extent of the other person's love, or to gain momentary assurance of a love already known to exist. The 'punishment' of another person by inflicting injury or damage upon oneself is another example of this, for it is the other's concern for the person injuring himself which is used as a means of punishing him. Although this type of behaviour (in its more violent forms at least) is confined in our society to pathological cases, being especially familiar as a symptom of hysteria, it is curious that in China and Japan it has actually become a national custom. It is not unusual there for someone to kill or mutilate himself, thereby invoking the general sympathy of the populace, in order to 'punish' a powerful personage. Under the old imperial regime in China the cause of the Revolution was advanced by a large number of these 'punitive suicides'. Analogous to this is the custom of Japanese women who frequently kill themselves when ill-treated by their husbands, so that the latter may be held up to obloquy through general sympathy with the deceased.

Chapter X

THE MORAL VALUE OF FELLOW-FEELING

GENUINE acts of fellow-feeling have positive moral value, though this is by no means true of heteropathic emotions in general. The degree of such value is determined:

(1) According to the level of the emotion, which may be a spiritual, mental, vital or sensory type of sympathy.

(2) According to whether the pity is of the first type ('pity with someone') as distinct from mere 'pity for someone'.[1] The value of emotional infection is negative rather than positive, its only effect being that of increasing the total amount of suffering present.

(3) According to whether the fellow-feeling is directed upon the centre of self-awareness and self-respect in the other's personality or merely towards his circumstances.

(4) In addition, the total value of an act of fellow-feeling varies according to the worth of the value-situation which is the occasion of the other person's sorrow or joy. In other words, to sympathize with joys and sorrows which are appropriate to their circumstances is preferable to sympathizing with those which are not. By the same token, it is better to have sympathy for a person of superior worth than for someone of lesser value.

Fellow-feeling possesses this value in its own right; it is not occasioned by the acts of beneficence which come about through fellow-feeling, and pity especially. For 'A sorrow shared is a sorrow halved; joy shared is joy doubled' is one of the few proverbs which brook examination from the moral point of view. However, it *is* one of the marks of *genuineness* in pity, that it should lead to acts of beneficence.

The foregoing evaluation is naturally quite different to that of

---

[1] Cf. pp. 12–13 *supra*.

138

the *Ethics of Sympathy* which holds that sympathy is the *source* of moral value generally. On this view, sympathy has literally no positive value, though all moral values are said to acquire their value only by virtue of their connection with sympathy.[1]

[1] Cf. *Der Formalismus in der Ethik.* These principles once established, it is easy to expose the errors of Schopenhauer and Nietzsche in their respective views and valuations of sympathy. This has been admirably done by E. Kramer in 'Das Phänomen des Mitgefühls in der modernen Philosophie' (Dissertation, Cologne, 1922).

Chapter XI

THE RELATIONSHIP OF LOVE AND FELLOW-FEELING

O NE of the gravest errors of almost the entire school of British moralists lies in their departure from Greek and Christian ethics in seeking to derive the facts of *love* and *hate* from fellow-feeling.[1] This has usually come about through putting sympathy into the foreground, and thereupon substituting *benevolence* (often called 'disinterested benevolence') in place of love. The slippery notion of 'benevolence', often based, in practice, upon pity (though far less so upon rejoicing), offers, as it were, a seeming approach to love, just as malevolence does to hatred. But 'benevolence' is by no means the same as love. Firstly, it is not at all necessary or essential to love that it should seek the (material) 'benefit' of its object. Love is entirely concerned with the positive values of *personality*, and with welfare only so far as it promotes such personal value. We also love things, such as beauty, art or knowledge, for which it would be meaningless to feel 'benevolence'. We love 'God', though it would be ridiculous to 'entertain benevolence towards Him'. Love of other people can lead to one 'wishing them well', but this is then a consequence of love. Nor is 'wishing them well' the same thing, phenomenologically speaking, as 'benevolence'. 'Benevolence' includes an element of *remoteness* and superiority on the part of the well-wisher, a certain 'condescension' which may easily rule out the possibility of love. This remoteness resembles that whereby our ordinary 'pity for someone' differs from our 'suffering in common with him'. Moreover the feeling of 'benevolence' also involves the

[1] Cf. my *Das Ressentiment im Aufbau der Moralen*; C. Stumpf's *Über ethischen Skeptizismus* and the criticism of the Ethics of Sympathy in E. von Hartmann's *Phänomenologie des Bewusstseins* are also relevant.

making of an effort towards the well-being of the other; it is not properly a volition, but an impulsive tendency to self-exertion (the 'seeds', the 'stirrings' of benevolence, as we say). But there is no sense of effort in love, as such, even though it does have the character of movement, which we also find in effort. There is no more 'exertion' in the act of loving than there is a counter-exertion in the act of hating. Love is certainly a movement towards positive value, but so far as the *nature* of love is concerned it makes no difference whether this value already exists or not. In all endeavour there is a content to be realized, which is inherent as its goal (or 'purpose', when we will).[1] Love does not have this at all. What does a mother seek to 'realize' when she gazes lovingly at her bonny child asleep? What is supposedly 'realized' in loving God? or in loving works of art? Love may give rise to all kinds of effort, desire, or longing for the beloved object, but these are no part of it. It follows an *opposite law to that of effort*. Whereas the latter exhausts itself and comes to rest once it is satisfied, love either remains the same or increases its activity, becoming ever more engrossed in its object, and ever more perceptive of values not at first disclosed. It makes no sense to talk of the act of loving being 'satisfied', unless we mean something quite different, namely, the satisfaction or gratification felt upon completion of the act of love. This equivocation has a most evil source, therefore, in that concept of love as a duty upheld in part of the ethical teaching of the church. This having proved a mistaken demand for the impossible, it has been replaced by benevolence, if not by mere *good works* of a practical kind. Kant, on the other hand, excluded love from the whole field of morally valuable conduct because it cannot be imposed as a duty, and because he (wrongly) thought it possible to base the concept of moral value upon obligation and duty alone.[2]

How then, are fellow-feeling, love and hatred actually related to one another? First of all, love has an intrinsic reference to *value*, and for that reason alone it cannot be a fellow-feeling. Even 'self-love', as distinct from mere egoism, has reference to value, and cannot, by its very nature, be 'sympathy for oneself'. Secondly, love is not a 'feeling' (i.e. a function), but an *act* and a *movement*.[3]

---

[1] See *Der Formalismus in der Ethik*, p. 26 ff., on the relation between purposes and goods, endeavour, value and goal.

[2] In my *Formalismus in der Ethik* the erroneous character of these principles of Kantian ethics is exposed in detail. Instead of overcoming the legalism of Old Testament ethics these errors have led to its replacement by a *new* law, differing only in content. Cf. the treatment of this subject in Fr. v. Baader's *Religiöse Erotik*, ch. 9.

[3] It therefore makes sense to describe love and hatred as emotions, but not as 'feelings', and certainly not as 'affects'.

All feeling is passive or receptive, whether it be feeling for values or for circumstances (e.g. suffering, enduring, tolerating, etc.), and we describe it therefore as a 'function'. But love is an emotional gesture and a spiritual act. It does not matter here whether, phenomenologically speaking, the gesture is mainly called forth by its object or is felt to proceed from the self. The conception of 'act' employed here does not relate to the self, but to the person, which can never be treated as an object. Love can also make itself felt as an 'attractive' or 'inviting' quality in its object, which feeling can never do. This is the sense in which Aristotle thinks of love, as when he says (in the Metaphysics) 'God moves the world as the beloved moves the lover'. But love is above all a *spontaneous* act, and remains so even when given in response, whatever the grounds for this may be. Fellow-feeling, on the other hand, is always a *reactive* condition. Thus one can only have fellow-feeling for that which is *subject to feeling*, whereas love is altogether free from this limitation.

Admittedly the two things are intimately connected in some essential respects, of which the most important is that all fellow-feeling is *based* upon love of some sort and vanishes when love is altogether absent: but the converse does not hold. Fellow-feeling, therefore, may vary in level and in *degree of penetration* into its object; it may extend to peripheral conditions, or to the inmost depths of personality, and with feelings of a sensory, vital or spiritual kind; but this is entirely dependent on the antecedent category of the love which underlies it—i.e. according to how *love is directed* upon that particular level.

The first point may be gathered from the obvious rule whereby our fellow-feeling varies according to the measure and depth of our love. Where our love for the object of fellow-feeling is no more than superficial, fellow-feeling soon reaches its limit, and certainly does not extend to the centre of personality. But we certainly do not mean to imply by this that we must already have love for the object of our fellow-feeling. All we are concerned with here is a law of dependence relating to the *essential nature* of the acts. We often have fellow-feeling for someone we do not love. In conveying our regrets to someone, for instance, there is no trace of love, nor is there in our ordinary pity 'for' him. But even here the stirrings of sympathy are based upon love; a love which in this instance relates either to a *whole* of which he is a part or member (a family, a nation, or mankind), or else to a *general category* which he exemplifies for us (as a compatriot, a relative, a human being, or even as a living creature). In other words, the phenomenological object to which love is directed does not have to coincide, in intention, with the object of sympathy. But the act of fellow-feeling, if it is to amount to more than mere understanding or vicarious emotion, must be rooted in an enveloping act of love. The effect of this addition is precisely what makes it perfectly possible to sympathize with someone we do not love; the really impossible thing is for sympathy to be lacking where love is present already.

The scope of the act of love therefore determines the sphere in which fellow-feeling is possible. Two conclusions may be drawn from this: first, that it is essentially impossible to hate and to sympathize in *one* combined act. In hatred, we rejoice at pain and injury, and give vent to a range of heteropathic, *negatively* valuable feelings, such as envy, spite, etc. Secondly, it can be seen how, in a case where we do have love indeed, but not for the object of our sympathy, the effect on the pitied one is to create a sense of 'injured pride', shame and humiliation. It is not, as Nietzsche says,[1] pity as such that is wounding to our shame, but pity without love for the pitied one. The only thing that makes pity *bearable* is the love it betrays. In the case referred to the pitied one feels that the love (which underlies pity) is not directed upon him in a concrete sense at all, but upon a generalized object—mankind, his family, his country, his membership of a class. It is this general or collective concept which continues to be loved and is the indirect occasion of pity; regarding the pitied one as merely a 'case' or 'instance', its effect, when viewed in relation to the *individual* suffering to which that pity refers, is to awaken shame. For this always follows once a value is transplanted from the cosy darkness of individual privacy into a field that is in any sense a general or 'public' one.[2] It is a matter of common observation, how a lessening in our love for an object makes for a corresponding forfeiture of its claim upon our sympathy, and this is a sure indication that if our love for a thing is nil, our sympathy for what is only indirectly involved in it will also be nil. It can therefore be seen that in the *absence* of love for a person, the expression of pity for him will be felt, even by the pitier himself (if he is morally sensitive), to be an act of brutality. If he cannot at the same time love what he pities, the sensitive man will *hide* his feelings of compassion. This gives some indication of the complete fallacy involved in supposing it possible to account for love in terms of fellow-feeling.

But wherever this theory has arisen, one may safely take it that the real basis for it is *vindictiveness*, which regards the sufferer as all the better for his suffering, and so gives rise to a perverse taste

---

[1] Cf. 'Of the compassionate' in Nietzsche's *Thus spake Zarathustra*, and also E. Kramer, op. cit.

[2] [Cf. the essay 'Über Scham und Schamgefühl' (1913), published in *Nachlassband* I.]

for suffering itself. We find this in Schopenhauer, for instance, and wherever the profoundly influential (Christian) idea of suffering 'gladly' (for something whose value outweighs the sacrifice and suffering involved), is distorted into the perversely vindictive notion that suffering and those who endure it are especially deserving of love (e.g. that those in poverty and distress are particularly 'well-pleasing' in the sight of God).[1] For love is extended, not to the suffering of those in distress, but to the *positive values* inherent in them, and the act of relieving their suffering is only a consequence of this. On the other hand, it is just such a compassionate emotion of love for those who suffer, as such, which furnishes the most questionable basis for all such attempts at deriving love from pity. Conversely, when we have the experience of being lovingly pitied by someone else, it is not for his acts of kindness that we first take him to our heart, but for the love and good-will which inspire them, and which his outward compassion only serves to disclose. As F. von Baader aptly says: 'Effective good-will is already itself a benefit, being the very heart and principle of beneficence, and therefore the greatest boon that a free and independent being can bestow on another, without which all other benefactions are vain and engender no gratitude.'[2]

[1] Cf. my essay 'Das Ressentiment im Aufbau der Moralen', and also my essay 'Vom Sinn des Leides'.

[2] *Die religiöse Erotik*, p. 1.5

PART TWO

LOVE AND HATRED

Chapter I

TOWARDS A PHENOMENOLOGY OF
LOVE AND HATRED

(I) NEGATIVE CONSIDERATIONS

We may have said enough to dispose of the idea that love
and hatred can be derived from fellow-feeling; but it
is equally out of the question to derive them from more
elementary facts of any kind, or to regard them as a 'complex'
of such elements. Any attempt to seek their origin in a complex
of feelings and impulses is doomed to failure. Consider, for instance,
the complete futility of Spinoza's definition, that love is '*quædam
lætitia concomitante causa externa*'. Malebranche was already justified
in asking of this whether we therefore love a fruit which we
consume and know to be a cause of pleasure?[1] In love (and
hatred) between human beings these acts remain wholly independent of changes in the state of feeling, as is shown by the fact
that throughout such changes they *remain fixed* upon their objects,
as with a steady, unwavering light. Our love for someone does
not alter, for all the pain and grief the loved one may cause us,
nor our hatred, for all the joy and pleasure the hated one may
afford. And throughout all the daily vicissitudes of joy and sorrow
among men their ties of love and hatred persist unaltered. One
can only say this about it, that a beloved object offers more
abundant possibilities of joy as well as sorrow. But the same is also
true of our hatreds; the more we hate a person, the more galling
his happiness and prosperity, the more gratifying his misery and
failure, and the more abundant the possibilities he offers for our
sorrow and our joy.

Quite a different set of facts is involved once the love and

[1] Cf. N. Malebranche : *Recherche de la Vérité.*

hate-relationships are regarded as *causes* of emotional states (and not as their effects). It now becomes plain that the *pursuance* of these acts is itself the deepest of all sources of joy and sorrow, bliss and despair. Thus, even when love is 'unhappy' in the sense of being unrequited, the act itself is still accompanied by a feeling of great happiness—and equally so when the loved one occasions pain and sorrow. And conversely, even where the distress of a hated person is a source of joy (as in envy, malice, spite, etc.), the *pursuance* of the act of hatred itself is still felt to have a sombre and dismal quality about it.

Even if, abstaining from consideration of love and hatred as emotional states, we merely enquire if they represent a feeling 'of something' in intention, this question must also receive a negative answer. For a thing can certainly be felt to have positive value without therefore arousing love. It is the merit of Franz Brentano to have recognized that love and hatred are by nature acts, and acts of an elementary kind. He actually regards them as prior even to judgement itself. We are the more ready to stress this here because it is our conviction that this one small observation shows how vastly Brentano's insight into these matters transcends the misconceptions now prevailing in psychology, whereby love and hatred are successively assigned to the spheres of feeling, conation and affect, or construed as a medley of in-gredients from all three. Yet we cannot follow him in equating them, as he does in *The Origin of the Knowledge of Right and Wrong*,[1] with 'preference' and 'rejection'. The relationship of these acts to love and hate has been fully explained by me in another work.[2] Here I would only emphasize that preference and rejection belong to the sphere of *value-apprehension* (and indeed to the apprehension of grades of value), whereas love and hatred cannot be reckoned as acts of apprehension *at all*. They represent a unique attitude towards objects of value, and it is certainly not just a cognitive function. They may indeed serve as a basis for the apprehension of value (as we shall see), but they are not themselves apprehen-sions of this kind. Moreover, these attitudes are not directed intentionally towards value, let alone 'higher' value, as when we prefer one value to another; they refer to *objects* inasmuch and insofar as these possess value. It is never values we love, but always something that possesses value.

In Malebranche's admirable discussions of love and hatred[3] they are taken to be feelings, but of a kind in which a value-judgement is presupposed, as to whether the object is worthy to

[1] *Der Ursprung sittlicher Erkenntnis* [tr. by C. Hague, Constable, 1902].
[2] *Der Formalismus in der Ethik*, p. 63 seq., p. 260 seq.
[3] Op. cit.

arouse a certain degree of joy. From this point of view he engages in criticism of Spinoza's theory. It is easy to see that this position involves a *mistaken rationalization* of love and hatred.[1] There may be emotional acts which presuppose the passing of a judgement (or rather, an evaluation). Respect, for instance, seems to me to be one of these. It presupposes that initial detachment from the object, which alone makes it possible for a value-*judgement* to precede the onset of the emotional act; and it also requires a specific awareness of the presence of the value by which it is evoked. But this detachment is just what is lacking in love and hatred. They are entirely *primitive* and *immediate* modes of emotional response to the value-content itself; so much so that, phenomenologically speaking, they do not even disclose a process of apprehending value (e.g. feeling, preference, etc.), let alone the making of a value-judgement. In particular, the value in question is not specifically envisaged beforehand, as it is in the case of *respect*. Nothing shows this better than the extraordinary perplexity which can be seen to ensue when people are asked to give 'reasons' for their love or hatred. It is then that one sees how these 'reasons' are invariably looked for after the event, and how the whole inventory of them is never sufficient to account for the nature and intensity of the acts they are alleged to justify. It is also noticeable that though other objects may have value-qualities identical to those alleged as reasons for love or hatred, no such emotions are addressed to them. Love and hatred necessarily fasten upon the individual core in things, the *core of value*—if I may be allowed the expression—which can never be wholly resolved into values susceptible of judgement, or even of distinct apprehension in feeling. On the contrary, our standards for the appreciation of value-attributes are governed by our love or hatred of the things exhibiting these values; it is not our appreciation that governs our love or our hate. Indeed, curious as it may appear, we feel it a kind of offence and transgression, a profane intrusion upon love (*and* hatred), that we should apply conceptual categories of valuation to the values of objects we love or hate, or should observe others doing so. When reading a letter from a loved one it is out of the question to judge it by ordinary standards of grammar, æsthetics or style. It seems 'disloyal' to do so. The qualities, the

[1] H. Blüher has made the assertion, which reappears in almost all his writings that 'Love is directed to the (whole) man, regardless of value'. If his intention was only to repudiate *this* fallacious rationalization, he would be quite right; but not if he means to imply that the act of love itself takes place without reference to value. Baader shows much greater insight in observing that beauty (loveliness) is derived from love and ugliness (the hateful) from hate, while *charis*, or grace(fulness), is identical with *charitas* (graciousness) (*Religiöse Erotik*, p. 15).

activities and the achievements of the loved one acquire all their value from him or her alone, as the object in which they inhere or the subject who carries them out.

From the rationalist point of view this is sufficient reason for regarding love and hatred as 'blind'. But this tells us very little. For the fact that the inner 'spiritual vision' of love and hatred should see something *other* in values, high or low, than that which the 'eye' of reason can discern, is no indication that we are merely getting a worse view here of the *same* thing which the eye of reason would discern more clearly. Love and hatred afford an *evidence of their own*, which is not to be judged by the evidence of reason. Only those to whom this evidence is denied, or who are constitutionally liable to vacillation about it, will be disposed to attribute the fact to a general 'blindness' of functions and acts, rather than to shortcomings in their own individual *exercise* of them.

It has already been emphasized that love and hatred do not represent acts of conation. It is precisely the element of 'uneasiness' in conation which is increasingly expunged from love and hatred, the more definite, pure and lucid they become. Nor do they contain any consciousness of something 'to be realized'. But more of this later.

The most important thing to notice is the way in which love and hatred differ, *as* acts even, from all other acts and from each other; the point being that they do not first *become* what they are by virtue of either their exponents, their objects or their possible effects and results. No other truth has been more grievously flouted by our current habits of thought. It is implied in the foregoing, firstly, that love and hatred are *in no sense relative* to the polar co-ordinates of '*myself*' and '*the other*'. In other words, love and hatred are *not intrinsically social dispositions*, as are the functions of fellow-feeling, for example.[1] Thus, one can 'love or hate oneself', but cannot have fellow-feeling for oneself. For if it is said of someone that he 'pities himself' or that he 'rejoices to find himself so happy today' (statements which undoubtedly designate phenomena of a quite specific kind), a closer analysis invariably discloses the presence of an element of phantasy, in which the person concerned regards himself '*as if he were someone else*' and shares his own feelings in this (fictitious) capacity. Thus I can fancy myself in the position of taking part in my own funeral, etc. But even then the act of fellow-feeling remains, phenomenologically, a social one. No such illusion is necessary in the case of self-love and self-hatred. Hence it is by no means a necessary condition for the occurrence

---

[1] Other examples of intrinsically social acts are those of promising, obeying, commanding, pledging oneself, etc. Cf. the penetrating analysis of 'psycho-social' acts in H. L. Stoltenberg: *Soziopsychologie*, Berlin, 1914.

of love and hatred, that the act should be directed on someone else, or that there should be any consciousness of human relationships. If acts that are addressed to others, as such, are described as 'altruistic', then love and hatred are in no way intrinsically altruistic acts. For the primary orientation of love is towards values, and towards the objects discernible, through those values, as sustaining them; whence it is essentially a matter of indifference whether the values concerned belong to the self or to others. The basic contrast is therefore between love, whether of self or others, and hatred, of self or others likewise. Conversely, acts addressed to others, as such, are by no means necessarily loving. For envy, malice and spite are so addressed. If by 'altruism' be meant an orientation towards other men, a predominant tendency to aversion from the self and its subjective experience, there is nothing in such a 'social' attitude to connect it, as such, with a 'loving' or 'kindly' one. Moreover, if love for others is based in this way upon an act of aversion, it must equally be founded upon a still more ultimate *hatred*, namely of *oneself*. Self-aversion, the *inability* to endure one's own company (of which the 'clubman' is a typical example), has nothing to do with love.[1]

But if it be no essential part of love that it should address itself to others, there is equally little necessity for it to relate to the *group*. There is such a thing as love for a group, and that in a twofold sense, namely love for the group as a whole, and love for each of its members, as 'belonging to the group'. But this can also co-exist with a quite independent love for the individual himself, considered without reference to a group of any kind, or, it may be, in actual opposition to one. (Love for the uniquely private self.) The group, in all its aspects, is thus only *one* object of love among others. If, by a 'social outlook' one is taken to mean a special liability to preoccupation with social matters, this also has nothing whatever to do with *love*. Though it is certainly possible for love, of a kind, to be realized in a 'social outlook'. Thus one may wish to benefit an entire nation, profession, community or race, 'out of love for them' (but never a class, for this is an embodiment of interests and, as such, valueless); but in doing so it should be realized that this involves a total exclusion of love or goodwill towards *individuals*. For it is a commonplace of observation that one may hate a group while loving certain of its members—not because they are members of the group, but in their individual

---

[1] In my essay 'Das Ressentiment im Aufbau der Moralen' I have exposed the limitless confusions inherent in the positivist equation of love and 'altruism'. Conversely, many of Nietzsche's arguments against love, in the chapter on 'Love of one's neighbour' in *Also sprach Zarathustra* are applicable only to this positivist misrepresentation of love as altruism.

capacity. Hence antisemitism, germanophobia, gallophobia, etc., are quite consistent with love for individuals in any given case.

Self-love and self-hatred are therefore no less fundamental than love or hatred of others. Nor is *'egoism'* the same as 'self-love'.[1] For in 'egoism' the given object of love is not my individual self, released from all social ties and thought of as merely a vessel for such supreme categories of value as those which find expression, for instance, in the concept of 'salvation'. Its object is simply myself, as one in competition with others, who thereupon simply 'fails to observe' that others have any value. It is typical of Egoism that it implies a *glance at other people* and their values and goods, and consists in just this *'failure to observe'* the claims engendered by these values (which is already a *positive* act, and not just a failure to perform one). Egoism does not consist in behaving 'as if one were alone in the world'; on the contrary, it is taken for granted that the individual is a member of society. The egoist is a man so taken up with his 'social self' that he loses sight of his individual private self. It is not that he loves this social self; he is merely 'taken up' with it, i.e. *lives* in it. Nor is his concern for his own values, as such (for it is only by chance that he finds them in himself); it is for *all* values, in things or in other people, but only *insofar* as they are, or might come to be *his*, or have something to do with *him*. All of which is the very *opposite* of self-love.

(2) POSITIVE DELINEATION OF THE PHENOMENA[2]

The ultimate essences of love and hatred, as inherent in acts, can only be *exhibited*; they cannot be defined.

In the first place love and hatred cannot be radically distinguished on the grounds that hatred is simply love for the non-existence of a thing. For hatred is really a *positive act*, involving a presentation of *disvalue* no less immediate than the presentation of *positive* value in the act of love. But love is a movement, passing from a lower value to a higher one, in which the higher value of the object or person suddenly flashes upon us; whereas hatred moves in the opposite direction. It can be seen from this that hatred looks to the possible existence of a lower value (itself of

[1] Compare Aristotle's penetrating discussion in the chapter on 'Self-love' in the Nichomachean Ethics. How vastly superior he is, on this point, to all who advocate a 'sociological' explanation for love and hatred!

[2] Karl Jaspers' treatment in the chapter on 'Die enthusiastische Einstellung in die Liebe' of his *Psychologie der Weltanschauungen* (Berlin, 1919), is in agreement on all fundamental points with the analysis presented in this chapter. On the problem itself, cf. Alexander Pfänder: 'Zur Psychologie der Gesinnungen' [*Jahrbuch für Philosophie und phänomenologische Forschung*, Vol. III. Niemeyer, Halle, 1916].

negative value, on that account), and to the removal of the very possibility of a higher value (which again has a negative value). Love, on the other hand, looks to the establishment of higher possibilities of value (which itself has a positive value), and to the maintenance of these, besides seeking to remove the possibility of lower value (which itself has a positive moral value). Hate, therefore, is by no means an utter repudiation of the whole realm of values generally; it involves, rather, a *positive* preoccupation with lower possibilities of value.

This 'higher' or 'lower' quality of values is something inherently given, requiring no such comparison of value as is always involved in 'preference', for example. Preference is not choice, nor is it in any sense a conative act, but an act of emotional cognition.[1] We can prefer Beethoven to Brahms, for instance, without actually choosing anything. Choice always relates to volition—never to objects as such. But preference always assumes the existence of two values A and B, of which one is then preferred to the other. This is not the case in love and hatred. For love is that *movement of intention* whereby, from a given value A in an object, its higher value is visualized. Moreover, it is just this *vision* of a higher value that is of the essence of love. In its ultimate nature, therefore, love is not just a 'reaction' to a value already felt, such as 'happiness' or 'grief', for example, nor is it a modally determinate function, such as 'enjoyment', nor yet an attitude to a pair of previously given values, such as 'preference'. Though all preference is based on love, inasmuch as it is only in love that the higher value flashes out and can thereafter be preferred.

Those who treat love as a merely consequential 'reaction' to a value already felt, have failed to recognize its nature as a *movement*, of which Plato was already so shrewdly aware.[2] Love does not simply gape approval, so to speak, at a value lying ready to hand for inspection. It does not reach out towards given objects (or real persons) merely on account of the positive values inherent in them, and already 'given' *prior* to the coming of love. For this idea still betrays that gaping at mere *empirical* fact, which is so utterly uncongenial to love. Of course there *is* an awareness, in love, of the positive value of the things loved, for instance, the beauty, the charm and the goodness of a person; but we can also be aware of this without any love at all. Love only occurs when, upon the values already acknowledged as 'real' there supervenes a *movement*, an intention, towards potential values still *'higher'* than those

---

[1] Cf. on this *Der Formalismus in der Ethik*, p. 63 seq., p. 260 seq.
[2] In his definition in the Symposium (205), according to which it is 'a cause whereby anything proceeds from that which is not, into that which is' [Shelley's translation].

already given and presented. These additional values are *not* yet manifested as positive qualities, being merely envisaged concurrently as potential ingredients of a corporate structural pattern. In so doing, love invariably sets up, as it were, an '*idealized*' *paradigm of value* for the person actually present, albeit conceiving this at the same time as an embodiment of his 'true' nature and 'real' value, which only awaits confirmation in feeling. To be sure, this 'paradigm' is *implicit* in the values already disclosed empirically in feeling—and only the fact that it is so implicit keeps it free from interpolation, empathic projection, etc., and hence from delusion. But, for all that, it is not empirically 'latent' in them, save as an appointed goal, an objective ideal challenge to a better and more beautiful fulfilment of the whole.

It is essentially as a movement tending to the enhancement of value that love acquires its significance (already explicit in Plato), as a creative force. This is not to say that love first creates these values or itself enhances them. Certainly not. But in all feeling and finding of values, all preference even (in relation, that is, to the spheres of feeling and preference), it is love that within *these* spheres of experience brings utterly new and superior values into existence; as it also does for the whole field of will, choice and action to which preference gives rise. Love, in short, is *creative* of 'existence', relative to these spheres. Hatred, on the other hand, is in the strictest sense *destructive*, since it does in fact destroy the higher values (within these spheres), and has the *additional effect* of blunting and blinding our feeling for such values and power of discriminating them. It is only because of their destruction (within these spheres) by hatred, that they *become* indiscernible.[1]

We now proceed to justify these remarks in more detail.

(a) Love and hatred as essentially appertaining to value

Believing as we do, that love and hatred are acts having an essential reference to objects in respect of their value (the nature of the process can be ignored for the moment), we expressly reject all views proclaiming that these emotions represent *specifically* '*human*' characteristics; that they are to be found only in man and in conjunction with his distinctive psychological make-up; and that it is only man who can figure, in the *primary* sense, as an *object* of love or hatred in any case. Now it is the central feature in the great humanitarian movement of modern times, that it is felt as a love *proceeding* from men as such, and *directed*, likewise, upon other men; the various positivistic theories are but a product

---

[1] As Jaspers pertinently remarks: 'In love we do not discover values, we discover that everything is more valuable', op. cit.

of this emotional trend in social history, and merely give systematic expression to the historical forces at work.[1] But the fact of the
matter is that love relates, in the first instance, to *what has value*,
and to man only to the extent that he is endowed with value and
capable of advancement in this respect. These acts and their laws
can be investigated (by means of a phenomenological reduction),
while entirely discounting the very existence of man as a being
endowed with love or hatred, and oblivious of the empirical fact
that many of these acts, as men actually perform them, do indeed
concern other men. For the fact remains—and even the doctrine
of modern 'humanitarianism' can do nothing to abolish it, that
we love all kinds of things (and spontaneously too), which have
nothing to do with man, and whose values and the appreciation
thereof are as utterly independent of 'man' and his values as they
are of the appreciation of such values in the human sphere.

We therefore fail to recognize the essential character of these
acts if, unlike acts of thought, we attribute them *specifically* to man,
as their sole agent and recipient. We do this if, taking our cue
from the naturalistic theory of love and hatred (to be outlined
below), we claim that man is the sole original object of human
love, and that it can only be extended to other things *inasmuch* as
they are credited with human ways of life by virtue of the '*pathetic
fallacy*'. Thus our love of natural objects, living or dead, is alleged
to be wholly based on our habit of projectively endowing these
objects with our own human feelings, and of looking at them in
terms of pictures and analogies drawn from human life. The same
thing applies, according to this theory, to works of art, 'knowledge', etc., for again it is only as 'forms of expression' for human
life, or as 'means of promoting' it, that these awaken our love;
and this is equally true of God, our idea of Him being (according
to Feuerbach), merely the result of attributing a human consciousness to the universe as a whole or to its ultimate principle.
Now these suppositions plainly have a bearing on matters of fact;
but the facts in question are represented, not by a genuine love
of Nature, Art, Knowledge or God, but by a merely *spurious* and
spectral form of this, namely the '*sentimental*' variety. *True* love of
Nature, for instance, is disclosed in the fact of Nature being made
an object of love *for her own sake*, for what is peculiar to herself
and hence alien to man. This is what distinguishes the genuine
love of Nature from its spurious 'sentimental' form.[2] This is why
such things as brutality towards the organic forms of Nature,

---

[1] Cf. my treatment in the essay 'Das Ressentiment im Aufbau der Moralen',
op. cit. Cf. also above.
[2] Seen at its most painful, for example, in the descriptions of *Love-life in
Nature*, by W. Bölsche (English translation by C. Brown, 1931).

animal and vegetable, do not become 'wicked' merely through being regarded as a symptom of 'potential' brutality towards men, but are actually wicked in themselves. There may also be 'Love of Art' of a sort, engendered likewise by an insincere 'gushing' over the work, a self-conscious regard for one's own feelings in the matter, rather than for the values inherent in the work itself (and accompanied by the delusion that these 'feelings' *are* its values). But in genuine love of art on the other hand we are concerned throughout with an *extra*-human element, with something which elevates man in his human capacity above himself and his experience. The same is most eminently true of the love of God; for this is devoted, not to 'man's own shadow' in the universe, but to the intrinsically Holy, Infinite and Good, which is by nature transcendent of man and all finite things.[1] Just as the theory of fellow-feeling earlier discussed, supposed it to be founded merely on the illusion that one is experiencing the joys or sorrows of others in oneself, so likewise does the present view suppose that all love of the extra- or super-human depends upon man being subject to the illusion that he is in loving contact with 'Another', while in fact it is never anything more than himself that he is adoring—his own face in a glass, darkly. This 'theory' of the love of God has been worked out by Feuerbach: and Auguste Comte's is like unto it.

(b) The givenness of value-objects in love and hatred

Love, we said, is a movement pointing from a lower value to a higher one, though it is *not* necessary for *both* values to be *given* in the process. Usually it is the lower value that is given, either in the intimation of value which produces the love, as in love at first sight, or as a sequel to the occurrence of an act of preference between several given objects. But whichever it may be, 'love' for the object or bearer of value concerned only begins with the commencement of that movement towards a potentially higher value in the beloved object; a movement which is as yet completely unconcerned as to whether this higher value is already in existence (having been merely unperceived or undiscovered hitherto, for instance), or whether it does not yet exist and merely 'ought' to do so (in an ideal, individual sense, not as a general obligation).[2] This *indifference* with regard to either possibility is a characteristic

[1] Cf. for this the highly relevant material in R. Otto: *The Idea of the Holy* (tr. by J. W. Harvey, Oxford, 1922). And cf. also our analysis of the 'religious act' in *Vom Ewigen im Menschen*.

[2] On the difference between the 'ideal Ought' and the sense of obligation, see the chapter 'Wert und Sollen', in my book *Der Formalismus in der Ethik*, p. 206 seq.

feature of love. It would therefore be wrong to depict love as an attitude of constantly prospecting, as it were, for new and higher values in the object, for this *could* only be due to *un*satisfied love. Yet it would be equally wrong to describe it as endeavouring actually to 'raise' the value of its object, either by merely wishing its betterment, or by actively willing and trying to secure this, as when we seek to 'better' a person or help them in any way to acquire a higher value. Though this too can certainly result from love. I said earlier in the case of personal love, that the movement of love itself 'sets up an ideal paradigm' of the person's value which is not 'drawn' from the empirical values he is felt to have, though it is erected upon that basis; but I do not take this to mean the same as an attempt to heighten the value of the beloved object, or a desire for its improvement. Such a desire for improvement implies (1) a 'pedogogic' attitude, which must immediately and necessarily banish whatever love is present; (2) a distinction drawn here between what the person concerned already is, and what as yet he is not, but supposedly ought to *become*. But this is the very distinction to which love is indifferent, and which is *never* to be found in it, any more than the distinction referred to previously, between the actual empirical values and the ideal 'paradigm'.

This brings us to the most difficult point of the problem. For in love there is no attempting to fix an objective, no deliberate shaping of purpose, aimed at the higher value and its realization; *love itself, in the course of its own movement,* is what brings about the continuous *emergence* of ever-higher value in the object—just as if it was streaming out from the object of its own accord, without any sort of exertion (even of wishing) on the part of the lover. We may take love to consist in the mere fact that a value already present beforehand comes to light at this point (as though love simply opens our eyes to such higher values, whereas hate closes them); *or* regard it, on the other hand, as a mere 'occasion' of the promotion and deliberate cultivation of these values, by education, for instance; or we may suppose it to create the new values effortlessly, out of itself. But all such attempts to confine this *basic phenomenon* to an either-or are but crude and inadequate characterizations, serving only to obscure the thing itself. For *love* is not present in any of these cases. It can certainly be said that true love opens our spiritual eyes to ever-higher values in the object loved. It enables them to *see* and does not blind them (as is suggested in a most foolish proverb, which obviously thinks of love in terms of a mere impulse of sensual passion). The blinding element in an empirical infatuation is never the *love*, but the sensual *impulses* which always accompany love and by which it is actually constricted and confined. But this 'wide-awakeness' is no more than a *consequence* of love, occurring in the varying degrees of 'interest', 'attention', 'notice', 'heed' and so on. In love itself there is no such seeking for new values in the object loved. On the contrary, to search around for higher values like this would undoubtedly indicate a prevailing *absence* of love. It would involve both an increased interest in the merits of the object and a lessening of interest in its failings; but this would imply an attitude which is at least heading towards *illusion*. While the genuineness of love is displayed throughout by the fact that we do indeed see the faults of these objects as they stand, but love them all the same. If love were a search of this kind, how would it be if the higher values sought were not forthcoming? Then, at all events, disillusionment would set in, and the search would come to an end. But whatever ended at this point could certainly not be *love* for the object. For this simply does *not* come to an end, because a value sought is not encountered. Hence the fact of being wide-awake to higher values than those actually present does not make love what it is, being at most a consequence thereof, and that without looking for anything in particular. Love opens our eyes to values higher than those which 'interest' would discern, and even the latter is far more than merely 'increased attention', being itself the actual cause of such an increase.

But this conception of love would obscure the phenomenon in yet another important respect. We said that love is directed towards the 'enhancement of value'; but this is not the same as being directed towards 'a higher value'. If I seek a value in an object higher than the given one, such a seeking demands some grasp of this higher value in respect of its ideal *quality*. But the higher value with which love is concerned is in no way previously 'given', for it is only disclosed in the *movement of love*—at the end of this, as it were. All that it necessarily includes is the orientation towards an enhancement of value (which may be qualitatively determined in various ways).

The second interpretation, that love is essentially no more than an occasion for the promotion of higher values, by education, etc., is one I have already rejected. To this I would add that it is not in the nature of love, as such, to desire a change in the thing loved.[1] It is quite correct to say that in principle we love objects,

---

[1] In his book *Geist der Erziehung* (Teubner, 1919) Jonas Cohn has attributed to me the opinion that to love a child is 'inconsistent' with the recognition of capacities for value in him which ought to be developed. All I maintained, however, was that love and the pedagogic attitude cannot coexist as simultaneous phenomena. What follows (in Cohn's book) also rests on a misunderstanding.

men for example, as they are. We also regard it as no less characteristic of love that it accepts the object as it is, with the values which it has, and we deny that there is a value given in love as that which the object 'ought' to have. If any such requirement is made a condition of love, the nature of the latter is fundamentally destroyed. This is of exceptional importance, for example, for a correct understanding of the idea of love in the Gospels—as I have shown in more detail elsewhere.[1] Jesus does not tell Mary Magdalene 'Thou shalt sin no more: promise me this, and I shall love thee, and forgive thy sins' (as Paulsen, for instance, once supposed).[2] Instead, He gives her a *sign* of His love and forgiveness of sins and then says at the end, 'Go, and sin no more.' And even this saying of Jesus is intended only to show Mary Magdalene the new intimate bond with Himself and to let her see from this that she can now sin no longer; it is in no sense a binding imperative. Again, in the parable of the Prodigal Son, it is not the fact of the son's already complete repentance which is the reason and condition of his father's forgiving him and receiving him with love; it is the astonishing realization of his father's love which brings about the overwhelming repentance. Hence the statement that 'Love is directed upon things as they are' is undoubtedly correct. If one is entitled to expect *love* and encounters only the pedagogic gesture 'Thou shalt', the result is *obduracy* and injured pride. And that is quite to be expected. But this 'as they are' should not be misunderstood. It should not be equated with 'we love things, possessing the values we discern them to possess', or 'through the medium of these values'. For this is to deprive love of that character as a *movement* which assuredly belongs to it. The 'being' we are concerned with here is that '*ideal* being' postulated in love which is neither an empirical and existential one, nor one which it 'ought' to have, but a *third* thing, which is as yet indifferent with regard to *this* distinction; the same being that is implied, e.g. in the phrase 'Become what thou art', which means something quite different from 'Thou shouldst be thus and thus', while it is also quite different from the being of empirical existence, for what one 'is' in this latter sense, one does not need to *become*.[3]

The third interpretation, that love 'creates' the higher values in the other and is therefore in *this* sense a movement towards

---

[1] Cf. *Der Formalismus in der Ethik.*

[2] See Paulsen's criticism of Gustav Frenssen's novel *Hilligenlei*, based on the life of Jesus.

[3] This is explained more fully by my theory of the individual ideal value-personality and its 'vocation', as developed in *Der Formalismus in der Ethik* (p. 508 seq.). The empirical process of 'development' in a man is simply an 'unveiling' from the point of view of his absolute being and character. [Cf. also *Ordo amoris* (1916–17) in *Nachlassband* I, 1933.]

higher value, would also be utterly mistaken. For this could only mean that the lover draws upon values in himself, which are then imputed to what is loved, so as to endow it with more or less imaginary values which it does not in fact possess; in other words, that he 'projects his own values into the object'. That would make it an illusion. Such illusions do of course occur, but they are certainly not occasioned by love for the object, being brought about by the very opposite of this, namely the inability to free oneself from partiality to one's *own* ideas, feelings and interests. The lover's notorious propensity (particularly in the case of sexual love), to 'over-value', exalt and idealize the object of his love, is by no means always present where it is commonly alleged to be. It is usually only the 'detached observer' who arrives at this conclusion, because he fails to recognize the particular *individual* values present in the object, but discernible only to the sharper eye of love. The 'blindness' then, is all on the side of the 'detached observer'. Indeed, the essence of individuality in another person, which cannot be described or expressed in conceptual terms (*Individuum ineffabile*), is *only* revealed in its full purity by love or by virtue of the insight it provides. When love is absent the 'individual' is immediately replaced by the 'social personality', the mere focus of a set of relationships (being an aunt or an uncle, for instance), or the exponent of a particular social function (profession), etc. In this case it is the lover who actually sees *more* of what is present than the others, and it is *he* and not 'others', who therefore sees what is objective and real. Only a falsely subjective devaluation of the real and objective to a mere 'universality of application' or 'general validity', one of the gravest errors of Kantian subjectivism[1]—could necessarily lead to any other conclusion. In many cases, admittedly, this tendency towards 'idealization' really does exist. But so far as it is present, it is not properly attributable to *love* for the other person, but to the obstacles which love encounters in the besetting tastes, interests, ideas and ideals of the lover himself. But that is simply due to partial 'egoism', to a failure to transcend oneself and the mental processes coloured by one's own physical sensations and instincts, so as to make contact with the object and the values it contains. But one ought not to construe the pure and authentic case of love in terms of the delusions which may arise under these circumstances.[2] There is a supposed form of love, for example, which

---

[1] Cf. on this 'Das Ressentiment im Aufbau der Moralen', and *Der Formalismus in der Ethik*.

[2] Cf. my remarks in the essay 'Über Idole der Selbstwahrnehmung', op. cit., concerning the mistaken principle of judging the normal by reference to the specious.

is merely an attachment to somebody because we have 'done so much for them', have 'spent so much toil and trouble over them', etc.; this typically resembles the 'grudging' evaluation, that a thing is good if it costs a lot. There is a suppositious love based on habit, which is a factor in attachment, so-called; there is that which derives from the inability to endure solitude (the 'flight from the self'), or from having interests in common; these too can produce in the parties concerned the illusion of love for an object. There can be pathological infatuation with an object, due to its resemblance to some earlier love; or intellectual affinity, which does not necessarily involve love, since it may only be based on 'respect'; or there is the sense of a common destiny, as in comradeship, for instance—a very different thing from friend-ship, which is based on love. But the nature of love itself should not be construed in terms of any of these possible delusive forms.

By thus dissenting from these three false interpretations of the phenomenal aspect of love (as a movement tending to the enhance-ment of value), I trust I have made it easier to grasp the basic character of the phenomenon itself. If we now consider this phenomenon, stripped of all its empirical and other trappings, it can also be said that *love is that movement wherein every concrete individual object that possesses value achieves the highest value compatible with its nature and ideal vocation; or wherein it attains the ideal state of value intrinsic to its nature.* (Hatred, on the other hand, is a move-ment in the opposite direction.) We are not concerned here with whether the love in question refers to oneself or to others, or with any other distinctions which might be drawn in this connection.

Chapter II

BASIC VALUES OF LOVE AND THE 'LOVE OF GOODNESS'

Love applies, in general, to the entire range of objects within the domain of value. But the kinds of value whereby love is attracted to its objects do not always give it the character of a *moral* act. This may suggest that the love of beauty, or knowledge, for example, are acts of no moral value, whereas love of goodness is so. But this would be a great mistake. For what other value attaches to the love of beauty or knowledge if not moral value? Love of beauty is not itself beautiful, nor does love of knowledge have any cognitive value. These types of love do indeed have moral value, insofar as the acts involved are conceived as *personal acts*. But does not the love of goodness have priority in this respect? The primary question is surely whether *there is any such thing as a love of goodness per se*? This, as I have elsewhere shown,[1] marks the great turning-point between the ancient and the Christian conceptions of love. The former acknowledges a love of goodness; for the latter, love itself has the value of 'goodness' in its most fundamental sense. My answer to this question is therefore negative. Love extends to all values, or rather to all objects because of their value, but there is no such thing as 'love of goodness'. Indeed, the love of goodness, as such, is itself evil, in that it necessarily involves Pharisaism; for the formula of Pharisaism is the precept 'Love the good' or 'Love men, insofar as they are good', and 'Hate evil, and men insofar as they are evil'. 'Love all men, inasmuch as they are bearers of values' is what Christianity rightly enjoins us, 'and especially the wicked'.[2]

---

[1] Cf. 'Das Ressentiment im Aufbau der Moralen'.

[2] It might be thought that one should love both the virtuous and the wicked,

Yet why is this so? For the simple reason that a person's moral 'goodness' (in the ultimate sense of the term), is determined according to the measure of his *love*—and only by this, on the absolute plane; just as the moral value of a community, for instance, varies in proportion to the total resources of love at its disposal. There can therefore be no such thing as love '*for*' a 'good', considered as a potential love-object, simply because love, of all acts, *possesses* the value of 'moral goodness' in the most eminent and ultimate sense of the term. If such a thing as a genuine love of goodness were possible, love itself could never possess the value of moral goodness in the most ultimate sense. But it is of all acts the *most ultimate* possessor of 'goodness'. For it is in its very movement from lower to higher value that 'goodness' first appears as a value. Hence there can be no question either, of loving one's own state of goodness; for one cannot have love for the self-love of another person. Let us put ourselves in the position of one who declares himself a lover of goodness: would he help a person, for instance, of whose moral goodness he was not already convinced? But, supposing the man is found to be in some sense a bad man, *who* can say that he would have been such, if he had only been loved enough, either by himself or others? Who can say that he would not have become a better man, in and through the act of loving? This marks the crucial distinction between Pharisaism and a genuine morality. We have shown elsewhere[1] that there is no willing of the good for its own sake. A person who helps another, as Kant says, 'not as if the interest or well-being of others were any of his concern', but in order to be 'good'; who regards the other as an opportunity for exercising his own goodness, beneficence, etc., is neither good nor well-conducted, but simply lives and acts in such a way as to be able merely to judge himself 'good' without there being any actual appearance of goodness, as a value, in his nature, volition or conduct. 'The world', as Shaw wittily observes,[2] is not 'a moral gymnasium, built expressly to strengthen your character in.' The Pharisee wishes to seem 'good' in the sight of himself, or others, or God; it is not that he *is* good, in doing so. We have also shown in the same connection, that there is no such thing as wanting to make others good, for the simple reason that 'good' is a value belonging intrinsically to spontaneous free acts and the nature of

but nevertheless love goodness and hate evil. But this is inacceptable, for there is no such thing as love and hatred for values or ideas of value as independent objects. Love and hatred invariably relate to concrete existents.

[1] Cf. 'Das Verhältnis der Werte "gut" und "böse" zu den übrigen Werten' in *Der Formalismus in der Ethik*, p. 19 seq.

[2] [*Man and Superman*, Act I.—Tr.]

personality alone, both of which are *in principle immune* from outside influence. It is just the same here. It is *in* the exercise of love that goodness shines out in the lover as an ultimate value. The conscious objectification of 'goodness' in the act of love can only mean one of two things: either we are deluded in thinking it to be goodness rather than some other value that we are objectifying, *or* we mistakenly suppose that the act in which that goodness appears is love rather than some other act, such as merely thinking of goodness, feeling it, rejoicing at it, and so on.

This also applies in relation to God. The love of God in its highest form is not to have love 'for' God, the All-merciful—for a mere concept, in effect; it is to *participate* in His love for the world (*amare mundum in Deo*), and for Himself (*amare Deum in Deo*); in other words it is what the scholastics, the mystics and Saint Augustine before them, called '*amare in Deo*'. If we wish to ascribe the highest of moral qualities to God, in the infinite mode of being, we can only do so by following Saint John and Saint Augustine, in treating love as the inmost essence of God Himself, and *identifying* Him as Infinite Love. It is to this heart and centre of the Divine activity that His infinite mercy and absolute moral perfection belong as attributes. Hence there is but one basic moral relationship between men of good-will: as fellow-servants, *partisans of a common Ideal and co-partners in a common Love.*[1]

With this state of things we may conjoin the (non-empirical) postulate that all love (once it is somehow perceived), evokes a loving response, and thereby brings a new moral value into being —for a loving response also possesses moral goodness, as an instance of love; and hence there emerges a principle which we propose to call the '*principle of the solidarity of all moral beings*'. It implies that with regard to their respective moral values, each is answerable, in principle, for all, and all for each; that where it is a question of mankind as bearers of all moral values, in collective responsibility to the Idea of the morally perfect Being, all stand proxy for one and one for all; so that each must share the blame for another's guilt, and each is *party from the outset* to the positive moral values of everyone else.

This principle is a corollary of the fact that the love of goodness is a myth; and from this it follows that the occurrence of wickedness always has a communal basis, which may or may not be empirically demonstrable, in a culpable *general want of love* for the wicked one on the part of others. For since love evokes an answering love, once it is seen—and the laws of intersubjective understanding always allow of this, in principle, without having to

---

[1] Cf. my discussion of the love of God in 'Probleme der Religion', in *Vom Ewigen im Menschen*.

postulate *beforehand* the bodily reality or causal interaction of the parties concerned—the occurrence of wickedness implies a concomitant absence of answering love, which is itself due to want of love in the first place. These assertions are in no way affected by men's actual empirical contacts with one another; nor are they relevant to the question of who is actually to blame in the concrete instance and who not, who has the moral credit and who not. They do not even depend on the fact that man happens to be a terrestrial living creature. There is thus a *collective moral guilt* and likewise a *collective merit* attaching to the moral community of persons as such, which is never a mere sum of their moral value as individuals.[1]

But if love of goodness is not moral love, how is the scope of the latter defined? For surely it is not every kind of love that has moral value as an act, even if its value is always positive, as in the love of beauty, knowledge, nature, art or concrete values generally? These acts certainly do not possess an immediate moral value, though as spiritual acts they may have values whose superiority to lower values is itself a contribution to the moral perfection of the persons who practise them. My answer to the question is that love has a specifically moral value *insofar as it represents a relationship between persons.*

[1] In 'Das Ressentiment im Aufbau der Moralen' I have pointed to the historical importance of this idea, as compared with the 'modern' conception of morality.

Chapter III

LOVE AND PERSONALITY

THERE are types of value which are essentially related to personality as their vehicle, and which can only attach to a person; 'virtues', for example, are values of this type. But in addition to this there is the value of the person as such, i.e. as that which essentially possesses these virtues. *Love for the value of persons,* i.e. for the person as a reality mediated in personal value, is *moral love* in the full sense of the term. I have given a detailed analysis of the concept of personality in another work.[1] Here I only wish to emphasize that the love which has moral value is not that which pays loving regard to a person for having such and such qualities, pursuing such and such activities, or for possessing talents, beauty or virtue; it is that love which incorporates these qualities, activities and gifts into its object, because they belong to that *individual person.* And it is therefore the only love that is '*absolute*', since it is unaffected by the possibility that these qualities and activities may change.[2]

Wherever we encounter the individual we meet with an *ultimate* which cannot be manufactured in any way out of features, qualities, activities, etc. Conversely, in that very mode of discernment which alone discloses the individual, it is always the features, qualities and activities which retain a merely abstract and general character, so long as we do not know the individual to whom they belong. It is characteristic, however, of individual personality that we only become acquainted with it *in* and *through* the act of loving, and that its value as an individual is likewise only disclosed

[1] Cf. the chapters 'Zur theoretischen Auffassung der Person überhaupt' and 'Die Person in ethischen Zusammenhängen' in *Der Formalismus in der Ethik.*

[2] The point was brought out clearly long ago by Aristotle, in the profound chapter on Friendship in his Nichomachean Ethics.

in the course of this act. Being an 'object' of love represents, as it were, the only objective status wherein personality has existence and can therefore be manifested. Hence the utterly misguided 'rationalism' of seeking to account for one's love for an individual person in any such terms as those relating to his qualities, acts, achievements or dispositions. Indeed the very attempt to do so has the effect of bringing the phenomenon of individual personal love sharply home to us. For we always find out in the process, that we can imagine every single one of these details to be altered or absent, without being a whit the more able, on that account, to leave off loving the person concerned. We also realize that if we consider these qualities and activities separately, and add up our liking for each of them, their total value for us is nothing like enough to justify our love of the person. There is always a surplus we cannot account for. (The same thing also applies in hatred, of course.) Moreover, the curious inconstancy of the reasons we are accustomed to offer ourselves in justification of our love for somebody, is a further indication that all such reasons are merely trumped-up after the event, and that none of them provides the real explanation.

How else then, is personality disclosed to us in love? Let us begin by getting this much clear: love is the most personal of attitudes, but a thoroughly *objective* one none the less, in the sense that in it we are 'objective' insofar as we free ourselves (in an unaccustomed fashion), from bondage to our own interests, wishes and ideas; but for all this the element of the personal in man can *never be disclosed to us as an 'object'*. Persons cannot be objectified, in love or any other genuine act, not even in cognition. Personality is that unity of substance, baffling observation and eluding analysis, which the individual experiences as inherent in all the acts he performs; no 'object' therefore, let alone a 'thing'. That part of others which does present itself objectively to me is never more than (1) the physical body; (2) its corporeal unity; (3) the self and the (vital) 'soul' belonging to it. And the same applies to everyone in respect of himself. The person of another can only be disclosed to me by my *joining in the performance* of his acts, either cognitively, by 'understanding' and vicarious 're-living', or morally, by 'following in his footsteps'. The moral core of the personality of Jesus, for example, is revealed to one man only: His disciple. This is the only path which can lead to such a disclosure. It may be vouchsafed to a disciple who knows nothing of an 'historical' kind about Jesus, nothing of His outward life, or even of His historical existence; for even to be *aware* of oneself *as* a disciple, which naturally implies an awareness of one's master as having an historical existence, is already a different thing

167

from *being* a disciple. The theologian, on the other hand, for all his knowledge of Jesus' career (including His inner life), is forever precluded by his office from any such insight; it necessarily transcends his field of view. A thing which is continually forgotten by the learned theological intellectualism of our day!

The values attaching to the physical, the corporeal and the mental can all be given us objectively, and may even be so given in the process of loving those who possess them. But this does not apply to purely personal values, i.e. the value of the personality itself. So long as we continue to 'objectify' someone in any way, his personality eludes our grasp, and only its trappings remain. Admittedly, we can still have love in an objective sense for the non-moral values of a personality itself, as an intellect for example, or an artistic force, for these we can grasp by reliving them in ourselves. But we can never grasp the purely moral value of a person in this way, for it is carried, in principle, only by his act of love. Hence this ultimate moral value of a personality is only disclosed to us when we associate ourselves with its own act of love. In order to elicit this moral value in our original, we must love what he loves, and love it *with* him. There is but one other case in which we may receive an 'objective' impression, not of the person as such, but of the self, and receive it by other means than those of discerning it immediately by way of expressive phenomena. Wherever the person loved is felt by us to be far more exalted than we are, it is noticeable how we seize hold of his personal existence by associating ourselves in his own acts of self-love and then scrutinizing the content given in these concomitant acts. It is this type of loving participation, namely in the love with which God loves Himself, which Brentano has recently claimed, in his book on Aristotle, to be already discernible in the Metaphysics; and which some of the mystics and schoolmen refer to as '*amare Deum in Deo*'. But we are also familiar with the corresponding state of affairs at the human level. It can happen, under certain circumstances, that we love a man more than he loves himself. Thus many people who hate themselves, are in fact loved, though any conjoint participation in their acts of self-hatred ought to mean 'hating them'. Yet these are cases in which a man's self-hatred may dissolve at the implied reproach of one who loves him and whom he loves in return: viz. 'that he ought not to hate a thing so, when the other, who loves him, is so very fond of it'. But so long as a man has love for himself, rather than hatred, the act of 'joining in' with such self-love is certainly *one* of the forms which other people's love for him may assume.

Chapter IV

THE FORMS, MODES AND KINDS
OF LOVE AND HATRED

WHAT we have hitherto treated as the acts of love and hatred, are merely the *bare essentials* of identity in those acts which remain the same throughout all the differences they may exhibit. But we can now characterize these differences by means of a three-dimensional classification, into what I shall describe as the *forms*, *modes* and *kinds* of love and hatred.

Corresponding to the basic division of all acts into vital acts of the body, purely mental acts of the self, and spiritual acts of the person, we also find love and hatred existing in three *forms*: spiritual love of the person, mental love of the individual self, and vital or passionate love. Although vital, mental and spiritual acts are intrinsically different in themselves, and are felt as different, without prior reference to their source, they do have an essential affinity with these sources, namely the body, the self and the person. At the same time, these emotional act-forms also have an essential reference to particular kinds of *value* as their noematic counterparts; vital acts to the values of the 'noble' and the 'mean' or 'base'; mental acts to the values of knowledge and beauty (cultural values); and spiritual acts to the values of the 'holy' and the 'profane'. The highest form of love is accordingly that which relates to objects (or persons), having the intrinsic value of holiness; mental love is that which the self has for cultural values of any kind; while vital love relates to the 'noble'. Objects whose value is simply that of being 'pleasant', engender neither love nor hatred. There is just a feeling of pleasantness (including reflexive modes of this, such as 'enjoyment'), together with an 'interest' in things that are pleasant, or indirectly pleasing, and so 'useful'; but there is no love for them.[1] For although we may speak, colloquially, of 'loving' a food, the expression is quite unsuited to the phenomenon it describes. Merely 'pleasant' things cannot be suitable for love, seeing that they are incapable of an enhancement of value in the sense implicit in the nature of love. Hence there is no such thing as 'sensual love', so far as the word 'sensual' in this expression is taken to denote a particular kind of love, and not just a way of saying that love, in this instance, is accompanied and interspersed with sensual feeling and emotion. A purely 'sensual' attitude to a person, for example, is at the same time an absolutely cold and *loveless* attitude. It necessarily treats the other as merely subservient to one's own sensual feelings, needs and, at best, enjoyment. But this is an attitude wholly incompatible with any sort of intentional love for the other, as such. Such an attitude is quite justified, from the ethical point of view, in relation to objects having no other value in themselves than that of being pleasant, which means, in effect, to things that are, and appear to be, 'dead'. But if it relates to an object which is manifestly susceptible of other and higher values than that of being pleasant to the senses—be it only the smallest and most trifling instance of vital value in plant or animal; and if it is present, moreover, *by itself* and not as a mere concomitant of other emotional intentions, such an attitude is 'evil', or 'wicked' (and most evil of all when it concerns a person). This naturally applies also to any attitude of this kind in relation to oneself.[2] There is, of course, no self-love present in such a case, but a debasement of body and spiritual personality precisely similar to that which is involved in the corresponding attitude to others.

The profound differences between these three forms of love are clearly brought out by a variety of circumstances. Firstly, by the fact that the same person can be the object of hatred *and* love, in each of their three forms, on all these *levels* of existence and value *at the same time* (while sensual attraction may take yet another course of its own). Thus we can love a person deeply, for instance, without his inspiring a 'passionate attachment' in us, indeed while finding his whole bodily aspect extremely repellent. It is equally possible to be fired with a violent passion for someone—not just a sensual attraction—without thereby finding anything to love in his mentality, the cast of his emotions, his intellectual interests, or the nature of his spiritual make-up. It is a type the poets have

[1] As Malebranche rightly saw, in the *Recherche de la Vérité*.
[2] As Kant rightly points out in reference to onanism: cf. *Metaphysische Anfangsgründe der Tugendlehre* (tr. in T. K. Abbott: *Kant's Theory of Ethics*, 6th ed., 1909).

often depicted, the man who combines a passionate love for another with hatred of their soul, while despising himself that he needs must love what, at higher levels of being and value, he cannot but abhor. On the other hand, even the deepest hatred embracing all levels save that of the person itself, may still retain a loving concern for the other's 'regeneration'. Hatred which extends even to this highest level of existence, is 'diabolical'; where it attaches to the mental, it is 'evil', while vital hatred is merely 'wicked'. People who display such an evident disparity and *conflict* in their love and hatred are usually described as 'maladjusted' characters. But this very fact that there can be such a variety of 'maladjustments' here, suggests that these functions of love are essentially *separable*, and continue to be so even when they actually work together in harmony and have but *one* object. A 'well-adjusted' character is to that extent a special gift of fortune. If it be objected that such maladjusted characters are so uncommon that one cannot use them to establish the separability of these forms of love as a general law, we may reply that a character perfectly adjusted in this respect is certainly no less uncommon. If Goethe, for instance, is an embodiment of the one type, there are other great men, such as Schopenhauer, Luther and St. Augustine, who are equally representative of the other. Again, the oft-mentioned *ambiguities* in the use of the word 'love' are traceable to these three forms. Thus in the first place we speak of 'love' in that highest sense of the word implied, e.g. in Buddha's discourses or in the Gospel's injunction to 'Love God before all things, and thy neighbour as thyself'. In trying to visualize such a love we have a conspectus of all that is finest and holiest in man's history. Secondly, we use the word in contexts such as those of friendship, marriage and the family, in which it is always love for the other as an individual soul that is implied. Lastly, we use the word 'love' without qualification to denote the amorous passion of a man and a woman. But language itself marks the contrast of this and all other forms of love from ties of a purely sensual kind.

From these 'forms' of love, let us now distinguish its '*kinds*'. They relate to those differences which make themselves felt to us as particular qualities of the emotion *itself*, without needing to consider the various *objects*, or common characteristics of these, to which such emotions refer. Thus we maintain that e.g. maternal and filial love, the love of home and country, and love in the implied sense of 'sexual love', are already distinct from one another as actual emotions, and not merely by the fact of being exercised in different fields, like a love for art, for the state, etc. If we consider what these words denote, we find that the very *stirrings* of love in such cases already evince *separate and distinct qualities*, and that at a stage of development where they still lack objects, or at least where the empirical aspect, the character of the object, has hardly yet been given. The (German) language frequently marks this difference by combining the name of the object with the word '*liebe*' (love) in one and the same verbal unit, the object-word being placed first.[1] Thus we cannot speak of *Staatenliebe* (love of the state), on the analogy of *Heimatliebe* (love of home) and *Vaterlandsliebe* (love of country), but only of *Liebe zum Staate*; there is *Gottesliebe* (love of God) but no *Kunstliebe* (love of art). Again, we do not have a *Vaterliebe* (father-love) corresponding to *Mutterliebe* (mother-love); the word 'father-love' actually leaves us in doubt as to whether the father is the loving or the loved one, whereas 'mother-love' is absolutely definite in referring to the mother's love for her child. The authenticity of the various kinds of love is warranted by their being recognizable as stirrings, *without* a semblance of the object to which they are directed having been given in any way. They are genuine *qualities of the acts themselves*. Thus a person having neither home nor country can still experience the characteristic stirrings of love for these things, even when they lack an object and persist therefore as yearnings without fulfilment. Again, when abroad for instance, one may be suddenly overtaken by a feeling of nostalgia, though without having any 'thought' or 'idea' of home in mind. Here we experience a powerful and peculiar hankering for somewhere far away and are overcome with tenderness for something which commends itself to us as fond and familiar. Perhaps we may endure this unsatisfied longing for a considerable time, without realizing that it is our home that we are yearning for. *Mother-love*, however, provides a particularly clear instance of a genuine *kind* of love in this sense. The occurrence of this affection (like that of the instinct associated with it), is quite unconnected with any form of experience with children on the part of the woman concerned. The presence of this specifically 'motherly' disposition is not contingent upon the woman in question having children of her own, nor would the affection disappear, as such, if she had never seen children, or had absolutely no conception of the process of child-bearing. It is only these genuine kinds of love therefore, that are capable of true '*fulfilment*' in a given object. Those, on the other hand, which can only be distinguished according to their objects, are incapable of 'fulfilment'. Hence there is no 'father-love' corresponding to 'mother-love'. And hence, too, a man's love for his child is much more powerfully affected by his love for the child's mother than is the mother's

[1] [There is, unfortunately, no way of reproducing this argument convincingly in English.—Tr.]

love for her child by her love for the child's father; just as it also depends to a far greater extent on the appearance and character of the child itself. His love for the child is also conditioned, of course, by the fact that it is 'his own' child, but this only comes about by means of an act of judgement, and not in the immediate fashion characteristic of mother-love. This immediate feeling for the child as 'hers', like the original longing for fulfilment of a love already evinced beforehand, is an intrinsic feature of the feminine consciousness as such, and has no analogy in the masculine frame of mind. Correspondingly, it is only in woman that the procreative urge has the form of an innate *instinct*, whereas in man this urge has merely the character of a wish, and not that of an instinct or drive; in other words, it is always based on grounds of some kind.[1] This can also be seen in the fact that in most cases the first awakening of the father's love for the child occurs at a more advanced stage of the child's development than the mother's, for it only begins when the mental and spiritual personality of the child has begun to assert itself more plainly.[2]

Lastly, we distinguish the kinds of love from the mere *modes* thereof, which consist in nothing more than *conjunctions* of acts of love, notably with social dispositions and feelings of sympathy. These too have left their mark on language in such expressions as 'kindness', 'goodwill', 'liking', 'fondness', 'grace and favour', 'amiability' (whose colloquial meaning is not that of 'worthiness

---

[1] To a man, conception and gestation are essentially no more than a 'consequence' of the sexual act, and do not appear to be due to a genuine procreative instinct; as has also been justly observed by the gynæcologist Hugo Sellheim, in *Das Rätsel des Ewig-Weiblichen.*

[2] Some authors unjustifiably deny the presence of a procreative urge or instinct even in women; Max Marcuse, for instance, in his very valuable *Wandlungen des Fortpflanzungsgedankens und-Willens.* Topp goes too far the other way in supposing a degeneration of 'the healthy natural procreative instinct into the sexual instinct' (in men as well), and this within historical times. (See *Mitteilungen der mediz, Zentralzeitung,* 1906, 10). But it is true, at all events, that in the course of animal evolution the sexual instinct was 'predominantly shaped and guided' by a procreative instinct (as Marcuse also admits). According to Marcuse, Landmann, in his *Grundfragen der Lebensform,* has adduced the following five principles with respect to temperate-zone mammals: (1) the beginning of puberty and of sexual feeling coincides with the completion of bodily growth; (2) the mating season (rut) is retroactively determined by the most favourable season for birth; (3) birth always occurs at the season which gives mother and young the best chance of subsistence; (4) sexual desire disappears in the female after conception, and once the secretion of the characteristic odour ceases, the male also lacks an inducement to copulation; (5) the sexual impulse remains dormant in the mother so long as the young still require to be fed. Landmann believes that it was only during the Ice Age that the sexual instinct freed itself from the rutting-cycle and thereby parted from the procreative instinct. How far some traces of periodicity may yet persist in man as he is today, is still largely an open question. (See the bibliography in Marcuse, op. cit.)

to be loved', but implies an active attitude), 'affection', 'courtesy', 'friendliness', 'devotion', 'attachment', 'loyalty', 'intimacy', 'gratitude', 'filial regard' and so on. A proportion of these terms denote attributes which are not part of the basic fabric of human nature, but only exist in the context of a given framework of historical development. Kindness, goodwill, gratitude and affection, for example, are assuredly modes of love which are common to *all* men, and do not depend for their emergence on the level of historical development. But it is otherwise with amiability, courtesy, filial regard, etc. There are modes of hatred corresponding to these modes of love, but I shall not enter into their details here. Finally, we may distinguish these modes from mere emotional complexes in which love and hatred are simply ingredients, and do not thereby impart an underlying flavour to the whole. Such, for instance, are fidelity and humility (in regard to love), and envy, jealousy and suspicion (in regard to hate).

Chapter V

THE LIMITATIONS OF THE
NATURALISTIC THEORY OF LOVE

IN the course of examining the theories of sympathy we have already rejected:

(1) Theories which derive love from fellow-feeling (by way of benevolence), while seeking to ascribe the latter to imitation, reproduction and empathy, or to an illusion.

(2) Theories which seek to explain fellow-feeling by reference to the social instinct and impulse; this originally 'phylogenetic' type of theory has now been supplemented, in the earlier and later versions of positivism (from Feuerbach onwards) by

(3) A range of ideas concerning the philosophy of history; which again serves to pave the way, historically, for

(4) A very recent ontogenetic theory of love which—if correct, would make nonsense of our whole account; this being the theory of Sigmund Freud.

I venture to describe these four theories, taken together, as *the naturalistic theory of love.*

There is one instinct and impulse which, in bisexual creatures at least, always functions simultaneously (even in non-gregarious animals), as a social impulse: that is the mutual attraction of the sexes. This has been considered sufficient to justify the inference that it is the source of every kind of social instinct—a very questionable conclusion, for the very fact that all bisexual animals possess the sexual instinct but do not all have the social instinct, does more to indicate their independence of one another. There is no refuge to be had in supposing the non-gregarious animals to be somehow furnished with sexual or procreative instincts (which we do not separate here), of a feebler kind. Feuerbach attempts, nevertheless, to show that all social instincts and the concomitant heteropathic emotions, which he also identifies, wrongly, with sympathetic emotions, are established (along with the 'forms of sociality' based thereon), in the following manner: the sexual instinct, insofar as it is in any way *checked* in its activity, splits up into sectional impulses, initially concerned with the children and chiefly felt by the mother, which then spread to the father as well in respèct of the children and their mother—over and above their passing contacts in a specifically sexual context. Maternal love, already widely prevalent in the animal kingdom, (and occurring even in the absence of conjoint parental love for the young) is taken, along with its associated parental instinct, to be the second source of the various forms of social instinct and sympathy. Hence there arise thirdly, the reciprocal love of children for their parents and for one another, and the ties of love which operate within the family. And in so far as these impulses extend to an ever-widening circle of those whose relationship to the family has an effect upon its welfare and destiny, there arises a further love for one's own kindred, native stock, people and fatherland, a process which can only seek and find its eventual outcome in engendering a universal love of mankind. A successive '*expansion*' of these impulses and sympathetic emotions by '*transference*' from the original object to those which are in some way causally linked with its interests and welfare; that is the principle on which to explain the 'evolution' of love in its various forms. The primary rôle assigned to maternal love seems to be corroborated by the fact, particularly stressed by Bachofen, and confirmed in many societies, that all such societies have passed through a phase of law, custom and culture to which Bachofen gives the name of 'matriarchy', since in it the mother is the centre of the family, the bridegroom enters the daughter's house, and the daughter is also the primary heir.[1] But the love of God, for Feuerbach, is never more than love for an imaginary being, in whom the 'idea of humanity' is hypostatized, and whose content is entirely dependent on the particular historical experience of the race concerned.

Thus far the 'naturalistic' theory has acquired three mutually-supporting components: (1) the early British theories of fellow-feeling (imitation, empathy, reproduction, illusion, etc.); (2) the phylogenetic theories of Darwin and Spencer; (3) the historico-philosophical theory whose further ramifications we shall not pursue here.

But the keystone of this 'naturalistic' theory, which first gave it a completely self-contained unity, came by addition of a still

---

[1] See Bachofen: *Das Mutterrecht* (Stuttgart, 1861).

very recent *ontogenetic theory* of the varieties of love; adopting and relying upon the general conceptions of explanatory principle current in British associationism and its theory of sympathy, it has sought by their aid to trace the typical and also the atypical course taken, in a human being, by the development of the love-impulses towards their various objects, and in their various kinds and forms. This has been the achievement of Sigmund Freud and his school.[1]

I do not intend at this point to give a detailed exposition or criticism of the Freudian theory. I merely wish to take a brief look at its principles of explanation. The theory itself proceeds from a group of facts which were indeed all-too-little known before Freud's time; from the fact that man seems to have a propensity originating not merely in adolescence, but from the very moment of his birth, for the sensation of sexual pleasure. Thus according to Freud, the infant at the breast has blissful sensations of this kind in the act of suckling ('sensual sucking')—and similarly in all stimulation occasioned haphazardly by mechanical or other means (in the course of daily care, bathing, etc.), of those bodily zones which Freud calls 'the erotogenic zones of infancy'; areas which do not by any means begin by coinciding with the genital organs, being far more widely extended over the surface of the body. These sensations which, once evoked by *accidental* stimuli, become the object of secondary desires for their revival and repetition, are now said to comprise, as it were, the ultimate *material for the construction* of all such kinds of love and sympathetic feeling as are actually observable in maturity, up to the highest, most sublimated and most spiritual forms. The driving impulse to the provision of these sensations is called 'libido' by Freud. Thus 'libido' is by *no* means equivalent to 'sexual instinct'. Freud does not say that the sexual instinct is the source of all kinds of love. On the contrary, he regards the sexual instinct in general, not as an innate and simple 'drive', but as a very complicated psychical *construct*, which is engendered and acquired anew in the life of every individual, and which in the strict sense of the word (as a hetero-sexual impulse), is not in fact always acquired, as is indicated by the remarkably significant fact of sexual *perversion*.

---

[1] The chief work in this field is Freud's *Three Essays on the Theory of Sexuality* (authorized translation by James Strachey, Imago, 1949). Of late the Freudian-school has returned to its historico-philosophical starting-point, in applying these principles to the historical interpretation of myth, religion and the evolution of law. Cf. especially the periodical *Imago*. Cf. also Freud's *Totem and Taboo* and his work on group-psychology already quoted. A good introduction to the theoretical aspect of Freud's work has been given by Kuno Mittenzwey in *Zeitschrift für Pathopsychologie* (ed. W. Specht). Cf. also C. G. Jung: *Psychology of the Unconscious* (tr. by Beatrice M. Hinkle), Kegan Paul, 1921.

The 'perversions', however, according to Freud, are not the aberrations of an implanted sexual instinct, but a *fixation* of still more fundamental attitudes which are generally current in childhood. Wherever, in fact, an object evokes sensations of the above-mentioned kind, libido is directed upon that object. Once it has developed more fully, it does not immediately direct itself generally upon the other sex, but gropes about, as it were, in all possible directions. Hence Freud's remark that 'man is born polymorphously perverse'. That it eventually finds an 'object-choice' in a member of the other sex is again, according to Freud, only a particularly fortunate *chance*, though on the whole a very frequent one. Every perversion is therefore both '*infantilism*', an arresting of normal development, and a fixation of an earlier stage. The neuroses are also largely ascribed by him to such arrested development. Interest in the other sex only sets in if the typical normal decline of sensitivity in all the 'erotogenic zones of infancy' reaches a vanishing-point, so that the sensation of sexual pleasure is retained only in the genital organs. This generally occurs on reaching puberty, whereupon the normal sexual impulse usually makes its appearance. There is no need to go into the details of this evolution here. It is only the concepts of 'libido' and 'sexual impulse' that are of interest in our present context.

How are the various kinds of love to be developed from this? Freud's answer involves two fundamental explanatory notions: (1) '*repression of libido*'; and (2) '*sublimation of libido*'. The forces which are supposed to effect this repression are, firstly, those feelings and impulses which life itself has developed, in order to restrain libido in a manner conducive to the maintenance of the species. These include disgust, shame and 'the structures of morality and authority erected by society', such as the feelings which lead to the taboo on incest. They see to it that the impulses of libido are repressed and *dammed*, as it were, but it still continues active in the 'Unconscious', as is shown by the analysis of dreams (sleeping and waking). The ætiology of most of the neuroses is supposed to be due to this repression of the libido and of all the contents upon which it is directed. They come about wherever the libido retains its original content (whether normal or perverse) in the Unconscious, but 'repressed' and without attaining satisfaction. In this case, according to Freud, the accumulation of repressed affects (impulse *plus* emotion) is transformed into the numerous expressive signs and symptoms of neurosis (such as convulsions, etc.).

But the case is altered if the libido and the instinctive energy it contains is set free from its original content, the pleasurable sensation and all objects connected with it, and is transferred through ever more refined vestigial reproduction of the pleasure-sensations (from which Freud ultimately derives all consciousness of value in general), to other objects, which are now loved '*on their own account*', independently of all connection with the original feeling of pleasure. Freud calls this process '*sublimation*'. All cultivation of social habits, knowledge, art and civilization is said to depend on this 'sublimation' of repressed libido, insofar as it is the mental flywheel which propels all these activities. Only where 'sublimation' does not come about normally, and where repression nevertheless occurs, do we find neurosis, or perversion, through fixation at an earlier phase of development.

Chapter VI

A CRITIQUE OF THE NATURALISTIC THEORY, AND OUTLINE OF A THEORY BASED ON THE PHENOMENA

(1) LOVE AND INSTINCT

IN order to evolve an *explanatory* theory, we must now suspend the phenomenological reduction; we are no longer, that is, to abstract ourselves deliberately from the real nature of the subjects who frame these acts and from the purport of their contents. On doing so it will be obvious that love and hatred, in their essence no less than their respective forms, modes and kinds, can only make their appearance in the concrete and extremely complex facts involved in the special character of the human constitution and its objective environment. Thus vital love, for example, with its domain of values—'nobility' and 'baseness' (or 'badness')—is a genuine essence, and not merely an act of loving as such. For 'life' is itself an essence, and not merely a concept abstracted from empirically existent organisms. The establishment of biology on a phenomenological basis may well confirm that not only such basic biological concepts as those of living form and movement, but also those of 'birth', 'death', 'growth', 'heredity' and many others, are concepts having a *specifically phenomenological basis* which owes nothing to observation of terrestrial organisms or to induction from these observations. The same applies to vital love, which our previous discussion has shown to consist of nothing but a movement tending to the enhancement of value from the base to the noble. But the way in which this movement is effected in *actual* organisms of any given kind, the nature of its accompanying circumstances, and the manner of its causal realization, are matters which lie altogether *beyond* the scope of phenomenology. The fact that in man, for instance, as in all bi-sexual animals, vital love is intimately connected with sexual love, though this is qualitatively of quite another kind, is certainly *not* a matter of intrinsic connection; I leave open here the difficult question whether 'male' and 'female' are themselves examples of genuine essences, or merely empirical concepts. It may be a matter of empirical fact that human sexual love should lead to such-and-such activities, and be accompanied by such-and-such organic sensations; there may equally be a question as to the organs involved, and as to the manner and means whereby the instinctive energies behind these activities are reconciled with those of other instincts, in view of the limited nature of man's vital energy and of the outlets permitted by his organic structure. But these are questions which must confront a descriptive and explanatory theory of the ontogenesis and also phylogenesis of human sexual love; they are no longer the concern of phenomenology.

But before tackling this ontogenetic problem and the way it is treated by the naturalistic theory, let us first apply the critical axe to the roots of that theory itself.

In addition to the view we have already rejected, that the act of love can be generally explained as a 'complex' or 'evolutionary outcome' of more elementary mental factors, the roots of naturalism lie in its complete failure to recognize the ultimacy not only of 'spiritual' and 'sacred' love, but also of 'love for the individual soul'. The error of naturalism does not consist in having actually recognized the facts so designated, while offering a false and inadequate 'explanation' of them. The fact is that it simply does not see them at all, being quite peculiarly *blind* to such things. It has no eyes for phenomena exhibiting a level of action and value which is *transcendent*, not only of our actual vital organization, but of the nature of all life, and (in sacred love) of the nature of all that belongs to the mental plane as well. It matters not at all at what stage of development in human history this level emerges, nor whether it makes its appearance in many people or only a few. If the naturalistic theory were aware of the phenomena of spiritual and sacred love, it would immediately recognize also that one cannot explain or derive them from any circumstance associated with the vital sphere or with love on that level. But here as elsewhere, the fundamental error of naturalism consists in the fact that its whole approach precludes it from realizing that completely *new* acts and qualities can and do appear in the course of organic and human evolution; and that these qualities inevitably appear *abruptly* and can never be regarded as merely gradual developments of the previous state, as is possible, in principle at least, when dealing with the bodily structure of the organism concerned.[1] Its approach also blinds it to the fact that in the course of vital evolution essentially *new and deeper planes of being and value* may come within the purview of life as it develops, so that whole realms of *objects* and values are opened up in the process; indeed that these realms of being and value already begin to open and disclose their wealth of qualities ahead of life's own advance. But for the naturalistic theory this can only amount to a continual piling-up of illusory contents (colours, sounds, values, etc.), *between* the organism and the world. On this view an organism perceiving only matter and motion would have the closest contact with 'things in themselves'; every additional quality would be just a further illusion. The naturalistic theory is utterly oblivious to the fundamental fact that the 'real' world is always 'richer' than any 'given' one. Like naturalistic philosophy generally, it is essentially deflationary in its outlook. It approaches everything on the false assumption that whatever happens to be simplest and least valuable must also have the character of *ontological priority* and causal antecedence; now it is true enough that such things are easiest to grasp from the point of view of a 'human understanding' bent on controlling and dominating the world, simply because they are the most tractable, widespread and easily communicable, as compared with the more complex and valuable factors; but that is no reason for supposing that being and value are arranged to suit the convenience of an intelligence operating in terms of practical ends. The phenomenon of 'sacred love' is certainly rare—rarer, even, than intellectual genius of any kind; it is, moreover, absolutely uncontrollable and cannot be produced 'experimentally' or by education. Even when present and observable, it is only perceived by the few; and as we have seen, a full and adequate grasp of its value already involves a corresponding genius for discipleship. But the content and values which proclaim its assignable rank in an order of existence relative to the absolute, no less than its place in the ascending and descending scale of objective value, have nothing at all to do with its frequency, communicability or 'general validity' so-called, nor yet with its degree of 'intelligibility' relative to and in terms of the practical aims of men; for its absolute quality and degree of value are entirely determined by its inner phenomenological character.

[1] For an acute exposition of this point see C. Stumpf: *Die Entwicklungsidee in der Philosophie*. Cf. also my lectures (to be published shortly) on 'Entwicklungsstufen der Seele'. [Cf. *Die Stellung des Menschen im Kosmos* (1927).]

The essential characteristics of sacred love are these: we may see how those imbued with it do not chafe and struggle against suffering and death, but embrace it willingly and gladly. They are not men who no longer value life—for in that case how could they sacrifice it? They love it well, but esteem it less than some other and greater thing. They endure suffering indeed, not because they are inured to it, but because the love and loyalty they evince for what is holy to them crowns their suffering with a beatitude before whose radiance all the joy and happiness of life pale into insignificance and seem of little worth. Again, we may see how freely this sacred love takes poverty upon itself, as Buddha or St. Francis did—not as an evil, which it assuredly is from the vital point of view, but 'as a radiant mistress and a bride', as St. Francis saw 'My Lady Poverty' before his first conversion, after the festive banquet with his gallant young companions, of whom each had addressed a song to his future bride; 'a radiant mistress' because the burdens she imposes on the act of sacred love which St. Francis felt pouring so strongly from his inmost heart, are lighter than those of wealth, which turns the spirit to material things and besets it in worldly toils.[1] To such facts and a thousand like them, involving the phenomenon of sacred love, the psychology and ethics of naturalism can offer only a very limited range of interpretations: it can treat them as a 'perversion' of the normal vital impulse, a 'morbid' tendency of action and emotion, an inner symptom of decadent vitality, or a form of 'resentment'. (It might be alleged, for example, that Francis was incapable of administering his fortune or of doing what his father asked of him, and hence, on realizing his incompetence, may be supposed to have declared that he would sooner live in complete poverty so as to save himself the trouble!) Again, the phenomenon may be regarded as a basically illusory 'sublimation of libido' into 'love of God', 'general benevolence', 'universal ministry' and the like. 'Is it not obvious,' it may be said, 'how his vision of poverty as a "bride and mistress", his own conception of himself as the "troubadour of God", his spiritual liaison with St. Clara, and many other things, all bear witness to the universal power of libido?' The explanation in terms of perversion and resentment is too utterly absurd in this case to deserve attention. Why should anybody love God and the world and be kind and loving to every living thing, merely because of his inability to administer his own possessions? The frivolous spendthrift and the bon-viveur are equally incapable in this respect. And what is there in common between an embittered love and esteem for poverty because of a felt inability to acquire and

[1] There is a good treatment of 'love without desire' in Walter Rathenau's book, *Mechanik des Geistes*.

manage wealth, and the attitude of the rich young man in the Gospel whose example St. Francis followed? It is not poverty as such that has any positive value for him, but the free *autonomous act of the spirit* in *giving away* his fortune (and giving it generously); an act whereby the rich young man does not despoil himself of value, but is immeasurably the richer; for has he not adorned himself with a value whose nature and essence lie far above all that life has to offer? As for 'sublimation', it merely exposes the persistent confusion in naturalistic ethics between shadow and substance. The saints have sought to convey their glowing love for the sacred and divine to others, and even to themselves, in words of a language not devised for matters so rare; and when, in doing so, they make use of images, expressions and metaphors derived from a sphere in which even the ordinary man feels that glow of love which they evince for things of the spirit, it is at once supposed that this can be nothing other than a covert, disguised, or sublimated sexual instinct! But why should it have taken this form in the case of the young, handsome, powerful, rich and universally beloved Francis? Why did he not do as his friends and companions did? We know how worn-out old men and pious old spinsters are accustomed, as the proverb has it, to make a virtue of necessity, which like all pharisees they then account to themselves as a genuine virtue. But what bearing has it here?

Similar considerations apply to the love of the soul. For of course the naturalistic theory can give no account of that love for the individual soul, be it rooted where it may, in friendship, marriage, etc., which persists unaltered throughout the vicissitudes of passion (in old couples, for instance, despite the altered ties of affection between them). For compared with a love which is solely concerned and engaged in the promotion of *vital* values, the love of the individual soul can *only* appear an 'aberration', a misguided fixation and infatuation, as it were, with the individual self of another person. For all the forces inherent in life and its promotion and maintenance, are primarily concerned with the furtherance and preservation of the *species*, and not the individual, let alone the individual soul. Whence it is perfectly intelligible that wherever the sexual relationship is wholly or predominantly judged in terms of biological value, marriage and other forms of sexual union are regarded as *mere* 'modes of propagation'; as when Tacitus, for instance, tells us in his *Germania* of the German women, that they do not love their husbands as individuals, but as fathers of their children. This is still the case in Japan, for example, where the idea of sexual *love* for another individual is almost unheard of, and the idea of a pure and absolute monogamy equally so in consequence.[1] The Japanese have no notion of a specific individual love between the sexes: they resolve a man's individuality into a set of attributes consisting primarily of physical features (his stature, hair, walk, voice, etc.); and sexual love is explained (in accordance with the ancestor-cult), by the fact that the loved one exhibits characteristics which were once loved by the lover's ancestors in their own day. This also makes it readily intelligible that it is mainly the parents who arrange the marriage-contract; they are in a position to do so since the tendency of their children's affections is supposed to be merely an inherited proclivity of their own. This explains why it should have been a law until recently that a marriage could actually be dissolved at the mother-in-law's request; why the marriage-bond in general is regarded as an entry into the family as a whole rather than the family as an outcome and product of the marriage; why a given individual is even described by name as merely the 'son of so-and-so', and much else besides.

The idea of 'monogamy' even, is simply incapable of derivation from naturalistic premises. For only love for the individual is 'singular' in its reference. If there is no such thing, monogamy is simply a baseless and irrational compulsion. Virtually all current proposals for the abandonment of monogamy (e.g. von Ehrenfels'), on the ground that it is 'harmful to the species', are based upon naturalistic presuppositions of this kind.[2] Monogamy only acquires an ultimate phenomenological basis if marriage is thought of as an institution, based on a relation of love between *souls*, for the purpose of procreation, and if sexual love is likewise regarded, not as an analogous love which merely obtains between two beings of physically opposite sex, but as a mode of love already having properties peculiar to the soul alone. For only so does it acquire a justification independent of contingent features in the human organism, such as would still render it valid even in a universe where these features were entirely different. The old saying that 'marriages are made in heaven', is but a mythological expression of the fact that 'monogamous marriage' is based on the possibility of an essential relationship subsisting between two *individuals* (male and female) as such, considered as entities, and not as initially identifiable only through their physical structure. Whence it follows that all the empirical hazards of time, place, social background, etc., which bring the couple together, must be regarded

---

[1] This connection between monogamy and love of the individual soul comes out very clearly in the case of polygamous societies such as the Mohammedans. Cf. the Koran, which denies, moreover, that women have souls.

[2] Cf. my address on 'Bevölkerungsprobleme als Weltanschauungsfragen', op. cit., on the occasion of the Cologne conference on population-policy, 1921.

simply as means to the attainment of that insight which first sets
the seal upon their union; while the actual institutions of monogamous marriage must be considered as merely defining the terms,
relative to a civilization and culture, under which the state or the
established church are prepared, on the average, to recognize the
fact of such an intrinsic bond of union. All proposals for 'temporary marriage', as was once the practice in Japan, or for 'trial
marriage', and so on, are therefore based on assumptions in which
the conception of sexual love as interfused with love of the
individual soul, is still wanting.[1]

Let us return once more to the basic aberration of the naturalistic theory; how are sacred love and the love of the soul related
to our *system of instincts*? All effort, all 'tendency' even (the phenomenological basis of the concept of vitality), is based upon acts
involving some kind of *evaluation* (there being also an awareness
of this value, in the case of effort); there need be no 'idea' or
'conception' of this even in the most formal sense (such as that
of Leibnitz), as has been supposed by those intellectualistic philosophers who have wrongly sought to derive the notion of value
from those of 'being' and 'perfection'. This intrinsically formal
element is present in all concepts of 'growth' and 'development'
and especially in that of 'progress' (a concept which already differs
from the vital concepts mentioned above in making use of positive
material assumptions, and the idea of purpose). Those effortful
impulses of a purely involuntary kind which do not proceed from
the self, but appear, phenomenologically, to be received by it,
are doubtless 'blind' in the intellectual sense, but not in the sense
of possessing an *underlying trend towards value generally*. Indeed we
may say that in the sequence of development of an impulse, the
trend towards value is already present at a level of consciousness
where *consciousness* of the effort itself may still be lacking, so that
there may be repression of the subsequent effort, leaving only this
consciousness of value as evidence of its initial generation.[2]

The naturalistic theory, however, is oblivious to all this, and
therefore seeks to derive love from impulses which are not only
blind intellectually, but blind to value as well, in attempting to
establish the concept of value in general on the basis of an affinity
between a valueless object and a prior (and inherently blind)
impulse. But *love and hatred form the basis for all* other kinds of

[1] This does not rule out the possibility of a positive legal dissolution of
marriage; for the civil or ecclesiastical regulations on the subject do no more
than state the *conditions* under which either a marriage has not been legally
contracted, or it must be presumed that the essential marital tie has never
subsisted.

[2] Cf. the chapter on 'Zwecke und Werte: Streben, Wert und Ziel', in *Der
Formalismus in der Ethik*, Pt. I, ch. I, 3.

evaluation (feeling, preference, or value-judgement), and are naturally at the very root of all effort and tendency, since these are themselves based upon an apprehension of value. Everything strives for what it loves, and against what it hates. It does not love what it strives for, nor hate what it repels. The way in which love or effort present themselves (in form, kind or mode) has no bearing on this at all, and the manner in which they are realized empirically is equally irrelevant.

Moreover the relationship of love and instinct is different in principle from that assumed by the naturalistic theory, viz. that love is itself an instinct or a genetic product of instincts and instinctive associations. It is altogether different, and may be formulated as follows: (1) an act of love occurs in a given bio-psychic organism only where an instinctive urge is also present towards the same region of value as that to which the movement of love is directed. (2) From the given realm of objectively sub-sistent value-qualities, the only values which stand out as 'potential love-values' for a real entity, are those whose actual physical possessors are in some way also subject to a system of instincts.[1] To that extent the instinctive system certainly determines the specific content of these values, as regards their *selection* and differentiation, but not their phenomenological content. The instinctive system with its 'degrees of urgency' remains responsible for the *ordering* of this selection but in no sense for the act of loving itself, nor for the value-content, nor for the higher or lower status of the value. It therefore determines, firstly, the actual way in which the act of love is evoked and secondly, the choice and order of preference among values, but it has no bearing upon the act of loving and the content thereof (value-qualities), nor upon the superiority of the value and its position in the scale of values. Figuratively speaking, the instinctive impulses are like torches casting a light upon those objectively subsistent value-contents which may come to determine the objects of love. Hence the essential status of love in relation to instinct is by no means that of a positive product, as if it were brought into being by instinct, or proceeded from thence; the effect is one of limitation and selection. What was ambiguously referred to above as 'evocation' is not a causal relationship, but a relation of relevance to existence.

[1] In his admirable description of the emotions and emotional behaviour of the chimpanzees he studied at Teneriffe, Wolfgang Köhler has given convincing evidence of the presence, even in animals, of love and cognate behaviour at the vital level (e.g. in the sharing and 'giving away' of food). Cf. *The Mentality of Apes* (tr. Ella Winter, Kegan Paul, 1925). But the facts reported make it equally clear that the display of such love is dependent on instinctive factors (e.g. sexual periodicity), and also confined to the immediately present. Animal 'affection' (such as that of a dog for its master) has nothing to do with love.

Actual empirical organisms of any particular kind are only able to love what is at the same time appropriate to their specific instincts and of importance to them.

There is a basis of justification for these theoretical remarks in phenomenological insight, though they are in no sense due to such insight themselves.

It is undoubtedly a factor in the strength of the naturalistic theory that it appears to account for a set of facts which might at first seem inexplicable on our present premisses, though properly seen, they do but *confirm* them. They can be grouped together under the heading of that 'perspective of interests' which governs all our actual human impulses of love (and all stirrings of sympathy and value-judgements as well). How is it that fellow-feeling varies or seems to vary so strongly according to the felt nearness or remoteness of the beloved object? And also according to that nearness or remoteness which is not just spatio-temporal, though likewise expressed in that form, the significance or insignificance of an object for our instinctively conditioned 'interests'? If we do not see someone we love for a long time, our attachment for him slowly diminishes. We may read in a newspaper that a thousand Japanese have been drowned, or even that twenty million Russians are starving, but this normally has less effect on our sympathies than when our wife cuts her finger or young Johnny has a stomach-ache. Why does the witnessing of an accident have such a very different effect from the mere report of it? How comes it that so often in history family-love is seen to militate against love of the clan, love of the clan against love of one's own country and people, and this in turn against love of mankind? And that even the love of God itself should conflict with true love of humanity? Why, again, do love and fellow-feeling broaden out so *slowly* from the narrower to the wider sphere? And what is meant in this instance by 'wider' and 'narrower'? Presumably (1) the degree to which our instinctive system is responsive to the field of objects in question, (2) the urgency of the 'instinct', and (3) the strength of the 'impulse'.

There can be no doubt as to the facts—but the question is: (1) What appearance do they actually present? How are we to improve upon our indefinite grasp of them? (2) How are they to be understood?

The naturalistic theory explains these facts in terms of a gradual 'expansion' of love and fellow-feeling by 'transference' of the direction of the instinct (Feuerbach, for instance, traces it from the sexual object to the child, from thence to the father, and ultimately to the family, the clan, the race, and so on); this is to treat this expansion as a mere increase of reciprocal interaction and interdependence among instincts and interests. Spencer adopts the same principle. But has the theory got the facts right in the first place? I do not think so.

(2) THE FACTS CONCERNING THE 'PERSPECTIVE OF INTERESTS'

To begin with, this theory is governed by a fundamentally erroneous estimate of love in terms of the sheer *size* and breadth of its range of objects: it supposes, for instance, that love of country, as such, is inferior to the general love of mankind, that family-love, as such, is inferior to love of country, that self-love is inferior to friendship, and so on. This is due (1) to the fact that the naturalistic theory does not recognize these types of love as genuine kinds of love-emotion, and believes it possible to derive them from one and the same kind of love, together with a quantitative enlargement of the group to which it refers. (2) The theory not only disregards the fact that love is intrinsically concerned with values and their enhancement, but also the fact that, as the circle is enlarged, the values which can still be discerned and correctly assessed within it become increasingly 'peripheral' and 'inferior' ones, passing from 'personal value' into the sphere of physical circumstances, and that this law has nothing to do with the increase or decrease in the number of those possessing these central or peripheral values. So far as it relates to the species as a whole, the love of humanity (however comprehensive it may be, according to the varying total of the world's population), can only subsist upon those values which are and *can* be attributed individually and collectively to men as mere 'specimens' of humanity, not as Frenchmen, Englishmen, Germans and so on. But at the same time these are invariably the more inferior vital values and above all the values of sensory attractiveness, not those of nobility, which are primarily associated with the racial unit and its subordinate categories; still less do they include spiritual and sacred values. (3) The theory in question fails to realize that in turning away from individuality and its values, love itself must necessarily decline in value also; and that the value of the individual as a member of the larger group can no longer be given with the same degree of adequacy as in the smaller one. This is not merely due to variations of historical circumstance, but is a *necessary* consequence (and in no way dependent on the number of members in the group). I am thinking here not only of the private individual, but also of the 'total individuality' of a given 'collective'. Thus the actual race of 'mankind' can be thought of as a *collective unit*. This is not the same as the *concept* of 'humanity'.

This 'unit', then, is the whole human race throughout the entire course of its history, one vast living, struggling, suffering entity, set over against the whole universe! As such it can be an object of love. Such an 'individual unit' would actually incorporate all the values of history, including the very highest. It would in fact be more worthy of love than any one people. But *who* is acquainted with this 'individual' and its values? In my opinion the varying adequacy of our apprehension of value in such units as 'humanity', 'the nation' and 'the family' is not due to relationships which are affected by positive historical processes, nor to variations in the numerical extension of any group so described, nor to any actual difference in the ties of interest which bind us to these groups. These 'basic groupings' of mankind are the *constituent elements* of history, and it cannot do away with them.[1] Assuredly, mankind as a whole is intrinsically more worthy of love than any one nation or country! But it can then no longer be assumed that he who exercises this act of love is specifically human in doing so. For it is already implied of man that in his specific capacity as a bearer of values he can never apprehend the whole of the generic unit to which he belongs with the same adequacy as those partial collective units of which he is *necessarily* a member. Hence a man's love for his country, for instance, has an intrinsically greater value than his love of mankind; and this because his country affords an intrinsically greater positive value-content than 'humanity' for the possible experience of any man whatever. God alone has a greater love for humanity as an historical collective unit than for any one people; God alone may do this, and is, as it were, 'entitled' to do so.

Moreover, the 'general benevolence' of the positivistic schools is quite unlike this 'love of mankind' we have just been describing, viz. love for a unitary *individual*, a spatio-temporal whole whose members, on the principle already enunciated, are of one body, one with another, wheresoever and whensoever they may actually have lived. It is that very questionable prior form of love for a given *cross-section of this enduring unit*, i.e. for mankind as at present constituted, whose members are thereupon considered only in respect of those values they have '*in common*'; and likewise in respect of what is common to the various qualitatively different cross-sections throughout the course of time. But by this resolution of differences in value the *highest* values in the scale are the *first* to be eliminated, till all that remains at the end of the thought-process is the (pure) craving for the mass as such! I have shown elsewhere[2] that love for the 'greatest number' (as Bentham puts

[8] Cf. my account of the essential types of group in *Der Formalismus in der Ethik*, p. 547 seq.
[9] Cf. the essay 'Das Ressentiment im Aufbau der Moralen'.

it, for instance), is really hatred; hatred for the positive values, given as such, which are inherent in 'home', 'people', 'country' and 'God'; a hatred which, in so far as it simply plays off humanity against these possessors of specifically higher values, is only able to pass as 'love' by virtue of an illusion. This idea of 'mankind as an individual', this great whole, as a *single* suffering, rejoicing, struggling entity united against the world, whose value can be adequately grasped by God alone, and which only His love can encompass, must therefore be distinguished from the notion of the 'mass of mankind'. To put love for the latter before people and country, and even before God, is not only evil and immoral, but actually the outcome of a malign reversal of values which necessarily betokens a progressive disparagement of the value of mankind as an individual. One further point: since the love of mankind as an individual relates to an object whose total value is accessible to God and *God alone*, there is but *one* mode of loving humanity so conceived: that which is *mediated through God*, which associates itself with God's love for mankind, though he who thus associates himself can never be aware of what is known only to God and in His love. The true love of mankind is rooted in the act of 'loving all things in God'.

This 'perspective of diminishing intensity' in love and fellow-feeling does not therefore depend on spatio-temporal remoteness, or lack of causal efficacy, or on a defective community of interests. Nor does it depend on factors which may fluctuate widely in history, due to the progress of civilization, the improvement of communications, the greater dovetailing of human aims and interests at any given time (or even the intensification of historical consciousness, represented by a more vivid insight into the life of the past, which has nothing to do with the mere advance of knowledge about the past); for its source lies in the nature of man as such. Indeed, apart from special cases, such as love of family or country, etc., it rests upon an even more exalted basis: as an instance of the 'perspective of interests' in general it derives from, and is essentially bound up with, *the nature of all living things*, to which any system of instincts of a positive type must necessarily belong. Hence it is not the perspectival character of the system that is peculiarly human, but only the *specific units* (such as family, clan or country) to which it is applied. In other species these are replaced by other units. But such a perspective will also continue to hold for any further evolutionary developments which may take place, including even the 'superman', if and when he appears.

This then is the basis of the assertion that 'where living beings are concerned, it is better to love what lies nearest in the perspective of interest, rather than that which is farther away'. The same idea is expressed in the concept of 'loving our neighbour' for which Nietzsche was so misguidedly anxious to substitute the 'love of them that are farthest'.

(3) THE PROBLEM OF 'TRANSFERENCE'

But the naturalistic theory misconceives the facts in quite another way. It overlooks the phenomenological law that it is by way of *values* that love is directed upon any thing, and that such love embodies a movement towards the '*enhancement* of value', even where the character and quality of this higher value is not yet apprehended. Since love is primarily directed upon concrete things, *by means of* values, the as yet unfelt and unacknowledged factors of this value in things are always *included* in the intentional content of love. In other words, for any pattern of value actually felt, there is always a sort of '*background of value*' gradually fading away into the 'perspective of interests'. Thus the eye of love sees something 'alive' in every living organism (the word being used here to denote only the particular value-quality of 'livingness' as such). Since it is only where signs of life are present that we actually describe whatever shows these signs as 'alive', or as an 'organism', we only apprehend vital value in practice where the signs of this value are present. It is thus an essential characteristic of love that its object, as phenomenologically apprehended in the act, always *exceeds* the values which the lover actually feels at the time. Hence there is no need of that 'mechanism whereby love is transferred from one thing to another', from one range of objects to the next, which is postulated by the naturalistic doctrine. The instinctive mechanism of 'transference' serves only to animate the content already included in the act of loving, so as to make it stand out from the accompanying background and attach it to some particular object. Naturalism takes no account of this transcendent consciousness of value; it ignores the fact that we can love and hate what we have never 'experienced' as something encountered through its actual presence and effect upon our senses; and indeed that love and hatred largely determine *what* we shall experience from among the endless possibilities available. It also overlooks the existence of that 'sense of fulfilment', which supervenes when we actually meet with what was previously adumbrated in the intentional content of love: 'This is the thing I love.' This is profoundly illustrated in connection with the love of God by Pascal's: 'You would not seek me if you had not found me.'[1] Nor does the naturalistic theory recognize that love is a *movement* and not a static condition capable of mechanical 'trans-

---

[1] [*Pensées*, sect. vii, 553. Misquoted in the original.—Tr.]

ference' from object to object (or from one part of an object to another), like the so-called diffusion of feeling-tone in a 'mood', for example; nor, again, that it is a movement essentially concerned with enhancing the value of the beloved object. But once these facts are admitted, there is no further need for any such 'transference' as that postulated by the naturalistic theory.

By way of example, let us consider the transference alleged by Feuerbach. The sympathetic delight in the object which accompanies the performance of the sexual act, but dies once it is over, is supposedly transferred, in the first instance, by the mother to the child, as the outcome of the process and primarily as 'part of herself', to be subsequently extended from the child to the father, and so on. But the woman (in this case) will never have regarded her partner 'in the first instance' as merely a negligible cypher providing physical pleasure; however crude the conception of humanity involved, she will always have given heed throughout to the living quality of the man, the 'nobility' or 'baseness' of his particular attributes, and his value as a human being. And the pleasure concerned will always have been felt as the 'fulfilment' of an impulse of sexual love, the satisfaction of a desire which (even though it may have included pleasure previously evoked by 'accidental' stimuli), was not first occasioned by the sense of well-being, but found its only satisfaction therein. Even a man and woman having no knowledge or experience of sexual intercourse would have felt the type of desire known as sexual attraction and love. But in man at the present day the maternal qualities of mother-love and the desire for motherhood are entirely independent of this. Inasmuch and insofar as it is inspired by *love*, the procreative instinct always includes the aim of improving the breed by choosing a partner of the highest quality. Like mother-love, it exists in its own right and requires no transference of love from the begetter to the child (many mothers have love for their children, though none for the father); nor is such love an 'enlarged form of egoism' extending to what was once part of the mother's own body, and is still felt to be so through a sort of illusion, as it were. Such an illusion certainly does occur. We find it very frequently in the mother who is loath to acknowledge her children as individual selves having independent lives of their own, even when they have begun to grow up, and who tends to go on treating them as small children even when fully adult. She cannot think of them as independent beings, but only in this foolish organic way as though they were still really 'part of herself'. But mothers like this are not *truly* maternal at all; they make the worst mothers, not the best. But we also know the perhaps rather resigned, but deep and quiet maternal feeling of women who have brought up an adopted child as their own, having never had children themselves. We find this maternal quality in many virgins and saints, and as a symbol of 'pure' motherhood at least, the Christian image of the Virgin Mother of all mankind has a profound truth and lofty value of its own. There is equally little in the notion that the love of children for their parents was ever a mere 'transference' of the pleasurable feelings occasioned by the benefits of their upbringing to those responsible for them; on the contrary, such filial love has always been notably *independent* of the amount and kind of pleasure-feeling experienced. Hence, among all peoples, the commandment to love one's parents has always been completely independent of the parents' treatment of their children. Even 'gratitude', which owing to the element of love it involves inevitably goes far beyond any idea of 'recompense' (for indeed it is *necessarily* beyond the bounds of possibility that children could ever 'recompense' their parents), is not sufficient to cover the whole emotion. There is another element in it, which can be seen in children who have been well brought-up by foster-parents, having lost their mother at birth, for instance, and their father being already dead, in their longing for 'real' parents; a love for those who 'brought them into being'. Historically, therefore, matricide, and later patricide, appear as the most heinous of crimes—even where the parents have given every kind of provocation for the deed. Similar considerations apply to the love between brothers and sisters.

Thus the 'family' as a whole is a fabric built out of love, which *from its outset* could only have existed as a *whole* and whose foundations in the human soul are *qualitatively distinct* from the very beginning. Moreover, every member of the family is similarly loved by every other member of it against the value-background of the *whole* family (however large or small it may be). This is the only explanation of that reinforced *solidarity* in shame or glory, which is strongest of all in the primitive family. Even among ourselves, where family life has been so largely destroyed by industrialism and the increase in powers of disinheritance, this strong sense of solidarity still persists, e.g. in the event of dishonour or injury to a member of the family.

And what is true of small matters is also true of great ones. The family itself is always loved against an ever-present background of value in the clan and the race, the race against the background of the nation, the nation against the background of humanity. There has never been a people which felt itself to be all alone upon earth—alone in time and space under the stars. Even if they had had no *empirical* acquaintance with other peoples, and had never faced the question whether they were indeed alone, if one of their number had said to the others 'we are altogether alone in the world', they would all have been filled with horror. And their very horror would have made it plain that the original object envisaged in their love was greater and wider than the tribe itself.

But even humanity has never at any time been considered as the sole object of value in human love. For it has always included some form of the 'divine' as a background of value. This direction of its love upon the characteristic value of divinity is in no way dependent on positive notions about 'the gods', and anticipates the formation of these ideas.[1]

Once the facts are correctly viewed, therefore, this notion of 'transference' is no longer required.

(4) THE PARALLEL EXTENSION OF LOVE AND HATRED

But the positivistic theory is false in yet another respect. Like Darwin, in his phylogenetic approach, it forgets that 'enlargement of the group' has the effect of extending not only love, but also hatred: that an increasing 'community of interests' cannot increase the amount of love in the world by a hair's-breadth, but at most has the result that with increasing solidarity the increase in physical well-being, which was previously made possible by love alone, is now no longer attainable solely in this fashion, but can be effected by a *mechanical gearing-together of instincts*. And certainly a satisfactory division of labour in the absence of love is better for the physical *well-being* of the community than a bad one even where love is present.[2] Thus the antiseptic treatment of wounds saves a great deal of 'love' in caring for the injured. But is the effect of this, as Herbert Spencer supposed, that love and all the ultimate 'forfeiture' of pleasure that it entails will therefore become increasingly *superfluous* in the world, the final aim being a world 'entirely free from love' in which all interests are completely integrated (Spencer's 'social equilibrium')? Here the naturalistic theory once more fails to realize that love is a *movement towards the enhancement of value*. It thereby overlooks the fact that once a form of beneficence or any other realization of values has become instinctive, love immediately turns to higher values which have not yet become so, striking upwards into regions of value still unknown. But that is part of its very nature. Hence the idea of 'the ultimately satisfactory moral state of mankind as one without

[1] Cf. 'Probleme der Religion' in my book *Vom Ewigen im Menschen*.
[2] As Adam Smith rightly says—and it will always be the task of economic policy to raise this integration of interests to the highest level of perfection.

sacrifice and without love' is a nonsensical one. Even if there should be a state of civilization which was 'perfect' in respect of the civilized values, the task of love would never be 'completed'. For it is part of its phenomenological essence to transcend the given positive values by pointing above and beyond them. Moreover, a completely civilized world could at the same time be *absolutely brimful of hatred*, a 'kingdom of the devil', in fact.

The Freudian theory is the latest addition to the doctrines of naturalism, but the fundamental assumptions with which it operates are no less unsound than before.

(5) FREUD'S ONTOGENETIC THEORY[1]

To embark, as Freud has done, upon an *ontogenesis* of sympathy and love is certainly an enterprise of the greatest value as such. Indeed, it is a task which has been almost entirely neglected hitherto. It is also an indubitable merit in the work of Freud and his school to have paid particular attention to the capacity for feelings of sympathy and love, and more especially those of the erotic and sexual type, in early childhood (up to the age of six). An entirely new tract of the child-mind has actually been discovered thereby. At all events it has been duly recognized that the stirrings of what is usually described as the 'sexual instinct' proper are preceded, in the period before puberty, by other erotically tinged attachments to objects, which deserve investigation on their own account. Freud and his school have also provided a great deal of factual evidence to show that the 'fixation' of such attachments (in contrast to the typical successive shedding of them in the normal course of development), can have a most important influence on the shape of the subsequent love-life of the individual, and his general career. Freud was enabled thereby to acquire a *genetic* understanding of many forms of mental illness, and also of many types of sexual perversion, which had previously been ascribed forthwith to an innate disposition—and this meant, of course, the abandonment of any attempt to cure the sufferer.

And here, before entering into details, I should like to mention a point in which Freud's ideas seem to me to have furthered our conception of *mental causation in general*. Freud's method may perhaps one day bring us closer to an altogether new understanding of that peculiar thing which we call a man's *'destiny'*.[2]

[1] Freud's theory of the genesis of different types of love is only briefly dealt with in this book. A more detailed study will be provided in the second part of this work, which deals with the emotion of shame. [Cf. *Über Scham und Schamgefühl* (1913) in *Nachlassband*, I.]

[2] On the laws which govern the shaping of 'destiny' in the individual and the group, cf. the theory of the influence of 'ideals', which I shall develop in the

'Destiny' is by no means comparable with those influences and stimuli which affect us from without. Nor is it in any sense a matter of conscious choice. It seems to be the general notion underlying all that we commonly mean by saying that this or that 'could only have happened to someone of that kind'. 'Destiny' is the series, the host of happenings which, though we have in no way sought, anticipated, expected or chosen them, are yet felt in a quite peculiar way to be *characteristic of us*, once they have happened; taken together, they represent a single pervasive theme running throughout a career, whose total pattern bears the individual stamp of the person to whom that career belongs. Of 'destiny' in this sense, Freud takes the view that its main lines are quite specifically laid down in the impressions and above all, he would say, in the *erotic impressions of early childhood*. On deeper consideration, it appears that Freud has here come close to an idea which may perhaps prove capable both of reconciling the enduring conflict between empiricism and the doctrine of innate ideas, and of replacing them by a new fundamental hypothesis. 'Empiricism' hitherto has made a point of assuming that, so far as the nature and magnitude of the effects are concerned, it does not matter when or at what stage in the total sequence of mental history the experience in question occurs. But this assumption is *fundamentally* incorrect.[1] Every experience, down to the simplest sensation, possesses, according to the nature and magnitude of its effect in shaping the total life of the individual, a definite and peculiar positional value in the typical development and maturation of a human being. Thus the effect of a childhood experience can be utterly different from that producible by a similar objective stimulus and the resultant experience-content, should they occur *later on* in the life of the same person. The childish experience can be 'dangerous', the other 'harmless'; the one may affect the whole life, the other may just have a momentary or short-term significance, or the individual may think nothing of it. This is not meant to imply that an experience, occurrence or impression is by nature dependent, for its total effect on the self, upon earlier experiences which the individual recalls, for example, or whose traces he encounters. *This* obvious fact, and the resultant variations in the effect of experiences at different stages and periods of human development, are things that even empiricism has never, of course, overlooked, and the only things, indeed, that it

second volume of my book *Vom Ewigen im Menschen*, under the title *Vorbilder und Führer* [published in *Nachlassband*, I, where cf. also the section on the 'Ordo amoris' and the shaping of destiny (1916–17), ibid.].

[1] Cf. the important distinction made by Koffka between 'learning' and 'maturation' in *The Growth of the Mind*, op. cit., ch. II, I.

recognizes. Its error lies simply in this, that instead of attributing one sort of diversity in the effect produced by an impression to variations in its positional value within a typical life-history, it has thought it possible to derive every kind of diversity from the fact that the impression has here or there encountered a variety of traces from experiences of different kinds.

Now the fact is that it is part of the essential character of psychic causality that every experience is and can be what it is on one occasion only, and only *once* exerts its characteristic effect. This peculiarity of psychic causality now acquires a singularly pregnant meaning through Freud's percipient observation that a psychic experience is partially conditioned, as to the nature and magnitude of its effect (and quite apart from the specific character of earlier psychic experiences), according to the *positional value* which it has within the *total* development of a man. An impression—in so far as it may occur at an immature stage of development, where the individual still approximates to the marginal case, roughly describable as one in which 'anything can be made of anything'—affects his life, particularly in one respect, quite otherwise than it would if met with at a more developed stage. It becomes like a '*mode of apprehension*', a kind of 'category', as it were, for all the later phases and potentialities of life; it sets limits to the possibilities and opportunities of later life in a remarkable way. It ensures that a certain range of happenings, of 'destined conditions' as it were, from now onwards enjoy a greater expectation of entering experience, while other happenings and experiences are, for that very reason, permanently excluded. An 'empiricism' which would adopt as its guiding principle an accurate evaluation of the significance of impressions and experiences, from the first moment of existence onwards, always according to the existing condition of maturity and immaturity in the individual concerned, would perhaps be in a position to make much intelligible, which remained a closed book to empiricism of the earlier type; for it was only in the *accumulation* of experiences and their association together, that the latter found principles for understanding their diversity of effect. Thus, for example, the strange and remarkably perverse statements dished out to us by Schopenhauer about 'women', are assuredly based on experiences which he had himself had in the course of his life. Like many others in such cases, who rely upon the evidence of their 'knowledge of life', he allows himself to appeal to his 'own experience' throughout. But that Schopenhauer should have had just *these* experiences and no others, that his disposition was such that of all the manifestations of feminity he met with, none could become part of *his* 'experience' save those which fitted in with his later opinions—this is a point which is wholly unaffected by any question as to whether these views are based upon objective 'experiences' (as distinct from imagination, illusion or misapprehension). It seems to us beyond doubt here that his negative and recalcitrant attitude towards his mother, dating from his early years ('the failure', as Freud would say, 'of the normal transference of libido to the mother'), created in Schopenhauer a negative, mistrustful *mode of apprehension*, governed by negative values. Hence it became his 'fate' to take an interest in, to get to know, and to form his judgement upon, such women as were alone adapted to this 'mode', and who did in fact correspond to the 'prejudice' already set up by his early childhood impressions on the subject.

On the other hand, Freud's distinction between the concepts of 'libido' and 'sexual instinct' has not so far attained to any kind of clarity. What sort of special fact does the word 'libido' stand for exactly, inasmuch as it is by no means intended to presuppose the fact of sexual instinct, this being rather to be regarded only as a particular phase in the development of libido, occurring 'in the majority of cases'? If one assumes, as Freud does, that the sensation of voluptuous pleasure and the accompanying sensory affect is an ultimate specific quality, and that such sensations are first aroused mechanically by chance stimulation of the infant's erotogenous zones, one might be inclined to describe all effort towards a repetition of sensations of this kind in terms of libido. Quite apart from the difficulty of determining whether the sensations in the infant corresponding to these stimuli possess this particular quality, we must begin by rejecting from the outset the idea that 'libido' does not represent an *original desire* (which might be satisfied by the occurrence of these sensations), but only *arises* on the basis of experience of such sensations. It has been a characteristic procedure in the evolution of Freudian theory, that the more the concept of 'libido' has been called upon in explanation of the various love-relationships, the greater the degree of *formalization* to which it has been subjected. Thus Freud's disciple, C. G. Jung, remarks somewhere that, properly speaking, one should mean nothing more by the term 'libido' than 'striving' as such.[1] It is fairly obvious that little can be done with such a concept, bereft of all its characteristic features. But if libido is understood to mean a primordial desire for sensations having the quality of voluptuous pleasure, it must be objected to this that striving is never directed in the first instance towards the realization of sensations, but always upon some sort of *content*, whose realization thereafter may well be accompanied by such sensations.[2]

[1] See C. G. Jung: *Psychology of the Unconscious*, op. cit.
[2] Cf. my analysis of striving and willing in *Der Formalismus in der Ethik*, p. 25 seq.

The concept of 'libido' may therefore be most readily inter-preted by ascribing to it any act of exertion whose realization is accompanied by sensations having the quality of voluptuous pleasure. But now the facts adduced by Freud do nothing to show that libido does not *coincide* with the primary impulsive form of the sexual instinct. Certainly it may be taken for granted that in infancy such impulses are not associated with any sort of imagery of the other sex or those of its aspects which are of especial rele-vance to the satisfaction of the instinct. To that extent these impulses can be regarded as objectless, or in the later phases of development as still largely fluid in regard to their object. But for all that we find here already an infusion of that quality which is characteristic of the mature sexual impulse, and such impulses already involve a similar tendency towards the specific qualitative values of the opposite sex.

Hence, the assertion that the sexual instinct first *emerges* at some point in individual life from something entirely different, namely a striving after a particular kind of pleasure, and that this emer-gence is due to a more or less fortuitous combination of external mechanical circumstances, in whose absence there would actually be no sexual instinct, is a conclusion which does not follow in the slightest from the facts produced by Freud. All that can properly be said is that the stage at which the sexual instinct has found its appointed object in the image of the opposite sex is preceded by another at which this has not yet taken place; a stage in which the instinctive impulse is directed to the values of hetero-sexuality merely, these values, though already determinate in quality, being unattached, as yet, to particular object-images. The transi-tion from one stage to the other can be seen very clearly in the course of the child's development. The stage of taking a definite interest in the physical presence of the other sex is preceded by a premonitory and still groping stage of consciously-felt *enquiry* as to the nature of these instinctive impulses whose innate tendency has already been felt, and that distinction between the sexes which has already been discovered. This groping attitude, which is later resolved by some sudden experience of *fulfilment*, connected with some kind of real relationship to the other sex, is extremely characteristic of a particular phase in the development of the consciously orientated sexual instinct. But these facts meet with no sort of comprehension in Freud's theory. His postulated 'libido', and the sexual instinct alleged to result from it, consist of nothing more than a very crude application of the notion of effort current in the traditional association-psychology. Here again, the fact of hunger in the infant is thought to have arisen more or less as follows: The infant's lips are first brought into contact with the mother's breast in a quite mechanical fashion and this leads to an equally automatic release of the mechanism of sucking, followed by a tasting of the sweetness of the milk and the pleasure it affords, whereupon the initial state of merely contingent discomfort is brought to an end; at every recurrence of this discomfort the whole sequence of experiences leading to its elimination is repeated; hence the mother's breast comes to be associated with the sensations previously encountered in sucking, and the fact of hunger is supposed to have first originated in this way.[1] But in point of fact 'hunger' is from the beginning a *directed* impulse, involving appetite and the possibility of disgust, nor is it simply eliminated by satisfaction, so much as 'pacified' thereby; moreover it carries from the beginning a sense of the *value* of food, even though there is no thought of food itself or of the activity and outward circumstances necessary in order to obtain it. It is not the fact of effort merely that is irreducible to sensation, feeling and imagery; the *qualitative direction* of the effort, and in this case, the local physical exertion are also *basic* facts. Hence it is impossible to explain how what Freud calls 'libido' should ever have arisen from the merely casual and mechanical production of pleasurable sensations. Libido itself is an equally *basic* example of a drive whose object is determined by an impulse of vital love, which is altogether distinct from the drive itself. And this remains true even when it has not yet developed into conscious sexual instinct (any more than vital love has become sexual love), and contains reference to the opposite sex only in the shape of a still imageless tendency towards value. In this sense therefore, the sexual instinct is wholly 'innate'. The 'unfolding', 'ripening' and 'development' which occurs does not consist in associating a quite indeterminate striving after pleasure with the general idea of the opposite sex; it is simply the gradual process whereby an instinct already concerned *in general* with the opposite sex, is brought to bear upon a *particular* member of that sex.

Freud thinks that by pointing to the fact of *perversion* in all its various forms, he is able to reinforce his view that the sexual instinct in general is only gradually built up in each individual. For him the facts in question are not due, as the term 'perversion' would suggest, to deviations and aberrations on the part of an inborn sexual instinct; on the contrary, they represent *primitive forms* of the libidinous impulse as such, having a quite general distribution and providing the material, as it were, from which the normal sexual instinct is ordinarily built up. On Freud's view,

[1] Koffka has shown in detail that the sucking movements of the child are likewise based on genuine instincts and not on reflexes; his treatment of 'instinct' in general is also noteworthy. Op. cit.

in fact, the perversions represent merely fixations at an infantile level of development. They are not aberrations of an original instinct, but relics of levels of development which are usually abandoned, in the normal case, at some definite point in time. Freud puts it by saying that 'Man is born polymorphously perverse'. But it is in fact the perversions which tell most strongly against the Freudian point of view; precisely because they continue to show, in all their forms, that here too the *direction* of the impulse towards '*hetero*sexuality' is still retained, even though the corresponding *values* are not found and sought in a member of the opposite sex proper, but either in the agent himself (autoeroticism) or in what is (actually) the *same* sex as his own. In all homosexual perversions for instance, we find that there is in fact a differentiation of sexual qualities, in that one partner always takes the part of the man, and the other that of the woman. It is not for nothing that effeminacy of mind and body is in general a necessary concomitant of masculine homosexuality. This is not the place to enter upon a more detailed description of the various types of perversion; but up to now it has been the chief defect in all descriptions of them to have merely defined them objectively, instead of starting from their *intentional* and evaluative tendencies. Yet it is easy to show, for example, that even actual heterosexuality is by no means incompatible with a homosexual intention.[1] The same applies, moreover, to all Freud's assertions as to the *stages* whereby the still quite aimless libido is supposed to develop its *normal* orientation towards the opposite sex and its characteristic sexual attributes. Among such stages he includes, for example, the love of a son for his mother, of a daughter for her father, or brothers and sisters for one another, and so on, impulses which, though originally sexual in character, are assumed to be later capable of sublimation, once the normal fixation upon the object has taken place. The only sound point in these observations is that before the normal fixation of the sexual instinct upon a real sexual object other than a member of the family, the instinct does make groping experiments of many different kinds. But a perversion, at whatever stage of development it occurs, is always a more or less pathological *aberration* of the normal instinct, so that it cannot be in any way described as a *generally* 'inborn' characteristic. Thus it may often happen, for instance, that filial love, of a son for his mother, say, or a daughter for her father, which has quite different emotional and conative origins, is at times confused or mingled with impulses of sexual desire and love. But Freud's claim that filial love *originates* in these impulses, or

[1] Cf. the above-mentioned works of Kurt Schneider, which were occasioned by what is said here.

represents at best a mere 'sublimation' of them, and that the love of brothers and sisters has a similar origin, must be rejected as a misapprehension of the facts in question. The fact of the matter is that from the outset there are *basically different kinds* of love, which cannot be derived from one another, and in which the most elementary qualitative relationships between man and his fellows are prefigured as it were, within the *structure* of the soul itself. Here, as so often elsewhere in his work, Freud commits himself, in all his inferences on this subject, to the *methodological fallacy* of seeking to explain the normal case in terms of the abnormal one, and hence of turning the facts upside down.

Within certain limits, however, we must defend the Freudian position against *one* objection to which it has often been exposed. What is the point (it has been urged), of giving priority to the *sexual* instinct in attempting to account for the various qualitative love-relationships among human beings? For the part played by the sexual instinct in establishing these relationships is not essentially different from that of hunger and thirst, for instance, or any other instincts of a more or less inborn kind, such as the instinctive desire for the approval of others, or the craving for respect, power, dominance and so on. When we *love* people to whom we are sexually attracted, this is not essentially different from our loving those who nourish and care for us (as the 'family retainer' loves those he serves), or who help to satisfy our desires in any other way. There are two major flaws in this analogy. Firstly, there is the notion that sexual love can be fashioned out of a quite general undifferentiated affection (or goodwill) and a wholly blind and unselective sexual instinct; the latter becoming 'individualized' only when *conjoined* with this affection, whose concern is essentially with factors such as beauty, vigour, etc., which are not sexual at all. Lipps, for example, has sought to interpret sexual love in this fashion as 'spiritualized desire', i.e. as a combination of purely spiritual sympathy (which is then explained by 'empathy') with the (intrinsically unselective) sexual instinct.[1] To this I reply that no such 'combination' is to be found in sexual love, for it is a specific kind of love, in the sense previously explained. And it must also be emphasized that, simply by virtue of being the central function of vital love generally, sexual love discriminates among the possibilities it encounters, preferring the *noble, the flourishing and the vigorous* to the life that is mean, feeble or decadent; and it does so regardless of all ties of spiritual sympathy (and hence of any sort of 'empathic' attribution of personal characteristics to the physical appearance of the other). It may be that an absolute individualization of sexual love, such that it is directed upon *one*

[1] Cf. Theodor Lipps: *Die ethischen Grundfragen*, Hamburg/Leipzig, 1899.

person only, in whom it is entirely realized, can never occur unless the other's individuality is also grasped in an act of spiritual love, transcending the sexual sphere. But even if this does *not* occur, sexual love is assuredly '*love*', and not a mere general instinct, and is already capable, as such, of exercising a *choice* among the possibilities available, which far outreaches the powers of a blind and generalized sexual instinct. Secondly, moreover, it is certainly no accident that in the vital sphere generally, sexual love is commonly spoken of simply as 'love',—unlike that love which may, for instance, be felt towards those who feed and care for us. For sexual desire and love are *primary* factors in the system of our vital instincts and in the corresponding system of love-impulses; and they are also *fundamental*—as Freud has, on the whole, rightly discerned—in the sense that as this central impulse of life declines there is a *corresponding* loss of energy and relapse into a certain degeneracy and decay on the part of all the other kinds of vital love and vital instinct.[1] Even the love of 'life' itself, the soul's responsiveness in vicarious and companionate feeling to every manifestation of life, the unsophisticated love of Nature even, cannot be cultivated without a certain measure of activity in this cardinal impulse. Every check upon its development in some way hampers the approach to *all* vital values, and has a coarsening effect upon all types of vital emotion. To that extent sexual love is not just one kind of vital love among others, but the *archetype and basis* of them all, and, as it were, the key-function among them. Hence it is that despite the greater urgency of hunger, for instance (from the point of view of individual self-preservation), the indulgence of this and of other importunate instincts is commonly neglected for the gratification of sexual desire, directed, through love, upon a particular individual. There is scarcely any sacrifice of other vital values which has not been made in certain circumstances for the sake of sexual love. There is a desire for food, and there is a desire for sex, but there is no 'love' for food, or for those who provide it, corresponding to sexual love. Any attempt to compare them therefore neglects a number of important facts.

Sexual desire, as such, has an undiscriminating reference to the opposite sex, whereas sexual love is essentially selective, opting, in principle, for the 'superior' qualities of life. Nor can its function

[1] There is admittedly no certain proof, as yet, of the theory that ageing in general is a sexual process; thus there has been no explanation, so far, of the fact men should have about the same expectation of life as women, although they do not lose their sexual powers until so much later than women do. But there is so much evidence in favour of the theory that it has every prospect of eventual confirmation. Steinach's rejuvenation experiments also bear it out, as do the results of comparative research on the relation between age and fecundity in similar plant and animal stocks under varying conditions.

in this respect be in any way superseded by rational eugenic arrangements, based upon scientific and objective knowledge of the best methods of propagating the species. This must be insisted upon as a virtual axiom, in opposition to a whole string of contemporary versions of ethical and political 'racialism'. In virtue of this there can be no such thing as a policy directly aimed at eugenic improvement, i.e. one that attempts to bring together those who by virtue of some outward trait are thought fittest for procreation, without considering the immediate choice which love and love alone can make, to be a decisive reason for their union. These ideas are backed, moreover, by a wholly fallacious mechanical conception of life itself. All efforts and undertakings aimed at the improvement of the race should avail themselves, rather, of that selective power of love which is inherent in man and every other bisexual species, and must reckon with it as something which cannot be replaced. Hence the true and proper 'racial policy' consists simply in eliminating, where possible, by correct education, the misdirection of love's basic impulses, whether this be due to utilitarian calculation, a tendency to mere gratification of desire, a one-sided preoccupation with sensual pleasure, or any other similar factors. Here it is not 'experience' and the scientific assurance it provides, which can lead to a real eugenic advance, but in a certain sense the very opposite, namely a removal of the restraints and disguises imposed by 'experience' and mere intellectual reflection upon the instinctive impulses of sexual love.

It follows from this that the Freudian attempt to derive the various qualities of love from that single quality he calls 'libido', must be regarded as a complete failure. And, as we have seen, it is equally impossible to reduce love in general to a mere instinct. Freud, however, does think it possible to provide such a deduction of the 'higher' qualities from libido, notably by calling upon the concept of 'sublimation'. Once an impulse of the libido has been 'repressed' or automatically checked, the energy it contains can be diverted, so Freud says, to other objects and tasks, to those of a spiritual character, for instance, or to any kind of cultural or vocational activity. All higher forms of love, all gifts of the spirit, for instance, are alleged to represent such a sublimation of repressed 'libido'. Now the problem which chiefly troubles us here is to see how, on Freud's premisses, any sort of constraint or repression of the 'libido' could ever come about. Freud tells us that some of these 'repressive forces', disgust and shame, for example, are self-created by the individual in the course of his own development, while others constitute a 'stock of moral ideas' acquired from without; the most important of these are the rules of sexual morality current in his *society*, such as the prohibition of incest, or marital customs—these rules being attributable to economic or religious causes. Now if, as Freud says, the term 'libido' is ultimately meant to include the *whole* field of mental forces, it is very difficult to see how it could ever come to generate forces whose very office, for Freud, is to hamper and repress the libido itself! The libido really acquires an almost mythological status at this point; it is exactly like the Fichtean Ego 'setting limits to itself'. It is even harder to see where this 'stock of moral ideas' has come from, whereby the individual libido is supposedly subject to external limitation and restraint on the part of 'society and the state'. For where do society and state originate, if not in the soul of man? And how, on Freudian premises, can 'moral ideas' be possible in any case? There is an obvious *circularity* in Freud's explanation here: All higher moral feelings and activities, and hence, presumably, all moral motives as such, are allegedly due to the 'sublimation of libido'. But in order to account for the 'sublimation' itself, Freud proceeds to postulate the existence of a 'morality' *at the behest* of which the repression of libido can be effected, and its diversion to 'higher activities' take place![1]

But the main question is: What is the meaning of the word 'sublimation' in this context? It looks, from Freud's account, as if he were assuming the acts of spiritual activity involved in all knowledge, all artistic or vocational pursuits, to be occasioned by repressed libido. If that were really Freud's opinion, there would be nothing more to be said: for a spiritual alchemy capable, by its arts, of conjuring 'thought', 'goodness' and the like out of 'libido' has been utterly beyond our ken till now. Hence it may be taken for granted, not only that the whole field of such acts generally must be *presupposed* in any case, but that in every case where this theory is invoked to explain the life-history of an individual, his special talents and the special fields of interest in which they are exercised must also be taken into account. Thus in seeking, for instance, to give a Freudian explanation of how the military and political genius of Napoleon was ultimately *manifested* in his campaigns and his actual statesmanship, we may conclude that it would never have *been* so displayed if he had been happier with Josephine Beauharnais than in fact he was. But to try to account for that talent itself, or the growth of his military and political ambitions, etc., in terms of the disappointments attaching

---

[1] For the considerable element of truth in Freud's theory as a philosophy of history, in contrast to the one-sidedness of the economic, political or purely ideological conceptions of history, cf. the essay on 'Die Ordnung der historischen Kausalfaktoren' in my *Zur Soziologie und Weltanschauungslehre*, Vol. IV. [This work has not been published: cf. instead Part I of *Probleme einer Soziologie des Wissens*, op. cit.]

to this affair and the repression of his earlier leanings towards 'idyllic love' in the manner of Werther and Rousseau, would naturally be an absurd undertaking. If, therefore, the word 'sublimation' is to have any reasonable meaning here, it can only refer to the fact that this process of libido-repression has *diverted* to spiritual capacities and interests *already present* in a dispositional sense, an *energy* which would not have been available if it had been unreservedly devoted to 'libido'.

Now since no one has more than a limited amount of psychical energy, there can be no doubt that the successful pursuit of intellectual, cultural or vocational activities, no less than the exercise of the higher forms of sympathy and love, does actually depend to some extent on keeping the sexual instinct under a certain discipline and control. But it is not this old-established truth that Freud has in mind, even if the concept of 'sublimation' be taken in the second and more reasonable sense. The peculiarity of his view consists rather, in his assumption that the various types of spiritual activity have no intrinsic 'energy' of their own, so that whatever energy they do possess can only have been diverted to them at the expense of libido itself. He therefore assumes the basic relationship between 'libido' and 'spiritual activity' to consist in the fact that the one can *only* acquire energy at the expense of the other. If Freud were correct in this assumption, it would constitute an *absolutely* tragic element in *human nature*. For our consciousness of value permits us to recognize that spiritual values are manifestly superior to all merely sensory or vital values.[1] And yet the greater man's practical devotion to this immediate awareness of value, the more he would necessarily destroy both himself, as a living creature, and the living roots of his existence and survival as a species. He would simply be left with a *choice* between either abandoning spiritual activity in favour of a primitivism which would bring him ever nearer to the beasts, the more closely he pursued it, or else a cultivation of spiritual activity which would mean his neglecting the central source of vitality, the joys it brings (and ultimately the propagation of his own kind). Every advance in the spiritual culture of the individual or the group would condemn those who made it to continence and ultimately to extinction: and *power* would eventually accrue to those peoples which had refrained from devoting their energies to spiritual activity and thereby weakening the forces which promote fertility. But Freud appears to be wholly mistaken in assuming this relationship in the first place.[2] In our view, all levels of mental life, from

[1] Cf. on this *Der Formalismus in der Ethik*, p. 84.
[2] We shall be treating the matter in more detail in a special monograph in this series.

sensory apprehension up to the highest acts of the spirit, are derived from an independent fund of mental energy, which is in no way borrowed from the instinctive energy of libido. Certainly, in view of the limitations upon a man's total mental energy, if more is demanded at one level than is consistent with the harmony and balance of the mental powers, this may well lead to a loss of energy at other levels; but only so far as the energies belonging to these various levels partake in the limited total energy of the individual, and can only be supplied from this source in accordance with the energy available and its internal laws of distribution. This rule serves to explain the numerous occasions in history where one instinct has *predominated* over the others, and also accounts for the formation of 'surrogates'. But the relationship involved is very much more complicated than Freud supposes. So far as the birth-rate does actually fall off in proportion to the increase of intellectual culture, this can well be accounted for in terms of the basic relationship we have postulated. Wherever the correlation is particularly marked, it also depends on the fact that the 'cultural ideal' which predominates among the people in question is a *one-sidedly* 'intellectualistic' one. It does not follow, however, that a true and genuine culture must necessarily lead to similar results: for its effect is to bring about a corresponding discipline and refinement of the emotional powers, and hence of those forces which promote the required selection of those best fitted to propagate. But if Freud's basic assumptions were correct, we should expect to find the highest degree of spiritual energy, and a correspondingly high level of cultural achievement, in cases of protracted sexual *asceticism*, as practised in monasteries, for instance; for this is well known to result in the decay and disappearance of sexual sympathy and desire. But for all the achievements of the monasteries, experience does not bear this out. Or alternatively, the repressed energies of libido should have found the other outlet which Freud regards as equally open to them, and should necessarily have brought on a mental illness, namely a neurosis. But here, too, experience affords no evidence in confirmation of the Freudian law.

What we look for in vain in Freud is any precise indication of the way in which a justifiable and necessary 'control' of libido and the sexual instinct *differs* from that 'repression' of the same which he considers to be a primary source of mental illness; nor do we find any definite account of the differentiating *conditions* under which repression of libido is said in the one case to make for 'sublimation', and in the other to result in 'disease'. In the absence of any exact and precise clarification of these two points, the Freudian theory is a source of considerable danger: on the one hand it may impose upon ethics the quite fictitious dilemma of 'primitivism' versus 'asceticism'; on the other, there is the no less serious danger of blurring the distinction between a morally necessary and justifiable control of the sexual instinct, and a misguided 'repression' of it, whose effect is to promote disease.[1]

[1] For an attempt to survey and interpret the facts uncovered by the Freudian school from a philosophic standpoint very different from their's and closely related to our own, see the recent essay by James J. Putnam, Professor of Neurology at Harvard University: 'Über die Bedeutung philosophischer Anschauungen and Ausbildung für die weitere Entwicklung der psychoanalytischen Bewegung' (Cf. *Imago*, 1912, Part 2).

PART THREE

OTHER MINDS

Chapter I

NATURE AND SCOPE OF THE PROBLEMS

IT is only in the course of many years' work on the problems touched upon in the Appendix to the first edition of this book, that we have come to realize the full force and meaning of what can be briefly described as the question as to the *grounds of the nature, existence and knowledge of the ties of connection between the spirits and souls of men.* Theodor Lipps has already done well to emphasize that only by the solution of this question can *sociology* be established on a philosophical basis.[1] It will be seen in what follows to be no less important (particularly in its epistemological aspects), for the theory of the *mental sciences*, and Oswald Külpe, in the second part of his *Die Realisierung*, was right to insist upon this. Wilhelm Dilthey,[2] Erich Becher[3] and Eduard Spranger[4] have also recognized the fact—though far from appreciating the extent and degree of its importance for the theory of our knowledge of other minds; nor for such questions as that of whether and how far our understanding of others is based upon our knowledge of Nature and belief in its reality, or again, as to the general *limits* of this understanding and its particular limitations within specific types of social group or under specific historical circumstances.[5] Benno Erdmann, in his celebrated Academy

[1] Theodor Lipps: *Das Bewusstsein von fremden Ichen*, op. cit.
[2] Wilhelm Dilthey: *Der Aufbau der geschichtlichen Welt in den Geisteswissenschaften*, Gesammelte Schriften (ed. Georg Misch), Berlin, 1905.
[3] Erich Becher: *Geisteswissenschaften und Naturwissenschaften: Untersuchung zur Theorie und Einteilung der Realwissenschaften*, Munich, 1921.
[4] Eduard Spranger: *Lebensformen*, 2nd ed.
[5] This is very obvious in Oswald Spengler, who, having assumed that the knowing mind, and hence the scope of its understanding, is completely governed

213

lecture on the subject, and in his last book, *Grundzüge der Repro-duktionspsychologie,*[1] has likewise dwelt upon it as constituting a fundamental problem, indeed *the* fundamental problem in the establishment of the mental sciences. That the solution of the *axiological* problem as to the relation of individual and community necessarily involves a settlement of this question, both on its ontological and epistemological sides, is clearly pointed out in my own *Formalismus in der Ethik,* in the course of my attempt to establish the 'principle of solidarity' as the primary axiom of all social philosophy and ethics. Münsterberg's Fichtean solution of our problem, in his *Psychology, General and Applied,* and Kronfeld's work on the epistemology of psychology,[2] have shown clearly that the question is fundamental to the theory of knowledge and methodology of empirical *psychology* and *psychiatry.* These sciences actually *presuppose* the existence and intelligibility of mental pro-cesses in other people; and it should be obvious, therefore, that they cannot themselves dispose of the *philosophical* problems involved. Only an accurate determination of the nature and structure of the soul can reveal the *limits* of would-be objective psychology in general (and experimental psychology in particular) and provide thereby a rational answer to the false pretensions of these sciences; only so can we define the limits of observation in general, and the limits attainable, moreover, by the pure reaction-experiment (in which the observer *conducts* the test), the experi-ment based on systematic introspection (in which he is the *subject* of the test), and lastly the (non-inductive) phenomenological experiment, which merely assists the contemplation of a 'thought'. It has, moreover, been admirably shown by Driesch,[3] that our problem is of no less interest for the epistemology and metaphysics of *biology*; for it is only by giving an account of the evidence and the 'criteria' for postulating 'consciousness', 'sensation' and 'men-tality' in general within the range of living organisms, that we can discover how far consciousness, mind, etc., and their basic forms and modes of connection, are distributed in the world, and how they may be investigated in the psychology of the child, the animal and perhaps even the plant (as parts of an independent evolutionary biology).[4] Again, the *philosophy of expression,* the

by the 'spirit' of its 'culture', is quite unable to explain how he himself (as a product of latter-day Western culture) is *able* to understand the alien cultures which he claims to 'interpret'. Cf. *The Decline of the West* (tr. C. F. Atkinson, Allen and Unwin, 1926).

[1] Berlin, 1920.
[2] Arthur Kronfeld: *Das Wesen der psychiatrischen Erkenntnis,* Berlin, 1920.
[3] In *Science and Philosophy of the Organism,* op. cit.
[4] Koffka has lately made a valuable and relevant contribution to this subject. Op. cit.

problem of the origin of language, and the philosophy of signs and symbols (semiotics), are most intimately concerned with our question. While the extent to which it enters even into the major ontological problems of philosophy can be gauged from the account already given of the post-cartesian development of two false theories, each providing the other with a semblance of support: a mechanistic metaphysics of the organic world, and an objective theory of empathy seeking to interpret the appearance of life as due to projective empathy—life itself as an objective fact of nature having been already explained away in mechanical terms.

But our problem has a quite special significance (which would still be primary even if all these other aspects were to lose their interest), for men in their capacity *as men*. For what men can be (or might become), to one another, and what they can not, in love or in hate, in unity and concord or in strife; what they can understand of one another, and how it is that some things can be understood, while others can only be accounted for; in what kinds of group-association, moreover, a man can grasp and appreciate this or that level of being or experience in his neighbour or colleague—all this depends on what kind of ultimate *ties* there are and can be between man and man, at the various levels of relative status among men themselves, and ultimately on the absolute plane of existence. The *metaphysic of men's knowledge of one another*, of what they can have in common—the problem, that is, of how the deep-lying ontological and epistemological relationships among men are adapted to the cosmic order, and of the types of human intercourse which that order permits and furthers, and those it does not—this alone is what ultimately determines the nature and significance of man for his fellow-men. Max Weber and Ernst Troeltsch have given a most valuable descriptive account of the rôle played by metaphysical and religious systems of knowledge, with their variety of answers to this question, in the history of *social* theory and of actual social systems. But only scattered attempts have so far been made to develop a purely *concrete meta-sociology*,[1] and here we are still largely dependent on relics inherited from religious and metaphysical systems of the past (e.g. the Leibnitzian metaphysics of monadic and spiritual individualism, or the systems of Hegel and von Hartmann). And these relics, however worthy of respect, are no longer adequate, in my opinion, to what we know already or are capable of knowing in the future.[2]

[1] There are good things in N. Hartmann's *Metaphysik der Erkenntnis* (Berlin, 1920).
[2] I shall try to show how important this is for a 'sociology of knowledge' in my

The chief defects in previous treatments of the subject, of which we were ourselves guilty at times in the first edition of this book, are as follows:

(1) Failure to separate the problems clearly enough.
(2) Misconception of the order in which to approach them.
(3) Failure to relate the solutions in a systematic way.

So far as the *first* point is concerned, there are *six* questions to be distinguished, which have been too readily confused until now. They may be listed as follows:

(1) What is the essential relationship between the self and the community in general—both in the ontological sense and in our knowledge of the essences involved? Or rather, is there an *essential* relationship of manifest connection between them (quite apart from the existence of any *particular* given self or given community), or is the association always a merely factual one? Are there, moreover, genuine essential ties of a *distinct kind* uniting men as vital creatures and as spiritual or rational beings, or is one of these two relationships a merely contingent one?

(2) There is the question which strictly belongs to logic and the *critique* of knowledge: By what right is a particular individual —for simplicity let us say myself (the present writer), entitled to postulate the existence (*a*) of any *given* community, and (*b*) of some other given person? Progress in the matter has been greatly obstructed by the fact that this question has rarely been distinguished from that relating to the nature of the entities referred to,[1] which must already have been settled, if this present one is to have any meaning. Theodor Lipps assimilated this epistemological question too closely to questions concerning the origin and psychological provenance of our knowledge of other selves, though it has little connection with *either* of these. This has been clearly recognized since by Oswald Külpe, Erich Becher and others. What has hardly been recognized at all, however, is that the answer to this question offers no sort of solution to three altogether different problems:

(a) What constitutes the *reality-factor* in an object generally, and how does it *present* itself, in principle, to a conscious subject as such?[2]

(b) What constitutes the *mental or spiritual reality* of a conscious

contributions to a collection of essays to be published by the Cologne Forschungsinstitut für Sozialwissenschaften [Dunker and Humblot, Munich, 1924. Cf. 'Probleme einer Soziologie des Wissens' in *Die Formen des Wissens und die Gesellschaft*].

[1] Cf. the following chapter.
[2] [Cf. the chapter entitled 'Metaphysik der Wahrnehmung und das Problem der Realität' in the essay 'Erkenntnis und Arbeit' (1926) and further the study 'Idealismus-Realismus' in the *Philosophischer Anzeiger*, Heft II, Bonn, 1928.]

self, and of self-consciousness generally (whether in myself or another), as distinct from mere *awareness* 'of' that reality, and how is this reality given?

(c) In what way and by what means are we first acquainted with the reality of the mental and spiritual centre in *others* generally, apart from a merely discursive knowledge of the other's conscious self and its contents? For it is a great illusion of epistemology generally (and not merely with regard to other minds), to suppose that the problem of the nature and giveness of reality is itself resolved in some way once criteria are established for the *conditions* under which reality may be attributed to an object of an already-determinate character (or to something that cannot itself be an object, such as an act, an act-centre, or a *Persona*), or conversely, the conditions under which a particular character may be assignable to the already-given reality of something (= X). Even in the extreme case of the pathologically 'autistic' individual (represented by some of Bleuler's cases, for example), no doubt is entertained as to the fact that other conscious subjects exist, although the patient may periodically lose all sense of the *reality* of his human environment.

(3) There is the problem of the *origin* of our social and other-consciousness generally, i.e. the transcendental psychological problem of our knowledge of other selves; this has no more to do with the question of our right to postulate their existence than it has with the problem of the empirical genesis and development of other-consciousness in the course of individual life from infancy to maturity. Here, as in all true questions of origin, it is a question, rather, of that point in the order of *dependence* among cognitive intentions (or the corresponding spiritual acts of the person), at which social and other-consciousness *commences*, i.e. what kind of cognitive acts must already have been accomplished before awareness of others can appear. Does, e.g., a knowledge of self in others necessitate, in general, a prior awareness of self derived from one's own case? (We shall be answering in the affirmative.) Does it also require self-consciousness in the first place? (We shall be denying this.) Again, does it either presuppose a (purely formal) awareness of God, or are both equally fundamental, or does it take precedence over the latter? (We think it possible to show, as against Descartes, that it is subsequent to the consciousness of God.) Again, does the knowledge of others (as other *minds*), presuppose a knowledge of the natural order and a consciousness of 'reality' in this order (i.e. the reality of the external world), or do both originate together, or does knowledge of others have priority? So far as the minds of others are concerned we shall find it necessary to accept the third alternative. The only thing we can concede as

a prior condition for accomplishment of the act of knowing other minds is what we may call a sense of the 'ideal meaning of signs' in general. Matters will be altered, however, in dealing with the question of the origin of our knowledge of other human (or sub-human) subjects at the level of *vital consciousness*. Here too the question is: Does this knowledge precede, accompany or follow the knowledge of Nature (both as to its order and its reality)? Our answer will be that our primary knowledge of Nature is itself a knowledge of the *expressive aspect* of living organisms; mental phenomena therefore (which are invariably presented only within a structural context), are always given, in the first instance, in unities of expression. Again, does such knowledge precede, accompany or follow a knowledge of the (inanimate) physical world? Our answer will be that it precedes it. Thus the primitive, like the child, has no general acquaintance with 'deadness' in things: all his experience is presented as *one* vast field of expression, in which particular expressive unities stand out against the background. Does this knowledge, moreover, precede, accompany or follow an acquaintance with organic form (the body, in man), and all that goes along with it (the environment, the occurrence of spontaneous movement, etc.)? We shall hold that they go together. It is only from the total unity of the 'animate' body that we go on to differentiate our knowledge of our fellow-man into an acquaintance with his physical body on the one hand, and his 'inner life' on the other.

It will be clear from this what we understand by the question of origin. It is a peculiarity of all the highly important questions of origin in the theory of knowledge (as distinct from the critique of knowledge, which is concerned with questions of criteria and justification), that they can and should be raised in *abstraction* from the particular *contingent* objects of knowledge; and they are no less independent of the actual phases of *empirical* development in any particular concrete individual, as regards his knowledge of these contingent real objects; (for instance, the genesis and development of knowledge in a particular child concerning the mental existence of his mother and the content of her inner life). The mere *order of sequence* governing the emergence of acts making for a unity of character among the objects of experience (e.g. space, time, material objects, etc.), *separates off each* phase in the empirical development of a man's knowledge over a period of time; it also marks the development from one individual to another by means of inherited dispositions. It has nothing to do with the scope, the simplicity or the complexity of this knowledge, with its adequacy or inadequacy (or completeness), and least of all with any judgement concerning its truth or falsity (both in the material and the formal sense). And yet the question of origin is the epistemological question *par excellence*; not so the questions of 'criteria' and 'justification', which are merely concerned with the logical *critique* of knowledge.

The problem of the origins of our knowledge of other minds, past, present and future, includes a range of questions almost unnoticed hitherto, concerning the genetic order in our knowledge of the various *essential group-forms* which have to be distinguished in the study of human social groups.[1] Thus it can be shown that a knowledge of the existence and character of mental life in the group comprising the 'community of irreplaceable spiritual persons' already presupposes a knowledge of the existence and nature of other people within 'society'; that the indirect knowledge of others which occurs in the social type of group, again presupposes the much more immediately given knowledge of others which can only be obtained from a communal mode of life (primarily in the family). Even this knowledge, however, can only arise because, in the early stages of infancy, our mental pattern corresponds to that which must also be ascribed to the herd, the horde and the mob; for at that time we absorbed unconsciously, by means of true identification and a genuine 'tradition', certain contents and functions of other minds (or dispositions to revive such contents and functions), which we should have been quite unable to acquire at a later stage, or in any other psycho-social group-structure than that of the horde, the mob and the herd. There is also the question of ascertaining the *different depths* in the mental and spiritual personality of the other, to which our knowledge of him can penetrate. They terminate at that which is utterly unintelligible in him, those personal acts which can no longer be 'construed' (and can at best be merely *imitated* or *reproduced*); they terminate also at the level of absolute privacy of content in the spiritual being of the other person, which can no longer be conveyed to us even by a free act of disclosure on his part.[2] However, the various degrees of intelligibility which lie within these absolute limits are closely connected with the form of the group concerned (as found in friendship, comradeship, acquaintance and even in the distinctions embodied in different forms of address; again in the ties of marriage, the family, the home, the clan, the tribe, the people or the nation and in religious or cultural communities, etc.). And among these groups, moreover, there are fundamental relationships *governing* the possibility of their knowledge of one another. While similar relationships also determine the possibility of acquiring knowledge of supra-individual communities in the

---

[1] I have already begun to lay the foundations of this in my *Formalismus in der Ethik*, p. 547 seq.　　　　　　　　　[2] Ibid., p. 585 seq.

past, as disclosed to us by an inherited capacity for understanding, by a genuine handing-down of tradition, and by the merely historical interpretation of evidence (sources, monuments, etc.).

This investigation of the order of origin and precedence in our knowledge of the social field is also fundamental to the *theory of stratification* which ethnology attempts to establish in relating cultural achievements to the mental and spiritual status of the groups to whom they belong, and to the special relationships between individual and community which obtain therein. The socio-psychology and psycho-sociology[1] of primitive thought, volition and feeling can only be elucidated, once it is established empirically what can be known in this field, by means of this philosophical theory of origin. A fundamental flaw in previous philosophical and epistemological treatments of our problem as to the origin of our knowledge of other minds has been that most of the solutions offered could only be taken seriously with reference to educated Northern Europeans of the present day. This, as we shall see, is obviously the case with the analogical theory, conceived as a theory of origin (and not as providing a 'justification' merely, or a purely psychological account); but it is equally true of Theodor Lipps' theory of imitation and empathy, and of the purely associative theory of reproduction put forward by Benno Erdmann. Hence incompatible theories have often been upheld as *absolutely* valid, which have only a *relative* validity within particular patterns of group-structure. Once account is taken of their limited significance, relative both to specific types of group and to specific planes (as distinct from chronological periods) of history, it can be seen that they are not really incompatible at all. Lipps' theory is not simply false; for in application to the pattern of crowd-psychology it is approximately correct. When applied to Europeans in the setting of 'society', and to the scientific pattern of that society, the analogical theory is not inaccurate, as a theory of origins, and even within limits, as a psychological account. The theory developed below, which I call the 'Perceptual theory of other minds' is again applicable only to the mode in which men encounter one another in communal life. But this ascription of relativity to the many previous theories as to the origin of our knowledge of other minds does nothing, of course, to imply that such relative theories are all we can look for. On the contrary, there is certainly an absolute theory as well, which only needs to be sufficiently formal to incorporate these relative theories as partial accounts referring to special groupings and phases of development in the field of human relationships.

[1] This pertinent distinction is made by H. L. Stoltenberg in his *Soziopsychologie*, Part I, Berlin, Curtius, 1914.

(4) A problem entirely different from those already mentioned is that which relates to the *empirical psychology* of the individual (including both normal and differential psychology or psychopathology), and the empirico-genetic psychology of human nature, with regard to the emergence and development of knowledge on the part of actual men concerning the minds of those about them.

It can be seen at once that, taken by itself, empirical psychology offers no entry to the philosophical questions dealt with here. For in all its enquiries it begins by naïvely taking *for granted* everything that is here in question. It presumes that there actually *are* other men and animals, possessed of a mental life open to observation. And it does so in just the same way as it assumes a real passage of mental events in objective time—the existence, not only of conscious experiences, which cannot be anything but present, but also of real experiences, past, present and future, which make a (more or less adequate) entry into consciousness and progress from this to internal awareness, attention and observation. Finally, it assumes the communicability of everything vouchsafed in internal awareness and the reflexive act or function, and of the data afforded to observation by the immediate retention of experiences, and subsequently expressed in propositional form; and it also assumes that such information can be understood.

Empirical psychology is unable by itself to determine the nature of internal awareness or to explain how this allows the object of such awareness to be strictly identified in a multiplicity of acts on the part of a multiplicity of percipients. This is the concern of a *mental ontology* and of the *theory and critique of psychological knowledge*. The same applies to knowledge of the conditions of our internal awareness of a mental fact, the limits of this awareness, and the conditions under which its adequacy can be increased. We shall describe this as the problem of 'inner sense'.[1] Nothing, I should say, is more certain than the fact that there can be no such thing as a science of unidentifiable objects. The oft-proposed definition of the mental as that which is accessible to one person only, would therefore, if correct, put an end to *all* empirical psychology whatsoever. For the mental datum present to the individual must not only be identifiable throughout a multiplicity of acts on his own part, but by many other people as well. Only a *realistic* psychology, in which the content of internal awareness is accurately distinguished from that of which we are aware, namely the actual mental state, can carry us beyond the immediacy of the conscious present. Let it not be forgotten that consciousness as such is *necessarily* only a consciousness of the

[1] Cf. the essay 'Die Idole der Selbsterkenntnis' (1913) in *Vom Umsturz der Werte*, Leipzig, 1915.

present (even though consciousness of past, present and future may be included as elements within it). Apprehension, attention and observation, which presuppose one another in that order, can never relate, in the genetic order of acts of mental cognition, to the object of internal awareness itself, but only to what is preserved in retention; so that once again their nature and limits of operation cannot be investigated by empirical psychology itself—for it already makes use of them as a source of knowledge. These are problems which belong to the epistemology of psychology. Is self-observation by nature prior to, simultaneous with, or later in origin than the observation of others (in the way that internal self-awareness is certainly prior to a corresponding awareness of others)? Or is it merely a corresponding attitude towards ourselves, 'as if we were another',[1] as Hobbes said—and rightly so, in our opinion? Again, the epistemology of understanding is equally a presupposition for empirical psychology, not an object of enquiry. The reports made by the experimental subject as to what he may have found in self-observation, based on experiment, have still got to be understood first of all, and even shared and reproduced by the person conducting the experiment, before the report itself has any claim to establish a 'scientific fact'. It is not for empirical psychology to provide an account of this understanding, sharing and reproduction of thought, for it is socially and epistemologically *presupposed* in its own procedure.

The reason why we are still lacking in clear and certain ideas as to the ultimate limits of knowledge in empirical psychology is simply that we have only the first feeble rudiments of *an ontology of mental reality* and an *epistemology of psychology* in general and of experimental psychology in particular. There is the problem, for instance, as to whether mental processes can be *repeated* in a number of subjects, and as to which kinds of process are in general 'repeatable' and capable of experimental revival, and which not; we also need to know at which levels of development in the individual and the group such repetition is still possible, and to what degree of accuracy;[2] all this must be cleared up beforehand if we are to have any conception of the abiding limitations to knowledge derived from inductive experiment. It is far too little recognized at present that every act of possible observation pre-supposes a *scrutiny of the nature* of the fact to be observed.

Above all, we feel the lack of any clear insight into the onto-logical *limits as to what can be objectified within the mental field*. For

---

[1] Internal observation also constitutes an artificial interruption of the con-tinuity of experience, a way of treating present experience 'as if' it were already over and done with.

[2] Cf. Koffka, op. cit.

only a part of our total mental and cognitive existence is capable of becoming an object for us, and only a very small proportion of that part can itself be observed and repeated (without intrinsic modification of its character); while only a part of what is mentally observable lends itself to deliberate experiment, governed by a prior analysis of the nature of its variable elements. We are very often told nowadays by those experimental psychologists who occupy themselves in enquiring into the 'higher' functions (of thought, will, religious activity, etc.), that the whole of mental and spiritual life must be submitted to experimental investigation. But to this it must be replied that the full significance of *cognitive* activity is not, and never can be accessible to internal awareness, or to apprehension, attention or observation, let alone to experimental interference; not by reason of any avoidable limitations of knowledge or method, but because of its *intrinsic nature*. Hence it is virtually a betrayal of that essentially human attribute in man which divides him from the beasts, namely reason itself, to declare that 'nothing shall be held to exist which is not open to experimental investigation'. Whatever lies open to experiment is exclusively confined to the field of being and becoming at the automatic, teleological, *vital level* of the mind, which lies *beneath* the domain of the free acts of the spiritual personality. It is only the effects of the latter on being and becoming at the vital level on the one hand, and the conditions governing the occurrence of certain types of personal activity on the other, that still fall within that potentially objective field of existence which is the sole concern of experimental psychology. It certainly represents a considerable advance that recent psychology should have begun to recognize the limitations of that scheme of mechanical associationism (with its objective counterpart, the operational and behaviouristic principle), upon which Münsterberg attempted to found it. It is also an advance to have realized that the 'pure' sensation never occurs as a fact, being only a hypothetical limiting case, gradually arrived at by abstraction from differences of attention and anticipations of value, as well as from a diversity of intentional patterns. And it is a further gain to have recognized that contiguous association, and mechanical reproduction by means of associative dispositions, merely represent a more or less considerable inhibiting factor upon the automatic operations of a mental life governed by aims and ends, by instinctive impulses and volitional acts. But such a psychology would be committing itself to a major error, in my view, if in so doing it were to suppose itself to have passed beyond the vital plane of mentality, as a potential counterpart of inner sense, and to have arrived at an investigation of the *cognitive and spiritual order*. For this constitutes a whole region of being which lies entirely *beyond the comprehension* of empirical psychology (experimental or otherwise), and this by virtue of its *ontological* status.

It is not simply (as Windelband, Münsterberg, Natorp and others have thought) that psychology differs from the study of the intellect in its method and point of view. For there are two decisive points at issue here: (1) The (spiritual) person, as such, is intrinsically incapable of being *treated as an object*, for its mode of being is only accessible by virtue of *participation* (or reproduction) in thought, volition or feeling, just as an act is; (personality is, in effect, a non-spatio-temporal collocation of acts, a concrete whole conditioning each individual act, and a whole whose variations are reflected in those acts: or, as I am wont to put it, personality is the substance of which acts are attributes). It is *this* participation alone which serves to replace our knowledge of objectively knowable facts, and is able to do so, since knowing itself is but another mode of participation in being, namely in that which can be treated as an object. While 'consciousness', in the subjective sense, is again simply a *form* of knowing, based on reflection upon the content of the knowledge-giving act. The person, however, and its intellectual (or spiritual) activity can only be understood in terms of its attributes, and the outward manifestations of intelligence. '*Understanding*' therefore constitutes an ultimate source of facts and intuitive data at least on a level with 'awareness' (and hence 'internal awareness' as well), the latter being itself a prior condition, in the genetic sequence of acts, for all internal scrutiny and self-observation. Understanding is not confined to the understanding of others (on the strength of what I have already perceived in myself). It is equally ultimate as an understanding of oneself. The understanding of others is simply that which is based upon an 'understanding', namely the receipt of a free and spontaneous disclosure, which cannot be made good in its absence by spontaneous knowledge and insight on the part of the percipient. Understanding, whether of an *act* or of its objective *significance*, is a basic type of participation, distinct from and in no way based upon perception, whereby one essentially spiritual being can enter into the life of another one, just as self-identification and co-operation represent the basic mode of entry into its existence.[1] Hence an intuitive psychology aiming at a knowledge of actual persons and the significance of their actual trains of thought is

---

[1] If God is thought of as a Person, it is equally inconceivable that there should be objective knowledge of Him; it is only by a *cogitare, velle, amare in Deo*, i.e. by a reliving of the divine life and the reception of His word, through which He first reveals His existence as a Person, that such knowledge is obtained. Cf. 'Probleme der Religion' in *Vom Ewigen im Menschen*.

distinguished, not merely by its method, but by its *subject-matter*, from any psychology dealing with potentially objective mental realities. It is an error to believe therefore, that an experimental and observational psychology could succeed, at any stage of its development, in providing what an intuitive psychology has to offer by way of a foundation for the social sciences. But it is also decisive, (2) that personality and spirit represent something which is quite unlike the inorganic and organic fields in being intrinsically *beyond the bounds of spontaneous scrutiny*, since it is *free to decide* whether to make itself available and knowable or not. Persons, in fact, can be silent and keep their thoughts to themselves, and that is quite different from simply saying nothing. It is an active attitude, whereby they can themselves conceal their qualities from spontaneous scrutiny to any desired extent, yet without this necessarily involving any automatic expression or physical symptom to that effect.[1] Nothing in Nature can 'hold its peace' in this way; which is why Nature, including happenings at the vital level of mentality, which always have a strictly unambiguous counterpart in physiological bodily processes, is open, in principle at least, to spontaneous scrutiny.

Thus empirical psychology has only a very limited application to our problem.

(5) A complete theory of our knowledge of communities and of minds (the real self or soul) in others, would also have to include *a metaphysic of this knowledge* and hence of the operative relationships between one soul and another (at the vital or spiritual levels). Erich Becher[2] is wrong, in my view, in thinking it possible to make a complete separation between the epistemological problem (which he also equates with the logical and critical one), and the metaphysical problem. As a matter of method it may well be possible and necessary to do so, but it cannot be carried through in practice. Here is an example to illustrate the point. Just as the strict epiphenomenalistic parallelism which denies all reality and causal connection to mental events ought logically to postulate an analogical inference in order to justify (if not actually to account for), all self-knowledge extending beyond the moment of consciousness, so Becher has to adopt a similar postulate in order to provide grounds for assuming

---

[1] Self-understanding, which is a prior condition for a person's being able to make himself available and accessible to understanding by others, in respect of what he is, thinks, wills, loves, etc., is therefore largely bound up with the practice of silence. Hence the *sanctum silentium* in so many metaphysical and religious communities (Buddhism, Christian monasticism, the Quakers, etc.). See the admirable study by Odo Casel, O.S.B., on the *sanctum silentium* within the mysteries of antiquity. (Dissertation, Bonn.)

[2] *Vide* E. Becher, op. cit., p. 283 seq.

the existence of consciousness in others. The 'veridical' chains of continuous physical causation which account for the epiphenomenal data of consciousness, would then differ, as between internal and intersubjective causality, purely as regards their length, so to speak. An idealistic or strictly monistic parallelism would seem to require telepathy both real and apparent (the latter at least the *appearances* of telepathy), and both theories would virtually make it a perpetual miracle that an actual physical linkage is always present, under normal circumstances, in men's knowledge of one another. A theory of justification by an analogical argument would be out of place in either of these metaphysical speculations, since it invariably proceeds on the assumption that it is not the concrete whole of the other's embodied self that is primarily given to us (as Wundt, for example, maintained, in full accordance with his parallelism), but simply the physical signs presented by the bodily organism. Again, Becher's own metaphysical belief in a supra-individual mind seems to me quite irreconcilable with his use of the argument from analogy. If there is apparently supposed to be a direct metaphysical connection between the substrates of a pair of selves, by way of the 'supra-individual mind', what is the point of bringing in an analogical argument from physical signs, not to account for the psychological origin of this knowledge, which would be intelligible even in Becher's case, but in order to justify it? The (traditional) argument from analogy is merely an epistemological tailpiece tacked on to *one particular system of metaphysics*, namely the Cartesian and Lotzean dualism of interacting substances, which does *not* postulate a supra-individual mind. It is the same with the epistemological idealists (such as Rickert, Husserl and others); either they accept an unaccountable miracle, in assuming the reality of other selves at all (granted, that is, that the self is admitted to be intrinsically individuated, and not merely by virtue of its empirical content or relationship to the body; for the latter, combined with an idealist theory of consciousness would inevitably lead to solipsism); or else we have another unaccountable miracle, namely that within the total content of 'consciousness in general' (which is supposed to contain each individual self as part of its objective content), there should still be individual centres of consciousness which are obliged to take special cognizance of their own existence.

These examples are only intended to show that our problem calls for a certain *unity of logical style* in dealing with its epistemological and metaphysical aspects, and that it will not do to suppose that any theory of knowledge is compatible, in this connection, with any kind of metaphysics. For since, in the last resort, we have to furnish a metaphysical explanation for all knowledge whatsoever, a metaphysic of our knowledge of other minds represents the only final solution to our problem. To be sure, it is then so closely connected with the mind-body problem that it is virtually impossible to separate the two. But since our methods and procedures must conform to the facts and not vice versa, this difficulty in keeping the problems separate, which is so troublesome in all philosophy, is quite unavoidable.

It is therefore all the more important to be quite clear as to the *objective order of those problems*, whose consideration can alone direct us to this ultimate solution of the question. This order (which we believe to be common to all metaphysics—or rather, to all the metasciences), is as follows: the common basis for the epistemological as well as for the metaphysical enquiry must consist, firstly, in an ideal scrutiny, without reference to actual existence, of the essential relationships between self and community in general; and secondly, in an exact determination of the situation within the field of natural experience. This is succeeded at once by the epistemological question as to the origin of our knowledge of other minds, and this in turn by a critical justification of this knowledge in respect of the empirical evidence. Not until both these questions have been settled is it possible and necessary to give a hearing to the claims of intuitive and observational psychology.

(6) Lastly, the problem of individual and society, and of self and other as conscious subjects, is also, in its most fundamental sense, a problem of *value*, an ethical as well as a juristic problem. Indeed there is a whole group of philosophers who have sought to establish the existence of other persons in general primarily from this point of view—and who would consider any other grounds for their existence to be merely derivative from that which is designated by the idea of a 'responsible being' in general. Fichte is the clearest, acutest and most radical exponent of the problem from this point of view. He argued more or less as follows: the central core of the Pure Ego consists in a *primordial consciousness of duty*, or pure consciousness of obligation; (in virtue of his interpretation of the 'primacy of practical over theoretical reason' this constitutes, for him, as it does for Kant, not only the prior condition of all apprehension of value and practical decision, but also of all theoretical assertion and denial of matter of fact); this consciousness of duty entails that there must also be other conscious subjects towards whom the Self can have duties of some kind. All theoretical insight into the existence of the other self is dependent on this practical evidence of my consciousness of duty, prior to any theoretical attribution of existence. This idea of Fichte's has been quite seriously revived of late, particularly by Münsterberg.[1]

[1] Cf. *Psychology, General and Applied*, Part I.

For Münsterberg also, our primary conviction of the existence of other people is due neither to inference nor to perception, nor to empathy, imitation, etc., but to an act of 'recognition' (in the moral sense), and 'appreciation' of the other person as a point of origin (X) for free acts of possible recognition and appreciation on his part as well. This recognition and appreciation of other responsible wills is already presupposed in the objective discrimination both of 'Nature' and of 'mind' (as that residual content of consciousness which has not as yet been attributed to Nature, being accessible to one person only). Aloys Riehl's view may also be described as a primarily ethical theory of other minds, which seeks to explain our conviction of their existence in terms of sympathy.[1] Nor is Hermann Cohen far removed from this position in deriving the existence of personality in general from the recognition that man (as a purely natural object), plainly has a juridical personality as such, so that a person could not be considered to exist (as a private, moral or religious agent), so long as he had not been acknowledged as a 'juridical person' of this type.[2]

Such exclusively ethical or even juridical theories must be wholly rejected. They are nothing but a revival of the old Platonic and Aristotelian identification of the 'good' with the 'existent' (*Omne ens est bonum*), and of the level of positive value with the level of existence; an equivalence so vividly represented, for example, in the Greek word ἐσθλός (the noble and free), i.e. he who 'is'. We have elsewhere repudiated the one-sidedness and perversity of both these theories, and given reasons for our rejection.[3] But this rejection should not blind us to the *relative* truth-value of these two theories. I see it in this, that though, in the ontological order, the existence of a person, while contemporaneous with his character as an individual, is necessarily prior to his value in the order for us (πρὸς ἡμᾶς), the value of the person is actually given prior to his character, though not, as this ethical theory claims, prior to the givenness of his existence. It is intrinsically impossible for the value of personality to be given in advance of its existence (and not merely of its character), for there can be no such thing as value apart from existence, either in appearance or in reality. And this applies still more once the further error is committed of attempting to base this givenness of value upon acts of recognition and appreciation, when all ideal obligation and all recognition of such obligation imply that such

[1] *Principles of the Critical Philosophy* (tr. by Dr. A. Fairbanks. London; English and Foreign Philosophical Library, 1894). Cf. Külpe's criticism in his book *Die Realisierung*, Vol. II.

[2] *Ethik des reinen Willens*, 1904.

[3] Cf. *Der Formalismus in der Ethik*, pp. 385 seq., 541, 585.

value is already given. This act of 'recognition and appreciation' would be a complete shot in the dark if the personal existence of something (X), and the value of this, were not already *given in advance*.

Now though there is little reason for thinking that the person (as a free and morally responsible centre of action), would count for anything, or deserve recognition, *prior* to its existence, or even to awareness of such existence, there is one point in which this theory is quite correct: namely that pure value-relationships and the corresponding evaluative ties between persons do engender *unique* (i.e. autonomous) *sources of emotional evidence* independent of (theoretical) grounds for existence, *in favour of the value* (and hence the existence)[1] of other persons and personal communities. Thus it would, in effect, be a major error to assert that a being capable only of feeling, loving, hating and willing (without any trace of a theoretical capacity, i.e. for the apprehension of objects), could have no sort of evidence for the existence of other people. By virtue of the necessary connection subsisting between existence and value (or between existential and evaluative judgements), a being thus confined (in imagination) to evaluative and practical activity might well succeed, by indirect methods, in establishing the existence of that to which he feels responsibility, duty, sympathy, etc. Taken by itself indeed, the moral consciousness offers a 'guarantee' that is not direct, let alone primary, but *indirect*, not only for the possibility of value, but also for the existence of other people. Nor does this apply to some one moral act or another, but to all morally relevant acts, experiences and states, in so far as they contain an intentional reference to other moral persons; obligation, merit, responsibility, consciousness of duty, love, promise-keeping, gratitude and so on, all refer, by the very nature of the acts themselves, to other people, without implying that such persons must already have been encountered in some sort of experience, and above all without warranting the assumption that these intrinsically social acts (as we shall call them), can only have occurred and originated in the actual commerce of men with one another. For on closer examination it appears, rather, that these acts and experiences are such that they cannot be reduced to a combination of more elementary acts and experiences of a *pre*-social kind, together with some sort of experience of other human beings. They demonstrate that even the *essential* character of human consciousness is such that the community is in some sense implicit in every individual, and that man is not only part of society, but that society and the social bond are an essential

[1] In as much as the presence of value in a thing necessarily implies the existence of that thing.

part of himself; that not only is the 'I' a member of the 'We', but also that the 'We' is a necessary member of the 'I'.[1] Indeed we ought to ask whether this intrinsic orientation of the particular individual towards a possible society is not also a *multiply qualified* one, such that by a purely immanent scrutiny of the intrinsic activity of *any* given self, prior to and apart from any chance empirical acquaintance or actual intercourse among men, one might discover in it a further orientation towards a multiplicity of groups and communal interests of very different kinds. There is one particular kind of communal relation which stands out as a condition, both fundamental and supreme, for the ideally possible occurrence of all the others, namely the community of each person with God as the Person of Persons; a community based upon the religious acts of love, awe and fear of God, the sense of individual and collective responsibility towards Him or of guilt, gratitude, etc., in His regard.[2] In particular, the moral evidence for the obligation to keep promises remains wholly unintelligible without reference to God, as the partner in a personal relationship which precedes all others. And it is also clear that the way in which this social and communal relationship to the Supreme Being is intuited, felt and conceived of, in terms of a particular religious attitude to God and the world, must have a crucial effect upon all other moral relationships subsisting between the person and the various kinds of human community (and also upon his attitude to the non-human organic world of Nature). This supreme principle, both of the sociology of religion and of any theory of the religious attitude to God and the world, is not derived from historical experience: on the contrary, such experience must be analysed under its guidance and direction if one is to disentangle the inner necessities of connection which hold between religious systems and the various modes of communal life.[3] Just as to every epistemological theory of other minds there corresponds, as we have seen, a particular metaphysics of real social relationships, so to both of these there corresponds again an ideally appropriate system of religion (or anti-religion).

Here again we fall into serious errors in attempting, like the south German school, for example, to deal with problems of value in isolation from problems of existence; as if any notion you please

[1] This happy expression of my view may be found in J. Plenge's *Über christlichen Sozialismus*.

[2] The defining characteristics of the 'religious act', i.e. the symptoms whereby love, fear or gratitude take on a 'religious' character, are fully dealt with in 'Probleme der Religion' in *Vom Ewigen im Menschen*, op. cit.

[3] An excellent factual account of the relationships of Christian churches, sects, etc., within such groups, has been given by Ernst Troeltsch in his *Social Teaching of the Christian Churches* (tr. Olive Wyon, Allen and Unwin, 1931).

as to the metaphysical relationship of individual and community were compatible with any evaluative theory of the relation between personal and communal values. Is it possible, in all honesty, to deny the metaphysical existence of the spiritual person as a substance (as Spinoza, Hegel, Schopenhauer and von Hartmann do), considering it to be a mode or function of one and the same infinite Mind, while at the same time giving it priority over the whole community to which it belongs, in the manner of personalism or evaluative individualism? Or conversely, is it possible to affirm this substantial existence of the person as a metaphysical entity, while remaining a socialist as regards value, in the sense of maintaining that personality only acquires its value through the relationship in which it stands to the community as a whole, or its collective will (cf. Wundt, for instance)? There is a pretty close connection between pluralistic materialism and the values of a competitive individualism (which is also exemplified in the 'class-struggle' of Marxian socialism[1]); and there is a similar parallel between the harmony of individual interests and egoistic conception of value in classical English liberalism for example, and the philosophy of deism. Monism, pandaimonism and pantheism in all their forms imply the system of values of a genuinely organic socialism (in which the private individual exists only for the sake of the whole); while a personalist view of human brotherhood entails theism (according to our account, whereby person and whole exist on their own, yet also for one another, though never *merely* for one another, since both exist together for God as a Person, and it is only 'in God' that they too can exist for one another).[2] There is a similar correlation of thought, of a kind disclosed by a purely a priori study of the general attitudes in question, between theories of knowledge and systems of ethics. Thus the old theory of the 'social contract' which derives historically from Epicureanism, has its counterpart in the theory of analogical inference, and the doctrine of the subjectivity of qualities and forms (together with the conceptual nominalism which goes along with this). For if I can knowingly have any content of consciousness—e.g. the blue of the pencil lying in front of me—*identically* in common with someone else, and not just in the sense that there are 'two' blues which merely represent the similar effects produced by an object without qualities upon our respective minds and nervous systems, then the 'argument from analogy' is no longer needed to account for every item in the consciousness of another.

[1] Historically, this connection is clearly exhibited in Democritus, Epicurus and Lucretius, who account for Nature as well as society in terms of a clash of forces among their ultimate constituents—as Hobbes also does.

[2] Cf. *Der Formalismus in der Ethik*, p. 540 seq.

Such parallels and others like them should therefore be taken seriously. Although the progress of systematic philosophy does not necessarily call for a 'history of philosophy' proceeding on chronological lines, it certainly needs a *philosophical study of general attitudes*, both pure and applied, which without pronouncing on their truth or falsehood would pursue an independent enquiry into the intrinsically necessary parallelism of ideas between the parts within the various typical systems of philosophy.[1]

A fully-developed theory of the grades of sympathy, from identification to non-cosmic personal love, could also yield philosophical enlightenment on everything in the history of manners, custom and law from primitive times to the present day, that is involved in the great problem of 'social cohesion', the dissolution of old loyalties and the formation of new ones (the association and dissociation of groups). The various systems of exacting vengeance, for example, which culminate in the statutory penalties of the criminal law, are all based upon different *patterns of sympathetic attitude*.[2] Their history is a continuous dissolution of earlier states of identification into an ever more distant sense of fellow-feeling, and finally into indifference.[3] The 'expansion' of sympathies, and their qualitative sublimation and spiritualization (positively, in love, and negatively in hate), always implies a further formation and dissolution of *solidarity in individual groups*. Even the partial truths embodied in successive philosophical theories of society itself must be read in the light of previous changes in the pattern of sympathy. Thus the contract theory, for example, is assuredly based in origin upon a feeling of estrangement from the social environment with which one has to deal (just as the psychological theory of analogy is). It has probably arisen in the first place wherever the population of a region or self-contained territory has increased more rapidly by aggregation from *without* (immigration, etc.) than from its own resources. Hence it finally becomes

---

[1] Cf. my essay 'Weltanschauungslehre, Soziologie und Weltanschauungssetzung' (1921) in *Schriften zur Soziologie und Weltanschauungslehre*, Vol. I, *Moralia*.

[2] I have shown in *Der Formalismus in der Ethik*, p. 372 seq., that the idea of retribution and the impulse towards it, which are necessary constituents of the notion of punishment, can in no sense be derived from the sympathy of a third party with the vengeful impulses of the person unjustly injured. Cf. also the chapter on 'Reue und Wiedergeburt' in *Vom Ewigen im Menschen*.

[3] The 'stranger' can be roughly defined (in a phenomenological sense), as one for whom it is no longer possible to feel any spontaneous affinity, in respect of the experiences manifested at first sight (i.e. prior to reflection or judgement) in his aspect, bearing or dress. This uncertainty about him (and even a foreign accent can have this effect upon a native member of the community), makes it easy for those whose judgement is still at the mercy of their feelings to regard him as an enemy or at least as an alien; one who no longer has any part in the material outlook common to the community in question.

pre-eminently the theory of a *social mode of existence*. Conversely, Aristotle's theory of man as a political animal was developed by the ecclesiastical natural lawyers who adhered to Aristotelian and Stoic ideas into a doctrine of natural human instincts, whereby man has an innate moral and juridical tie with the community prior to any sort of promissory or contractual relationship. And this is equally obviously a mere formalization of the cognitive and moral relations of men engaged in a *communal mode of life* (bound together by ties of blood, tradition, place and a speech that is natural and not consciously cultivated), and an extension of this to mankind at large. Hence we may discount the claims of either of these theories to universal validity.

Chapter II

THE GENERAL EVIDENCE FOR THE 'THOU'

In my *Formalismus in der Ethik*,[1] I put a question to a supposed (epistemological) 'Robinson Crusoe', a man, that is, who has never in any way perceived beings of his own kind, or any traces or signs of them, and has no other evidence for the existence of such beings. The question was whether or not such a 'Robinson Crusoe' could know anything of the existence of a community or of conscious subjects resembling himself; and whether he could further be aware of 'belonging' to such a community. I answered both questions in the affirmative and maintained that such a Robinson Crusoe would never think: 'There is no community and I belong to none: I am alone in the world'. He would not only possess the notion and idea of community, but would also think: 'I know that there is a community, and that I belong to one (or several such); but I am unacquainted with the individuals comprising them, and with the empirical groups of such individuals which constitute the community as it actually exists.' In the Appendix to the first edition of this book (which appeared *before* my *Formalismus*), I did not make a sufficiently accurate distinction between these two questions: knowledge of the *nature* of the community, and of the existence of others *in general*; and knowledge of the *contingent* existence of a member of a community, or of some particular historical community. But since, in all my discussions of the subject after the first edition of the *Formalismus*, I have always stated my views in terms of a very sharp distinction between these two questions and the answers to them, it was no blame or reproach to me, but rather a source of particular pleasure, to find

[1] p. 542 seq.

234

in Johannes Volkelt's *Das ästhetische Bewusstsein*[1] a clear recognition, not only of 'a primary conviction of the Thou', but also of 'an intrinsic connection between the self's conviction of its own identity and its certainty regarding other people'. To be sure, the grounds of Volkelt's assertion are quite different from those already adduced in my *Formalismus*, and still more so from the rather more elaborate account presented here. Volkelt speaks of 'an intuitive certainty', or, to quote the more comprehensive and exact description given in his *Gewissheit und Wahrheit*,[2] of an 'immediate apprehension of something that cannot be experienced'. Since I have nothing in common with Volkelt's epistemological doctrines (or his theory of 'intuitive certainty'), and more particularly am unable to accept an 'immediate apprehension of something that cannot be experienced', and indeed must consider this doctrine as a piece of objectivistic dogmatism, whose consequences would be wholly unpredictable, there is little point in entering upon a critical discussion of the subject here. According to my *Formalismus*, Crusoe's evidence of the existence of a Thou in general and of his own membership of the community is not merely a contingent, observational, inductive 'experience', but is certainly *a priori* in both an objective and a subjective sense and has a definite *intuitive basis*, namely a specific and well-defined consciousness of *emptiness* or absence (as compared with the presence of some genuine entity already there), in respect of emotional acts as represented, for instance, by the authentic types of love for other people. In the case of conative acts one might also refer to the consciousness of 'something lacking' or of 'non-fulfilment' which would invariably and necessarily be felt by our Crusoe when engaged in intellectual or emotional acts which can only constitute an objective unity of meaning *in conjunction with* the possibility of a social *response*. From these necessarily specific and unmistakable blanks, as it were, where his intentional actions miss their mark, he would, in our opinion, derive a most positive intuition and idea of something *present to him as the sphere of the Thou, of which he is merely unacquainted with any particular instance.* There is and has been no reference here to any 'innate idea' (virtual or actual), and still less to an 'intuitive certainty of something that cannot be experienced', since it is wholly by means of specific *experiences* in himself (though viewed and regarded in an ideal sense), and by means of the positive sense of vacancy they engender, that Crusoe fashions these ideas of the 'Thou' and of the community generally.

In his *Science and Philosophy of the Organism*, Hans Driesch has

---

[1] p. 117 seq. (Munich, C. H. Beck, 1920).
[2] p. 539 (Munich, C. H. Beck, 1918).

dealt in a very interesting fashion with Lipps, with Volkelt and with my own earlier treatment in the 'Appendix'. Nor is he satisfied with the empirist theory of analogical inference. As to the point which he makes against me, that 'the intuition of a particular Thou is at least mediated by the manifestly perceived movements of its body', I grant it entirely as regards the existence of other 'psychoids' (to use Driesch's term), and the strictly parallel operations of their mental or conscious inner life. But I cannot concede it for the assumption that spiritual persons exist, since this assumption (as will later appear), only requires a rational content of meaning in *some* sort of objective sign-material —and by no means necessarily involves that the body should itself be present. Driesch himself, in addition to the analogical argument (which he retains in a secondary capacity), relies upon: (1) the a priori and merely intuitive category of 'wholeness', which is exemplified empirically in the first place, both by my own body and by that of another, and also applies to my own mental life; (2) the knowledge of a primary 'parallel correspondence' between my body and my mind as separate wholes. Both of these being given for me, I now infer by analogy to the existence of mind in others and to the conscious processes which underlie this. What we are saying (in our own terminology), is simply that the world of the Thou, or of the community, is just as much an *independent sphere of essential being* as are the spheres of the external world, the internal world, the bodily environment and the realm of the divine. But *every* truly irreducible sphere of being must necessarily be given as a whole *beforehand*, as a 'background' to the positing of the reality of any possible object within it; hence it does not simply comprise the sum of all the contingent facts within it. This doctrine of the prior givenness of particular spheres of being standing in strict correlation to quite specific types of act, and indeed to any sort of human knowledge about anything, represents, as will appear more precisely in another connection, a general cognitive presupposition for the whole theory of knowledge put forward here. This question of 'spheres' must be sharply distinguished throughout (1) from the problem of reality (i.e. the reality of the external world, of the divine, etc.); (2) from the question of *what* particular real facts or events are actually present in any one of these pre-given spheres.[1]

In my *Formalismus* and in the 'Appendix', I gave no account (or at least no adequate one), of the very important *distinction between the givenness* of the unitary psycho-somatic *vital* centres in others (an aspect which relates equally to men, animals and plants), and

[1] [Cf. the essay 'Idealismus-Realismus' in *Philosophischer Anzeiger*, Vol. II, 3 (Bonn, 1927), and also *Erkenntnis und Arbeit* (1926), op. cit.]

the givenness of their *spiritual centres* of personality; nor did I determine how far there is an a priori factor in both these cases, or only in one of them. For it is not only the sphere of spiritual acts (of a cognitive or moral type, for example), that gives rise to the question of the prior givenness *a priori* of the Thou in general; it is equally appropriate to the sphere of all those psycho-somatic forms of knowledge (instinct) and tendency (basically impulsive factors of a directed kind), which have an existence, nature and orderliness quite independent of acts and laws of the cognitive type. Is there an implanted vital instinct in every organism with regard to every living thing, and a corresponding impulse (hostile or friendly) among living creatures generally, which precedes any specific experience? Do men have an instinct for one another generally (and a correspondingly general human gregarious impulse)? Or is their impulsive and instinctive associa-tion (in concord or in conflict), merely an objective consequence of generic instincts and impulses, such as the procreative and sexual instincts? Or does it derive from more specialized predatory appetites, implanted from the beginning and prior to all experi-ence in particular types of creature, and from analogous impulses to power, domination and control, and the impulses to service, devotion, surrender and imitation which go along with them?[1] The stirrings of these instincts and impulsive factors can only be regarded as *pre-empirical* elements in awareness of the vital soul in another if they: (1) precede any sort of sensation or perception of the other's body; (2) already condition and direct the emergence of sensations and perceptions which are only a 'potential' outcome of stimuli and sensory processes; (3) provide, as it were, a pre-empirical meaning and 'interpretation' for the resultant contents of bodily perception, e.g. sensations of the sexual organs, and sexually conditioned expressions thereof, such as the mating-call, or the song of birds in the courting-season.

---

[1] It has already been mentioned that the concepts of specifically purposive impulse (pre-empirical effort), and of specifically purposive instinct (pre-empirical vital knowledge), do not involve any suggestion of 'innate ideas'. Cf. Freud: *Group Psychology and the Analysis of the Ego*, op. cit. Freud denies the existence of a universal gregarious instinct.

Chapter III

THE PERCEPTION OF OTHER MINDS

THE difficulties of this problem are mostly self-engendered, owing to the assumption that each of us is 'primarily' aware only of his own self and its experiences, and that among these only a proportion of such experiences, images, etc., are related to other individuals. The question then arises: (1) how can this portion be distinguished from that other portion which relates only to the self and its own experience? (2) How does the portion relating to others acquire a title to make us acquainted with the actual existence of other people? There have been two ways of resolving these difficulties hitherto: the theory of analogical inference, whereby, on perceiving expressive movements similar to those which we experience in ourselves in consequence of our own individual self-activity, we infer a similar self-activity in others; and the theory especially associated with Theodor Lipps, whereby this assumption involves a belief in the existence of mind in others, based upon a process of empathic projection of the self into the physical manifestations evinced by the other.[1] Neither of these theories succeeds in achieving its object.

As a theory of origins, the *analogical argument* has already been subjected to damaging criticism by Riehl and Lipps. For one thing—as Hume had already noted—this belief is undoubtedly found in animals as well, though they certainly do not perform analogical inferences. Wolfgang Köhler, in his *Mentality of Apes*,

---

[1] Lipps also relies upon a blind belief to substantiate the existence of mental life in the past, of which, again, we only have an interpreted picture, in the shape of a memory image. And he gives similar grounds for assuming the existence of an external world. This is at least consistent. For Lipps ensures thereby that the existence of other selves is at any rate no less and no different in its certainty than the existence of minds in the past and of the external world.

says that 'by suddenly showing signs of the greatest terror, while staring at a certain spot as though possessed, it is not difficult to make all the chimpanzees in the station look at the same place at once. Immediately all the black company starts as if it had been struck by lightning, and proceeds to stare at the same spot, even though there is nothing there at all to be seen.' According to the usual view, this involves an analogical inference concerning 'my consciousness'. It is hardly possible to attribute inference by analogy to a twenty-five-day old baby. Yet Miss Ghinn[1] says of her niece that she already showed signs of an interest in human faces at about this time, long before she reacted to simple colour-stimuli. Again, it is the inflections of the human voice and not just the simple auditory stimuli thereof, which first arouse attention and interest. According to W. Stern's studies of the psychology of childhood, it is already observable in the second month of life that the child does not remain indifferent to the face and voice of his mother, but responds with 'a gentle smile'. By the middle of the first year it is possible to notice a variable response to different facial expressions on the part of the parents. Koffka very rightly says of this: 'It would appear therefore, that phenomena such as "friendliness" and "unfriendliness" are extremely primitive—even more so perhaps, than that of a blue spot.'[2] From these facts and others like them, we conclude that 'expression' is indeed the very *first* thing that man apprehends of what lies outside him, and that he only goes on to apprehend sensory appearances of any kind, inasmuch and insofar as they can be construed as *expressions* of mind. Not only is there no question here of an analogical inference; there can be equally little room for the complicated 'processes of assimilation', postulated in the works of Erdmann,[3] in order to account for the first stages of 'understanding'. The rags and tatters of sensation from which associationism endeavours to piece together our picture of the world are just pure fictions. In the case of the primitive, so well described by Lévy-Brühl, we might perhaps go further and say that everything whatsoever is given, for him, as 'expression', and that what we call development through learning is not a subsequent addition of mental elements to an already-given inanimate world of material objects, but a continuous process of disenchantment, in that only a proportion of sensory appearances retain their function as vehicles of expression, while others do not. Learning, in this sense, is not *animation*, but a continual '*de-animation*'. One should

---

[1] M. W. Ghinn: *The Mental Development of a Child*, University of California Studies, Vol. I, 4.

[2] Cf. Koffka, op. cit., p. 134.

[3] Benno Erdmann: *Grundzüge der Reproduktionspsychologie*, Berlin, 1920.

not impute to children or primitives the world-view of a civilized adult, and then go on to postulate real processes in order to transform this picture back into that of the child or the primitive. Lévy-Brühl has rightly censured this procedure in Herbert Spencer and others.[1] Moreover, we are indeed conscious of our expressive movements, but apart from mirrors and suchlike, such consciousness takes the form, merely, of intentions to *move*, and of the consequences which follow from sensations of movement or state; while in the case of others, the primary data are represented by the visual images of such movements, which have *no* sort of immediate resemblance or similarity to the data encountered in our own case. The fact of the matter is, then, that we only make analogical inferences when we already take the existence of some other animate beings for granted, and are acquainted with their inner life, but are in doubt, on encountering expressive movements which resemble those of other beings better known to us, as to whether a given movement has an expressive significance (in the case of the lower animals, for instance). But even in this case (which resembles the situation in which we construe the gestures of the insane, or where we suspect someone of 'putting it on'), the analogical inference never yields a presumption of the existence of mind in general, but only a conjecture as to its presence in this particular case,[2] or as to the particular kind of experience that may be going on just now, such as remembering, attending, enjoying, etc. Thirdly, there can be no doubt that we also assume the presence of mind in creatures whose expressive movements (and 'actions') have no resemblance to our human ones (e.g. in birds, fish and so on). Lastly, this argument from analogy—even if it were used, and the data for it were available, and it were always employed wherever this assumption is made—would never lead to the content of the assumption in question. For such an argument would be logically correct (and not a fallacy of four terms), only if it implied that on the occurrence of expressive movements similar to those I perform myself, *it is my own self that is present here as well—and not some other and alien self.* If the conclusion refers to an alien self distinct from my own, it

---

[1] Cf. Koffka's excellent comments, op. cit., pp. 336–55, on the 'world of the child'.

[2] Becher remarks on this point that if mind is present in another in any particular case, the existence of other minds in general is confirmed thereby. This is undeniable. But the crucial point is that to treat a movement or bodily occurrence as an 'expression' is already to presuppose the presence of mentality in the organism as a *whole*, and that a particular attribute (pleasure, etc.) can only be inferred if the actual presence of mind, as well as the specific relationship between experience and expressive attribute, is already taken for granted.

is a false conclusion, an instance of the fallacy of four terms.[1] Finally, let us consider what is involved in this assumption. It entails that there are other conscious individuals, who, as such, are different from myself. But the analogical argument can never, in any case, imply the existence of other selves, except in so far as they are like myself; and hence it can never establish the existence of other conscious individuals.

But the *theory of belief and empathy* is equally nugatory in this respect. It provides a hypothesis concerning the manner in which this assumption is arrived at. But it can never assure us of the *legitimacy* of the assumption itself. For all that the theory seeks to establish is a 'blind' belief, not a self-evident intuition or even a rational postulate (such as would naturally be the outcome of the analogical argument). For it would be pure chance that the process of empathy should coincide with the actual presence of mind in the bodies so perceived. Hence the theory of empathy is wholly incapable of pointing to any sort of difference which may exist between that group of cases in which we wrongly impute a self or a soul to something (as, for example, in the 'animism' of primitives and children, and of mythology), and those other cases in which mind is actually present, as for instance in our fellowmen. Nor can the theory distinguish empathy as a source of our knowledge of other minds from the merely *æsthetic* projection of content and character on the part of the self, into a portrait, for instance, or the embodiment of Hamlet, a personage belonging to the world of art, in the gestures of an actor. Indeed there is no telling here, which data are supposed to set off the process of empathy in oneself. Will *any* sort of visual content do for this purpose? Assuredly not, for we do not 'project' ourselves into any visual content we please. The theory is that perception of '*expressive movements*' is required, or at least the behaviour of a *living* creature of some kind. But this answer does not help matters. For the realization that certain seen movements represent expressive movements already presupposes knowledge of the presence of another mind of some kind. The recognition that they are 'expressive' is not the source but the *outcome* of this belief. Moreover, the reference to 'living creatures' will not do here, for the empathy theory itself denies the existence of an independent, objective

[1] Becher's attempt (op. cit) to prove that there is no such fallacy here does not seem to me to be successful. It is not a question of how we come to postulate the occurrence of isolated experiences which are simply not our own, but of how we arrive at the notion of another self, which does not have 'our' experiences, just because they are *his*, i.e. those of another self. This existence of the other self is given to us prior to the particular experiences enjoyed by this other self. The step from one's own self to another's is quite unlike the step from any such given self to a second, a third and so on.

phenomenon of 'life', given in external perception, whose manifestations are taken to be 'alive' because they exhibit this *primary phenomenon*. For even the appearance of life itself is likewise to be explained in terms of an empathic projection of our own *feeling of life*, i.e. of a psychological fact.[1] We should therefore have to reckon with a two-fold process of empathy here: firstly, a projection of our 'feeling of *life*' into certain sensory complexes, and secondly, a projection of *selfhood* which is then imposed upon the whole of this already 'animate' complex. But this is merely to shift the problem. For it must now be asked: in the presence of which objective data can the projection of a 'feeling of life' be justified?[2] When all is said, the theory of empathy offers no grounds for assuming the existence of other selves, let alone other individuals. For it can only serve to confirm the belief that it is *my* self which is present 'all over again', and never that this self is other and different from my own. It could only confirm the latter by virtue of a misconception.[3] We should also pay heed to the fact that we not only know that there are other individual mental selves, but also that we know we can never grasp these adequately in their unique individual essence. For we certainly do know this. It is not a matter of apprehending the self as a particular individuality merely because we encounter it in association with another body; we know that the self we apprehend is itself an *individual*, and one that is distinct from our own self, and only so do we know it to be 'another's'. We do not take it to be an individual, because it is another's. To know of the existence of an individual self it is quite unnecessary to be acquainted with its body. For wherever we meet with *signs* or *traces* of its spiritual activity, in a work of art, for instance, or in the felt unity of a voluntary action, we immediately encounter in this an active individual self. Xenophon rightly observes that if, in order to establish the existence of an historic personage, it were necessary to start from the reports of those who had actually seen him in the flesh, we would not be able to credit the historical existence of Pisistratus, for example, since none of the authors of our sources ever saw him. But in spite of this, we

[1] I propose to show elsewhere how wrongly the facts of life have been interpreted by the empathy theory, closely associated as it is with the mechanistic outlook of post-Cartesian biology. There are few more important tasks for present-day philosophy than to provide a phenomenological basis for the knowledge of life, and hence to give biology a place in the field of epistemology that is independent of physics and chemistry, no less than of psychology.

[2] Moreover, how are we to give an exact account of the 'feeling of life', if the appearance of 'life' is first derived from a process of empathy, which cannot therefore be guided by an already prior notion of the appearance of life?

[3] But once this mistake was realized, solipsism would be the only logical outcome.

can clearly trace the individual unity of his political influence in Athenian politics: and this allows us to assume that he did really exist. As against this, we do not believe in the existence of the devil, for instance, although a great many people have claimed to have seen him in the flesh.[1]

There is, in general, no warrant at all for the assumption that consciousness of the self as an individual is first presented by way of its expressive activity, or through the *bodily* consciousness associated with this— or, objectively speaking, through physical correlates in the nervous system and the fact that they relate to one particular body, or again by virtue of the particular empirical *contents* of experience (as given in inner perception); for apart from these differentiating elements, such a self would be simply the *idea* of a consciousness in general, the mere 'form of a consciousness'. Whereas it might be the case that absolutely identical bodies and contents of physical consciousness were associated with quite different individual selves. Even identical behaviour and attitudes may have quite different mental associations. I am not, of course, saying (as Lipps does) that my body is 'mine' only because I am acquainted with 'myself' as an individual, and thereby know myself to be active as this experiencing individual. This seems to me to overstate the case. What happens, rather, is that I experience my body as mine (and the body of another as belonging to someone else), because I know that both self and body (in its mental and physical aspects) belong to one and the same concrete individual person. Both self and body acquire their ultimate individual character from their evident connection with the unitary *person*.[2] And hence it is not the content of consciousness (what I think, feel, will and so on), which serves to individualize the self. Exactly the same experiences (as they would appear to an ideally perfect inner perception), could still belong to quite different individual selves. An individual mind is never the mere 'collection' or 'sum' of its experiences; or a synthesis of such experiences whose subject is supposed to be a so-called 'supra-individual' conscious activity, a 'consciousness in general'. On the contrary, an experience only becomes a concrete experience (and not just the notion or semblance of such a thing), inasmuch as I thereby apprehend an individual self *in* it, or as it becomes a *symbol* to me for the presence of such an individual.[3] Hence it is not just isolated

[1] Ultimately, wherever we find 'rational' unities of meaning exhibited in some 'material' form, we are necessarily obliged to postulate certain relevant acts, and to attribute these acts to a centre of personality which has imposed this 'meaning' on the material.

[2] On the concept of personality see my *Formalismus*, op. cit., ch. VI.

[3] Cf. my essay on 'Idole der Selbsterkenntnis' op. cit.; and H. Bergson: *Introduction to Metaphysics* (1913).

experiences that I apprehend in another, but always the individual's mental character *as a whole* in its total expression. Small quantitative variations in the organs (such as the nose, mouth, eyes, etc.), which exhibit this, can alter this character completely, whereas greater changes elsewhere leave it wholly unaffected. I can tell from the expressive 'look' of a person whether he is well or ill disposed towards me, long before I can tell what colour or size his eyes may be.

But now let us enquire if the twofold starting-point of these two theories is *phenomenologically accurate*: (1) that it is always *our own self, merely, that is primarily given to us*; (2) that what is primarily given in the case of others is merely the *appearance of the body*, its changes, movements, etc., and that only on the strength of this do we somehow come to accept it as animate and to presume the existence of another self.

Both assumptions commend themselves as self-evident, and both readily appeal to the fact that 'it could not be otherwise'. How indeed could we think any other thoughts, feel any other feelings than 'our own'? And how else should we come to know of the existence of another human being if not by first perceiving his body? What else is there to perceive of him except his body? It is only from thence that our sense-organs receive stimuli, and only by means of such physical processes can there be any intercourse between individual minds.

Let us remember, however, that there is nothing of which the philosopher must be more wary than of taking something to be self-evident, and then, instead of looking to see what *is given*, turning his attention to what 'can be given' according to some supposed realistic theory. For it will be evident that the foregoing assumptions involve a complete departure from the phenomenological standpoint, replacing it—and covertly at that—by a realistic one.

(1) For who can say that it is our *own* individual self and its experiences which are 'immediately given' in that mode of intuition, by which alone the mental, a self and its experiences, can possibly be apprehended, namely in inner intuition or perception? Where is the phenomenological evidence for this assertion?[1]

What is the meaning of the proposition that 'a man can only think his own thoughts and feel his own feelings?' What is 'self-

[1] The act of 'inner perception' is of a different *polarity* from that of 'outer perception' (and one in which there is no necessity for it to operate through sensory functions, let alone the sense-organs). This distinction obviously has nothing to do with what is 'inside' or 'outside' for any given individual. 'Inner perception' is essentially concerned with apprehension of the mental, and it makes no difference to this whether perception is of oneself or another. On this subject cf. also the essay on 'Idole der Selbsterkenntnis', op. cit.

evident' about it? This only, that if once we postulate a *real substratum* for the experiences, of whatever kind, which I may happen to have, then all the thoughts and feelings which occur in me will in fact belong to this real substratum. And that is a tautology. Two real substrata, two soul-substances, for instance, or two brains, certainly cannot enter into one another, or switch from one to the other. But for the moment let us leave such questionable metaphysical hypotheses to one side. However, if we do seriously abandon these and all the presuppositions of realism in general, and stick to pure phenomenology, our proposition loses all semblance of being 'self-evident'. For nothing is more certain than that we can think the thoughts of others as well as our own, and can feel their feelings (in sympathy) as we do our own. Are we not for ever distinguishing 'our own' thoughts from those we have read or which have been told to us? 'Our own' feelings from those we merely reproduce, or by which we have been infected (unconsciously, as we later realize)? 'Our own' will from that which we merely obey and which is plainly manifest to us at the time as the will of another, just as we distinguish our own true will from that which we are deceived into thinking our own, though it has been suggested to us by someone else, in hypnosis, for instance? Even in these very trivial examples we find a string of 'possible' cases of what is supposed, on present assumptions, to be 'self-evidently' impossible. It may well be that our thoughts are presented 'as' our own, and those of others as theirs, e.g. in merely understanding a piece of information. That is the normal case. But it may also happen that the thought of another is not presented as such, but as a thought of ours. Such is the case, for instance, in 'unconscious reminiscence' of things read or communicated. It also occurs when, imbued with a genuine tradition, we accept the thoughts of others, e.g. of our parents or teachers, as thoughts of our own: we then 'reproduce' such thoughts (or feelings) vicariously, without being explicitly conscious of the function of intellectual or emotional reproduction. And hence they appear to us as our own. It may also happen that one of our own thoughts or feelings is presented as belonging to someone else. Thus the mediæval writers were often given to reading their own thoughts or those of their own time into the sources and documents of classical antiquity, thereby fathering Christian modes of thought upon Aristotle, for example. Whereas the tendency in modern times has been to take up ideas which have been unconsciously acquired and thought a thousand times, and put them forward as new and original, the older (mediæval) habit was to extract ideas which actually were new and original from such authors as were invested with special authority. The latter represents the case of 'delusive empathy'. Just because the process of empathy is not explicit here, the individual's experience appears to him as having been derived from someone else.

It is possible, therefore, as these examples show, for the same experiences to be given both 'as our own' *and* 'as someone else's'; but there is also the case in which an experience is simply given, *without presenting itself either as our own or as another's*, as invariably happens, for example, where we are in doubt as to which of the two it is.[1]

Yet it is this level of 'givenness' which represents the common starting-point for the elaboration of an ever nicer distribution of the material of experience so given between ourselves and other people; an ever more precise appropriation of 'our own' and repudiation of what belongs to 'others'. It is not the case therefore, as these theories suppose, that we have to build up a picture of other people's experiences from the immediately given data furnished by our own, and then to impute these experiences, which have no intrinsic marks of 'foreignness' about them, to the physical semblances of other people. What occurs, rather, is an immediate flow of experiences, *undifferentiated as between mine and thine*, which actually contains both our own and others' experiences intermingled and without distinction from one another. Within this flow there is a gradual formation of ever more stable vortices, which slowly attract further elements of the stream into their orbits and thereby become successively and very gradually identified with distinct individuals. But the essential links in the process are simply the facts: (1) that every experience belongs *in general to a self*, so that wherever an experience is given a self is also given, in a general sense; (2) that this self is necessarily an *individual self*, present throughout every experience (in so far as such experiences are adequately given), and not therefore primarily constituted by the interconnection between them. (3) that *there is an 'I' and a 'Thou' in a general sense*. But which individual self it may be, that owns a given experience, whether it is our own or another's, is something that is not necessarily apparent in the experience as immediately presented.

But if there is a general human *tendency* to err in one of these two directions rather than the other, it is certainly not the error of empathy, so-called, whereby we impute our own experience to others, but the *opposite* tendency, in which we entertain the experi-

[1] To be sure, even a thought so given is related to the self in a purely formal sense, for that is part of its nature. But this 'self' is merely a cypher in the formal multiplicity and unity of consciousness—not something experienced, let alone one's 'own' self, which can only be presented by contrast, in relation to some 'other' or 'alien' self.

ences of other people as if they were our own. In other words, a man tends, in the first instance, to live more in *others* than in himself; more in the community than in his own individual self. This is confirmed by the facts of child-psychology, and also in the thought of all primitive peoples. The ideas, feelings and tendencies which govern the life of a child, apart from general ones such as hunger and thirst, are initially confined entirely to those of his immediate environment, his parents and relatives, his elder brothers and sisters, his teachers, his home, his people, and so on. Imbued as he is with 'family feeling', his own life is at first almost completely hidden from him. Rapt, as it were, and hypnotized by the ideas and feelings of this concrete environment of his, the only experiences which succeed in crossing the threshold of his inner awareness are those which fit into the sociologically conditioned patterns which form a kind of channel for the stream of his mental environment. Only very slowly does he raise his mental head, as it were, above this stream flooding over it, and find himself as a being who also, at times, has feelings, ideas and tendencies of his own. And this, moreover, only occurs to the extent that the child *objectifies* the experiences of his environment in which he lives and partakes, and thereby gains *detachment* from them. The mental content of experience that is virtually absorbed 'with one's mother's milk' is not the result of a transference of ideas, experienced as something 'communicated'. For communication entails that we understand the 'communicated content' as proceeding from our informant, and that while understanding it we also appreciate its origin in the other person. But this factor is just what is absent in that mode of transference which operates between the individual and his environment. For in this case we do not primarily 'understand' the passing of a judgement or the expression of an emotion, or regard it as the utterance of another self. We fall in with it, without being consciously aware of the element of co-operation involved. And the effect of this is that we begin by regarding it as our *own* judgement or emotional reaction. It is only in recollection that the experience normally comes to have the character of something acquired from without, depending on how far we have succeeded by then, through maturity rather than knowledge, in separating our own experience (and its individual contents) from that of other people. But long before the child has ever reached the stage of being capable of a more precise *distinction* between himself and his mental environment, his consciousness is already filled with ideas and experiences of whose real origin he is completely unaware; and once he has begun to lay hold of experiences of his own which lie beyond this original communal threshold, he can call upon such ideas in order to make

sense of his environment, because that is just where they have
come from in the first place.[1]

A similar immersion in the spirit of the community and conformity to the shapes and patterns of its flow, can also be seen in
all primitive peoples. Just as speech exerts a profound influence
on the silent and solitary life of the soul, so that if there is no *word*
or other socially valid expression for an experience, the latter
usually fails to stand out plainly from the stream of experience,
so too, the possible *social relevance* and importance of an experience
tends to intrude itself, like a selective form of apprehension, between pure internal perception and the experience itself, and
hence virtually overshadows the private life of the individual, and
conceals it, as it were, from the possessor himself. Though we
nowadays regard it as a 'pathological' symptom (of hysteria, for
instance), when a man's inner life appears to be involuntarily
shaped according to the attitudes and standards of his environment, what is now held to be a 'pathological' trait is characteristic,
like so many other similar features, of all primitive life whatsoever.[2]
Thus the vengeful impulses of a member of the family or tribal
unit in respect of any insult or injury towards a fellow-member of
the same unit, is not due to fellow-feeling (which already postu-
lates the apprehension of the suffering *as* endured by someone
else), but to an immediate awareness of this insult or injury as
affecting himself; a phenomenon which is directly based upon the
fact that the individual begins by living in the community to a
much greater extent than he does in himself.

But how then is it possible to observe the mental life of another
person? Let us now go on from the phenomenological fact that a
mental experience may be presented in 'internal perception'
regardless of whether it is 'my' experience or (characteristically)
someone else's, to the question how such a thing is possible. For
is not 'internal perception' necessarily also a perception of *oneself*?
Is it possible to have internal perception of the self and the inner
life of *another* person?

This question has hitherto received an unhesitatingly negative
answer for the simple reason that no distinction has been drawn

[1] This is why a *complete* understanding of the mental history of a people (or a
religious community) can only be attained, in the last resort, by those who belong
to the group in question and have been imbued with its traditions. Lamprecht
also reaches this conclusion in his essay 'Kulturpolitik' (*Deutsche Revue*, December 1912).

[2] This primitive element must again be taken into account nowadays in the
phenomena of crowd-psychology, which could easily be shown to contain much
that would have to be regarded as 'pathological' in an individual case. Thus it
is possible, for example, to rediscover in the mental processes of crowds a whole
range of phenomena characteristic of hysteria.

between the sphere of internal intuition (or those of internal perception, representation, feeling and the like), and the sphere of 'inner sense'. But 'internal intuition' can certainly not be defined by reference to its object, by saying that a person engaged in such intuition is perceiving 'himself'. For I can perceive myself in an external sense just as much as I can perceive anyone else. Every glance at my own body, every touch upon it, confirms the fact. If I touch my thumb with my middle finger, the double sensation still consists of one and the same sensory content at the surfaces of the two separate parts of the body. Thus internal perception represents a polarity among acts, such acts being capable of referring both to ourselves *and* to others. *This polarity is intrinsically capable of embracing the inner life of others as well as my own,* just as it embraces myself and my own experience *in general,* and not merely the immediate present. To be sure, certain conditions are required before the experiences of others can be presented to me in the act of internal intuition. But these are equally necessary if I am to be aware of my own personal experience. They certainly include the ontological condition that my body should be subject to effects whose causes are located in, or proceed from, the other's body. For instance, the air-waves set in motion by his utterances must reach my ear if I am to understand what he says. But there is no reason why this condition *should entirely determine the act whereby these words are understood.* The condition itself can be explained by reason of the facts: (1) that every act of possible internal perception is associated with a similar act of possible external perception; and (2) that the act of external perception does in fact have an external sensory basis as well. The process whereby individual A is apprised of an experience in individual B must operate, in these circumstances, 'as if' this experience must first have evoked certain physical modifications in B, and these a similar series of modifications in A, to be followed, in consequence, by an experience in A similar or comparable to that possessed by B. But in actual fact the internal perception of A is intrinsically capable of apprehending B's experience *immediately,* and these causal processes serve only to determine when the act in question shall take place, and again to select its particular content from within the possible field of internal perceptions of other people.[1]

If the above-mentioned account of the matter were true, the

---

[1] Even in external perception the stimulus never determines the character of the thing perceived, but only the perception of this and no other character; and the same is true of the relationship between remembering and reproduction or association. But this can only be shown in the context of the general theory of knowledge which underlies what is said here. [Cf. on this the chapter 'Zur Philosophie der Wahrnehmung' in *Erkenntnis und Arbeit* (1926), op. cit.]

objective course of events could only follow the course already indicated, whereby internal perception is wholly confined to one's own mental experiences, and the transference of an experience from B to A can only come about, objectively speaking, if B's experience affects his body, and this affects A's body, which then influences his 'soul' and thereby causes the production of a *similar* experience in him; so that A's knowledge of B's experience would depend upon inference, or the empathic projection of his own experience into B. But according to *our* account we are committed to saying that A's act of internal perception embraces not only his own mental processes, but has both the power and the right to take in the *whole* existing realm of minds—initially as a still unorganized stream of experiences. And just as we start by apprehending our present self against the background of our *whole* temporal experience, and do not manufacture it by a *synthesis* of our present self with earlier remembered states of itself, so too do we always apprehend our own self against the background of an ever-vaguer all-embracing consciousness in which our own existence and the experiences of everyone else are presented, in principle, as included together. It is not, therefore, the perception of other selves and their experiences, but only the particular content that stands out vividly at any time from this vast total content, the emergence of a self and of its experience from the great collective stream of universal consciousness, which is in fact conditioned by the bodily transactions which take place between us. From this point of view we gain a quite new insight, not to be found in the previous theory, into that strange interdependence between our self-knowledge and our understanding of others, described in the words of Schiller:

> 'If you would know yourself, take heed of the practice of others;
> If you would understand others, look to your own heart within
> you'.[1]

Anyone learning a foreign language realizes that only in doing so does he become aware of the special character of the meaning-units and other basic peculiarities of his own tongue. And is this any less true of all those other tendencies in experience and behaviour that are governed by national, local or professional concerns or otherwise unified in terms of a group? It is by virtue of *precisely the same act of discernment within an as yet undifferentiated whole* that we come to a clear realization *both of what is ours and of what belongs to others.*

---

[1] 'Willst du dich selber erkennen, so sieh, wie die andern es treiben,
  Willst du die andern verstehn, blick in dein eigenes Herz.'

It is a fundamental weakness of theories which seek to derive our knowledge of other minds from inferences or processes of empathy, that they have an inveterate tendency to under-estimate the difficulty of self-knowledge, just as they over-estimate the difficulty of knowing other people. It is no longer realized in such cases that it is self-knowledge which has always been reckoned the most difficult, so that Nietzsche, for example, could utter the pregnant words, 'every man is farthest of all from himself' (from knowing himself, that is, and I should add that this is just *because* he is closest to himself in *practice*). What has been overlooked is that the degree of vividness necessary even in one of our own mental processes, before it can stand out from the vague whole of our own total experience at any time, is no more dependent on the mere act of internal perception than is a mental process in someone else; for both are *equally* dependent on their ability to occasion specific causal *changes* in the peripheral areas of the *bodily* self (or animate body). We only pay special attention to an experience of our own in so far as it discharges itself in intended movements, or at least in expressive tendencies. Thus it can easily be confirmed that when the expression of an emotion is violently repressed, this invariably has a tendency to repress it simultaneously from internal perception as well. When joy or love are inhibited in their expression they do not simply remain the same from the internal point of view, but tend to evaporate. If it were possible (which it is not), to go on to annihilate the *inner* expressive phenomena localized within the animate body, the experience would still continue to modify the field of internal awareness in some way, though it would no longer be accessible to individual inspection. Internal reading-movements are so closely bound up with the understanding of what is read, that if the tongue is immobilized, even the understanding of a newspaper is greatly impaired. These facts and others like them show that even prior to self-directed internal perception such an experience does not succeed in emerging from the total stream of life immediately, but only by means of the effect it has on the state of the *body*. In this respect, therefore, there is, at bottom, no very crucial difference between self-awareness and the perception of mind in others. Such perception occurs, in both cases, only so far as the state of the body is modified in some way and so far as the mental state to be perceived is translated into some sort of *expression* or other physical modification. Thus it is not merely another person's artistic intentions, for example, that I grasp through the process of their depiction and the result produced; for even my own artistic ideas only mature *in* the process of depiction and only attain a definite shape *in so far* as they are bound up with this process.[1] Just as the painter does not first see in order to depict, but only penetrates into the full colour and chiaroscuro of his overt subject in the process of depicting it, so likewise is self-perception possible only when its subject-matter is first translated into expressive tendencies.

It would therefore be quite wrong to suppose that we first simply perceive ourselves and our experiences, and then go on subsequently to take additional account of our expressive movements and tendencies, our actions, and their effect upon our bodily states. Such a purely 'intra-mental' self-perception is a complete fiction. The fact is that the articulation of the stream of consciousness and the ascription to it of those specific qualities of vividness which bring certain parts of it into the focus of internal perception, are *themselves governed* by the potential unities of action and expression (and the physical significance of these), which they are able to induce. Even the nature of our moral character is not apprehended by means of some pure antecedent self-intuition, completely divorced from the sphere of action, but only in the course of our actions themselves. It will also be evident from this how largely the actual direction of self-perception at any time, the selection of what we shall or shall not observe in ourselves, is dependent upon the prevailing fields of *attention* which the *environment* imposes upon us. An experience whose general character, whether of pity or vengeance, shame or joy, we know to lie, in general, within our environmental field of attention, even though we need not be attending to it at the moment, stands a much greater chance of being observed by us, even within ourselves. Without our realizing it, our experience largely shapes itself according to the disposition of our environmental fields of attention. Language again, with its psychological unities of meaning, intrudes its network of order and articulation between what we see and what we experience. Anything in our experience which can be put into words is always something which, having been singled out by common language, must also be accessible to others; and such experience presents a quite different appearance in internal perception from anything that is 'ineffable'. It is given *prior* to the ineffable. For this reason poets, and all makers of language having the 'god-given power to tell of what they suffer',[2] fulfil a far higher function than that of giving noble and beautiful expression to their experiences and thereby making them recognizable to the reader, by reference to his own past experience in this kind. For by creating new forms

---

[1] Cf. Karl Fiedler's æsthetic theory, more especially his book, *Ursprung der Kunsttätigkeit*. [Cf. also, in *Nachlassband*, I, Appendix to *Vorbilder und Führer*, the sections on the artist, and on conception and the process of representation.]

[2] [Goethe, *Marienbader Elegie*.]

of expression the poets soar above the prevailing network of ideas in which our experience is confined, as it were, by ordinary language; they enable the rest of us to *see*, for the first time, in our own experience, something which may answer to these new and richer forms of expression, and by so doing they actually *extend* the scope of our *possible* self-awareness. They effect a real enlargement of the kingdom of the mind and make new discoveries as it were, within that kingdom. It is they who open up new branches and channels in our apprehension of the stream and thereby show us for the first time *what* we are experiencing. That is indeed the mission of all true art: not to reproduce what is already given (which would be superfluous), nor to create something in the pure play of subjective fancy (which can only be transitory and must necessarily be a matter of complete indifference to other people), but to press forward into the whole of the external world *and* the soul, to see and communicate those objective realities within it which rule and convention have hitherto concealed. The history of art may be seen, therefore, as a series of expeditions against the intuitable world, within and without, to subdue it for our comprehension; and that for a kind of comprehension which no science could ever provide. An emotion, for example, which everyone can now perceive in himself, must once have been wrested by some 'poet' from the fearful inarticulacy of our inner life for this clear perception of it to be possible: just as in commerce things (such as tea, coffee, pepper, salt, etc.), which were once luxuries, are nowadays articles of everyday use in general supply.

There are two metaphysical theories of the mind-body relationship which chiefly obstruct our understanding of the facts concerning our knowledge of other minds. The one is the old notion of interaction between two substances, i.e. the theory of a self-contained 'soul-substance', which can only operate on the soul of another via its causal influence on its own body, and the effect of the latter on the other's body. The other is that of 'psycho-physical parallelism', so-called, whose main postulate is that every mental event in A is accompanied by a corresponding event in A's body, so that a mental influence of A upon B would equally have to take place by way of the effect of their respective bodies on one another. Both theories would rule out the internal perception of other minds. For each of them, everyone lives immured in his own mental prison and must wait upon whatever the metaphysical causal nexus may spirit into it.[1] But

[1] If this parallelism is taken to imply a univocal interdependence of all mental and all physical events, we should also have to postulate 'mental' correlates for the sound and light waves which enable us to see and hear the other person,

both these theories misapprehend the facts and neglect the *phenomena*.[1]

Anything given in internal and external intuition that has physical (objectively observable) concomitants is not the pure qualitative content of such intuition, but only the givenness of that *portion* of its total content which continues to have an effect upon the body. Only the actual (though not therefore necessarily 'given') vital motor-impulses of the body and its various states are accompanied by parallel occurrences in the nervous system. The reason for this is simply that modification of the (internal) bodily system is itself a condition for the *emergence* of mental processes from within the field of internal intuition into the sphere of possible perception; hence it is indirectly the case that for every (perceptible) distinction, selection or abstraction within the total stream of consciousness, there are corresponding physical nerve-currents, which are a necessary condition, not for the content of the experience itself, but for the perception thereof. Thus the body as a whole simply serves to analyse, not only the givenness of the external world and what is 'picked out' from it, but also the stream of consciousness which continually tends to overflow its limits. Hence the brain and nervous system and all the events occurring in them merely determine what is *perceived*, but not the occurrence and content of mental processes. The function of the nervous system on the physical side is not essentially different from what it is on the mental. It is the condition for the *perception* of its character, not for the character itself, let alone for its existence. Just as there are no specific bodily processes governing the existence and character of the sun and moon, without which these bodies could not exist, it being only the manner in which they are presented to us (as discs of light in the sky) that is determined in this fashion, so too there are no specific conditions in the nervous system governing the existence and character of mental processes; though there *are* definite conditions determining the manner in which they are presented in internal perception. In other words the body and its changes merely condition the appearance or aspect that our experience presents to inner sense, but never the experience itself.

though these would naturally have been invented merely for the sake of the hypothesis. Such an assumption would also involve the acceptance of telepathy, as Sigwart has already done well to emphasize (*Logik*, Vol. II). There is much on this subject in T. K. Oesterreich's book on occult phenomena (*Possession, Demoniacal and Other*, Kegan Paul, 1930).

[1] The theory of mind and body so vaguely outlined above will only be rendered intelligible in the second volume of my Metaphysics which I shall shortly be preparing for publication. [Cf. *Die Stellung des Menschen im Kosmos*, 1927, and also, for the theory of perception, *Erkenntnis und Arbeit*, op. cit.]

Hence there is no immediate causal connection, nor even a specific relation of dependence, between mental experience and events in the nervous system. All there is, in fact, is an indirect relationship of dependence between such events and the actually given content of inner sense-perception (i.e. the faculty of distinguishing among the data of internal intuition). This relationship is due to the fact that all changes in the body are accompanied by two other sets of changes: (1) nervous processes in the physical body, (2) changes in the bodily consciousness, which serve to determine which part of the totality of inner life is to enter internal awareness.[1]

Now this enables us to account for a number of facts to which little attention has been paid hitherto. The only thing we can never perceive in our observation of others is their experience of their own *bodily states*, especially their organic sensations, and the sensory feelings attached thereto. It is these things which account for that particular *kind* of separateness among men which the above-mentioned theories attribute to the *whole* of mental life. Though there have been misguided attempts to draw a general distinction between the mental and the physical by asserting that the 'mental' is what can only be given to 'one' person at a time, this statement only applies, in fact, to organic sensations and sensory feelings.[2] The pain of another person, or the sensory enjoyment of his food, is something I can never perceive directly. All I can do is to reproduce a similar sensation of my own, and infer that in the presence of comparable stimuli the other person has a similar experience. But I cannot share it or reproduce it vicariously, as I can, for instance, the spiritual emotion of grief. The various states of the body in sensation and feeling are wholly confined to the body of the individual concerned. Hence an identical sorrow may be keenly felt (though in one's own individual fashion), but never an identical sensation of pain, for here there are always two separate sensations. Again, one may see the same shade of red as another person (without actually reducing the colour to wave-motions), or hear the same sound of C. But the aural and ocular sensations involved are accessible only to the possessor of the organs in question.

To the extent, therefore, that a man is predominantly concerned with his own bodily states, he will remain cut off from the

[1] Exactly the same situation arises in external perception. It is an error to suppose that Nature, its object, is dependent on the body in a manner intrinsically different to that of mental happenings. For all natural phenomena are equally made up of elements that are dependent on the body for their existence and others that are not so.

[2] For the notion of 'sensory feelings' (as distinct from vital, mental and spiritual feelings), cf. *Der Formalismus in der Ethik und die materiale Wertethik*, ch. V, § 8, 'Zur Schichtung des emotionalen Lebens'.

mental life of his fellows (and indeed from his own). And it is only so far as he *surmounts* this and views his body with detachment, clearing his mental life of its ever-present sensory accompaniments, that the facts of mental life in others will become increasingly visible to him.

The act of internal perception, therefore, is not by nature an act which can only be directed upon the mental life of the percipient himself, as if 'internal perception' and introspection amounted to the same thing. Our claim is, rather, that so far as concerns the act and its nature and the range of facts appearing within it, everyone can apprehend the experience of his fellow-men *just as directly* (*or indirectly*) as he can his own. It is only the inescapable difference in our physical circumstances, in so far as they govern the selection of that part of our purely mental life which appears in internal perception (in which capacity we describe them as 'inner sense'), which determines that though B may have had the same actual experience as A, the 'picture' that he has of it is always different from A's.[1]

There have been a number of different attempts to establish that we can only have knowledge, or a clear conception of the constituents of mental life, by previous recourse to the defining properties of the object as it exists in *external* nature. Thus Natorp, in his *Einleitung in die Psychologie*, took the view that psychology must always be preceded by an 'objectification' of the given into an external natural object (by means of a 'transcendental synthesis') and that only from this standpoint is it possible, by means of a reconstructive process, to provide either a descriptive or an explanatory account of the mental experience; a sensation, for example, must be referred to its physical stimulus. Münsterberg also wishes to define the natural object as the element X which remains identifiable throughout a multiplicity of private acts or intersubjective transactions—so that the concept of the mental becomes, as it were, characteristic of what can only be given in one subjective act at a time, and therefore, in effect, to one person at a time. Such theories would make it impossible, by definition, for us to perceive the mind of another: indeed, even the perception of our own mental life could only be achieved indirectly, by taking the external natural object as our starting-point, in order to identify our experience as correlative to it. The logical consequence of such views is that the mental field has no sort of organic unity of its own, either in the subject himself, or in his relation to others; for, according to them, the only thing that can be regarded as 'mental' is that contingent residue of the 'given' which does not

---

[1] This 'picture' is not, of course, a particular real object but only a limited 'aspect' of the other's experience.

happen to be included in the structure of the natural object or the regular causal connections within the body, so that there can therefore be no reason to think of it as constituting a continuous intelligible sequence on its own account. In short, the natural conclusion to be drawn from these premises is epiphenomenalism, with its methodological aim of accounting for all rational connections within mental experience by reference to corresponding physiological and physico-chemical processes in the nervous system.

But all that these theories ultimately show is that from the 'natural point of view', in which, from the start, we are wholly absorbed in the external world, we often succumb to the illusion of taking a thing for a mental experience when it is actually given only as a physical object. It is Bergson's especial merit to have shown how we are all inclined to import a quasi-spatial multiplicity into the mental field, despite the fact that the two things are utterly unlike.[1] These theories therefore transform a particular and perhaps inveterate tendency to illusion on the part of internal perception into a 'condition of mental experience in general'. A further conclusion to which these theories are led is that, instead of regarding the body and its changes as a merely limiting condition for the perception of actual mental life, they think of it as a wholly determinant, independently variable causal sequence, such that mental events are themselves alleged to depend upon its interconnections. These conclusions are due to the misguided notion of the 'mental' as that which is only given to one person at a time, or cannot be identified throughout a multiplicity of subjective acts. But if the mental were only given to one person at a time, it could never be communicated. It is here that we notice how these theories assert of the mental in general what in fact applies only to physical sensations and sensory feelings.[2] Hence they invariably relapse in practice into sensationalism, the impossible attempt to trace the whole of experience back to 'sensations' and their derivatives.[3] It is actually a complete mistake to

[1] Henri Bergson: *Time and Free Will* (authorized translation by F. L. Pogson) London, Macmillan, 1910.

[2] I pass over the fact that it is a complete error to suppose, with Münsterberg, that the principle of Identity is sufficient to justify the reduction of the phenomena to mechanical terms. For the same sound can certainly be perceived, imagined or remembered, and may equally be sensed by a number of subjects, without any need to characterize it, merely for the sake of identification, as a wave-motion. As to the real reasons conducing to this mechanistic reduction of natural phenomena, I shall give the gist of the matter below. [Cf. *Phänomenologie und Erkenntnislehre* (1913) and *Lehre von den drei Tatsachen* (1911) in *Nachlassband*, I (1933), and also *Erkenntnis und Arbeit* (1926).]

[3] Hence it is quite intelligible that Münsterberg should allot to psychology the task of ultimately 'recasting' all mental phenomena, including volition, into sensations. I am at a loss to know what 'recasting' may mean in this context.

suppose that a mental experience cannot remain identical through-out a multiplicity of acts. Can we not feel the same sorrow or love, to a greater or lesser extent at different times, or remember the same experience many times over, and thereby actually relive and reproduce the same identical feeling, for instance? Are we not given to saying, in psychology, that the same optical sensation is sometimes manifested as a visual content or constituent thereof, and sometimes (as in hysterical blindness) is not so; that it is sometimes observed or attended to and at other times overlooked? Anyone who holds it to be an essential feature of the mental that it can never persist identically throughout a multiplicity of acts, has begun by confusing the sphere of mental phenomena with that of mental *reality*; and he is also confusing the sphere of *phenomena in general*, i.e. that which is immediately given in any objective field, with the *mental* as such. This is what Wundt did, in equating the mental with what is immediately experienced and the physical with what we arrive at indirectly. But in fact there are levels of mediacy and immediacy among the objects of external *and* internal perception, and hence in the natural world as well as in the mental one.[1]

But just as the same mental content can be present in a multi-plicity of acts, so it can also be present to a number of *different* individuals. Just as we can revive, recall and grieve, more or less, over the same painful experience at different periods in our life, so we can also join with others in grieving at one and the same experience. To be sure, we can never experience the same (physic-ally localized) sensory pleasure or pain. These states are confined to the individual in whom they occur, and can only be like one another, never identical. But two people may very well feel the same sorrow; a strictly identical, not just a similar one, even though the experience may be differently coloured in each case by differing organic sensations. Anyone who holds that mental events are only accessible to one person at a time will never be able to explain the exact meaning of phrases like: 'All ranks were fired with the same enthusiasm', 'The populace was seized with a common joy, a common grief, a common delight', and so on. Custom, language, myth, religion, the world of the tale and the saga—how can they be understood on the assumption that mental life is essentially private?

---

[1] O. Külpe has recently adopted a similar account of the matter in his book *Die Realisierung*. Cf. also in my essay 'Die Idole der Selbsterkenntnis' (op. cit.), the note on Edmund Husserl's essay in *Logos* (1913). Cf. also the excellent treatment of the question in Moritz Geiger's 'Fragment über den Begriff des Unbewussten und die psychische Realität' (*Jahrbuch für Philosophie und Phäno-menologische Forschung*, IV, 1921).

What is shown by the above is that these theories confuse that aspect of our own (and others) experience which is presented in inner sense with the existence and character of the mental in general. But this error would be comparable with that of wanting to define Nature as merely the sum of those parts of it which fall within the scope of human sense-perception. For the case is actually just the same as this. Even in external perception (as an independent intentional act), we grasp a given portion of its character only against the background of the whole of Nature: in *every* such act we have assurance of the existence of the whole realm of Nature, without the need of any 'inference' or 'empathic projection'. And here, too, the body and its unity of sensibility interposes between the perceiving subject, which has both the power and the right to address itself to the whole of Nature, and its actual object. It is 'outer sense', in other words, which limits the content of perception to whatever may have a bearing upon the possible activities of the body. And although such 'contents' vary from one individual to another, even when the objects are the same, we take it for granted that it is one and the same Nature which we perceive in these contents.[1]

It is a crucial objection to the view that mental life is essentially private that if its premisses were correct, we ought equally to be led to the conclusion that Nature is also a private affair. 'Subjective idealism' does in fact lead to this conclusion, and it has been very properly objected to it that if its reasoning were correct we should have to deny not only the existence of matter and the external world, but also the existence of past contents of consciousness, and of other selves. The only incorrigible certainty would be the existence of the solipsist's own momentary self. Now we actually approach such a solipsism of the moment the more we confine our existence to our own body. And there is another conclusion of no less importance than this: anyone who denies our ability to perceive other selves and their experiences, must equally be prepared to deny the perceptibility of matter. Nor is it without interest to observe how in the history of philosophy the existence of a real external world has been far more frequently denied than the existence of other selves; and this though no one has denied our ability to perceive Nature, while practically everyone has disputed our powers of perceiving mental life in others. The reason for this is that *our conviction of the existence of other minds is earlier and deeper than our belief in the existence of Nature.*

[1] We are not referring here to the way in which things are presented as 'real', for this, in our opinion, has nothing to do with whether these 'fields' exist, and only arises in the shape of 'resistance' to our volitional behaviour towards the given. Cf. note on p. 236.

(2) But let us now turn to the other 'self-evident' assumptions made by these two theories. What else, it may be asked, can I be supposed to perceive of another man apart from his '*body*' and the movements he makes?

Now to begin with, it only needs the simplest of phenomenological considerations to show that at any rate there is nothing self-evident about this. For we certainly believe ourselves to be directly acquainted with another person's joy in his laughter, with his sorrow and pain in his tears, with his shame in his blushing, with his entreaty in his outstretched hands, with his love in his look of affection, with his rage in the gnashing of his teeth, with his threats in the clenching of his fist, and with the tenor of his thoughts in the sound of his words. If anyone tells me that this is not 'perception', for it cannot be so, in view of the fact that a perception is simply a 'complex of physical sensations', and that there is certainly no sensation of another person's mind nor any stimulus from such a source, I would beg him to turn aside from such questionable theories and address himself to the phenomenological facts. All he need do in the first place is to compare these examples with cases which actually *exhibit* what his theories lead him to accept *a priori* in the present instance, namely a *conclusion* amenable to proof. Thus, for example, the actions of a man with whom I have previously spoken, and whose feelings and intentions were, as I thought, plain to me, may yet compel me to the conclusion that either I have misunderstood him and deceived myself, or else that he has been lying or pretending to me. *Here* then I do actually draw conclusions about his state of mind. Again, by a similar inference from his looks to his thoughts and feelings, I may even prepare myself in advance, e.g. in dealing with someone whom I fear to be deranged or mad, or where I suspect dissimulation or an intention to deceive. I do this, in effect, wherever I find my internal and vicarious perception of his experiences unduly *checked* in any way, or where I am compelled for specific positive reasons, themselves derived (in the last resort) from perception, to postulate a *discrepancy* between inner experience and outer expression, an (involuntary or deliberate) breach of their symbolic interrelation—a relation which holds good regardless of the particular experiences or circumstances of the individual concerned.[1] It is at this point only that I begin to draw conclusions. But it should not be forgotten in this that the *material* premises for these conclusions are based upon my elementary perceptions of the person concerned or other people; and they therefore *pre-suppose* these immediate percep-

---

[1] On the connection between experience and expression, cf. the remarks of Koffka, op. cit. He also denies that the connection is merely learnt or acquired.

tions. Thus I do not merely see the other person's eyes, for example; I also see that 'he is looking at me' and even that 'he is looking at me as though he wished to avoid my seeing that he is looking at me'. So too do I perceive that he is only pretending to feel what he does not feel at all, that he is severing the familiar bond between his experience and its natural expression, and is substituting another expressive movement in place of the particular phenomenon implied by his experience. Hence I can tell that he is lying, for example, not merely by having proof that he must be aware that he is telling it differently, and that matters are other than he says they are; for in certain circumstances I can be *directly* aware of his lying itself, of the very act of lying, so to speak. Again, there is sense in my saying to somebody, 'That isn't really what you meant to say: you are expressing yourself badly', i.e. I grasp the *meaning* he has in mind, though here it certainly cannot be deduced from his words, since otherwise I should not be in a position to correct them by reference to the meaning already given beforehand.

It may be argued, perhaps, that although such differences occur, they do not represent a difference between perception and inference, but only the contrast between a simple, primitive or 'unconscious' form of inference and a more elaborate and conscious one. But enough of such objections, fabricated in the interests of a fallacious theory and capable of proving anything or nothing.[1]

Let us now go on to consider the claim that we can have no immediate perception of anything in other people except their bodies and physical movements.

Our immediate perceptions of our fellow-men do not relate to their bodies (unless we happen to be engaged in a medical examination), nor yet to their 'selves' or 'souls'. What we perceive are *integral wholes*, whose intuitive content is not immediately resolved in terms of external or internal perception. From this stage of givenness we can then go on, in the second place, to adopt the attitude of internal or external perception. But the fact that the individual bodily unity thus immediately presented should be

---

[1] It is easy to point to the psychological sources of this 'theory'. It comes down to us, historically speaking, as one of a number of theories typical of the Enlightenment (the contract theory of the state, the conventional theory of language, etc.), which all conceive of the origins of the community in terms of an 'artificial society' in which distrust has become a permanent attitude. Cf. 'Das Ressentiment im Aufbau der Moralen', op. cit.

It may be noted that we often make inferences with regard to our own experiences also; as when we say: 'What sort of man can I be to have done that?', or when we seek to account for a mood of our own which is not intelligible in terms of our present circumstances.

associated, in general, with a possible object accessible both to internal and external perception, is founded upon the *intrinsic* connection between these intuitive contents, a connection which also underlies my own perception of myself. It is not acquired through observation and induction from my own case. Such a connection holds good for the nature of all living organisms generally.[1]

The appearances presented by this individual bodily unity are originally no less inconclusive, as regards their psychophysical character, than the unity itself. They may be capable of further analysis, e.g. into unities of pure colour, shape and outline, or unities of change, movement and variation. But every 'expressive unity' at this level of appearance remains a unity belonging to the whole of this living organism as an individual *whole*. At this level, such an appearance has *no* sort of function as a symbol, either for the bodily unity (or its parts) as presented in external perception, or for the unity of the individual self and its experience (or its parts) as allocated to internal perception. Moreover, the appearances at this level are incorporated into *combinations and structures of quite a different kind*, according to whether they take on the symbolic function, in the act of external perception, of symbolizing the individual's body (and its reactions to other bodies in the environment), or whether they serve, in the act of internal perception, to symbolize the individual's self (and its reactions to other selves in the environment). Thus it is only within these different fields of perception—and depending on which of them is operative, that *one* combination of the same stimuli presents an appearance in which we perceive the other person's *body* (an appearance manifestly due to external impressions), whereas another combination of the same stimuli yields an appearance in which we perceive that person's *self* (an appearance manifestly expressive of his inner life). Hence it is intrinsically impossible ever to resolve the unity of an expressive phenomenon (such as a smile, or a menacing, kindly or affectionate look), into a sum of appearances, however large, such that its members could equally

---

[1] This also applies to the lower organisms. It is possible for a physiologist to give a completely 'mechanistic' explanation of the wrigglings of a severed worm, and to smile (like Jacques Loeb) at the notion that it is 'wriggling with pain' (since the headless portions also wriggle). But of course it is quite absurd to argue, from the possibility of this mechanico-causal explanation, that the movement is not also expressive of pain (by alleging that the worm cannot feel pain without its head). It would be as absurd as to argue that a man's blushing cannot be an expression of shame, since it can be explained mechanically (as indeed it can) as a rush of blood to the cheeks. For what bearing does a mechanico-causal explanation have upon symbolic functions, such as the phenomena of expression?

well comprise a unity of appearance in which we might perceive the body, or a unitary impression from the physical environment. If I adopt the approach of external perception, and rely upon the unities of appearance presented therein, they will enable me to form an impression of any part of the individual's body, however small; but in any combination of such unities I shall never come upon the unity of a smile, an entreaty, a threatening gesture and so on. Again, the shade of red which visibly covers the physical surface of a man's cheek can never present the unity of a blush, whose redness appears, as it were, as the outcome of the shame which I sense him to feel. If the cheek is red, merely, the same immediate appearance of redness might equally well betray over-heating, anger or debauchery, or be due to the light from a red lamp.

Perhaps this may give us a rather better understanding of the supposedly 'self-evident fact' that we can only perceive the bodies of other people. If we begin by treating colours, sounds, shapes, etc., as 'sensations', when they are really *qualities* appearing in conjunction with sensation: if again, we treat the perception based upon (though not composed of) such qualitative complexes, as a complex of sensations, though sensation plays no part in it; and if we then forget that on this (doubly erroneous) view of perception it is *no more possible* to perceive the body than it is to perceive the self, and still consider it feasible on these premises to do so, then we do indeed reach the remarkable conclusion that we can perceive the bodies of other people but not their selves. This 'result' is achieved by coupling a set of (partially) false factual premises with a fallacy of four terms.

We need not concern ourselves, in *this* context, with the *theory* of perception adopted in any given case. If anyone supposes the content of perception to be a complex of sensations and their derivatives, such as the evoked memory-traces of previous sensations, he need not fancy himself able to 'perceive' the body of another person. If anyone supposes that perception always implies a judgement, he should recognize that (strangely enough) it is also possible to make an 'immediate' judgement to the effect that somebody is ashamed. If it be said that perception involves an inference (albeit an 'unconscious' one), it should be admitted that such unconscious 'inferences' also figure in the perception of other minds.[1] The fact that my body must be affected by physical and

[1] Sensualism can be extremely naïve. Hume marvels at the fact that men should have hated and fought one another so much, simply because they were yellow or black or white. That is his conception of racial conflict and hatred! But we venture to suppose that the Americans do not hate the negroes because they are black—there being no evidence, as yet, that they also dislike the blackness of clothes or materials; they scent the negro under the blackness of his skin. (Cf. Hume's *History of England*.)

chemical stimuli emanating from another body, does not mean that I have to be aware of that body, or that I must first be conscious of some of the sensory appearances, sounds, colours, smells, etc., corresponding to these stimuli, before I can recognize an expression of friendliness, and so on.

The primary awareness, in ourselves, in animals and in primitives, invariably consists of *patterns of wholeness*; sensory appearances are only given in so far as they function as the basis of these patterns, or can take on the further office of signifying or representing such wholes.

INDEX OF SUBJECTS

INDEX OF SUBJECTS

Maternal love, 97–8, 172–3, 193
and instinct, 26 ff., 73, 107
social value of, 32, 176
Mechanistic view of life, 94, 104–5,
125 ff., 215, 257, 262
Melancholia, 14, 16
Mental parasitism, 43
Metaphysical monism, 35, 51–76
and fellow-feeling, 62 ff.
and individualism, 231
and love, 68 ff.
Microcosm, man as, 105
Monogamy, 185
Moral unity of mankind, xxx, 49, 128,
164–5, 190, 214
Mystery-religions, 20, 25, 34, 84, 85,
97
Mysticism, 33, 56, 78, 127

Nature, attitude to, in adolescence, 109
in Christianity, 84 ff.
Franciscan, 87 ff.
Greek, 79, 82 f., 89
Indian, 77, 79 f., 83
Jewish, 79, 84, 90, 94, 105
scientific, 82, 94, 104–6 (see Identification with the Cosmos)
Neurosis, 178, 208 f.
Non-cosmic love-mysticism, 79, 85,
87, 100
and benevolence, 99 ff.
Franciscan conception of, 87 ff.
and panentheism, pantheism, 91–3
Pauline conception of, 85–6
and theism, 102, 128 (see God, love
of)

Old age, 108, 204
'Ordo amoris,' l, 103–29
Organic view of life, 82, 90, 94, 104,
262
Other minds, knowledge of, xxxviii,
101–2, 121–3, 213–64
analogical theory of, 9, 220, 225–6,
231, 236, 238 ff., 251, 263
growth of, in children, 246–7
moral evidence for, 227 f.
perceptual theory of, 220, 245,
248 ff., 261 f.

Other minds, knowledge of, in solitary
individual, 234–5
and vital consciousness, 236–7

Panentheism, 66, 91, 92
Pantheism, xxxii, 63, 77, 89, 91, 93,
120, 127–8
Panvitalism, 25, 79
Parental instinct, 26 ff., 124, 176 (see
Maternal love)
Pathological states of feeling, 14, 16,
22, 23, 43, 48, 58, 73, 136 f., 144,
161, 178, 183, 196, 201–2
Patriotism, 100, 172, 190
Perception, 29 f., 58, 244, 249, 254,
259, 261 ff.
Perversion, sexual, 22, 136 f., 178,
183, 196, 201 f.
Pessimism, xxviii, 64, 79, 81, 135
Pharisaism, 162–3, 184
Pietas (see Ancestor-cults)
Pity (Commiseration), and fellow-
feeling, 8, 13, 37
intentional character of, 39 f., 41
and love, 142 f.
Schopenhauer's theory of, 51–5
types of, 135 ff.
value of, 17, 54, 62, 131, 136–8
Pre-existence, 124
Primitive thought, 19, 218, 239, 248
Privacy, of personality, 10, 33, 66 f.,
71, 121, 219, 225
of sensation, 13, 33, 255–8 (see In-
dividuality, Spiritual person)
Procreative instinct (see Sexual love)
Protestantism, xxi, 94
Psycho-analysis, 16, 18, 38 177 ff.,
196 ff.
Psychology, limits of, 214, 221 ff., 256
Psycho-physical parallelism, 253

Regret, 135
Rejoicing (-with) (see Pity)
Religious faith, xvii–xxiii, xxix, 32,
86, 230
Renaissance view of life, 89, 93 f., 109
Reproduced (vicarious) feeling, 9,
12, 13 f., 29, 31, 43, 45–7, 53,
67, 143, 245

INDEX OF SUBJECTS

INDEX OF NAMES

271

INDEX OF NAMES

Totals

HUMANITIES

	Asst	Assc	Prof	All
Amer Civ	0	0	0	0
Art History	0	1	0	1
Classics	1	0	0	1
Comp Lit	1	0	0	1
Drama/Thea	2	0	1	3
English	1	1	2	4
German	1	0	0	1
History	0	0	0	0
Ital/French	1	0	0	1
Linguistics	0	0	0	0
Modern Lang	1	0	0	1
Music	0	0	0	0
Nr East St	1	0	0	1
Orien/As St	0	0	1	1
Philosophy	1	0	0	1
Relig St	0	1	0	1
Rhetoric	0	0	0	0
Rom St/Lang	0	0	1	1
Russian Lit	0	0	1	1
Span & Port	1	0	1	2
Sub-total	11	3	7	21

SOCIAL SCI

	Asst	Assc	Prof	All
Afro-Am St	0	0	0	0
Anthropology	1	1	2	4
Asian-Am St	1	1	0	2
Economics	11	1	0	12
Geography	1	0	0	1
Govt/Pol Sc	4	1	1	6
History	2	0	4	6
Home Econ	1	0	0	1
Linguistics	0	0	2	2
Psychology	2	1	1	4
Region Sci	0	0	1	1
Sociology	2	0	0	2
Speech Comm	0	0	1	1
Sp & Hrg Sci	1	0	0	1
Sub-total	26	5	12	43

NATURAL SCI

	Asst	Assc	Prof	All
Astronomy	0	0	0	0
Molec Biol	0	1	1	2
Chemistry	0	2	0	2
Comp Sci	0	0	2	2
Ecol & Sys	1	0	0	1
Geology	0	0	1	1
Home Econ	1	1	1	3
Mathematics	0	1	1	2
Microb & Imm	0	0	0	0
Nrbiol & Beh	0	0	0	0
Physio & Ana	0	0	0	0
Physical Ed	0	0	0	0
Physics	2	1	1	4
Statistics	0	0	0	0
Zoology	0	0	0	0
Sub-total	4	6	7	17

	Asst	Assc	Prof	All
TOTAL	41	14	26	81

IVa. Retirements 1955-57

Number of Actions

	Public University A			Private University B			Public University C			Private University D			Private University E			Public University F		
	Asst	Assc	Prof	Asst	Assc	Prof	Asst	Assc	Prof	Asst	Assc	Prof	Asst	Assc	Prof	Asst	Assc	Prof
HUMANITIES																		
Art																		
Classics																		1
Decrtv Art			1															
Drama/Thea																		
English			1					1										1
Fine Arts																		
German		1																
Ital/French								1										
Music																		
Nr East St																		
Philosophy																		
Rom St/Lang					1									1				
Slavic Lang																		
Span & Port																		
Speech																		
Sub-total	0	1	2	0	1	0	0	2	0	0	0	0	0	1	0	0	0	2

IVa. Retirements 1955-57

	Public University A			Private University B			Public University C			Private University D			Private University E			Public University F		
Number of Actions	Asst	Assc	Prof	Asst	Assc	Prof	Asst	Assc	Prof	Asst	Assc	Prof	Asst	Assc	Prof	Asst	Assc	Prof
SOCIAL SCI																		
Anthropology																		
Economics				1														
Geography																		
History							2											
Home Econ																		
Journalism																		
Polit Sci																		
Psychology																		
Social Svc																		
Sociology																		
Sub-total	0	0	0	1	0	0	2	0	0	0	0	0	0	0	0	0	0	0

IVa. Retirements 1955-57

Number of Actions

NATURAL SCI	Public University A		Private University B		Public University C		Private University D		Private University E		Public University F	
	Asst	Assc Prof	Asst	Assc Prof	Asst	Assc Prof	Asst	Assc Prof	Asst	Assc Prof	Asst	Assc Prof
Astronomy										1		
Biochem	1											
Biol Sci												
Botany				1								
Chemistry										3		
Geology												
Home Econ												
Mathematics	1			1						1		
Physics				1								1
Psychology												
Zoology											1	2
Sub-total	2	0	2	1	0	0	0	0	0	5	1	3
TOTAL		4		5		4		0		6		4

IVa. Retirements 1955-57

Totals

HUMANITIES

	Asst	Assc	Prof	All
Art	0	0	0	0
Classics	0	0	1	1
Decrtv Art	0	0	1	1
Drama/Thea	0	0	0	0
English	0	0	3	3
Fine Arts	0	0	0	0
German	0	1	0	1
Ital/French	0	0	1	1
Music	0	0	0	0
Nr East St	0	0	0	0
Philosophy	0	0	0	0
Rom St/Lang	0	0	2	2
Slavic Lang	0	0	0	0
Span & Port	0	0	0	0
Speech	0	0	0	0
Sub-total	0	1	8	9

SOCIAL SCI

	Asst	Assc	Prof	All
Anthropology	0	0	0	0
Economics	0	0	1	1
Geography	0	0	0	0
History	0	0	2	2
Home Econ	0	0	0	0
Journalism	0	0	0	0
Polit Sci	0	0	0	0
Psychology	0	0	0	0
Social Svc	0	0	0	0
Sociology	0	0	0	0
Sub-total	0	0	3	3

NATURAL SCI

	Asst	Assc	Prof	All
Astronomy	0	0	1	1
Biochem	0	0	1	1
Biol Sci	0	0	0	0
Botany	0	0	4	4
Chemistry	0	0	0	0
Geology	0	0	0	0
Home Econ	0	0	0	0
Mathematics	1	0	3	4
Physics	0	0	2	2
Psychology	0	0	0	0
Zoology	0	0	1	1
Sub-total	1	0	12	13

	Asst	Assc	Prof	All
TOTAL	1	1	23	25

177

IVb. Retirements 1983-84

Number of Actions

	Public University A			Private University B			Public University C			Private University D			Private University E			Public University F		
	Asst	Assc	Prof	Asst	Assc	Prof	Asst	Assc	Prof	Asst	Assc	Prof	Asst	Assc	Prof	Asst	Assc	Prof
HUMANITIES																		
Amer Civ																		
Art History																		
Classics					1													
Comp Lit					1							1						
Drama/Thea																		
English		1			1				1									1
Fine Arts									1		1			1				
German														1				
History																		
Ital/French																1		
Linguistics																	1	
Modern Lang																		
Music																		
Nr East St									1									
Orien/As St									1									
Philosophy																		
Relig St																		
Rhetoric										1								
Rom St/Lang																		
Russ/Ur/Slav									1			1						
Span & Port																		
Sub-total	0	1	0	0	3	0	0	0	5	1	1	2	0	2	0	1	1	1

IVb. Retirements 1983-84

Number of Actions

	Public University A			Private University B			Public University C			Private University D			Private University E			Public University F		
	Asst	Assc	Prof	Asst	Assc	Prof	Asst	Assc	Prof	Asst	Assc	Prof	Asst	Assc	Prof	Asst	Assc	Prof
SOCIAL SCI																		
Afro-Am St																		
Anthropology			1															
Asian-Am St																		
Economics																		1
Geography																		1
Govt/Pol Sc									3									
History															1			
Linguistics																		
Psychology																		
Region Sci																		
Sociology			1			1												
Sub-total	0	0	2	0	0	1	0	0	3	0	0	0	0	0	1	0	0	2

IVb. Retirements 1983-84

Number of Actions

	Public University A			Private University B			Public University C			Private University D			Private University E			Public University F		
	Asst	Assc	Prof	Asst	Assc	Prof	Asst	Assc	Prof	Asst	Assc	Prof	Asst	Assc	Prof	Asst	Assc	Prof
NATURAL SCI																		
Astronomy																		
Molec Biol																		1
Chemistry															1			1
Comp Sci									2									
Ecol & Sys																		
Geology																		1
Home Econ																		1
Mathematics																		
Microb & Imm			1															
Nrbiol & Beh					1													
Physio & Ana																		
Physical Ed																		
Physics			1			1												
Statistics																		
Zoology																		
Sub-total	0	0	2	0	1	1	0	0	2	0	0	0	0	0	1	0	0	4
TOTAL	0	0	5	0	1	5	0	0	8	0	1	2	0	0	4	0	2	8

IVb. Retirements 1983-84

Totals

HUMANITIES	Asst	Assc	Prof	All
Amer Civ	0	0	0	0
Art History	0	0	1	1
Classics	0	1	1	2
Comp Lit	0	0	0	0
Drama/Thea	0	0	0	0
English	0	0	5	5
Fine Arts	1	0	1	2
German	0	0	1	1
History	0	0	0	0
Ital/French	0	1	1	2
Linguistics	0	0	0	0
Modern Lang	0	0	0	0
Music	0	0	0	0
Nr East St	0	0	1	1
Orien/As St	0	0	1	1
Philosophy	0	0	0	0
Relig	1	0	0	1
Rhetoric	0	0	0	0
Rom St/Lang	0	0	0	0
Russ/Ur/Slav	0	0	2	2
Span & Port	0	1	1	2
Sub-total	2	3	15	20

SOCIAL SCI	Asst	Assc	Prof	All
Afro-Am St	0	0	0	0
Anthropology	0	0	1	1
Asian-Am St	0	0	0	0
Economics	0	0	1	1
Geography	0	0	1	1
Govt/Pol Sc	0	0	3	3
History	0	0	1	1
Linguistics	0	0	0	0
Psychology	0	0	0	0
Region Sci	0	0	0	0
Sociology	0	0	2	2
Sub-total	0	0	9	9

NATURAL SCI	Asst	Assc	Prof	All
Astronomy	0	0	1	1
Molec Biol	0	0	1	1
Chemistry	0	0	1	1
Comp Sci	0	0	0	0
Ecol & Sys	0	0	0	0
Geology	0	1	0	1
Home Econ	0	0	1	1
Mathematics	0	0	0	0
Microb & Imm	0	0	1	1
Nrbiol & Beh	0	0	1	1
Physio & Ana	0	0	0	0
Physical Ed	0	0	0	0
Physics	0	0	2	2
Statistics	0	0	0	0
Zoology	0	0	0	0
Sub-total	0	1	8	9

	Asst	Assc	Prof	All
TOTAL	2	4	32	38

V. Respondents 1958, 1986

	Public Univ A	Private Univ B	Public Univ C	Private Univ D	Private Univ E	Public Univ F	Total
ASST PROF							
1958	5	1	7	7	3	8	31
1986	10	10	13	10	16	18	77
ASSOC PROF							
1958	7	2	6	8	9	3	35
1986	6	5	10	9	5	11	46
PROFESSOR							
1958	25	20	20	16	20	20	121
1986	30	29	33	25	29	37	183
TOTAL							
1958	37	23	33	31	32	31	187
1986	46	44	56	44	50	66	306

VI. Disciplines Represented 1958, 1986

Discipline	No. of Depts 1958	1986	Discipline	No. of Depts 1958	1986
Afro-American Studies	–	2	Microbiology and/or Immunology	–	2
American Civilization	–	1	Modern Language	–	1
Anthropology	3	5	Music	3	1
Art/Art History	1	3	Near Eastern Language/Studies	1	3
Asian-American Studies	–	1	Neurobiology & Behavior	–	2
Astronomy	2	2	Oriental/Asian Studies	–	2
Biochemistry	1	–	Philosophy	2	5
Biology (incl Molecular)	1	4	Physical Education	–	1
Botany	2	–	Physics	5	6
Chemistry	2	5	Physiology & Anatomy	–	1
Classical Studies	1	5	Political Science/Government	3	5
Comparative Literature	–	2	Psychology	5	4
Computer Science	–	2	Regional Science	–	1
Decorative Art	1	–	Religious Studies	–	2
Drama/Theatre Arts	3	3	Rhetoric/Speech	1	2
East Asian Language & Culture	–	1	Romance Studies/Language	4	2
Ecology & Systematics	–	1	Russian Literature	–	1
Economics	5	6	Slavic Studies	2	1
English	5	6	Social Service	1	–
Fine Arts	2	2	Sociology	–	5
Geography	2	3	Spanish & Portugese	–	3
Geology	2	3	Speech & Hearing Sciences	–	1
German	3	2	Statistics	–	1
History	5	5	Telecommunications	–	1
Home Economics	2	2	Uralic & Altaic Studies	–	1
Italian and/or French	1	3	Zoology	2	2
Journalism	1	–	TOTAL NUMBER OF DEPARTMENTS	78	131
Linguistics	–	4	TOTAL NUMBER OF DISCIPLINES	32	50
Mathematics	4	4			

183

VII. Data Summary by Institution 1958, 1986

	Public Univ A	Private Univ B	Public Univ C	Private Univ D	Private Univ E	Public Univ F	Total
APPOINTMENTS							
1958	20	14	16	15	11	15	91
1986	21	15	30	21	24	26	137
DISMISSALS							
1958	12	3	2	3	5	10	35
1986	2	1	4	5	15	16	43
RESIGNATIONS							
1958	7	11	12	21	9	7	67
1986	6	12	18	7	16	22	81
RETIREMENTS							
1958	6	5	4	0	6	4	25
1986	5	6	8	4	5	10	38
DEATHS							
1958	3	0	4	2	4	3	16
1986	1	1	3	0	0	0	5
ALL TERMS							
1958	28	19	22	26	24	24	143
1986	14	20	33	16	36	48	167
ALL ACTIVITY							
1958	48	33	38	41	35	39	234
1986	35	35	63	37	60	74	304
RESPONDENTS							
1958	37	23	33	31	32	31	187
1986	46	44	56	44	50	66	306
DEPARTMENTS							
1958	16	13	13	12	12	12	78
1986	24	20	28	17	20	22	131

VIII. Department Size by Institution 1986

	Public Univ A	Private Univ B	Public Univ C	Private Univ D	Private Univ E	Public Univ F	Average
HUMANITIES							
Amer Civ	–	–	–	–	9	–	9
Art History	13	14	–	8	–	–	12
Classics	18	15	–	8	16	19	15
Comp Lit	24	5	–	–	–	–	15
Drama/Thea	6	21	14	–	–	–	14
English	70	49	63	20	47	93	57
Fine Arts	–	–	34	3	–	–	19
German	–	–	–	–	13	23	18
History	–	28	–	–	–	–	28
Ital/French	7	–	20	–	–	29	19
Linguistics	–	–	–	–	11	–	11
Modern Lang	–	27	–	–	–	–	27
Music	–	–	–	–	13	–	13
Nr East St	17	11	5	–	–	–	11
Orien/As St	–	–	10	–	25	–	18
Philosophy	18	13	15	14	–	28	18
Relig St	–	–	16	–	7	–	12
Rhetoric/Sp	13	–	9	–	–	–	11
Rom St/Lang	–	17	–	–	19	–	18
Russ/Ur/Slav	–	4	14	6	–	–	8
Span & Port	15	–	17	–	–	35	22
Sub-total	201	204	217	59	160	227	
Average	20	19	20	10	18	38	20
SOCIAL SCI							
Afro-Am St	9	–	–	6	–	–	8
Anthropology	30	17	20	12	30	–	22
Asian-Am St	2	–	–	–	–	–	2
Economics	39	27	32	28	49	33	35
Geography	–	–	–	5	–	15	10
Govt/Pol Sc	–	27	30	27	18	44	29
History	–	–	45	27	29	49	38
Home Econ	–	–	10	–	–	–	10
Linguistics	13	–	12	–	–	20	15
Psychology	–	26	38	–	–	51	38
Region Sci	–	–	–	–	13	–	13
Sociology	19	15	25	–	28	32	24
Sp & Hrg Sci	–	–	11	–	–	–	11
Telecomm	–	–	19	–	–	–	19
Sub-total	112	112	242	105	167	244	
Average	22	22	24	18	28	35	25

	Public Univ A	Private Univ B	Public Univ C	Private Univ D	Private Univ E	Public Univ F	Average
NATURAL SCI							
Astronomy	–	–	7	–	–	22	15
Molec Biol	16	–	52	26	33	–	32
Chemistry	–	30	37	34	27	48	35
Comp Sci	–	–	18	–	–	35	27
Ecol & Sys	–	18	–	–	–	–	18
Geology	–	–	24	–	12	39	25
Home Econ	–	–	–	–	–	31	31
Mathematics	75	–	48	43	–	53	55
Microb & Imm	12	–	–	–	–	17	15
Nrbiol & Beh	–	15	–	9	–	–	12
Physio & Ana	17	–	–	–	–	–	17
Physical Ed	7	–	–	–	–	–	7
Physics	68	49	40	29	47	63	49
Psychology	–	–	–	–	28	–	28
Statistics	28	–	–	–	–	–	28
Zoology	31	–	–	–	–	64	48
Sub-total	254	112	226	141	147	372	
Average	32	28	32	28	29	41	33
TOTAL	567	428	685	305	474	843	
AVERAGE	23	20	24	18	24	38	25

	Public Univ A	Private Univ B	Public Univ C	Private Univ D	Private Univ E	Public Univ F
HUMANITIES						
Art History	6	17		23		
Classics	2	13		–	11	9
English	2	7	17	19	11	23
French/Rom	8	10	11		7	20
German					18	6
Linguistics	5		23		5	3
Music					6	
Philosophy	4	10	15	35		24
Span & Port	5	13	11			3
SOCIAL SCI						
Anthropology	1	17	32	11	4	
Economics	10	20	50	10	8	42
Geography				27		29
Govt/Pol Sc		11	17	13	30	26
History		15	14	18	12	23
Psychology		15	15		4	19
Sociology	3	19	12		12	17
NATURAL SCI						
Molec Biol	8		18	26	18	
Chemistry		11	18	12	29	17
Comp Sci			35			10
Geology			30			13
Mathematics	2		23	23		30
Microb/Imm	23					23
Physiol/Anat	22					
Physics	3	6	32	36	14	16
Statistics	1					
Zoology	2					9

*Jones et al. (1982)

Bibliography

Abrahamson, Mark. "Talent Complementarity and Organizational Stratification." *Administrative Science Quarterly* 18 (June 1973): 186–193.

Alpert, Daniel. "Performance and Paralysis: The Organizational Context of the American Research University." *Journal of Higher Education* 56 (May/June 1985): 241–281.

American Association of University Professors. "Report of Committee B: Methods of Appointment and Promotion in American Colleges and Universities." *AAUP Bulletin* 15 (March 1929): 175–217.

Baker, Paul J., and Mary Zey-Ferrell. "Local and Cosmopolitan Orientations of Faculty." *Teaching Sociology* 12 (October 1984): 82–106.

Baldridge, J. Victor, David V. Curtis, George Ecker, and Gary L. Riley. *Policy Making and Effective Leadership.* San Francisco: Jossey-Bass, 1978.

Baldwin, Roger G., and Robert T. Blackburn. "The Academic Career as a Developmental Process." *Journal of Higher Education* 52 (November/December 1981): 598–614.

Bernard, Jessie. *Academic Women.* University Park, Penn.: Pennsylvania State University Press, 1964.

Bess, James L. *University Organization.* New York: Human Sciences Press, 1982.

Blau, Peter M. *The Organization of Academic Work.* New York: Wiley, 1973.

———. "Recruiting Faculty and Students." *Sociology of Education* 47 (Winter 1974): 93–113.

Bok, Derek. *Higher Learning.* Cambridge, Mass.: Harvard University Press, 1986.

Bowen, Howard R., and Jack H. Schuster. *American Professors.* New York: Oxford University Press, 1986.

Boyer, Ernest L. *College: The Undergraduate Experience in America.* New York: Harper and Row, 1987.

Breneman, David W. "An Economic Theory of Ph.D. Production: The Case at Berkeley." Paper P-8 (June 1970). Berkeley: Ford Foundation Program for Research in University Administration, University of California.

Brown, David G. *The Mobile Professors.* Washington, DC: American Council on Education, 1967.

Bunnell, Kevin P. "Recruiting College Faculty Members: A Short-Range View of the Problem." *Educational Record* 41 (April 1960): 138–142.

Caplow, Theodore. "La Répétition des enquêtes: Une méthode de recherche sociologique." *L'Année Sociologique* 32 (1982): 9–22.

——— and Reece J. McGee. *The Academic Marketplace.* New York: Basic Books, 1958.

Carnegie Council on Policy Studies in Higher Education. *A Classification of Institutions of Higher Education.* Berkeley, Cal.: Carnegie, 1976.

Carson, Richard T., and Peter Navarro. "A Seller's (& Buyer's) Guide to the Job

Market for Beginning Academic Economists." Discussion Paper 87–6 (March 1987). Department of Economics, University of California, San Diego.

Cartter, Allan M. *Ph.D.'s and the Academic Labor Market.* New York: McGraw-Hill, 1976.

Clark, Burton R. "Organizational Adaptation to Professionals." In *Professionalization,* edited by Howard M. Vollmer and Donald L. Mills. Englewood Cliffs, NJ: Prentice-Hall, 1966.

————. *The Academic Life: Small Worlds, Different Worlds.* Princeton, NJ: Carnegie, 1987.

Clemente, Frank, and Richard B. Sturgis. "Quality of Department of Doctoral Training and Research Productivity." *Sociology of Education* 47 (Spring 1974): 287–299.

Crane, Diana. "The Academic Marketplace Revisited: A Study of Faculty Mobility Using the Cartter Ratings." *American Journal of Sociology* 75 (May 1970): 953–964.

Cyert, R. M. "Strategic Planning." Paper presented at American Council on Education Workshop, 14 October 1982.

Dill, David D. "The Management of Academic Culture: Notes on the Management of Meaning and Social Integration." *Higher Education* 11 (May 1982): 303–320.

————. "Research as a Scholarly Activity: Context and Culture." In *New Directions for Institutional Research,* edited by J. W. Creswell, No. 50. San Francisco: Jossey-Bass, June 1986.

————. "Theory Versus Practice in the Staffing of R&D Laboratories." *R&D Management* 15 (July 1985): 227–241.

Dornstein, Miriam. "Some Imperfections in the Market Exchanges for Professional and Executive Services." *The American Journal of Economics and Sociology* 36 (April 1977): 113–128.

Dressel, Paul L., F. Craig Johnson, and Philip M. Marcus. *The Confidence Crisis: An Analysis of University Departments.* San Francisco: Jossey-Bass, 1970.

Drucker, Peter. *Toward the Next Economics and Other Essays.* New York: Harper and Row, 1981.

Finkelstein, Martin J. *The American Academic Profession.* Columbus: Ohio State University Press, 1984.

Flango, Victor E., and Robert E. Brumbaugh. "The Dimensionality of the Cosmopolitan-Local Construct." *Administrative Science Quarterly* 19 (June 1974): 198–210.

Frank, Robert H. *Choosing the Right Pond: Human Behavior and the Quest for Status.* New York: Oxford, 1985.

Garvin, David A. *The Economics of University Behavior.* New York: Academic Press, 1980.

Goldberg, Albert I. "The Relevance of Cosmopolitan/Local Orientations to Professional Values and Behavior." *Sociology of Work and Occupations* 3 (August 1976): 331–356.

Gouldner, Alvin W. "Cosmopolitans and Locals: Toward an Analysis of Latent Social Roles—I." *Administrative Science Quarterly* 2 (1957–58):281–306.

———. "Cosmopolitans and Locals: Toward an Analysis of Latent Social Roles—II." *Administrative Science Quarterly* 2 (1957–58): 444–480.

Gross, Edward, and Paul V. Grambsch. *Changes in University Organization, 1964–1971.* New York: McGraw-Hill, 1974.

Hagstrom, Warren O. *The Scientific Community.* New York: Basic Books, 1965.

Hannan, Michael T., and John Freeman. "The Population Ecology of Organizations." *American Journal of Sociology* 82 (March 1977): 929–964.

Hargens, Lowell L., and Grant M. Farr. "An Examination of Recent Hypotheses about Institutional Inbreeding." *American Journal of Sociology* 78 (May 1973): 1381–1402.

Hargens, Lowell L., and Warren O. Hagstrom. "Scientific Consensus and Academic Status Attainment Patterns." *Sociology of Education* 55 (October 1982): 183–196.

———. "Sponsored and Contest Mobility of American Academic Scientists." *Sociology of Education* 40 (Winter 1967): 24–38.

Hook, Sidney. "On Discrimination: Part One." In *New Directions for Institutional Research,* edited by L. W. Sills, No. 3, Autumn 1974. San Francisco: Jossey-Bass, 1974.

Jones, Lyle V., Gardner Lindzey, and Porter E. Coggleshall, eds. *An Assessment of Research-Doctorate Programs in the United States.* Washington: National Academy Press, 1982.

Kanter, Rosabeth Moss. *The Change Masters.* New York: Simon and Schuster, 1983.

Kaplowitz, Richard A. *Selecting College and University Personnel: The Quest and the Questions.* ASHE-ERIC Higher Education Report No. 8. Washington, DC: Association for the Study of Higher Education, 1986.

Kasten, Katherine Lewellan. "Tenure and Merit Pay as Rewards for Research, Teaching, and Service at a Research University." *Journal of Higher Education* 55 (July-August 1984): 500–514.

Keller, George. *Academic Strategy.* Baltimore, Maryland: The Johns Hopkins University Press, 1983.

Kenen, Peter B., and Regina H. Kenen. "Who Thinks Who's in Charge Here: Faculty Perceptions of Influence and Power in the University." *Sociology of Education* 51 (April 1978): 113–123.

Kerr, Clark. *The Uses of the University.* Cambridge, Mass.: Harvard University Press, 1963.

Klugh, H. E. "Approaches to the Academic Market." *American Psychologist* 19 (August 1964): 670–674.

Lester, Richard A. *Antibias Regulation of Universities.* New York: McGraw-Hill, 1974.

Lewin, Arie Y., and Linda Duchan. "Women in Academia." *Science* 173 (3 September 1971): 892–895.

Lewis, Lionel S. *Scaling the Ivory Tower.* Baltimore, Maryland: The Johns Hopkins University Press, 1975.

Long, J. Scott, Paul D. Allison, and Robert McGinnis. "Entrance into the Academic Career." *American Sociological Review* 44 (October 1979): 816–830.

Love, Robert E. "Getting Your First Job: A View from the Bottom." *American Psychologist* 27 (May 1972): 425–430.

Mack, Raymond W. Review of *The Academic Marketplace*, by Theodore Caplow and Reece J. McGee. *Social Forces* 37 (May 1959): 364–365.

Marsh, John F., Jr., and Frank P. Stafford. "The Effects of Values on Pecuniary Behavior: the Case of Academicians." *American Sociological Review* 32 (October 1967): 740–754.

Marshall, Howard D. *The Mobility of College Faculties*. New York: Pageant Press, 1964.

Marwell, Gerald, Rachel Rosenfeld, and Seymour Spilerman. "Geographical Constraints on Women's Careers in Academia." *Science* 205 (21 September 1979): 1225–1231.

Massengale, John D., and George H. Sage. "Departmental Prestige and Career Mobility Patterns of College Physical Educators." *Research Quarterly for Exercise and Sport* 53 (December 1982): 305–312.

McGee, Reece. *Academic Janus*. San Francisco: Jossey-Bass, 1971.

Menges, Robert J., and William H. Exum. "Barriers to the Progress of Women and Minority Faculty." *Journal of Higher Education* 54 (March/April 1983): 123–144.

Miles, Matthew B., and A. Michael Huberman. *Qualitative Data Analysis: A Sourcebook of New Methods*. Beverly Hills: Sage, 1984.

Mitroff, Ian I. *Stakeholders of the Organizational Mind*. San Francisco: Jossey-Bass, 1983.

Mommsen, Kent G. "Black Ph.D.'s in the Academic Marketplace." *Journal of Higher Education* 45 (April 1976): 253–267.

Moore, William J., and Robert J. Newman. "An Analysis of the Quality Differentials in Male-Female Academic Placements." *Economic Inquiry* 15 (July 1977): 413–433.

Moore, William J., Robert J. Newman, John Raisan, and R. William Thomas. "A Quality-Adjustment Model of the Academic Labor Market: the Case of Economists." *Economic Inquiry* 21 (April 1983): 241–254.

Muffo, John A., and John R. Robinson. "Early Science Career Patterns of Recent Graduates from Leading Research Universities." *Review of Higher Education* 5 (Fall 1981): 1–13.

Murray, Stephen O., Joseph H. Rankin, and Dennis W. Magill. "Strong Ties and Job Information." *Sociology of Work and Occupations* 8 (February 1981): 119–136.

National Research Council. *Summary Report 1983: Doctorate Recipients from United States Universities*. Washington, DC: National Academy Press, 1983.

Otto, Luther B., Kenneth I. Spenner, and Vaughn R. A. Call. *Career Line Prototypes*. Boys Town, Neb.: Center for the Study of Youth Development, 1980.

Ouchi, William G. "Markets, Bureaucracies, and Clans." *Administrative Science Quarterly* 25 (March 1980): 129–141.

Patton, Carl Vernon. "Early Retirement in Academia: Making the Decision." *The Gerontologist* 17 (August 1977): 347–354.

Rafky, David M. "The Black Scholar in the Academic Marketplace." *Teachers College Record* 74 (December 1972): 225–260.

Reich, Robert B. *The Next American Frontier*. New York: Times Books, 1983.

Reskin, Barbara F. "Academic Sponsorship and Scientists' Careers." *Sociology of Education* 52 (July 1979): 129–146.

Roose, Kenneth D., and Charles J. Andersen. *A Rating of Graduate Programs.* Washington, DC: American Council on Education, 1970.

Sacco, William P., and Suzette Milana. "Increase in Number of Authors per Article in Ten APA Journals: 1960–1980." *Cognitive Therapy and Research* 8 (February 1984): 77–83.

Sawyer, Darwin O. "Institutional Stratification and Career Mobility in Academic Markets." *Sociology of Education* 54 (April 1981): 85–97.

Schein, Edgar H. *Career Dynamics.* Reading, Mass.: Addison-Wesley, 1978.

———. "How 'Career Anchors' Hold Executives to their Career Paths." *Personnel* 52 (May-June 1975): 11–24.

Shichor, David. "Prestige and Regional Mobility of New Ph.D.s in Sociology." *The American Sociologist* 8 (November 1973): 180–186.

Simon, Rita James, Shirley Merritt Clark, and Kathleen Galway. "The Woman Ph.D.: A Recent Profile." *Social Problems* 15 (Fall 1967): 221– 236.

Smelser, Neil J., and Robin Content. *The Changing Academic Market.* Berkeley: University of California Press, 1980.

Solomon, Warren E., and Allan T. Walters. "The Relationship Between Productivity and Prestige of Graduate Sociology Departments: Fact or Artifact." *The American Sociologist* 10 (November 1975): 229–236.

Spenner, Kenneth I. "Occupational Characteristics and Classification Systems: New Uses of the Dictionary of Occupational Titles in Social Research." *Sociological Methods & Research* 9 (November 1980): 239–264.

Stehr, Nico. "Ascriptive Career Contingencies of Sociologists: A Longitudinal Analysis." *The American Sociologist* 9 (November 1974): 206–211.

Thompson, Fred, and William Zumeta. "Hiring Decisions in Organized Anarchies: More Evidence on Entrance into the Academic Career." *Review of Higher Education* 8 (Winter 1985): 123–138.

Thurow, Lester C. *The Zero-Sum Solution.* New York: Simon and Schuster, 1985.

Touraine, Alain. *The Academic System in American Society.* New York: McGraw-Hill, 1974.

Trow, Martin, and Oliver Fulton. "Research Activity in American Higher Education." In *Teachers and Students*, edited by Martin Trow. New York: McGraw-Hill, 1975.

Van Maanen, John, and Stephen R. Barley. "Occupational Communities: Culture and Control in Organizations." *Research in Organizational Behavior* 6 (1984): 287–365.

Walton, Richard E., and Paul R. Lawrence, eds. *HRM, Trends and Challenges.* Boston: Harvard Business School Press, 1985.

Wilkins, Alan L., and William G. Ouchi. "Efficient Cultures: Exploring the Relationship between Culture and Organizational Performance." *Administrative Science Quarterly* 28 (September 1983): 468–481.

Wilson, Logan. *American Academics: Then and Now.* New York: Oxford University Press, 1979.

Youn, Ted Il Koo. "The Careers of Young Ph.D.'s: Temporal Change and Institutional Effects." Ph.D. Dissertation, Yale University, 1981.

Index

About the Author

DOLORES L. BURKE is Special Assistant to the President of Duke University. She is the winner of the 1987 Distinguished Dissertation Award for the Study of Higher Education. She has contributed to the *Review of Higher Education* and the *Yearbook of American Universities and Colleges*.